Hitler's *Volksgemeinschaft* and the Dynamics of Racial Exclusion

HITLER'S VOLKSGEMEINSCHAFT AND THE DYNAMICS OF RACIAL EXCLUSION

Violence against Jews in Provincial Germany, 1919–1939

Michael Wildt

Translated from the German by
Bernard Heise

berghahn

NEW YORK · OXFORD

www.berghahnbooks.com

Published by
Berghahn Books
www.berghahnbooks.com

German-language edition
©2007 Hamburger Edition
Volksgemeinschaft als Selbstermächtigung:
Gewalt gegen Juden in der deutschen Provinz 1919 bis 1939
By Michael Wildt

English-language edition
©2012, 2014 Berghahn Books
First paperback edition published in 2014

Library of Congress Cataloging-in-Publication Data
Wildt, Michael, 1954-
[Volksgemeinschaft als Selbstermächtigung. English]
Hitler's Volksgemeinschaft and the dynamics of racial exclusion : violence against Jews in provincial Germany, 1919-1939 / Michael Wildt ; translated from the German by Bernard Heise. -- 1st ed.
p. cm.
Includes bibliographical references and index.
ISBN 978-0-85745-322-8 (hardback) -- ISBN 978-1-78238-670-4 (paperback)
1. Antisemitism--Germany--History--20th century. 2. Jews--Persecutions--Germany--History--
20th century. 3. National socialism. 4. Germany--Politics and government--1933-1945. 5. Holocaust, Jewish (1939-1945)--Causes. 6. Germany--Ethnic relations. 7. Germany--History, Local. I.
Title.
DS146.G3W5513 2011
940.53'18--dc23
                                                                                            2011025039

British Library Cataloguing in Publication Data
A catalogue record for this book is available from the British Library

The translation of this work was funded by
Geisteswissenschaften International – Translation Funding
for Humanities and Social Sciences from Germany
A joint initiative of the Fritz Thyssen Foundation, the German Federal Foreign Office,
the collecting society VG WORT and the Börsenverein des Deutschen Buchhandels
(German Publishers & Booksellers Association).

Printed on acid-free paper.

ISBN: 978-0-85745-322-8 hardback
ISBN: 978-1-78238-670-4 paperback

For Brigitte

CONTENTS

Abreviations

BGB	(Bürgerliches Gesetzbuch) Civil Law
BDM	(Bund Deutscher Mädel) League of German Girls
BVP	(Bayerische Volkspartei) Bavarian People's Party
CAHJP	Central Archives for the History of the Jewish People, Jerusalem
C.V.	(Centralverein deutscher Staatsbürger jüdischen Glaubens) Central Association of German Citizens of Jewish Faith
CVZ	(C.V.-Zeitung) C.V. newspaper
DAF	(Deutsche Arbeitsfront) German Labor Front
DDP	(Deutsche Demokratische Partei) German Democratic Party
DNB	(Deutsches Nachrichtenbüro) German News Agency
EPA	(Einheitspreis AG) chain of discount stores modeled on the American five-and-dime stores
DNVP	(Deutschnationale Volkspartei) German National People's Party
DVP	(Deutsche Volkspartei) German People's Party
Gestapa	(Geheimes Staatspolizeiamt, Berlin) Secret State Police Agency, Berlin
Gestapo	(Geheimes Staatspolize) Secret State Police
HJ	(Hitlerjugend) Hitler Youth
HRG	(Handwörterbuch zur deutschen Rechtsgeschichte) Concise Dictionary for German Legal History
IMG	(Verhandlungen und Beweisdokumente des Prozesses gegen die Hauptkriegsverbrecher vor dem Internationalen Militärgerichtshof, Nürnberg 14. November 1945–1. Oktober 1946, 42 Bde.) Trial of the Major War Criminals before the International Military Tribunal, Nuremberg, 14 November 1945–1 October 1946, 42 volumes
Jungvolk	Subdivision of the Hitler Youth for boys aged 10-14
KdF	(Kraft durch Freude) Strength through Joy (Nazi leisure organization)
KPD	(Kommunistische Partei Deutschlands) Communist Party of Germany
KZ	(Konzentrationslager) concentration camp

MBliV	(Ministerialblatt für die innere Verwaltung) Ministerial Newsletter for the Internal Administration
MSPD	(Mehrheitssozialdemokratische Partei Deutschlands) Majority Social Democratic Party of Germany
NSBO	(Nationalsozialistische Betriebszellenorganisation) National Socialist Factory Cell Organization
NSDAP	(Nationalsozialistische Deutsche Arbeiterpartei) National Socialist German Workers' Party
NS HAGO	(Nationalsozialistische Handwerks-, Handels- und Gewerbeorganisation) National Socialist Organization of Crafts, Commerce and Industry
RGBl	(Reichsgesetzblatt) Reich Law Gazette
RM	Reichsmark
RMdI	(Reichsministerium des Innern) Reich Ministry of the Interior
SA	(Sturmabteilung) Storm Detachment (paramilitary organization of the Nazi Party)
SD	(Sicherheitsdienst) Security agency of the SS
SS	(Schutzstaffel) Defense Corps
SPD	(Sozialdemokratische Partei Deutschlands) Social Democratic Party
Stahlhelm	Steel Helmet (conservative paramilitary organization)
StdF	(Stellvertreter des Führers) Deputy Führer
USPD	(Unabhängige Sozialdemokratische Partei Deutschlands) Independent Social Democratic Party of Germany

INTRODUCTION

Marburg, 19 August 1933. Saturday afternoon. A man is being driven through the streets by the SA, a young man in a dark suit. He carries in his hands a large sign that reads: "I have defiled a Christian girl!" His facial expression (as far as one can tell from the photograph) appears rigid and mask-like, as if, by denying the situation as much as possible, he can keep the humiliation at bay. Without the placard, it would be difficult at first glance to recognize this procession as a political action intended to publicly demean a human being and make him contemptible. Marching in front of the SA is a brass band; teenagers accompany the parade, smirking and riding bicycles; curious spectators line the street—a mother holds her child in her arms, and another woman greets the column of SA troopers with her arm raised in the "German salute." Laughing and happy people are visible, but no one opposes the spectacle or looks away in disgust.[1]

It is impossible to know what the spectators in the photograph thought about this publicly staged humiliation of the young man. Perhaps some may even have felt disgust or pity, although such feelings cannot be recognized in the faces or gestures. The numerous spectators were not perpetrators like the SA who organized this procession and compelled the young man to move through the streets of Marburg wearing the sign. And yet they were participants nonetheless—for without an audience, with empty streets and closed windows, the SA action would have ineffectually fizzled out.

The onlookers, the curious, and the passers-by: regardless of their internal disposition toward the event, they were an indispensable component of this operation, one that took place openly in public so that this very public might be fundamentally changed. This kind of action compels a response, willing or not. Of course, perhaps there were people not visible in the photograph who turned away from the violence in silence. But they did not openly oppose the procession; instead, they let it occur. The excuse that would later be heard so frequently—namely, "What should I have done? I could not have prevented anything anyway"—undoubtedly involves a realistic assessment of the limits to one's power as an individual. But it also represents a helpless denial of one's own moral judgment, and at the same time this excuse reveals a surprising lack of concern regarding the threat to one's own personal integrity.[2] For one could not escape the compulsion to respond—which was precisely the point of the operation. All spectators who accompanied the procession, including those with inner reservations, participated in the performance. Admittedly, they did not become perpetrators, but they were active accomplices in anti-Semitic politics.[3]

The question of how "ordinary men" could become perpetrators has increasingly been a topic of discussion in recent years.[4] Yet upon closer consideration, the question is revealed as one about participation—types of involvement and ways of taking part that may very well be highly differentiated. In the photograph from the summer of 1933, the victim and the SA perpetrators are clearly recognizable. However, the generic notion of spectator or "bystander" does not sufficiently grasp all of the other participants who were necessary for the act of violence. Clearly, the levels of participation were too varied—for many people, participation did not mean merely watching but also taking part.[5] The current trend, which always searches for new perpetrators and groups of perpetrators, ultimately culminates with a totalizing effect in which German society between 1933 and 1945 is finally seen without exception as a "society of perpetrators."

To be sure, this characterization makes possible collective condemnation and establishes moral distance, but it offers no further analytical explanation. With this book, I would like to pursue a different course, namely to relinquish what appear as certain and unambiguous notions and to ask questions not about "perpetrators" but about actors, participation, involvement, and how they change—that is, I do not want to take the "Volksgemeinschaft" for granted as a presupposition, but to investigate the process of its creation.[6]

The "*Volksgemeinschaft*" was a fundamental political goal of the National Socialists; yet whether it ever existed justifiably remains a matter of contention within the historiography. In 1971 Hans Mommsen identified the *Volksgemeinschaft* as a propagandistic concept, arguing that the bourgeois middle classes in particular revealed a strong ideological susceptibility to its "illusion of social integration."[7] Thirty years later, Hans-Ulrich Wehler in contrast held that the "appeal of modernity" and the mobilizing impulse associated with the *Volksgemeinschaft* unleashed a transformative dynamic that contributed decisively to the legitimation of the regime, especially for younger generations.[8]

In the spring of 1933, German society was still deeply divided—in the elections for the Reichstag on 5 March, the majority of German voters did *not* vote for Hitler. Nonetheless, the rapidly growing approval of Hitler's politics was unmistakable.[9] The political expectations bound up with Hitler and the fresh start of the Third Reich were apparently so great that many—far too many—were prepared to give up their democratic rights and civil liberties. Without a doubt, the production of the *Volksgemeinschaft* was a process of social inclusion that was supported by promises of equality, economic prosperity, and symbolic recognition. Yet at the same time, *Volksgemeinschaft* meant dictatorial coercion, concentration camps, and secret state police. This dimension of terror is an inseparable part of the *Volksgemeinschaft*, and when making use of this concept the terror should never be suppressed. Yet the politics of the National Socialist *Volksgemeinschaft* reached far beyond the integration of German society through terror and materialism. "The concept of the National Socialist *Volksgemeinschaft* utopia," according to Detlev Peukert, "sought the formation of an ideologically homogeneous, socially conformist, performance-oriented and hierarchically structured society by means of educating the 'well suited' and 'eradicating' the supposedly 'unsuitable.'"[10]

In this racist project to create a *Volksgemeinschaft*, anti-Semitic politics occupied a central place, for they were both an objective (the creation of a "Jew-free" greater German Reich) and a means to completely topple the civil order in Germany. The exclusion of the German Jews from the *Volksgemeinschaft*—both as mandated by countless government measures and as carried out through everyday ostracism—did not merely draw an anti-Semitic boundary while leaving the non-Jewish part untouched. The everyday practice of exclusion changed the society itself. The bureaucratic discrimination and the legal ordinances that declared Jewish Germans to be citizens with reduced rights, and likewise the violent, anti-Jewish actions that are the focus of this book, destroyed the civil and constitutional order and transformed the German nation into an aggressive and racist *Volksgemeinschaft*.[11]

In particular, it was in the provinces—in the villages and small localities, where the Nazis had admittedly conquered the leadership positions but still had not attained political power—that the persecution of Jewish neighbors as "enemies of the people" and as "racial adversaries of the German people" was the central political instrument with which to attack the civil order and produce the *Volksgemeinschaft*. The countryside differed from the big cities, where, first, the administrative means and the presence of party organs could more strongly exert control and, second, the Jewish victims were more likely to find a place to hide within urban anonymity. Conditions in the provinces, in contrast, offered a field that was both easily surveyed and inescapable, where all actors were visible and recognizable. The production of the *Volksgemeinschaft* can be traced here much more clearly than in the large cities.[12]

With regard to political praxis in situ this meant first of all the creation of social distance, stigmatizing any kind of solidarity with and pity for the persecuted in order to isolate Jewish neighbors and to declare them to be without rights—indeed, fair game. If one views the interminable anti-Semitic operations of local NSDAP chapters in the years before the war—the vehemence and aggression with which they proceeded against Jewish merchants, citizens, and neighbors and likewise against the non-Jewish Germans who bought from Jews and maintained contact with them and were thus publicly denounced as "*Volksverräter*" (traitors of the people)—it becomes apparent that what this political transformation from a civil society to a *Volksgemeinschaft* literally meant for everyday life was humiliation and degradation and the existential threat to life and limb. The following pages investigate this process.

For a long time since Raul Hilberg's study,[13] in which he distinguished within the anti-Semitic politics of the NS regime a series of deliberate and successive phases (discrimination, appropriation, ghettoization, annihilation), the historiography has typically suggested that National Socialist politics against the Jews was a goal-oriented development consisting in the first instance of state measures, laws, decrees, and ordinances.[14] This engendered the problematic impression that the anti-Semitic politics of the NS regime were sharply defined and linear; such a schema also reflected a "top-down" view, whereby the persecution of the Jews is characterized as a series of governmental acts of repression—that is, politics is defined as state action.[15]

There is no doubt that the countless administrative measures, from the laws of the Reich regime down to the local ordinances, represented an essential moment in the National Socialist persecution of the Jews; for indeed it was in Germany that a hate-filled anti-Semitic party managed to become a governing power.[16] In contrast, however, apart from the early studies by Werner Jochmann and Ursula Büttner, the praxis of societal anti-Semitism—neighbors, colleagues, customers, acquaintances, and relatives—went unnoticed for a long time.[17] Yet since the 1980s, many local studies and investigations of the economic plundering of the German Jews have brought the societal dimension of the persecution of the Jews into the spotlight, above all the work of Avraham Barkai, who also drew early attention to the meaning of the National Socialist concept of the *Volksgemeinschaft*.[18]

Meanwhile, with Peter Longerich's comprehensive study on the "politics of annihilation" and his most recent volume concerning the Germans' awareness about the persecution of the Jews, and above all with Saul Friedländer's overarching representation of the Shoah, books are now available that pay attention to the quotidian violence against the Jews in Germany even during the prewar period.[19] Yet regarding the years of persecution from 1933 to 1939, Friedländer's book is mostly limited to the enumeration of violent actions, and Longerich arranges the acts of violence within the framework of National Socialist politics as developed and directed by the regime's leadership. My concern is to turn the perspective toward the "organizing" violence, that is, to the production of the *Volksgemeinschaft* through violence, especially through the anti-Semitic and everyday violence against Jews.[20] This allows the violent actions of the party, SA, or HJ (Hitler Youth) groups to be viewed systematically and not merely phenomenologically. At the same time, the observational focus fixes on the transformation of German society toward a *Volksgemeinschaft*.[21]

Only in recent years has the National Socialist concept of the *Volksgemeinschaft* entered the purview of historical research, although Michael Stolleis' postdoctoral study in legal history (which appeared in 1972) about National Socialist formulations of the "common good" was groundbreaking. And the study by Oliver Lepsius revealed once again the elucidating level at which legal historians are discussing the National Socialists' *Volksgemeinschaftsrecht* (Law of the *Volksgemeinschaft*).[22] Two Anglo-Saxon historians, David Schoenbaum and Tim Mason, advanced the thesis in the 1960s and 1970s that the social changes within National Socialist society may have created an actual basis for the *Volksgemeinschaft*.[23] Challenging popular explanations that maintained that the Germans in Hitler's Reich were coerced by terror and violence, Detlev Peukert, too, always returned to the question of whether there were actually numerous points of consensus with the NS regime, especially with its politics against "asocial" elements and "*Gemeinschaftsfremde*" (elements alien to the community).[24] Finally, the concept of the *Volksgemeinschaft* also became a subject in intellectual history about political rights, particularly in the work of Stefan Breuer.[25]

Since then the discussion in the historiography has noticeably gotten under way. Historians like Hans-Ulrich Thamer and Hans-Ulrich Wehler assign the *Volksgemeinschaft* an important place in their interpretations;[26] for Norbert Frei, the question about the *Volksgemeinschaft* leads to "the core of the problem."[27] And if nothing else, concepts like *Volkstaat* (people's state) (Götz Aly) and *Zustimmungsdiktatur* (consensual dictatorship) (Frank Bajohr) show that there is a new debate about the character of the political order of National Socialism. This book should contribute to that debate, whereby I have decided upon the concept of the *Volksgemeinschaft* because it points to political and emotional expectations, to the rift between collectivization and communalization and the hope that this rift might be overcome. At the same time, the concept reveals the anti-statist will of the National Socialists and avoids hastily answering questions about the political order of the NS regime with what seems like a foregone conclusion that this regime had something to do with a "state." Additionally, the concept of the *Volksgemeinschaft* points to a field of political semantics that also encompassed the non-National Socialist parties of the Weimar Republic, and thus may shed light on how the National Socialists succeeded in associating themselves with political hopes and desires.[28]

The major body of source material for this book is comprised of local and regional reports from the local chapters and regional associations of the Centralverein deutscher Staatsbürger jüdischen Glaubens (C.V.) (Central Association of German Citizens of Jewish Faith). With over 600 local chapters and close to 70,000 members, the C.V. was the largest secular German-Jewish association within the Jewish community in Germany.[29] It was founded as an association in 1893 in response to the rampant anti-Semitism of Wilhelmine Germany. And as the programmatic formulation of its name suggests, the organization quickly came to represent those Jews who were proud to be German but who did not want to disavow their Jewish faith and considered themselves to be on equal footing with German Catholics and Protestants. Most of these reports were directed toward the central office of the C.V. in Berlin. They not only describe the everyday reprisals to which Jews in the provinces were exposed, but also clearly demonstrate the endurance and courage with which C.V. members and functionaries took up the fight against anti-Semitism. They stood up for the rights of Jews in Germany before the courts and state authorities and strengthened the internal cohesion of the Jewish communities with a multitude of association activities, above all lectures and meetings. Last but not least, they also attempted to provide their non-Jewish neighbors with an authentic picture of the lives and perspectives of German Jews.

These records of the C.V. were confiscated by the Gestapo when the association was banned. Due to the bombing of Berlin, they were moved to a depot, probably in Silesia, where they were captured by the advancing Soviet army and brought to Moscow. Together with numerous other German documents, they were deposited in a "special archive" and kept secret for over fifty years for reasons that nobody today can say.[30] In the meantime, these C.V. records have been almost completely filmed and made available in the Central Archives for the History of the Jewish People in Jerusalem. I inspected a good part of these files in Moscow and evaluated most of them during my research stay during the winter of 2001/02 at the International Research Institute for the Holocaust, Yad Vashem, Jerusalem.[31] Here I had access not only to an abundance of materials pertaining to specific localities but also to the Pinkas Kehillot, a large and valuable collection of documents concerning the Jewish communities.[32]

The second body of sources, one that in certain respects gives voice to the NS regime, is the comprehensive collection of background and situation reports from government agents and agencies like mayors, district administrators, district presidents, and branches of the NSDAP, as well as reports from the secret state police and the security service of the SS (SD). This collection, which totals 3,744 documents, has already provided essential source material for the recently published volume by Peter Longerich.[33] My study systematically evaluates the material for the first time with respect to acts of violence and excesses, which were referred to in the language of the NS as "independent actions."[34] With good reason, Longerich has warned not to take these reports as authentic statements about the "mood" in German society.[35] But I am not examining these reports with this kind of question in mind. Rather, my interest concerns the manner in which the institutions of the NS regime reported on the acts of violence and the supposed reaction of the population—that is to say, how their own perspectives constituted their representations. In some instances, the contrast with the C.V. reports could hardly be greater, something that can be demonstrated in individual cases.

Finally, for each local case study I have used the respective regional and local archives. And above all I had access to the relevant library of the Institut für die Geschichte der deutschen Juden in Hamburg, which houses a wealth of local studies on the history of Jewish communities in Germany, including many accounts by dedicated city archivists and local researchers who meticulously gathered materials and conducted interviews with former Jewish residents who survived the Shoah.

Even though it is concerned with processes of social transformation, this is not a sociological book. The sources upon which it is based do not amount to the kind of systematic collection and quantifiable social-scientific data that could lead to a representative sociology of violence in German society from 1919 to 1939. Instead, I attempt to question the sources about what kinds of violent practices, practicalities, and changes can be observed, how these violent practices were supported, interpreted, and perceived, and what kind of knowledge was bound up with this praxis of violence. From this analytical-interpretive perspective, *Volksgemeinschaft* is not a concept that refers to the NS regime as a totality from the retrospective viewpoint of the historian; rather, it is supposed to outline a linkage between praxis and knowledge—it is something that was both historically produced (not merely through discourse but through violence) and that itself structured and normalized praxis and knowledge. *Volksgemeinschaft* as praxis and knowledge creates both real and imagined orders, which destroy and transform other orders (real and imagined) and make them disappear.

The investigation of such orders is exemplative, not representative. The local case studies should make changes apparent, not provide a total explanation of German society. Indeed, the historical data that forms the basis for this book does not allow for a quantitative-representative analysis of acts of violence in the German Reich from 1919 to 1939, for the data is not comprised of serialized sources but rather of information about predominantly local acts of violence. Yet this is precisely the reason why this data is especially valuable for the questions posed in this investigation, for it provides the necessary density of source material that makes the description of the processes of violence even possible. The choice of regions and localities is by no means arbitrary or coincidental, but rather is intended to bring the most highly varied parts of Germany into the picture—whether it be Protestant East Prussia or the Catholic Rhineland, East Frisia on the periphery or Hesse at the center, the Ruhr region as characterized by the workers' movement or Bavaria as shaped by the Catholic Church. While one certainly cannot thus claim the ability to make comparisons across the Reich, choosing such variable case studies surely addresses the danger that arises when concentrating on a single region, namely that of hastily proclaiming the particular to be a generality.

This book is also not a "prehistory" of the Holocaust, but rather an attempt to track transformations, continuities, and discontinuities, to elucidate options for radicalization that might have led to the practice of annihilation but were not predetermined to do so. Thus the book ends in 1939, for the war signified a clear caesura; without the war, the mass murder of the European Jews, the sick, the disabled, the prisoners of war, and others would hardly have been possible. Yet the book is still about the Shoah, for within the discontinuities—the disruption of (legal) orders—it tries to disclose the opportunities for creating a new (violent) order, the dimensions of which may very well have not been intended by the actors involved. Thus *Volksgemeinschaft* signifies both continuity and disruption, the desire for order and the praxis of exclusion; *Volksgemeinschaft* is both a conceptual projection and an operational term.

For this reason, this book does not merely portray the production of the *Volksgemeinschaft* chronologically, but rather attempts to elucidate this process from a number of different perspectives. So the first chapter deals with the origins of the myth of the *Volksgemeinschaft* during the First World War and the special way it influenced politics in the Weimar Republic, for during this precise moment in German history, when the people were elevated to sovereignty by the constitution, the counter-principle was prepared with the concept of the *Volksgemeinschaft* to destroy the constitutional democracy. Yet the state's constitutionality represents a decisive difference to the NS regime, a fact that determines the central question about the continuity and discontinuity of violence when investigating anti-Semitic violence in the Weimar Republic (Chapter 2). Thus the year 1933 unquestionably marks a break, for the vehement "*Gleichschaltung*" (synchronization) of state and social institutions and the explosion of violence in the spring that revealed National Socialism's strength of purpose fundamentally changed German society (Chapter 3).

While international and economic considerations forced the NS regime to restrain itself in urban centers, which were the focus of worldwide publicity, the boycott of Jewish merchants in the provinces provided a political arena, as described in Chapter 4, in which the local political order could successfully be transformed. The question about actors, participation, and involvement, then, lies at the center of Chapter 5; this is subsequently followed by an investigation of the new racist (legal) order that came to light particularly during the so-called "*Rassenschande*" (racial defilement) processions during the summer of 1935. With respect to practices, symbols, and forms of expression, this new order could make use of a rich reservoir supplied by the traditional practice of "*Volksrecht*" (people's justice) and honor justice (Chapter 6). No later than 1935, when acts of anti-Semitic violence during the summer finally led to the Nuremberg Race Laws, the political agenda included questions regarding the monopoly of violence (Chapter 7).

This self-created and irreconcilable dilemma—namely that, on the one hand, violence was the medium of politics and self-empowerment for the basic components of National Socialist rule, while on the other hand violence as an instrument was supposed to be subject to the controlled power of command—completely erupted in 1938, the year of the pogroms. After only five years of NS rule, the year of the pogroms revealed the great extent to which German society had become capable of brutal and devastating violence. Civil society in Germany did not disappear, but the lines of order were drawn anew, and the legal order was rolled back in favor of an order of violence, which established the preconditions for the war for "Lebensraum," something that Hitler had desired from the outset. In 1939 it became possible to move beyond Germany and begin the racist and mass-murderous restructuring of the whole of Europe.

I must first thank the International Institute for Holocaust Research, Yad Vashem, which made my archival work possible with a research fellowship in the winter of 2001/02. Above all, I would like to extend heartfelt thanks to Tikva Fatal-Knaani, David Bankier, who died much too soon in 2009, and Elliot Nidam-Orvieto for their professional support and friendly collegial assistance. Likewise, I thank the archive of Yad Vashem, Jerusalem, where my research began years ago and there in particular Yaacov Lozowick, Naomi Halpern, and Yaacov Borut as well as Daniel Fraenkel, Tamar Avraham, and Antje Naujoks from the Pinkas Kehillot project. I was able to discuss the basic outline of the project with Leni Yahil, Dan Michman, Yehuda Bauer, Israel Gutman, Yfaat Weiss, and other colleagues in Israel, and likewise with Reinhard Rürup in Berlin. I presented the project a number of times at the Hamburg Institut für Sozialforschung and thank all those who helped me move forward with their objections, advice, and encouragement, but especially Werner Konitzer, with whom I am bound in friendship by many intense conversations. Ellen Wesemüller participated actively in the project during her internship. I was able to present initial research findings in a number of essays in *WerkstattGeschichte* and *Mittelweg 36*. Early versions of the manuscript were read by Ulrike Jureit, Stefanie Schüler-Springorum, Alf Lüdtke, and Brigitte Salzmann, whose extensive critical and constructive advice was extraordinarily helpful.

I would especially like to thank Otto Dov Kulka, who made the NS background reports available to me before they were published and attended to this project with considerable involvement; and likewise Avraham Barkai, who early on had investigated the significance of the *Volksgemeinschaft* for the political order of National Socialism and who, through many years, has stood at my side, prepared to help with word and deed.

Notes

1. The photograph is from Klaus Hesse and Philipp Springer, *Vor aller Augen: Foto-dokumente des nationalsozialistischen Terrors in der Provinz* (Essen, 2002), 22. For the event itself see Günther Rehme, Konstantin Hasse, and Klaus Hesse, "… *mit Rumpf und Stumpf ausrotten"*: *Zur Geschichte der Juden in Marburg und Umgebung nach 1933* (Marburg, 1982). As recorded beneath the headline "Pilloried" in the *Oberhessische Zeitung* (24 August 1933), the victim, a Jewish student named Spier from Gemün-den, was compelled to march through Marburg by SA members. After the march, Spier was taken into "protective custody" and hauled off to a concentration camp. A facsimile of the article appears in Rehme, Hasse, and Hesse, "… *mit Rumpf und Stumpf ausrotten,"* 65.

2. See Jan Phillip Reemtsma, "'Wie hätte ich mich verhalten?' Gedanken über eine populäre Frage," in Jan Phillip Reemtsma, "*Wie hätte ich mich verhalten?" und andere nicht nur deutsche Fragen: Reden und Aufsätze* (Munich, 2001), 9–29.

3. On the concept of complicity as it is used here see Hannah Arendt's essay (first pub-lished in January 1945 in *Jewish Frontier*) "Organisierte Schuld," in Hannah Arendt, *Die verborgene Tradition: Acht Essays* (Frankfurt am Main, 1976), 32–45; see also in the same volume "Was heißt persönliche Verantwortung," 81–97.

4. Christopher Browning, *Ordinary Men: Reserve Police Battalion 101 and the Final Solu-tion in Poland* (New York, 1992); Daniel Jonah Goldhagen, *Hitler's Willing Execution-ers: Ordinary Germans and the Holocaust* (New York, 1996); currently see especially Harald Welzer, *Täter: Wie aus ganz normalen Menschen Massenmörder werden* (Frank-furt am Main, 2005). See also the research overview by Gerhard Paul, "Von Psycho-pathen, Technokraten des Terrors und 'ganz gewöhnlichen' Deutschen: Die Täter der Shoah im Spiegel der Forschung," in *Die Täter der Shoah: Fanatische Nationalsozi-alisten oder ganz normale Deutsche?* (Göttingen, 2002), 13–90.

5. The third part of Hilberg's book, *Perpetrators, Victims, Bystanders: The Jewish Ca-tastrophe 1933–1945* (New York, 1992), introduces such a heterogeneous group of people and behaviors that the notions "spectator" and "bystander" clearly do not suffice. Hilberg said himself that this book was important and that he felt it had too often been ignored; see R. Hilberg, *Unerbetene Erinnerung* (Frankfurt am Main, 2008), 11–14, 162–166.

6. This kind of formulation of the problem, in which one asks about everyday par-ticipation, involvement and forms of cooperation, is inspired by Alf Lüdtke, whose work has deeply influenced me and from whom I derived many insights and ideas during our many friendly conversations. See also, e.g., the following by Alf Lüdtke: "'Formierung der Massen' oder: Mitmachen und Hinnehmen? – 'Alltagsgeschichte' und Faschismusanalyse," in *Normalität oder Normalisierung? Geschichtswerkstätten und Faschismusanalyse*, ed. Heide Gerstenberger and Dorothea Schmid (Münster, 1987), 15–34; "'Ehre der Arbeit': Industriearbeiter und Macht der Symbole: Zur Reichweite symbolischer Orientierungen im Nationalsozialismus," in *Arbeiter im 20. Jahrhundert*, ed. Klaus Tenfelde (Stuttgart, 1991), 343–392; "Funktioneliten: Täter, Mit-Täter, Opfer? Zu den Bedingungen des deutschen Faschismus," in *Herrschaft als soziale Prax-is*, ed. Alf Lüdtke (Göttingen, 1991), 559–590; "The Appeal of Exterminating 'Oth-ers': German Workers and the Limits of Resistance," in *The Third Reich: The Essential Readings*, ed. Christian Leitz (Oxford and Malden, MA, 1999), 155–177.

7. Hans Mommsen, "Volksgemeinschaft," in *Lexikon zur Geschichte und Politik im 20. Jahrhundert*, vol. 2, L–Z, ed. Carola Stern et al. (Cologne, 1971), 830; also critical:

Bernd Weisbrod, "Der Schein der Normalität: Zur Historisierung der 'Volksgemeinschaft,'" in *Geschichte als Möglichkeit: Über die Chance von Demokratie: Festschrift für Helga Grebing*, ed. Karsten Rudolph et. al. (Essen, 1995), 224–242.

8. Hans Ulrich Wehler, *Deutsche Gesellschaftsgeschichte*, vol. 4: *Vom Beginn des Ersten Weltkrieges bis zur Gründung der beiden deutschen Staaten 1914–1949* (Munich, 2003), 681.

9. Gellately's assessment, however, that within only a few months after January 1933 a "social consensus" was reached in favor of Hitler and National Socialism that was henceforth "practically never" questioned, is clearly exaggerated and conceptually brings homogeneity into the foreground again instead of asking about actual differences. Robert Gellately, *Hingeschaut und Weggesehen: Hitler und sein Volk* (Stuttgart, 2002), 15; similarly Peter Fritzsche, *Wie aus Deutschen Nazis wurden* (Munich, 1999), 147–223.

10. Detlev Peukert, *Volksgenossen und Gemeinschaftsfremde: Anpassung, Ausmerze und Aufbegehren unter dem Nationalsozialismus* (Cologne, 1982), 295. Peukert drew early attention to "racism as social politics" with this book.

11. I am picking up on an idea of Ulrich Bielefeld, who in the third part of his book *Nation und Gesellschaft: Selbstthematisierungen in Deutschland und Frankreich* (Hamburg, 2003) analyzes the dissolution of the concept of the "nation" in the twentieth century in favor of race and *Volksgemeinschaft* on the basis of writings by Ernst von Salomon and Louis-Ferdinand Céline and thereby refutes the description of National Socialism as "extreme Nationalism" (M. Rainer Lepsius). But I go beyond his sociological determination of the *Volksgemeinschaft* as a "community of consensus and submission" (p. 351) that maintains its silence, for the focal point of my examination is the historical praxis of production, the empirical practices of violence that gave "voice" to the *Volksgemeinschaft*.

12. This is not negated by the fact that over half (54.5 percent) of ca. 550,000 German Jews lived in large cities with populations over 100,000, particularly Berlin and Frankfurt am Main; see Avraham Barkai and Paul Mendes-Flohr, *Aufbruch und Zerstörung 1918–1945*, vol. 4, *Deutsch-Jüdische Geschichte der Neuzeit* (Munich, 1997), 37–40. The present book is not concerned with a representative but rather an exemplative perspective, one that is supposed to elucidate the transformative processes and practices of violence. In any event, when compared with Austria, where 90 percent of all Jews lived in Vienna, urbanization had not proceeded as far. There still existed more than 1,600 Jewish congregations in the German Reich, and one-fifth of German Jews lived in localities with fewer than 2,000 inhabitants (ibid.); see also Christhard Hoffmann, "Verfolgung und Alltagsleben der Landjuden im nationalsozialistischen Deutschland," in *Jüdisches Leben auf dem Lande: Studien zur deutsch-jüdischen Geschichte*, ed. Monika Richard and Reinhard Rürup (Tübingen, 1997), 373–398.

13. Raul Hilberg, *The Destruction of the European Jews* (Chicago, 1961). The first German translation appeared twenty years later in a small Berlin publishing house, Olle & Wolter. The standard German edition still remains *Die Vernichtung der europäischen Juden* (Frankfurt am Main, 1990).

14. Coming from this perspective, the exceedingly thorough book by Uwe Adam has provided a reliable foundation for many years: Uwe Dietrich Adam, *Judenpolitik im Dritten Reich* (Düsseldorf, 1972). In his instructive overview, *Reichskristallnacht: Antisemitismus und Judenverfolgung im Dritten Reich* (Munich, 1988), Hermann Graml identified the following phases: annulment of emancipation, isolation, dispossession, approach to genocide. As an early critical response, however, see Karl Schleunes,

The *Twisted Road to Auschwitz: Nazi Policy toward German Jews 1933–1939* (Urbana, 1970).

15. In their focus on state action, "intentionalists" like Eberhard Jäckel and "structuralists" like Martin Broszat were thoroughly in agreement, even though their interpretations were diametrically opposed. This controversy can be reviewed in Eberhard Jäckel and Jürgen Rohwer, eds., *Der Mord an den Juden im Zweiten Weltkrieg* (Stuttgart, 1985).

16. The collection by Joseph Walk remains indispensable to this day: *Das Sonderrecht für die Juden im NS-Staat: Eine Sammlung der gesetzlichen Maßnahmen und Richtlinien: Inhalt und Bedeutung*, 2nd ed. (Heidelberg, 1996).

17. Werner Jochmann, *Gesellschaftskrise und Judenfeindschaft in Deutschland 1870–1945* (Hamburg, 1988); Ursula Büttner, ed., *Die Deutschen und die Judenverfolgung im Dritten Reich* (Frankfurt am Main, 2003).

18. Avraham Barkai, *Vom Boykott zur "Entjudung": Der wirtschaftliche Existenzkampf der Juden im Dritten Reich, 1933–1943* (Frankfurt am Main: 1988) and "The German Volksgemeinschaft from the Persecution of the Jews to the 'Final Solution,'" in *Confronting the Nazi Past: New Debates on Modern German History*, ed. Michael Burleigh (London, 1996). Exemplary for recent studies concerning "Aryanization" that include the aspect of societal anti-Semitism is Frank Bajohr, *"Arisierung" in Hamburg: Die Verdrängung der jüdischen Unternehmer 1933–1945* (Hamburg, 1997).

19. Peter Longerich, *Politik der Vernichtung: Eine Gesamtdarstellung der nationalsozialistischen Judenverfolgung* (Munich, 1998), English edition: *Holocaust: The Nazi Persecution and the Murder of the Jews* (Oxford, 2010) and *"Davon haben wir nichts gewusst!": Die Deutschen und die Judenverfolgung 1933–1945* (Munich, 2006); Saul Friedländer, *Nazi Germany and the Jews*, Vol. I: *The Years of Persecution, 1933–1939* (New York, 1997) and *Nazi Germany and the Jews*, Vol. 2: *The Years of Extermination, 1939–1945* (New York, 2007).

20. In what follows, violence is predominantly understood as physical violence, as *violentia*, even though the other literal meaning of violence, *potestas*, in the sense of power, always resonates and both meanings are also explicitly bound together in the thesis of the *Volksgemeinschaft* as self-empowerment; in this regard see Thomas Lindenberger and Alf Lüdtke, eds., *Physische Gewalt: Studien zur Geschichte der Neuzeit* (Frankfurt am Main, 1995); see also Armin Nolzen, "The Nazi Party and its Violence against the Jews, 1933–1939: Violence as a Historiographical Concept," *Yad Vashem Studies* 31 (2003): 245–285.

21. This kind of perspective, of course, is diametrically opposed to that of Daniel J. Goldhagen, who posits a preexisting German *Volksgemeinschaft* whose eliminatory anti-Semitism only needed to be put into practice after 1933.

22. Michael Stolleis, *Gemeinwohlformeln im nationalsozialistischen Recht* (Berlin, 1974); the main ideas of this study are already found in his essay: "Gemeinschaft und Volksgemeinschaft: zur juristischen Terminologie im Nationalsozialismus," *Vierteljahreshefte für Zeitgeschichte* 20 (1972): 16–38; Oliver Lepsius, *Die gegensatzaufhebende Begriffsbildung: Methodenentwicklungen in der Weimarer Republik und ihr Verhältnis zur Ideologisierung der Rechtswissenschaft unter dem Nationalsozialismus* (Munich, 1994); see also Bernd Rüthers, *Die unbegrenzte Auslegung: Zum Wandel der Privatrechtsordnung im Nationalsozialismus*, exp. 6th ed. (Tübingen, 2005).

23. David Schoenbaum, *Hitler's Social Revolution: Class and Status in Nazi Germany, 1933–1939* (Garden City, 1966); Timothy Mason, *Arbeiterklasse und Volksgemeinschaft: Dokumente und Materialien zur deutschen Arbeiterpolitik 1936–1939* (Opladen, 1975).

24. See especially Peukert, *Volksgenossen und Gemeinschaftsfremde*; Detlev Peukert and Jürgen Reulecke, eds., *Die Reihen fast geschlossen: Beiträge zur Geschichte des Alltags unterm Nationalsozialismus* (Wuppertal, 1981); see also Heide Gerstenberger and Dorothea Schmidt, eds., *Normalität oder Normalisierung? Geschichtswerkstätten und Faschismusanalyse* (Münster, 1987).

25. Uwe Puschner, *Die völkische Bewegung im wilhelminischen Kaiserreich: Sprache – Rasse – Religion* (Darmstadt, 2001); Stefan Breuer, *Ordnungen der Ungleichheit: Die deutsche Rechte im Widerstreit ihrer Ideen 1871–1945* (Darmstadt, 2001) and *Nationalismus und Faschismus: Frankreich, Italien und Deutschland im Vergleich* (Darmstadt, 2005); also Kurt Sontheimer, *Antidemokratisches Denken in der Weimarer Republik* (Munich, 1962).

26. Hans Ulrich Thamer, *Verführung und Gewalt: Deutschland 1933–1945*, rev. ed. (Berlin, 1994); Wehler, *Deutsche Gesellschaftsgeschichte*, vol. 4.

27. Norbert Frei, "'Volksgemeinschaft': Erfahrungsgeschichte und Lebenswirklichkeit der Hitler-Zeit," in *1945 und wir: Das Dritte Reich im Bewußtsein der Deutschen* (Munich, 2005), 107–128.

28. See Frank Bajohr and Michael Wildt, eds., *Volksgemeinschaft: Neue Forschungen zur Gesellschaft des Nationalsozialismus* (Frankfurt am Main, 2009); Frank Bajohr, "The 'Folk Community' and the Persecution of the Jews: German Society under National Socialist Dictatorship, 1933–1945," *Holocaust and Genocide Studies* 20 (2006): 183–206.

29. See Arnold Paucker, *Der jüdische Abwehrkampf gegen Antisemitismus und Nationalsozialismus in den letzten Jahren der Weimarer Republik*, 2nd ed. (Hamburg, 1969); Jürgen Matthäus, "Kampf ohne Verbündete: Der Centralverein deutscher Staatsbürger jüdischen Glaubens 1933–1938," *Jahrbuch für Antisemitismusforschung* 8 (1998): 248–277; and above all Avraham Barkai, *"Wehr Dich!" Der Centralverein deutscher Staatsbürger jüdischen Glaubens 1893–1938* (Munich, 2002).

30. See Avraham Barkai, "The C.V. Archives in Moscow: A Reassessment," *Leo Baeck Institute Yearbook* 45 (2000): 173–182; also http://www.sonderarchiv.de [accessed 7.12.006]; as well as the Russian-language homepage of the archive: http://www.rusarchives.ru/federal/rgva/index.shtml [accessed 12 July 2006].

31. Thus the sources referenced in the endnotes refer either only to the signature of the special archive in Moscow or to the signature of the CAHJP microfilm in Jerusalem, supplemented with the respective Moscow signature to make it easier to find.

32. A recent publication from this collection is Herbert Obenaus, ed., *Historisches Handbuch der jüdischen Gemeinden in Niedersachsen und Bremen*, 2 vols. (Göttingen, 2005).

33. Longerich, *"Davon haben wir nichts gewusst!"*

34. Otto Kulka and Eberhard Jäckel, eds., *Die Juden in den geheimen NS-Stimmungsberichten 1933–1945*, vol. 62, *Schriften des Bundesarchivs*. Düsseldorf, 2004 (Düsseldorf, 2004); English edition: *The Jews in the Secret Nazi Reports on Popular Opinion in Germany, 1933–1945* (New Haven, 2010); see also Otto Kulka, "Jewish Society in Germany as Reflected in Secret Nazi Reports on 'Public Opinion' 1933–1945," in *On Germans and Jews under the Nazi Regime: Essays by Three Generations of Historians: A Festschrift in Honor of Otto Dov Kulka*, ed. Moshe Zimmermann (Jerusalem, 2006), 261–279.

35. Longerich, *"Davon haben wir nichts gewusst!"* 23–53.

1

VOLKSGEMEINSCHAFT AS A POLITICAL CONCEPT

The Origins of the *Volksgemeinschaft* during the First World War

The entry *Volksgemeinschaft* in the German dictionary by the brothers Grimm records only a single source, namely Friedrich Schleiermacher.[1] Nonetheless, we also find the *Volksgemeinschaft* in Wilhelm Dilthey, Johann Caspar Bluntschli, and Friedrich Carl von Savigny, who understood the state as the "corporal form of the spiritual *Volksgemeinschaft*."[2] Ferdinand Tönnies used the term, as did Theodor Herzl in his book *The Jewish State*, albeit only in passing and with reference to persistent anti-Semitism. Herzl wrote that the Jewish people had made an honest attempt "to assimilate with the *Volksgemeinschaft* that surrounds us while only preserving the faith of our fathers. One does not allow it."[3] Hans-Ulrich Wehler sums up that during the Wilhelmine Empire the concept *Volksgemeinschaft* gradually took the place of the *Volksnation* (people's nation), which at that time already possessed the fatal flaw of being "constitutionally indifferent"—as much at home with the Empire as with the Weimar Republic and National Socialism—and did not guarantee an association with the rights of liberal freedom and democratic equality.[4] The kind of political potential lurking within the concept was already made clear before the First World War by the liberal Friedrich Nauman, who remarked ironically: "The *Volksgemeinschaft* is never larger or more flexible than when people must die together."[5] And in fact, the First World War can be seen as the actual hour of the *Volksgemeinschaft*'s birth.[6]

The final days before the mobilization on the first of August were filled with tension. As late as 28 July, the SPD staged an anti-war rally in which more 750,000 people participated, considerably more than in the patriotic processions of the previous days.[7] Faced with the threat of war, others were gripped by panic. Thousands withdrew their savings from the banks and hoarded foodstuffs.[8] "Deep into the night," proclaimed a typical newspaper report from Wattenscheid near Gelsenkirchen, "people waited for final news about the state of things. While at first an oppressive mood predominated, the tension gradually eased and disappeared into thin air with the singing of patriotic songs."[9]

Special editions then spread the news about the mobilization within the briefest time; people gathered, read the declarations aloud, and sang songs of imperial loyalty. The newspapers attested to the unanimity and steadfastness of the German people in the face of war and described the processions as expressions of the people's solidarity with the emperor. In this situation, addressing the large mass of people who had assembled on 1 August in front of the Berlin Palace, Wilhelm II found these words to say (which would later be cited again and again): "I thank you from the depths of my heart for the expression of your love and your faithfulness. In the battles that are now to come, I no longer recognize any parties in my people. Among us there are now only Germans." According to newspaper reports, these words were met with thunderous exultation.[10] In the Reichstag on 4 August, the emperor repeated this statement, and the parliament unanimously approved the war credits.

This internal truce that the SPD made with the imperial regime created the image of a unified nation, even though recent investigations of this myth of the entire German people closing ranks at the beginning of the war reveal significant gender, class, and regional differences; the myth should be evaluated more as media production than as a reality.[11] For young bourgeois men—especially academics—the war represented a test of character, a manly baptism of fire. The philosopher Karl Löwith, a young Bildungsbürger who reported as a volunteer, described his motives:

> The drive for emancipation from the bourgeois strictures of school and home, an internal discord with myself after the collapse of my first friendship, the appeal of "living dangerously" which enthused us because of Nietzsche, the desire to throw oneself into adventure and to test oneself, and

last but not least the alleviation of one's own being, which had become conscious through Schopenhauer, by participating in the totality by which one was surrounded—these and similar motives determined that I would welcome the war as a chance to live and die.[12]

The newspapers and intellectual public reinforced the image of national unity. The "Spirit of 1914" became a set phrase for the unified *Volksgemeinschaft* that, transcending parties and classes, glimpsed its strength in unity and coherence, with which it believed it could defy any enemy. The essays, books, brochures, speeches, and tracts of German intellectuals who proclaimed their enthusiasm for the war are legion.[13] In a keen historical comparison, the situation in 1914 was likened to the wars of liberation fought in 1813 against Napoleonic rule, while at the same time the rejection of the values of the French Revolution was codified: against the "democratic freedom" of the allies there was "German freedom" (Friedrich Meinecke), against civil equality there was soldierly comradery, against brotherhood there was Prussian socialism.[14] Johann Plenge wrote: "to will from a different will than that narrow will of your little I! That is the communal!"[15] Such demands that the individual be subjugated to the whole, together with the apotheosis of the German people as the manifestation of the Hegelian "World Spirit" leading a crusade for humanity, created a vision of community that combined arrogance with hubris.[16]

The close connection between the feeling of the *Volksgemeinschaft* and ostracism and persecution—the enthusiastic and emotionally laden inclusion linked with a vehement and violent exclusion—is revealed by the hunt for alleged spies. As early as the first days of August, newspapers spread reports of spies who were attacking bridges and poisoning drinking water.[17] Even though the imperial regime immediately denied such reports and told the populace not to believe everything that was written in the papers, the fever of the hunt spread everywhere. On 3 August sixty-four supposed spies were turned over to police at a Berlin train station, but they turned out to be nothing of the sort. Even the actress Asta Nielsen became the victim of a hysterical crowd while taking a walk, as she recorded in her memoirs:

Suddenly my hat was torn off, so that my black hair became visible. "A Russian!" cried someone from behind, and a hand grabbed me by the head. I cried out in fear and pain. Then a man turned in front of me and recognized me. He called out my name to the excited crowd behind me and they let me go and started berating each other.[18]

Similar incidents occurred in other cities as well. Rumors about alleged atrocities against German soldiers in Belgium further aggravated the mood. In the Thuringian town of Ohrdruf, a crowd lynched a Catholic priest who was accused of helping the Belgian army.[19]

Social Democrats as well as many German Jews hoped that by supporting the war they would finally be seen as equal members of the German Volk. In fact, the war could only be waged with accelerated industrial production, that is, with the help of the workforce. The conservatives mistook the national euphoria in Germany at the beginning of the war as an affirmation of the political status quo. But they were soon forced to learn (no later than when the defeat at the Battle of the Marne in September 1914 made a "lightning victory" unimaginable) that the recognition of the Social Democrats and the unions as equally legitimate powers within the state was a prerequisite for the necessary war effort. In turn, the leadership of the SPD took up as a leitmotif the idea that the class struggle could only be resumed once the stability of the society as a whole was secured.[20] "Standing together with the Volksgemeinschaft in misery and death" was a matter of course, according to Konrad Haenisch, who became the Prussian minister of culture after the war.[21] And, as another SPD leader added helpfully, "national solidarity" with the Volksgemeinschaft meant "subordinating all of the desires of the individual party to the question regarding the welfare of the Volk."[22]

Most Jews also joined the national euphoria, and not only because they hoped to attain their long sought-after integration with the Volksgemeinschaft through public displays of patriotism. They did so, rather, mostly because they were, in fact, patriots. At the worship service on 5 August, the synagogue in Berlin-Charlottenburg, which could hold 2,000 people, was overflowing; Leo Baeck gave the sermon and explained that this war would decide about the culture and civilization of Europe.[23] Even Martin Buber was gripped by the mood: "never has the concept of 'Volk' become such a reality for me as in these weeks."[24] More than 10,000 young Jewish men volunteered for the army immediately after the war began; all told, 96,000 Jewish solders served in the German forces during the First World War, of whom 12,000 died and 35,000 were decorated with medals.[25]

The directive on the "home front" was that one had to support the men "in the field." Throughout Germany, local committees were formed under the leadership of the Red Cross to collect donations. The National Women's Service (Nationaler Frauendienst) now included Social Democratic women's organizations, which had previously been denied the opportunity to collaborate.[26] Even children and adolescents were called upon to participate in the Volksgemeinschaft's war efforts. "What did we notice of the war?" Klaus Mann asked himself, having been eight years old when the war began:

Afternoons one went to the nearest corner to read the daily report. Two thousand prisoners captured on the Eastern Front, triumphant advances in the West: there were always only victories. The great victories were much like major holidays. When Hindenburg did that colossal thing in the Masurian swamp, the children were in buoyant spirits like on Christmas Eve.[27]

Remembering his childhood in Berlin, the later West German journalist and author Sebastian Haffner (born in 1907) wrote that the war was "a big and excitedly enthusiastic game of nations, which provided more meaningful entertainment and provoked more passionate emotions than anything peace-time could offer."[28] In his notes written in 1939 while exiled in London, Haffner confessed that for him the most lasting impression created by all the hardships and discomforts that the war brought especially to the cities—bad and often insufficient food, wooden soles for shoes, clothes worn inside out, collecting bones and cherry pits in school—was of the war as a game:

> It was a dark, secretive game, one with a never ending and vicious appeal that extinguished everything and declared real life null and void, with the narcotic effect of playing roulette or smoking opium. I and my comrades played it through the entire war, four years long, unpunished and undisturbed—and it was *this* game, not the harmless "war games" that we also played in the streets and playgrounds, that left its dangerous marks on all of us.[29]

The real fissures in the wartime society soon showed themselves.[30] The initial enthusiasm for the war was quickly followed by disillusionment. The drafted men were no longer available to provide for their families, and government assistance was often insufficient to keep up with the rising cost of living. Thus many women had to search for ways to earn income and took the workplaces in the factories that had been left behind by the men.[31] The horrors of the "turnip winter" in 1916/17—when for lack of bread, milk, butter, and meat the turnip became the primary source of nutrition—remained for decades a fixed part of the collective memory in Germany. And thirty years later it significantly influenced economic measures vis-à-vis nourishment on the part of the National Socialists, who during the Second World War feared that a similar catastrophic nutritional situation could decisively weaken wartime morale and encourage revolutionary resentment.

In Berlin, the first disturbances caused by food shortages occurred in October 1915, after which the series of hunger riots never let up. Women and adolescents took part in the looting of grocery stores and even engaged in violent confrontations with police. There were mounting complaints by public authorities about the "waywardness" of youth.[32] The year 1916 witnessed the first short strikes in the armaments industry, by which workers sought to reinforce their demands for cost-of-living adjustments and increased food rations. Finally, reports from the Russian revolution in the spring of 1917 reinvigorated anti-war sentiments. In April of that year, metal workers in Berlin, Leipzig, and other locations laid down their tools; in January 1918 the waves of strikes swelled to the largest protests in Germany during the war. In July 1918, the Magdeburg General Command complained:

> The previously large rift between the poor and the rich that had been pretty much sealed by the enthusiasm for the war early on grows increasingly larger with time. Among the poorer classes of the population, a decidedly harmful hatred has accumulated against the rich and namely against the so-called war profiteers, about which one can only hope that [this hatred] will not at some point come to a dreadful discharge.[33]

In this situation, the appeal to the "Spirit of 1914" served to strengthen the perseverance of the populace and reproduce the *Volksgemeinschaft* that was threatening to break apart. The Reich Chancellery founded its own propaganda institution, the German National Committee (Deutsche Nationalausschuß), which immediately organized a series of lectures in memory of the "Spirit of 1914," initially with prominent speakers like Max Weber, Ernst Troeltsch, and Friedrich Naumann.[34] The German Fatherland Party grew out of the National Committee in 1917 with Grand Admiral Tirpitz as party leader; its central purpose was to represent the "Spirit of 1914."[35] Within a year, the Fatherland Party gained almost half a million members and thus counted among the largest political associations during the war. With numerous propaganda operations and mass assemblies, with placards, leaflets, and brochures, it tried to strengthen the Germans' resolve for victory and to denounce any calls for a negotiated peace.

"All Authority Emanates from the *Volk*"

The collapse into defeat was correspondingly severe. At the end of September 1918, when the Supreme Command (Oberste Heeresleitung) suddenly admitted that the war could no longer be won and sued for an immediate cease-fire, the news struck the public like a shock, for until that moment the propaganda had always nurtured the hope for victory.[36] Now the artificial confidence collapsed, and the call for a quick end to the war spread like wildfire. When the admiralty reversed itself yet again and ordered continued fighting so as to preserve "honor" in defeat, the soldiers resisted the senseless dying. The revolution started in Kiel—on 4 November the sailors and soldiers had control of the city, and in following days workers' and soldiers' councils assumed power in many cities throughout the empire. The power structure of the old regime capitulated everywhere with next to no resistance. On 9 November the revolution finally reached Berlin.

Although the SPD leadership under Ebert believed for a short time that it could take over power within the framework of the October constitution and establish a Social Democratic/bourgeois cabinet, the events rolled over them as well. Around noon of 9 November, Max von Baden, without being authorized to do so, announced the abdication of the Kaiser, who had already fled at the end of October to the military headquarters in Spa, and turned over the office of the Reich chancellor to Friedrich Ebert. In the afternoon, Philipp Scheidemann dashed to balcony of the Reichstag and proclaimed the "German Republic," just a few hours before Karl Liebknecht proclaimed the "Free Socialist Republic" at the Berlin Palace.

Ebert's intention to hamstring the social revolution and support state authority expressed itself in an appeal to civil servants to stay at their posts and especially in his pact of mutual recognition with General Groener, the successor to Ludendorff in the Supreme Command. But a continuation of the old imperial cabinet was no longer conceivable. The Berlin soldiers' councils resolved on 9 November to elect workers' and soldiers' councils throughout Berlin and have them come together in their first large assembly. The SPD leadership reacted to its threatened loss of power and reached an agreement with the leftist USPD (Independent Social Democratic Party of Germany) on the afternoon of 10 November to create a Council of People's Representatives that would seat three members from each of the two parties, including Ebert and Scheidemann.[37] On the same day, the assembly of Berlin workers' and soldiers' councils confirmed the creation of a Council of People's Representatives and resisted the demands on the Left to exclude the majority Social Democrats from the leadership of the council.[38] One month later in Berlin, by a large majority, the first nationwide Congress of Workers' and Soldiers' Councils called for the election of a National Assembly to provide a constitution, thus making room for a parliamentary democracy.

On 12 November, one day after the signing of the cease-fire agreement, the Council of People's Representatives published an appeal to the German people, which became "the first constitutional document of the Republic" (Christoph Gusy). Apart from abrogating the state of siege and granting amnesty for political crimes, the document declared the freedom of association and assembly, the prohibition of censorship, and the freedoms of opinion and religion to be fundamental rights, as well as democratic elections by universal suffrage with equal, secret, and direct ballots.[39] The election of a National Assembly to provide a constitution was a clear objective of social democratic politics, but the SPD did not have a constitutional theory at its disposal.[40]

So it made complete sense that on 15 November, instead of a Social Democrat, it was Hugo Preuß, a constitutional lawyer and liberal, who was called to head the Imperial Ministry of the Interior and entrusted with composing a draft for a constitution.[41] In a daring treatise that received wide attention, Preuß (whose parents were Jewish) had already staked out a position during the war in opposition to the Wilhelminian authoritarian state. He had argued for a *Volksstaat* that was to combine national unity and the people's freedom, which in concrete terms meant a demand for electoral reforms and a parliamentary monarchy.[42]

Now Preuß pled his case anew in a programmatic article on 14 November 1918 in the *Berliner Tageblatt* against the traditional authoritarian state and against a Bolshevist class dictatorship, but for a *Volksstaat* that would help the Bürgertum and workers attain their political rights:

> Not classes or groups, not parties or estates in opposing isolation, but only the entire German Volk, represented by a German National Assembly which has proceeded from wholly democratic elections, can create the German *Volksstaat*. [The Assembly] must create it soon, lest an unspeakable disaster completely immiserate our wretched Volk. Certainly a modern democracy must be filled with the spirit of vigorous social progress; but its political foundation can never be created by class struggle or the suppression of one social stratum by another, but rather only by the unity and freedom of all *Volksgenossen* [people's comrades].[43]

Despite the Revolution, the debate about constitutional politics was still shaped by the German tradition of constitutional thought, at the center of which stood the state-as-power (Machtstaat).[44] "The constitution has changed, the state has remained. This is the only way to understand the German Revolution of November 1918," commented Gerhard Anschütz, a liberal specialist in constitutional law, in the important commentary he wrote at the time about the Weimar imperial constitution.[45] According to both right- and left-wing critiques, the "genuine" and "true" *Volkswille* (will of the people) could not be expressed by the principle of the majority—*Volkswille* was always more than the will of the majority. Thus the parliament could not be the only institution that articulated the *Volkswille*. The influential expert on constitutional law Robert Redslob wanted a "system of balance between the executive and legislative power." The parliament could not be allowed to impose its will on the regime, but instead could only possess the "right of criticism." Conversely, the regime could not be allowed to act against the expressed will of parliament. Only this kind of "system of duality" could make the Volk capable of sovereignty, whereas the head of state would assume the role of "the creative force in the [power balance] mechanism."[46]

Max Weber took a similar approach in a series of articles about "Germany's future form of state" in the *Frankfurter Zeitung* in November 1918. He developed the idea of a constitution in which the Federal Council, as a representative of the states, stood opposite a Reich president elected by the people, whereas the only responsibilities left to the Reichstag were matters of secondary importance, like controlling the budget.[47] Weber had already pressed for the "direct election by the people of the supreme bearer of authority" in 1917, for this was the only way to assure the political "selective choosing of leadership" (*Führerauslese*) in a modern mass democracy. Now, as Wolfgang Mommsen put it, he formally embarked on "the path toward a plebiscitary Führer democracy."[48]

Before deliberations began at the end of January 1919, in an article about Preuß's constitutional draft, the liberal historian Friedrich Meinecke also endorsed an "enlightened and energetic dictatorship of trust [*Vertauensdiktatur*]," whose leader could very well be a Social Democrat. Only a "unified and strong hand" would be capable of freeing "us from the co-government of the workers' and soldiers' councils, this scum of our public life." Meinecke supported the demand for a strongly positioned Reich president, who according to him should also be the Reich chancellor. "A strong and unified Reich chancellery authority at the head of the German republic—that would be the proper organic bond between the past and future of our national being."[49]

In the constitutional discussions in the Imperial Office of the Interior during mid December 1918 (in which Max Weber played a significant role), Hugo Preuß objected to an "inauthentic parliamentary system" in which the president was elected by parliament. Instead, Preuß espoused the election of a president by plebiscite.[50] One year later, on the occasion of the National Assembly's acceptance of the finalized constitution, Preuß again underscored the point that the constitution was not supposed to create "parliamentary absolutism"; rather, "next to the parliament as the supreme organ of the communal being" it quite deliberately positioned a "Reich president who was directly elected by the people."[51] Correspondingly, the first draft of the constitution that Preuß delivered to the Council of the People's Representatives at the beginning of January 1919 proposed a president directly elected by the people as a counterweight to the Reichstag.[52] The Council of the People's Representatives pushed above all for an explicit formulation of fundamental rights in the constitution. Thus on 20 January, one day after the elections for the National Assembly, a revised version was published as a kind of governmental draft that was essentially the same as the first, except that it was expanded to include a catalogue of fundamental rights.[53] In the appended memorandum, Hugo Preuß once again outlined his concept of a unified *Volksstaat*: "The German Republic can only be the democratic self-organization of the German people as a political whole.... There is no such thing as a Prussian or Bavarian, a Lippian or Reussian nation; there is only a German nation, which shall shape the form of its political life in the German Democratic Republic."[54]

This strongly unified character of the imperial constitution steadily diminished in the subsequent deliberations with the states, and the federal aspects of the empire drew more forcefully to the fore.[55] The changes in the paragraph regarding the sovereignty of the people were significant. In Preuß's version, it read: "all state authority lies with the German people [*beim deutschen Volke*]"; now it read: "state authority lies with the people [*beim Volke*]," which indeed could be understood as Prussian, Bavarian, or Lippian state people.[56] After repeated revisions, especially by the representatives of the states, the constitutional draft was submitted to the National Assembly.[57]

With 38 percent of the votes cast, the SPD emerged as the strongest force from the National Assembly elections on 19 January 1919. Together with the most successful bourgeois party, the liberal DDP (German Democratic Party), and the Catholic Center Party, it formed the so-called Weimar Coalition, which represented the Republic's hopeful anacrusis. The German Nationals and right-wing liberals lagged behind the electoral results they had enjoyed during the Wilhelmine Empire, and with their 7.6 percent even the left-wing Independent Social Democrats by no means attained the results they had hoped for. The conservatives—the DNVP (German National People's Party) and the right wing of the DVP—insisted on a return to the constitutional monarchy and the preservation of the social status quo; the Catholic representatives of the Center Party and the BVP (Bavarian People's Party) were committed to a state based on principles of Christian natural law and thus wholly opposed to the sovereignty of the people and "absolutism of the majority" (*Mehrheitsabsolutismus*). Therefore, for all intents and purposes, the Social Democrats and the progressive liberals of the DDP were the only ones with a clear commitment to a parliamentary-democratic republic. According to Ernst-Wolfgang Böckenförde, a mere 60 percent of the representatives could be counted as "actual supporters of the democratic foundations of the new order of the state."[58] The National Assembly gathered on February 1919 and, after passing the law concerning preliminary imperial authority on 10 February, it elected Friedrich Ebert as Reich president the next day.[59]

"All authority lies with people"—this was the weighty programmatic formulation in Article 2 of the constitutional draft that the National Assembly had to deliberate. With the Revolution and the abdication of the Kaiser the empire had obviously disappeared, yet the basic legitimating principles that would support the new state were hotly contested. In the plenary debate about the constitutional draft, the Social Democrat Richard Fischer emphasized that a new Germany had to be built on a foundation of freedom, law, and justice; it would be a new empire with virtually nothing in common with the old empire apart from its name. Consequently, the Social Democrats were in favor of speaking not about a "Constitution of the German Empire" but a "Constitution of the German Republic." Similarly, the DDP representative Erich Koch, the mayor of Kassel in Hesse, gave unqualified support to democratic constitutional ideas, which he traced straight from 1848 to 1918. In contrast, the representative of the Center Party Peter Spahn, formerly the Prussian minister of justice, expressly criticized the principle of *Volkssouveränität* (sovereignty of the people). The idea of the state, according to Spahn, was "rooted in moral human nature and thereby in the divine world order." Thus he found himself in opposition to the definition in the constitutional draft that all authority emanates from the people.[60]

The "constitutional conflict" about *Volkssouveränität* continued to preoccupy Catholics in the years to come. Above all, Heinrich Schrörs, a Church historian from Bonn, insisted in numerous publications that the constitutional principle that authority emanates from the people was fundamentally opposed to Catholic doctrine.[61] In turn, politicians from the Center Party, supported by part of the episcopacy, defended themselves and the pragmatics of the constitution. As the legal historian and Center Party representative Konrad Beyerle said defensively: "Where in Bismarckian constitution does it say anything in favor of freedom of conscience, Church, and Christian schools that even in the most remote way approaches the guarantees that the Weimar [constitution] provides for these religious areas of life?"[62] Others emphasized that the principle of *Volkssouveränität* did not signify the denial of divine guidance, but rather provided the initial impulse toward developing the "republican idea of the living *Volksgemeinschaft*" into an actual social ethos.[63] Article 1 of the constitution was merely a declaration of the *Volksstaat* in opposition to the former authoritarian state and not a legal-philosophical or theological statement about the origins of state power. Nonetheless, the circle of Catholic representatives still maintained a distance from the republican constitution.

The USPD noticeably withdrew from the 1918/19 constitutional discussion. While their representative, the Jewish Berlin lawyer Oskar Cohn, was active in the National Assembly with many critical but thoroughly

constructive criticisms,[64] in March 1919 the USPD party congress concluded that democratic legal forms within a capitalist social order were
a mirage, and thus the party would strive for the council system and the
dictatorship of the proletariat.[65] In another resolution, the party congress
(in which Oskar Cohn was not a delegate) declared: "The party congress
sees in the National Assembly in Weimar neither a *Volksparlament* [peo-
ple's parliament] nor an expression of the real proletarian Volk's will. An
administration like that in Weimar, which is only supported by bayonets,
must and will meet its imminent dissolution."[66]

During the debate, representatives on the political right swore by the
old Reich and the wisdom of the Bismarckian constitution, which could
no longer be discerned in the new constitutional draft. They advocated
a constitutional monarchy, which in light of the Kaiser's abdication and
the revolutionary changes sounded more like the swan song of a lost ep-
och than a political position within a National Assembly that was creating a constitution. While not actually avowing the Republic, the right-
wing liberals nonetheless managed with great difficulty to acknowledge
the political realities of the day.[67] Even during the final deliberations on
the constitution, the representative Heinze declared that the DVP had
not failed to cooperate in the creation of a constitution, but he promised
that when it came to establishing the Republic as the fundamental form
of state for the German Reich, the DVP would vote against Article 1 and
the constitution as a whole.[68]

Likewise, the German National representatives rejected the constitution because it was republican, although, as formulated by the representative and former justice minister of Baden Adalbert Düringer, they
would not let the republican form of state prevent them from "fulfilling
our responsibilities as state citizens." Yet at the party congress in mid July
1919, resistance mounted to even this distanced cooperation on the part
of the German National fraction in the National Assembly. Receiving
thunderous applause from the delegates, the extreme right-wing *völkisch*
constitutional lawyer Axel von Freytagh-Loringhoven demanded "of our
representatives that they vote against this constitution that seeks in the
end to establish this goddamned and cursed republic."[69]

It was also Freytagh-Loringhoven who fundamentally denied the Weimar constitution any legitimation whatsoever. According to him, the unauthorized abdication declaration of Wilhelm II as proclaimed by Reich
Chancellor Max von Baden and the proclamation of the Republic by
Philipp Scheidemann amounted to acts of high treason. The Council of
People's Representatives was just as illegitimate as the National Assembly it convoked. Freytagh-Loringhoven polemicized forcefully against the
recognition of the normative force of the de facto situation:

The Bolshevik's bloody regime of terror will never be transformed into legality, and neither will we Germans ever find legal the dictated Treaty of Versailles, even though our enemies have the power at the moment to give us laws. Precisely in light of the violence to which our Volk is being subjected, we cannot acknowledge that illegitimate power takes precedence over powerless legitimacy.[70]

To be sure, one could not avoid recognizing the power that stood behind the new republic, because abolishing it by force would provoke a civil war. But that only meant going along with the constitution "the way the population of a territory occupied by the enemy comes to terms with his ordinances so as to prevent greater harm."[71]

The Republic as an occupying force that suppresses its own people: this poisonous image—formulated in 1920 at the beginning of the Weimar democracy by an influential expert in state law—could hardly have more accurately described the deep aversion toward the Republic that predominated in many parts of Germany. In precisely that moment when the constitution extolled *Volkssouveränität* as the foundational principle of government, the fundamental opposition rallied around the notion of the Volk, paradoxically twisting the principle that all state authority emanates from the people in order to undermine the Weimar constitutional state. The nineteenth-century discussions of state law were characterized by a division of state and society that, as Christoph Gusy writes, assigned to the constitution a delimiting function that protected the respective features of one from access by the other, thus excluding society as the realm of individual freedom from the realm of politics. Now, instead of the "theoretical exclusion of the Volk from the political," constitutional law included the Volk. All of the supreme state organs were beholden to the Volk as the highest organ for the formation of the state's will, not merely in ideal terms but also procedurally.[72] But the Volk's entrance into the realm of constitutional politics did not mean that the political mutivalence bound up in the notion of the Volk had become civically unambiguous.

The pathos of the constitution's preamble allowed the appearance of a Volk quite different from a Volk comprised by state citizens:

The German Volk, unified in its tribes [*Stämme*] and animated by the will to renew and consolidate its Empire in freedom and justice, to attend to internal and external peace, and to promote social progress, has given itself this constitution.[73]

This Volk was obviously not first created politically by virtue of the constitution; it already existed earlier and gave itself this constitution.

And this Volk as a historically active agent defined itself differently from the assembly of free and equal citizens that Jean-Jacques Rousseau had in mind with his *contrat social*. In 1927 the Weimar expert on state law Hans Liermann wrote: "every attempt in this place to interpret the German Volk as some kind of soulless mere summation of individuals would be a slap in the face to what is meant in the preamble."[74] *Volkssouveränität* had to be understood in a higher sense than the commonly accepted notion, according to which the Volk participates in state authority. It is the recognition of the Volk as a "state-creating elemental power. The Volk is not, as in a democracy, situated *in* the state, but rather *above* the state. It is not an organ of the state, but rather its master."[75]

The plebiscitary vote of the Reich president, something that Max Weber in particular called for time and again, did not imply the creation of the position of an "ersatz Kaiser" or of a constitutional monarchy.[76] The position of the Reich president was not directed toward the past; on the contrary, it was directed toward an authoritatively formed mass democracy (Wolfgang Mommsen even discerned here a trajectory that led directly to the Führer dictatorship). The "much talked about 'dictatorship' of the masses," according to Weber, demands a "dictator," to whom the former subordinate themselves as long as he has their confidence.[77] Subordination of the masses to the leader that they elect themselves—this was the magical formula contained in Article 41: "The Reich president is elected by the whole German Volk." Of course, the Reich president was elected only by state citizens with the right to vote, and not by the entire German Volk. But the pathos evoked here by this holistic concept of Volk was purposefully formulated and intended to underscore the contrast to the elections for parliament. Whereas society's special interests stood for election in the latter, the former was concerned with the politically unified will of the entire German Volk.[78]

It was Carl Schmitt who polarized the ambivalence of the concept of the Volk in the Weimar constitution with an anti-liberal charge. The constitution was something essentially quite different from a social contract à la Rousseau.

> The democratic principle of the Volk's power to grant a constitution implies that the constitution comes into being through an act of a Volk that is capable of political action. The Volk must exist as a political entity and must be presupposed, if it is to be the subject of a power to grant a constitution.[79]

The political Volk, from which emanates all authority in a democracy, is not understood in liberal terms as something composed through the constitution from the collectivity of all citizens; rather, it needs much more to be presupposed so that it could even want a constitution. "The political being preceded the granting of the constitution."[80]

For that reason, the form of the state was for Schmitt of secondary importance, since it was the will of the Volk as a political entity that was fundamental. Thus the Imperial Constitution of 1871 possessed without a doubt the approval of the Volk, even if the latter did not yet have the will to abolish the monarchical principle and to declare itself sovereign. In this manner, Schmitt's argumentation could be taken further—even the Führer state was based in the will of the Volk, which had announced its approval by acclamation.[81] This political entity, namely the "Volk awakened to political consciousness and capable of action,"[82] accordingly remains a pre-constitutional and even pre-state entity, whose political character is determined neither by law, nor by the constitution, nor by the state; but rather by that definition of the political as provided by Schmitt himself: the distinction between friend and foe.

> The political enemy need not be morally evil or aesthetically ugly; he need not appear as an economic competitor, and it may even be advantageous to engage with him in business transactions. But he is, nevertheless, the other, the stranger; and it is sufficient for his nature that he is, in a specially intense way, existentially something different and alien.[83]

This difference precedes the constitution; it can be determined culturally by language and history and likewise "naturally" by race and blood. In a certain sense, it persists through every constitution, for the Volk can express its unity through a variety of state forms.

This concept of an extra-constitutional political unity of the Volk lies at the basis of the notion of the *Volksgemeinschaft*.[84] It could be used to justify inclusion as well as distance from and even animosity toward the Weimar constitution. The *Volksgemeinschaft* demanded an all-encompassing communalization and the production of a political unity—"one Volk, one Reich, one Führer"—and at the same time demonstratively set itself apart from the constitutional processes of forming the Volk's will that occur by means of parties and interest groups.

Constitutional democrats like Hugo Preuß still struggled to create a bond between the term *Volksgemeinschaft* and the new order. In a brochure published in March 1919, the Center for Home Service (the official political information distribution center for the imperial regime) even tried to establish the source of the *Volksgemeinschaft* as the Revolution itself: "The Revolution is the beginning of a new person. It is the beginning of the community of the Volk [*Gemeinschaft des Volkes*]."[85] But the erosion of the concept of Volk as defined in relation to state citizenship by the propagation of the *Volksgemeinschaft* is unmistakable. In the same precise moment when the principle of *Volkssouveränität* became the founding principle of a German constitution, the concept of *Volksgemeinschaft* brought together the critique of the Republic and its democratic constitution. When the political parties of the Weimar Republic, including the Social Democrats (notwithstanding their different motives), propagated the *Volksgemeinschaft*, they themselves were destroying the foundation that secured their constitutional existence. In any case, the ambivalence that is an inescapable part of the principle of *Volkssouveränität* and that also found expression in the Weimar constitution was something that they could at best have "worked with" but never have resolved.

Weimar Parties and the *Volksgemeinschaft*

With ranking members like Hugo Preuß among others, the liberal DDP was considered the party of the constitution par excellence, and it propagated an idea of the *Volksgemeinschaft* that was supposed to overcome the notion of class struggle and produce the social unity of the nation. The DDP entered the 1924 election campaign with the slogan "democracy means overcoming the idea of class struggle by virtue of the *Volksgemeinschaft*"; [86] in 1928, the left-wing liberals called out the vote with the following: "the basic idea of our internal politics, however, is for us at all times the notion of the *Volksgemeinschaft*, which we advocate in contrast to the parties which sharpen the oppositions between 'national' and Marxist, between town and country, between the races, denominations, and classes."[87]

What distinguished them from propagandists of the *Volksgemeinschaft* on the right was their position vis-à-vis the constitution. For the liberals, the *Volksgemeinschaft* was an inextricable part of the democracy. According to Gustav Schneider, a functionary for the union of white-collar workers speaking at the 1924 party congress in Weimar, the Weimar imperial constitution formed the "only [basis] on which a genuine *Volksgemeinschaft* is possible."[88] Using the attributes "genuine" and "true," they tried to set themselves apart from the parties on the right. In 1924, even Hugo Preuß once again emphasized that *Volksgemeinschaft* and party politics were not mutually exclusive and that the "obliteration of natural differences of principles, convictions, and objectives" would only lead to an "insipid broth of unity."[89] But the forceful reference repeated time and again to the "whole Volk," to the organic state as a "unified body" to which persons and communities should belong as "living cells and limbs" (as was stated in the party platform of 1919), allowed terminological differences to blur. Then with the transformation of the DDP to the German State Party (Deutsche Staatspartei) in 1930, the course was clearly set in the crisis of the Weimar Republic: "The German State Party rests on the basis of the *Volksgemeinschaft*. It rejects any ties to special groups of a denominational, economic, estate-based or class-based nature."[90]

The right-wing liberal DVP, in contrast, considering itself from the outset to be a bourgeois conglomeration against the "Left," as a defender of European culture against "Asiatic Bolshevism," called for a "fierce struggle against the Marxist social democracy." It did so in clear opposition to the bourgeois-liberal DDP, which had entered into a governing coalition with the SPD. "The enemy stands on the left!" proclaimed Gustav Stresemann in the 1920 election campaign. In this sense, the DVP was supposed to be the centrist party that according to Stresemann's intentions "wants to be neither on the radical right nor on the radical left, but consciously strives for a balance of interests."[91] Correspondingly, the party's call to action for the 1920 Reichstag election stated: "reconciling the estates rather than inciting them to hatred. Employers and employees must act together; the labor community [*Arbeitsgemeinschaft*] must become a *Volksgemeinschaft*."[92]

For the Catholic Center Party, the term *Volksgemeinschaft* did not lie close at hand, for it remained a political force based in the rural and Catholic population. Nonetheless, the Center Party understood itself as the order's Christian-democratic party, seeking with all its power to prevent a Bolshevist "class government." For that reason, the party supported the election of a National Assembly and hoped for a "democratic *Volksstaat*," described in the call to action in Berlin on 21 November 1918 as the "unification of the German tribes into a *Volksreich* that is carried by a strong national consciousness."[93] Four years later, this new and powerful concept had also gained acceptance in political Catholicism: "The Center Party is the Christian *Volkspartei*, which consciously stands for the German *Volksgemeinschaft* and is strongly resolved to realize the principles of Christianity in state and society, economics and culture." As with the Liberals, this implied in the first instance fighting against class struggle and class government: "The organic growth of the German *Volksgemeinschaft* rests on the solidarity of all classes and professions [*Berufsstände*]."[94]

Yet the Center Party also clearly turned against definitions from the right: "The Center Party wants the German *Volksgemeinschaft*. We deliberately set aside all divisive differences that split up our Volk. We are resisting a new division, called forth by a so-called 'neo-Germanic' spiritual world, which is confusing our Volk."[95] Perhaps for this reason the party grew more hesitant about using the concept of the *Volksgemeinschaft*. In 1925, the Center Party still presented its presidential candidate, Wilhelm Marx, as "president of the *Volksgemeinschaft*."[96] But after that, the concept mostly disappeared from the Center Party's calls to action; the party now represented itself mostly as a "true *Volkspartei*"—that is, literally at the center within a Volk split into two extreme political camps. Perhaps it was also the idea of a strong state—which in both substance and essence was a force for order that ultimately could only be based in God—that prevented a predominant orientation on the *Volksgemeinschaft*.[97]

Recently, Moritz Föllmer has appropriately drawn attention to the fact that the rhetoric of the *Volksgemeinschaft* and "national solidarity" often had no effect in the daily conflict between interest groups in a modern society.[98] The appeals to unity and a readiness to make sacrifices died away when it came to protecting respective interests. The entrepreneurial side of the Zentralarbeitsgemeinschaft (Central Association of Employers and Employees), founded in 1918 with the unions, continuously complained that the latter were going to withdraw from the *Volksgemeinschaft*; for their part, after the Zentralarbeitsgemeinschaft was dissolved in 1924, the employers proclaimed the entrepreneurial right of unlimited trade to be a national good. Henceforth "*Werksgemeinschaften*" (company communities) were supposed to represent the *Volksgemeinschaft* at the company level. The Economic Party (which in 1925 became the Reich Party of the German Middle Class) also failed in its attempt to pass off political lobbying for middle-class interests as actions for the *Volksgemeinschaft*. It proclaimed in grandiose rhyme:

> Lend a hand, a brotherly hand! It is for the German middle class! … Smash the false idols of these times that are spreading through the Volk, smash the discord and the disgrace in the sorely tried Fatherland!

> [*Reicht die Hand, die Bruderhand! Es gilt dem deutschen Mittelstand! Zerschlagt die Götzen dieser Zeit, die sich im Volke machen breit, zerschlagt die Zwietracht und die Schande im vielgeprüften Vaterlande!*]

Nonetheless, support for the Middle Class party collapsed during the elections of 1930 and it vanished into meaninglessness.[99]

Even the Social Democrats flirted with the *Volksgemeinschaft*. The unstable situation after the collapse of the Kaiserreich, in which the Social Democrats assumed political responsibility and felt themselves threatened by attempted revolutionary uprisings from the left, led to a rhetoric of internal coherence, unity, and defense against any kind of division. At the October 1920 party congress in Kassel, Adolf Braun presented the case to the party directorate for the necessity of expanding into a Volk's party. After acknowledging that the fathers of the Erfurt Program of 1891, which was officially still valid in 1920, had directed themselves toward industrial workers, Braun added:

Today we have become a political party that also includes white-collar workers and bureaucrats, and that ranges across industry, trade, agriculture, shipping, etc. We are a party of all kinds of people who work with their heads and work with their hands. In this hall we see workers, from university professors to unskilled laborers. Our future program must be shaped in a way that corresponds with this amalgamation.[100]

Consequently, the Görlitz Program of 1921 announced right from the outset: "The Social Democratic Party of Germany is the party of the working Volk in town and country. It strives to consolidate all physical and intellectual producers who are dependent on the proceeds of their own labor, to reach common understandings and objectives, [and] as a *Kampfgemeinschaft* (battle group) for democracy and socialism." In terms of political economics, the SPD demanded: "property, natural resources, and natural power sources that serve the production of energy are to be withdrawn from capitalist exploitation and put in service of the *Volksgemeinschaft*."[101] According to Paul Löbe in his speech at the Görlitz party congress, the SPD wanted to "capture the majority of the Volk" and to "win over the entire working Volk."[102]

The notion of class struggle was not even mentioned in the first draft of the program. And although it was later added, as Heinrich August Winkler notes, it read more like a historical justification than as a declaration of social war.[103] But the Görltiz Program did not escape criticism; the USPD in particular flatly rejected it. After the USPD split, with a majority switching to the Communist Party of Germany (KPD) and a minority returning to the SPD, the rhetoric of the Social Democrats moved to the left. Their politics would henceforth be animated by the aspiration "to gather all the strengths of the proletariat in a unified class struggle to win political power, abolish class rule, and realize socialism."[104] In the 1925 Heidelberg Program, the notion of *Volksgemeinschaft* no longer appeared.[105]

But the term had by no means disappeared from Social Democratic rhetoric. Friedrich Ebert, who was elected president in 1919, appealed on his first official day in office to the unity of the "*Volksgenossen*" (Volk comrades).[106] Until his death in 1925, the *Volksgemeinschaft* repeatedly cropped up in his speeches as something that was necessary to attain unity, solidarity, and self-affirmation.[107] Among younger Social Democrats as well, particularly those who came upon the socialists by way of the youth movement, there were many for whom socialism in the first instance meant adventure and community. Love of nature, anti-bourgeois habitus, play, dancing, elitist consciousness, and communal feeling—these all marked the young socialist groups emerging from the towns to wander the countryside on Saturday afternoons, with mandolins and guitars and greetings of "*Frei Heil!*"[108]

The occupation of the Rhineland by Belgian and French troops in January 1923 also led to an escalation of nationalist rhetoric and an evocation of the *Volksgemeinschaft* among young socialists.[109] At Easter a group of about one hundred—half of them from the occupied territories—gathered in Hofgeismar near Kassel to discuss "Volk and State" and, as one of the organizers put it, to realize a "new positive *Volksbewußtsein* [Volk consciousness]." Although the speakers (along with the chauvinistically German workers' poet Karl Bröer and the Marburg philosopher Paul Natorp, they included other prominent academics like Gustav Radbruch, Eduard Heimann, and Hugo Sinzheimer who were averse to the pathos of the *Volksgemeinschaft*) were opposed to any kind of aggressive nationalism, the *Volksgemeinschaft* nonetheless formed a key concept for the emotions that drove the participants.[110]

Emerging from that meeting was a circle of like-minded comrades who seized the political initiative in many groups—among them Theodor Haubach and Carlo Mierendorff, who would later be part of the resistance against Hitler.[111] The theoretician behind the "Hofgeismar Circle," the state-law expert Hermann Heller, defined class struggle as the workers' struggle to be recognized as a part of the nation and advocated a nationalistic socialism: "Socialism by no means signifies the end but rather the completion of the national community; not the destruction of the national *Volksgemeinschaft* through class, but the destruction of class by a genuinely national *Volksgemeinschaft*."[112] Admittedly, the Hofgeismar Circle was vanquished during the young socialists' internal altercations, whereupon some of its protagonists found a new home in the National Bolshevist circle around Ernst Niekisch. However, many remained loyal to the Social Democratic Party or, like Haubach and Mierendorff, switched to Reichsbanner Schwarz-Rot-Gold (Black, Red, Gold Banner of the Realm), which attracted these members of Hofgeismar Circle with its emphasis on national solidarity and its willingness to collaborate with all powers to defend the Republic.[113]

Yet despite semantic congruence, the Social Democratic understanding of *Volksgemeinschaft* was not synonymous with the political concepts of the right. For the Social Democrats, the *Volksgemeinschaft* was always an expression for the unification of all exploited social classes in opposition to a small exploiting class. The *Volksgemeinschaft* as a community that included all producers, bound by solidarity and a social economy—this was a way to transcribe the vision of a harmonious society, its classes reconciled.[114] In contrast, the political right imbued the concept of the *Volksgemeinschaft* with very different semantics and emotions.

Volksgemeinschaft as Exclusion

The development toward a society of economic classes took off so explicitly and relentlessly that many wanted to quickly and radically overcome modernity again and longed for a balanced, "just," and above all stable order. In the months of crisis in 1923, bourgeois principles like "good money for good work" or "saving means security for old age" turned to dust in the whirlwind of hyperinflation, which not only obliterated material savings of wealth but also the belief in the validity of bourgeois society's immaterial values. Never before, according to Martin Geyer in his investigation of the "tospy-turvy" world of 1914–1918, had the struggle of all against all and the challenge to help oneself been so strongly invoked as in those years of inflation. Those who could not help themselves could not help others and inevitably joined the losers. And self-help clearly did not meant a collective organization with principles of solidarity, but rather selfishness, ruthlessness, and violence.[115] "Nothing more heavily underscores the existence of the German society of economic classes, with its deep antagonisms and fatal economic fluctuations," writes Hans-Ulrich Wehler, "than the victory parade of this chimera that was the '*Volksgemeinschaft*' with its promise of a stress-free nation in which everyone would find a suitable and respected place."[116]

While the social and moral milieus of earlier political currents (liberal, conservative, Catholic, socialist) began to crumble, the NSDAP could exploit its initial marginal situation, for it was not bound to any clientele and presented itself rather as a "young" and class-transcendent "*Volkspartei*," one that did not seek to represent any particular interests but rather the *Volksgemeinschaft* as a whole. Yet in contrast to the Social Democrats, for example, who advocated an inclusionary understanding of the *Volksgemeinschaft* that was supposed to unify all producers in opposition to a few monopoly capitalists, the *Volksgemeinschaft* on the political right—especially the National Socialists—was determined by boundaries: by exclusion. The right was not so much concerned with those who belonged to the *Volksgemeinschaft*, but rather with those who were not supposed to belong—above all, the Jews.

In his commentary on the Weimar imperial constitution, Freytagh-Loringhoven had already denied Jews the rights of citizenship. He argued that a Volk was determined by lineage, common language, and a culture as generated and maintained by the leading stratum, as well as by a subjective moment, namely the will to a *Volksgemeinschaft*. When applied to Germany, this meant that the Jews did not belong to the German Volk. To be sure, they had adopted the German language and adapted to German culture, but their lineage had nothing in common with the German

Volk. They also lacked the will to a *Volksgemeinschaft*, for, on the one hand, large circles of the German people rejected community with the Jews, and on the other hand, large parts of Judaism aligned themselves with Zionism. Freytagh-Loringhoven's recommendations for a constitution based on principles of the Volk anticipated the anti-Semitic hierarchy created by the Nuremberg laws of 1935. He determined that only those who "stem from German blood" could be part of the state and considered citizens of the Reich. In his view, the Jews in particular could not possess any rights of state citizenship: they could not vote or be elected, and they could not hold public office.[117]

The concept of the *Volksgemeinschaft* first appeared in Hitler's public addresses in his programmatic speech "Why Are We Anti-Semites?" delivered in the ballroom of the Hofbräuhaus on 13 August 1920.[118] His talk centered on the concept of work. While work at an instinctive level as a drive for self-preservation was common to both humans and animals, a second level had developed among humans, namely work motivated purely by egoism. This level, too, was surpassed in favor of work motivated by an "ethical-moral sense of duty," an activity "that I do not engage in merely for myself, but for the benefit of my fellow human beings."[119]

Work appears here not in its sober definition as found in classical economics, which Karl Marx adopted as well, that is, as a material exchange between humans and nature. Hitler took his notion of work from a historical sketch of the "Nordic races," whose members, because of the inhospitable external living conditions, were compelled to work not only for themselves but for their entire clan. According to Hitler, for the "Nordic races" the struggle for existence developed further into a "purifying racial breeding" because the weak and the sick could not survive and what remained was a "race [*Geschlecht*] of giants in strength and health." Finally, the boundaries that limited their external sphere of operation entailed that the internal lives of these people developed all the more deeply. As a consequence of all three factors—work as duty, racial purity and health, and a deep internal spiritual life—the "Aryans" acquired the capability of forming states and developing culture. Yet the foundation was based on the notion of work.

By contrast, the Jews, who unlike the Nordic races were not "pure bred," were in no position to form states. Rather, they could only exist as "parasites on the bodies of other peoples [*Völker*]." These "vermin of the *Volksgemeinschaft*" did everything possible to destroy the racial unity, health, politics, economics, and culture of the German Volk. Hitler concluded in his summary:

We see that already here there are two big differences between the races. Aryanism means an ethical understanding of work and for that reason those things about which we speak so often today: socialism, a sense of community, putting the common good before self-interest. Judaism means an egoistical understanding of work, and thus mammonism and materialism, the very opposite of socialism. And in this characteristic, which he cannot transcend, which lies in his blood—he himself acknowledges this—in this characteristic itself lies the necessity for the Jew that he must present himself as destructive to the state. He cannot do otherwise, whether he wants to or not.[120]

This passage reveals a central element of National Socialist anti-Semitism: there is no escape for the Jews. As individuals they might be good or bad, hardworking or lazy, accommodating or head-strong, but it did not matter. The complete assimilation of the Jews as demanded by the older generation of anti-Semites was for Hitler an obsolete solution; indeed, it only hid from view the immutable Jewish "racial fate." According to Hitler, nothing could prevent it—neither education nor a merely economic struggle—nothing except for the action and organization of the masses.

We understood clearly, that if this movement does not penetrate into the broad masses and organize them, then all is in vain, then [we] will never be successful in freeing our Volk, and we will never be able to think about rebuilding our Fatherland anew. Salvation here can never come from above; it can and will come only from the broad masses, rising from below.[121]

The necessary social reforms in favor of those who "day after day work for the *Volksgemeinschaft*" must be accompanied by a "struggle against the opponent of every social institution: Judaism. Here, too, we know full well that scientific awareness can merely be prep work, but that behind this awareness there must be organization, which will one day move into action, and that action for us is unshakably firm. It is: the removal of the Jews from our Volk." The protocol notes at this point thunderous and enduring applause and hand clapping.[122]

Here lay the decisive difference from previous anti-Semites. While the Treitschkes, Stoeckers, and Marrs put their anti-Jewish poison on paper, writing it down and having it printed, Hitler called for action. The anti-Semites of the Wilhelmine Kaiserreich, according to Shulamit Volkov, were part of a written culture. They spent their energy on internal arguments and played at times with the idea of legal restrictions. Someone like Eugen Dührung pursued his theoretical considerations to the point of the physical destruction of the Jews. But none of this proceeded beyond the words on a page, for there was no organization, praxis, or action that could turn these ideas into reality. In contrast, Hitler was little inclined to the written word; "knights of ink" and "scrivener souls" earned his contempt. Hitler's medium was the speech, as he explained in detail in *Mein*

Kampf. But the rhetoric was not merely meant to convince listeners; the speech was a call to action.[123] "Our concern," announced Hitler, "must be to awaken, whip up, and incite the instinct against Judaism in our Volk, until it arrives at the decision to join the movement which is prepared to draw the necessary conclusions."[124] Indeed, National Socialist anti-Semitism proved itself in action; the *Volksgemeinschaft* was produced through praxis, not merely by Sunday speeches and glossy party brochures.

Hitler had the charisma of a "Führer" for an entire Volk, which was prepared to place its combined hopes for unity, salvation, transcendence of divisions, integration, and recognition on the promise of a future *Volksgemeinschaft.*[125] But from the very outset, the moment of inclusion in the *Volksgemeinschaft* was linked with the violent exclusion of the so-called "asocials," the supposedly genetically inferior, and most of all the Jews. What the memories of former "*Volksgenossen*" later preferably kept separate, namely the persecution of the Jews and the experiences of community in National Socialism, are inextricably linked—they were two sides of a political project: the destruction of civil society and the creation of a new racial order. The exclusion of the German Jews from the *Volksgemeinschaft*, not merely rhetorically but through acts of violence, formed the constitutive element in the National Socialist *Volksgemeinschaft.* For that reason, anti-Semitism and the persecution of the Jews cannot be separated from the inclusive moments of the *Volksgemeinschaft.* In the sense of National Socialist politics, neither could it simply be decreed by the state. The production of the *Volksgemeinschaft* was a matter for the "Volk" and it was a question of action, not law. Anti-Semitic violence was thus not merely a means of National Socialist politics; violence against Jews was the core of those politics.

Notes

1. Jacob Grimm and Wilhelm Grimm, *Deutsches Wörterbuch*, ed. Deutschen Akademie der Wissenschaften zu Berlin (Leipzig, 1951), vol. 12, sect. II, col. 481.
2. Quoted in Norbert Götz, *Ungleiche Geschwister: Die Konstruktion von nationalsozialistischer Volksgemeinschaft und schwedischem Volksheim* (Baden-Baden, 2001), 85.
3. Theodor Herzl, *Der Judenstaat: Versuch einer modernen Lösung der Judenfrage: Text und Materialien 1896 bis heute*, ed., afterword by Ernst Piper (Berlin, 2004), 17.
4. Wehler, *Deutsche Gesellschaftsgeschichte*, vol. 3: *Von der "Deutschen Doppelrevolution" bis zum Beginn des Ersten Weltkrieges 1849–1914* (Munich, 1995), 951.
5. Quoted in Götz, *Ungleiche Geschwister*, 87.
6. According to the book directory of the Market Association of Leipzig Book Dealers, the concept appeared in droves in book titles directly after the end of the First World War and in the early 1930s. Norbert Jegelka, "'Volksgemeinschaft': Begriffskonturen in 'Führer' ideologie, Recht und Erziehung (1933–1945)," in *Das Volk: Abbild, Kon-*

struktion, *Phantasma*, ed. Annette Graczyk (Berlin, 1997), 115–128; in particular, 115, note 3.

7. The Social Democratic *Hamburger Echo* warned on 30 July 1914: "The rallies that became noticeable in some of the large German cities should not be seen as an expression of the voice of the German *Volk*. For neither the workers nor the farmers are touched by this mood." Jeffrey Verhey, *Der "Geist von 1914" und die Erfindung der Volksgemeinschaft* (Hamburg, 2000), 61, note 24.

8. Verhey, *Der "Geist von 1914"*, 86–105.

9. Quoted in ibid., 108.

10. Ibid., 118. This scene in front of the royal palace had its orchestrated precedents, as shown in an essay by Alexa Geisthövel that investigates the experience of national unity induced by the proclamation of victory dispatches during the 1870 Franco-Prussian War by Queen Augusta from the balcony of the Berlin Palace. Alexa Geisthövel, "Augusta-Erlebnisse: Repräsentationen der preußischen Königin 1870," in *Neue Politikgeschichte: Perspektiven einer historischen Politikforschung*, ed. Ute Frevert and Heinz-Gerhard Haupt (Frankfurt am Main, 2005), 82–114; see also Thomas Lindenberger, *Straßenpolitik: Zur Sozialgeschichte der öffentlichen Ordnung in Berlin 1900 bis 1914* (Bonn, 1995), 359–381.

11. Verhey, *Der "Geist von 1914,"* 129–193; Wolfgang Kruse, "Kriegsbegeisterung? Zur Massenstimmung bei Kriegsbeginn," in *Eine Welt von Feinden: Der Große Krieg 1914–1918*, ed. Wolfgang Kruse (Frankfurt am Main, 1997), 159–166. For a clear treatment of the class-specific differences, see Wehler, *Deutsche Gesellschaftsgeschichte*, vol. 4, 14–17 (with many further references).

12. Karl Löwith, *Mein Leben in Deutschland vor und nach 1933: Ein Bericht* (Stuttgart, 1986), 1.

13. See Bernd Hüppauf, ed., *Ansichten vom Krieg: Vergleichende Studien zum Ersten Weltkrieg in Literatur und Gesellschaft* (Königstein/Taunus, 1984); Helmut Fries, *Die große Kartharsis: Der Erste Weltkrieg in der Sicht deutscher Dichter und Gelehrter*, 2 vols. (Constance, 1995); Wolfgang Mommsen, ed., *Kultur und Krieg: Die Rolle der Intellektuellen, Künstler und Schriftsteller im Ersten Weltkrieg* (Munich, 1996); Uwe Schneider and Andreas Schumann, eds., *"Krieg der Geister": Erster Weltkrieg und literarische Moderne* (Würzburg, 2000); Kurt Flasch, *Die geistige Mobilmachung: Die deutschen Intellektuellen und der Erste Weltkrieg: Ein Versuch* (Berlin, 2000); now also especially Steffen Bruendel, *Volksgemeinschaft oder Volksstaat: Die "Ideen von 1914" und die Neuordnung Deutschlands im Ersten Weltkrieg* (Berlin, 2003).

14. See Bruendel, *Volksgemeinschaft*, 115–124, 260–263.

15. Quoted in Axel Schildt, "Ein konservativer Prophet moderner nationaler Integration: Biographische Skizze des streitbaren Soziologen Johann Plenge (1874–1963)," *Vierteljahreshefte für Zeitgeschichte* 35 (1987): 523–570, here 535; see also Joachim Müller, *Die "Ideen von 1914" bei Johann Plenge und in der zeitgenössischen Diskussion: Ein Beitrag zur Ideengeschichte des Ersten Weltkrieges* (Neuwied, 2001).

16. Quoted in Schildt, "Ein konservativer Prophet," 533. In the summer of 1914, according to Plenge, "our new spirit [was] born: the spirit of the strongest aggregation of all economic and state powers into a new totality, in which everyone lives with an equal share. The new German State! The idea of 1914!" Quoted in Bruendel, *Volksgemeinschaft*, 71.

17. See Verhey, *Der "Geist von 1914,"* 133ff., 146–151; also Kruse, "Kriegsbegeisterung," 163.

18. Quoted in Verhey, *Der "Geist von 1914,"* 146.

19. Ibid., 147; on German atrocity propaganda, see Lothar Wieland, *Belgien 1914: Die Frage des belgischen "Franktireurkrieges" und die deutsche öffentliche Meinung von 1914 bis 1936* (Frankfurt am Main, 1984); now also especially John Horne and Alan Kramer, *Deutsche Kriegsgreuel 1914: Die umstrittene Wahrheit* (Hamburg, 2004).

20. See Gunther Mai, "'Verteidigungskrieg' und 'Volksgemeinschaft': Staatliche Selbst-behauptung, nationale Solidarität und soziale Befreiung in Deutschland in der Zeit des Ersten Weltkrieges (1900–1925)," in *Der Erste Weltkrieg: Wirkung, Wahrnehmung, Analyse*, ed. Wolfgang Michalka (Munich, 1994).

21. Ibid., 591. Similarly, Heinrich Cunow, the director of the *Neue Zeit*, wrote that the Social Democrats "apart from class-interests and class-feelings also possessed something like national-feelings, a feeling of *Staatsgemeinschaft* [state community] and *Volksgemeinschaft*." Quoted in Götz, *Ungleiche Geschwister*, 88; other references in Mai, "Verteidigungskrieg und Volksgemeinschaft," 591; see also Ben Möbius, "Das Vaterland der 'vaterlandslosen Gesellen': Sozialdemokratischer Patriotismus am Vorabend des Ersten Weltkrieges," in *Politische Gesellschaftsgeschichte im 19. und 20. Jahrhundert*, ed. Albrecht Henning et al. (Hamburg, 2006), 13–29.

22. Quoted in Mai, "Verteidigungskrieg und Volksgemeinschaft," 591.

23. Barkai and Mendes-Flohr, *Aufbruch und Zerstörung*, 16. There also were other Jewish voices, for example Sigmund Freud's "Thought for the Times on War and Death" (1915) which began with the sentences: "In the confusion of wartime in which we are caught up, relying as we must on one-sided information, standing too close to the great changes that have already taken place or are beginning to, and without a glimmering of the future that is being shaped, we ourselves are at a loss as to the significance of the impressions which bear down upon us and as to the value of the judgments which we form. We cannot but feel that no event has ever destroyed so much that is precious in the common possessions of humanity, confused so many of the clearest intelligences, or so thoroughly debased what is highest." Sigmund Freud, "Zeitgemäßes über Krieg und Tod," in *Studienausgabe*, vol. 9 (Frankfurt am Main, 1982), 35; see also Paul Mendes-Flohr, "The Kriegserlebnis and Jewish Consciousness," in *Leben in der Weimarer Republik/Jews in the Weimar Republic*, ed. Wolfgang Benz, Arnold Paucker, and Peter Pulzer (Tübingen, 1998) 225–237 and Ulrich Sieg, *Jüdische Intellektuelle im Ersten Weltkrieg: Kriegserfahrungen, weltanschauliche Debatten und kulturelle Neuentwürfe* (Berlin, 2001).

24. Quoted in Barkai and Mendes-Flohr, *Aufbruch und Zerstörung*, 17.

25. Ibid., 17.

26. Barbara Guttmann, *Weibliche Heimarmee: Frauen in Deutschland 1914–1918* (Weinheim, 1989).

27. Klaus Mann, *Kind dieser Zeit* (Berlin, 1932), 53. Heinrich Himmler (born 1900) viewed the war in similar terms as an exciting adventure game in which the Germans were predetermined to be the victors. A typical entry in his diary reads: "the Bavarians are said to have held themselves very bravely in yesterday's battle. In particular our 16th are said to have grappled admirably with their long knives. The whole city is decked out with flags. The French and Belgians could hardly have thought that they would be hit so hard." Diary of Himmler, entry for 8/23/1914, Bundesarchiv Berlin, N 1126/3; see Werner T. Angress and Bradley F. Smith, "Diaries of Heinrich Himmler's Early Years," *Journal for Modern History* 31 (1959): 206–224.

28. Sebastian Haffner, *Geschichte eines Deutschen: Die Erinnerungen 1914–1933* (Stuttgart, 2000), 21 (quotation translated by Bernard Heise).

29. Ibid., 20f. (quotation translated by Bernard Heise).

30. Jürgen Kocka, *Klassengesellschaft im Krieg: Deutsche Sozialgeschichte 1914–1918* (Göttingen, 1973); Wehler, *Gesellschaftsgeschichte*, vol. 4, 69–102.

31. On the soldiers' wives' self-perception and their new understanding of roles, see Birthe Kundrus, *Kriegerfrauen: Familienpolitik und Geschlechterverhältnisse im Ersten und Zweiten Weltkrieg* (Hamburg, 1995), 43–97; see also Belinda Davis, *Home Fires Burning: Food, Politics, and Everyday Life in World War I Berlin* (London, 2000).

32. Volker Ullrich, *Kriegsalltag: Hamburg im Ersten Weltkrieg* (Cologne, 1982), 51–62, 68–72; Robert Chickering, *Imperial Germany and the Great War, 1914–1918* (Cambridge, 1998), 123–125.

33. Quoted in Kocka, *Klassengesellschaft*, 45.

34. See Verhey, *Der "Geist von 1914,"* 257; Bruendel, *Volksgemeinschaft*, 146f.

35. Quoted in Verhey, *Der "Geist von 1914,"* 297. In opposition to the Fatherland Party, Max Weber, Delbrück, Meinecke, Troeltsch, and others founded the Volksbund für Freiheit und Vaterland (People's Association for Freedom and Fatherland) in December 1917 (see Bruendel, *Volksgemeinschaft*, 149–153).

36. At the same time on 1 October 1918 Ludendorff said that he asked Wilhelm "to now bring those particular circles into the regime whom we mainly have to thank that it has come to this.... They should now eat this soup that they have gotten us into." Quoted in Heinrich Winkler, *Weimar 1918–1933: Die Geschichte der ersten deutschen Demokratie* (Munich, 1993), 23. With that, as Hans Mommsen determined, self-delusion took shape right from the outset, namely that it was not the front that had failed, but the homeland. Hans Mommsen, *Die verspielte Freiheit: Der Weg der Republik von Weimar in den Untergang 1918 bis 1933*, vol. 8: *Propyläen Geschichte Deutschlands* (Berlin, 1989), 22.

37. As appointed Reich chancellor and as director of the Council of People's Representatives, Ebert represented a "bridge of legality," according to Ernst-Wolfgang Böckenförde, "Der Zusammenbruch der Monarchie und die Entstehung der Weimarer Republik," in E. Böckenförde, *Recht, Staat, Freiheit: Studien zur Rechtsphilosophie, Staatstheorie und Verfassungsgeschichte* (Frankfurt am Main, 1991), 306–343, here 321; Hans Mommsen speaks of a "double legitimacy" possessed by Ebert. H. Mommsen, *Verspielte Freiheit*, 41.

38. The drama during those weeks, as indeed the contemporaries so often experienced, especially in the revolutionary centers of Berlin and Munich, cannot disguise the fact that there was never really any danger of a Bolshevik takeover. The short-lived authority of the communist councils in Berlin stood on shaky ground and collapsed immediately with the arrival of the Freikorps; the January rebellion by the Spartacus Group in Berlin had no chance of a military victory, and the hoped-for support of the workers never materialized. The real power fell to the Council of the People's Representatives, particularly since most of the councils that were formed during the Reich were composed by a majority of SPD and USPD representatives and viewed themselves as transition committees exercising control over the authorities until democratic institutions could be constituted.

39. "Aufruf des Rats der Volksbeauftragten an das deutsche Volk vom 12. November 1918," in *Dokumente zur deutschen Verfassungsgeschichte*, vol. 4: *Deutsche Verfassungsdokumente 1919–1933*, ed. Ernst Huber, 3rd ed. (Cologne, 1992), vol. 4, 6f. (Document No. 7).

40. Susanne Miller, *Die Bürde der Macht: Die deutsche Sozialdemokratie 1918–1920* (Düsseldorf, 1978), 104–115; Sigrid Vestring, *Die Mehrheitssozialdemokratie und die Entstehung der Reichsverfassung von Weimar 1918/19* (Münster, 1987), 27–29a. Hans Mommsen makes the criticism that both the MSPD and USPD had declined taking the

process of providing a constitution into their own hands and thereby had lost sight of Lassalle's insight that constitutional questions are questions about power. H. Mommsen, *Verspielte Freiheit*, 64.

41. According to a dairy entry by Thomas Wolff (who was for many years the editor-in-chief of the *Berliner Tageblatt*) about a conversation he had with Preuß on the morning of 15 November, Friedrich Ebert supposedly told Preuß: "We cannot do that; we do not have people for that." Theodor Wolff, *Tagebücher 1914–1919*, ed. Bernd Sösemann (Boppard, 1984), 654.

42. Hugo Preuß, *Das Deutsche Volk und die Politik* (Jena, 1915); see also Bruendel, *Volksgemeinschaft*, 104–106; Jasper Mauersberg, *Ideen und Konzeption Hugo Preuß' für die Verfassung der deutschen Republik 1919 und ihre Durchsetzung im Verfassungswerk von Weimar* (Frankfurt am Main, 1991), 40–43. On Hugo Preuß see the 1955 dissertation by Günther Gillessen, *Hugo Preuß, Studien zur Ideen- und Verfassungsgeschichte der Weimarer Republik* (Berlin, 2000); also Detlef Lehnert, *Verfassungsdemokratie als Bürgergenossenschaft: Politisches Denken, Öffentliches Recht und Geschichtsdeutungen bei Hugo Preuß: Beiträge zur demokratischen Institutionenlehre in Deutschland* (Baden-Baden, 1998).

43. Hugo Preuß, "Volksstaat oder verkehrter Obrigkeitsstaat," in *Staat, Recht und Freiheit: Aus 40 Jahren deutscher Politik und Geschichte* (Hildesheim, 1964), 365–368, here 367f.; Preuß linked his constitutional concepts with the demand to abolish the states, particularly Prussia, and the creation of a unified national state, while simultaneously criticizing unlimited centralization. Instead, the "cultural diversity" of the German Volk was to be nurtured and the autonomous self-administration of communal and rural associations was to be strengthened. Preuß, "Denkschrift zum Entwurf des allgemeinen Teils der Reichsverfassung vom 3. 1. 1919," in *Staat, Recht und Freiheit*, 368–394; see Detlef Lehnert, "Verfassungsdispositionen für die politische Kultur der Weimarer Republik: Die Beiträge von Hugo Preuß im historisch-konzeptiven Vergleich," in *Pluralismus als Verfassungs- und Gesellschaftsmodell: Zur Politischen Kultur in der Weimarer Republik*, ed. Detlef Lehnert and Klaus Megerl (Opladen, 1993), 11–47.

44. See also Christoph Gusy, *Die Weimarer Reichsverfassung* (Tübingen, 1997), 62–66.

45. Gerhard Anschütz, *Die Verfassung des Deutschen Reiches vom 11. August 1919: Ein Kommentar für Wissenschaft und Praxis*, 3rd ed., 12th printing (Berlin, 1930), 1.

46. Quoted in Gusy, *Weimarer Reichsverfassung*, 64f., 372f.; see Ernst Fraenkel, "Die repräsentative und plebiszitäre Komponente im demokratischen Verfassungsstaat," in *Deutschland und die westlichen Demokratien*, ed. Alexander v. Brünneck (Frankfurt am Main, 1991), 153–203.

47. Max Weber, "Zur Neuordnung Deutschlands," in Max Weber, *Gesamtausgabe*, sect. I, vol. 1 (Tübingen, 1988), 91–146; see Wolfgang Mommsen, *Max Weber und die deutsche Politik, 1890–1920*, 2nd ed. (Tübingen, 1974), 356–370. According to the protocol of the Council of the People's Representatives for the morning session on 15 November, Max Weber was even considered as an alternative to Preuß for an appointment to state secretary for the interior. But then Ebert was assigned to continue negotiations together with Hugo Preuß, whose appointment was confirmed on the same day (ibid.; Mommsen suggests that Weber's public appearance in opposition to the government of the People's Representatives may have helped destroy this great political opportunity, about which Weber apparently knew nothing).

48. W. Mommsen, *Weber*, 364.

49. Friedrich Meinecke, "Bemerkungen zum Entwurf der Reichsverfassung," in *Werke*, vol. 2: *Politische Schriften und Reden*, ed. and with an introduction by Georg Kotowski (Darmstadt, 1968), 299–312.
50. For details see W. Mommsen, *Weber*, 380–396; also Mauersberg, *Ideen und Konzeption Hugo Preuß' für die Verfassung*, 60–77.
51. Hugo Preuß, "Das Verfassungswerk von Weimar," in *Staat, Recht und Freiheit*, 426. But compared to Weber's caesarian model, in Preuß's political thought the parliament retained its position as the "supreme organ of communal whole [*Gemeinwesens*]."
52. The text for this early draft is documented in Heinrich Triepel, ed., *Quellensammlung zum Deutschen Reichsstaatsrecht*, exp. 4th ed. (Tübingen, 1926), 6–8. This qualifies Böckenförde's argument that a preliminary decision in favor of a strong Reich president was first made with the law passed on 10 February 1919 regarding the provisional order of imperial authority, since the discussions at the end of 1918 had already provided for a president elected by the people who would act as a counterweight to the Reichstag. Böckenförde, "Zusammenbruch der Monarchie," 336.
53. "Entwurf einer Verfassung des Deutschen Reiches (Entwurf II). Vom 20. Januar 1919," in Triepel, *Quellensammlung*, 10–15. Recalling the long and procrastinatory debate over fundamental rights in St. Paul's Church in Frankfurt, Preuß dispensed with a catalogue of fundamental rights. Instead he wanted the new state to have a unitary character and sought, in particular, the dissolution of the state of Prussia. The Reichstag was to be comprised of a Volkshaus (House of the People), with "representatives of the unified German Volk" chosen in general elections, and a Staatenhaus (House of the States), whose representatives were delegated by each respective Landtag (state parliament).
54. Preuß, "Denkschrift," 370f.
55. This contest regarding the federal character of the new imperial constitution shapes the account by Horst Möller, *Weimar: Die unvollendete Demokratie* (Munich, 1985), 110–132; for a contemporary account of the legal critique of the unitary character of the first constitutional drafts, see Fritz Stier-Somlo, *Deutsches Reichs- und Landesstaatsrecht* (Leipzig, 1924), vol. 1, 248–258.
56. "Entwurf einer Verfassung des Deutschen Reiches (Entwurf III). Vom 17. Februar 1919," in Triepel, *Quellensammlung*, 17–27. Later in the constitution committee of the National Assembly, Preuß confirmed that the committee representing the states intervened against the formulation that the realm's entire authority lay with the German Volk because that would endanger the political existence of the states. *Berichte und Protokolle des Achten Ausschusses über den Entwurf einer Verfassung des Deutschen Volkes*, no. 21 of *Berichte der verfassunggebenden Deutschen Nationalversammlung 1919* (Berlin, 1920), 29.
57. "Entwurf einer Verfassung des Deutschen Reiches (Entwurf IV). Vom 21. Februar 1919," in Triepel, *Quellensammlung*, 27–31.
58. Böckenförde, "Zusammenbruch der Monarchie," 333f.
59. This established important trajectories for further constitutional deliberations, for as per earlier drafts, the law concerning imperial authority placed the Reich president in a strong position. He conducted the business of the empire (§ 6), he represented the empire in international law vis-à-vis foreign nations, and he convened the imperial administration (§ 8), although the imperial ministers needed to be confirmed by the National Assembly. This law, for instance, made no mention of a Reich chancellor. In any event, as early as 11 February Ebert commissioned Philipp Scheidemann to create an administration and thus created de facto the office of the Ministerpräsi-

dent (prime minister). The Weimar constitution reinstated the term "Reichskanzler" (Reich chancellor).

60. *Verhandlungen der Deutschen Nationalversammlung 1919/20*, vol. 326, pp. 371f., 379, 390f.; an instructive study of the National Assembly as a place of communication is provided by Thomas Mergel, *Parlamentarische Kultur in der Weimarer Republik: Politische Kommunikation, symbolische Politik und Öffentlichkeit im Reichstag* (Düsseldorf, 2002), 41–80.

61. Rudolf Morsey, *Die Deutsche Zentrumspartei 1917–1923* (Düsseldorf, 1966), 237. In terms of dogma, the point of departure for this debate is the well-known passage in Paul's epistle to the Romans (13:1): "Everyone must submit himself to the governing authorities, for there is no authority except that which God has established. The authorities that exist have been established by God." Significantly, Luther translated the Greek term which means power, violence, and lordship, as authority.

62. Quoted in Morsey, *Deutsche Zentrumspartei*, 238.

63. Ibid., 240.

64. Cohn repeatedly called for social and democratic corrective actions and for the "democratization of the life of the Volk." Nowhere should the attitude still prevail "that the Volk is only supposed to wait for the command of the authorities and then take its position and if necessary fall in line as commanded by the authorities." Rather it must become a commonplace that each individual is "the State," that each individual is a part of the Volk totality, and that the state is each individual. With regard to the right to protection for national minorities, he raised the question about whether this right should also apply to the Jewish minority. He opposed the notion that there was no "national Jewish question"; and in light of the Versailles peace conference, which was prepared to recognize the Jewish Volk as an independent nation, Cohn called for the consideration of whether the constitution should also provide for national minority rights for the Jews.

　　Born in 1869, Oskar Cohn was a Social Democratic representative in the Reichstag from 1912 to 1918 and from 1919 (as of 1922, again for the SPD) to 1924 a member of the Prussian Landtag; he was board member for the Human Rights League and active in Jewish organizations. He fled to Paris immediately after the National Socialists came to power and later to Switzerland, where he died in October 1934. See Ludger Heid, "'Er ist ein Rätsel geblieben': Oskar Cohn—Politiker, Parlamentarier, Poale-Zionist," in *Jüdisches Leben in der Weimarer Republik/ Jews in the Weimar Republic*, ed. Wolfgang Benz, Arnold Paucker, and Peter Pulzer (Tübingen, 1998), 25–48.

65. "Programmatische Kundgebung," in *Protokoll über die Verhandlungen des außerordentlichen Parteitages der Unabhängigen Sozialdemokratischen Partei Deutschlands vom 2. bis 6. März 1919 in Berlin* (Berlin, 1919), 3.

66. "Antrag 99, 1," in ibid., 270. This unequivocal mood in the USPD clearly led the fraction in the National Assembly (including Oskar Cohn) to reject the constitution in the final vote.

67. Gustav Stresemann, who in a letter in February 1919 categorically refused to consider himself a republican, stated in that same month in a election campaign speech that the form of the state had become a "question of action" and that this question had been decided in favor of a republic. Thus one could not abstain from cooperation with this republic. "But we want to make no bones about the fact that we are firstly opponents of the Revolution and will remain so." Quoted in Wolfgang Hartenstein, *Die Anfänge der Deutschen Volkspartei 1918–1920* (Düsseldorf, 1962), 48.

68. Meeting of 2 July 1919, *Verhandlungen der Deutschen Nationalversammlung*, vol. 327, 1223.

69. Quoted in Christian Trippe, *Konservative Verfassungspolitik 1918–1923: Die DNVP als Opposition in Reich und Ländern* (Düsseldorf, 1995), 88; see in the same place also a detailed account of the actions of the DNVP fraction in the National Assembly.

70. Axel Freiherr v. Freytagh-Loringhoven, *Die Weimarer Verfassung in Lehre und Wirklichkeit* (Munich, 1924), 15.

71. Ibid., 20.

72. Christoph Gusy, "Verfassungsumbruch und Staatsrechtswissenschaft: Die Verfassung des Politischen zwischen Konstitutionalismus und demokratischer Republik," in *Neue Politikgeschichte: Perspektiven einer historischen Politikforschung*, ed. Ute Frevert and Heinz-Gerhard Haupt (Frankfurt am Main, 2005), 166–201.

73. "Die Verfassung des Deutschen Reiches von 11.8.1919, RGBl. 1919, 1383" in Huber, *Dokumente*, vol. 4, 151–179. Naturally, the programmatic preface of the Weimar constitution also made reference to the preamble in the Imperial Constitution of 1871, whose creators were not the Volk but rather a federation of princes: "his majesty the King of Prussia in the name of the North-German Federation, his majesty the King of Bavaria, his majesty the King of Württemberg, his royal highness the Grand-Duke of Baden, and his royal highness the Grand-Duke of Hesse and by Rhine for the parts of the Grand-Duchy of Hesse that lie south of the Main, seal an eternal federation to protect the federation territory and the valid laws within the same, and to support the welfare of the German Volk. This federation will bear the name 'German Empire' and will have the following constitution." See Anschütz, *Verfassung des Deutschen Reiches*, 32f.

74. Hans Liermann, *Das deutsche Volk als Rechtsbegriff im Reichs- Staatsrecht der Gegenwart* (Berlin, 1927), 166.

75. Ibid., 170 (emphasis in the original). On Liermann, see Michael Stolleis, *Geschichte des öffentlichen Rechts in Deutschland*, vol. 3: *Staats- und Verwaltungsrechesweissenschaft in Republik und Diktatur 1914–1945* (Munich, 1999), 264.

76. According to H. Mommsen, *Verspielte Freiheit*, 71.

77. Weber, "Der Reichspräsident," in *Max Weber Gesamtausgabe* (Tübingen, 1988), sect. I, vol. 16, 220–224. This article appeared for the first time in the *Berliner Börsenzeitung* on 25 February 1919 and was reprinted by a number of newspapers in the days that followed.

78. It was the Social Democrat Richard Fischer who perceptively forewarned in the National Assembly against allowing oneself to be influenced by the fact that a Social Democrat now held this office. It could be possible that one day another man from another party would become the Reich president. Fischer did not want to rely on the Volk, for the Germans were not a free Volk—"a Volk must be educated for freedom, and the German Volk more than any other needs to educated for freedom"; Session on 28 February 1919, in *Verhandlungen der Deutschen Nationalversammlung*, vol. 326, 374. In opposition to the votes of Richard Fischer and Oskar Cohn, the constitution committee voted to establish a very powerful Reich president who was elected by the people. Bericht des Achten Ausschusses, Aktenstück Nr. 391 zu den *Verhandlungen der Deutschen Nationalversammlung*, vol. 335, 459.

79. Carl Schmitt, *Verfassungslehre* [1928] (Berlin, 1993), 61 (quote translated by Bernard Heise).

80. Ibid., 50 (quote translated by Bernard Heise). The research literature on Carl Schmitt and the German State-Law debate in the Weimar Republic is too extensive to be cited here; consider thus William E. Scheuerman, *Carl Schmitt: The End of Law*

(Lanham, MD, 1999). Suggestive for me in the context of this chapter was the essay by Ulrich K. Preuß, "Carl Schmitt – Die Bändigung oder die Entfesselung des Politischen?" in *Mythos Staat: Carl Schmitts Staatsverständnis*, ed. Rüdiger Voigt (Baden-Baden, 2001), 141–167.

81. See Ulrich Thiele, *Advokative Volkssouveränität: Carl Schmitts Konstruktion einer "demokratischen" Diktaturtheorie im Kontext der Interpretation politischer Theorien der Aufklärung* (Berlin, 2003).

82. Schmitt, *Verfassungslehre*, 27. "The political being preceded the granting of the constitution. That which is not available politically can not consciously make decisions. With respect to this fundamental act [the French Revolution, author's note] in which a Volk acted in a politically conscious manner, the political existence was presupposed and the act by which the Volk gives itself a constitution is to be distinguished from the constituting of the state." Ibid. (quotation translated by Bernard Heise).

83. Carl Schmitt, *The Concept of the Political*, trans. with introduction and notes by George Schwab (Chicago, 2007), 27.

84. For that reason I disagree with Steffen Bruendel, who distinguishes between an "exclusive" *Volksgemeinschaft* and an "inclusive" *Volksgemeinschaft*, in which he claims to recognize elements of participatory reform, a "foundation for future togetherness" in the "Spirit of 1914," and even the concept of a "democratic Volksgemeinschaft." It was not, as Bruendel maintains, the "inflationary usage by the National Socialists" that first "contaminated" the notion of the *Volksgemeinschaft*; instead, the "Volksgemeinschaft," based on identity and homogeneity rather than representation, was itself the antithesis of a liberal constitutional state. Bruendel, *Volksgemeinschaft*, 258–313.

85. Zentrale für Heimatdienst, ed., *Der Geist der neuen Volksgemeinschaft: Eine Denkschrift für das deutsche Volk* (Berlin, 1919), 4.

86. Jürgen C. Heß, *"Das ganze Deutschland soll es sein"* (Stuttgart, 1978), 332.

87. Quoted in Werner Schneider, *Die Deutsche Demokratische Partei in der Weimarer Republik 1924–1930* (Munich, 1978), 48, note 82.

88. Reichsgeschäftsstelle der DDP Berlin, *Staat und Wirtschaft: Rede von Gustav Schneider, Bundesvorsitzender des Gewerkschaftsbundes der Angestellten, auf dem Reichsparteitag der Deutschen Demokratischen Partei in Weimar am 6. April 1924* (Berlin, n.d.), 3; see also Heß, *"Das ganze Deutschland,"* 331.

89. Hugo Preuß, "Volksgemeinschaft?" in *Um die Reichsverfassung* (Berlin, 1924), 17–22, here 19.

90. "Manifest der Deutschen Staatspartei," in Wilhelm Treue, *Deutsche Parteiprogramme 1861–1954* (Göttingen, 1954), 148–152, quote on 148; see Burkhard Gutleben, "Volksgemeinschaft oder zweite Republik? Die Reaktionen des deutschen Linksliberalismus auf die Krise der 30er Jahre," *Tel Aviver Jahrbuch für deutsche Geschichte* 17 (1988): 259–284; for a survey see Konrad Jarausch and Larry E. Jones, eds., *In Search of a Liberal Germany: Studies in the History of German Liberalism from 1789 to the Present* (New York, 1990), and Eric Kurlander, *Living with Hitler: Liberal Democrats in the Third Reich* (New Haven, 2009).

91. Quoted in Hartenstein, *Anfänge der Deutschen Volkspartei*, 53, 207.

92. Quoted in ibid., 210.

93. "Aufruf und Leitsätze der Deutschen Zentrumspartei, 21.11. 1918 (Berlin)" in Herbert Lepper, ed., *Volk, Kirche, Vaterland: Wahlaufrufe, Aufrufe, Satzungen und Statuten des Zentrums 1870–1933* (Düsseldorf, 1998), 387–390, quote on 388.

94. "Richtlinien der Deutschen Zentrumspartei, 16.1. 1922," in ibid., 418–428, quote on 418f.

95. "Wahlaufruf der Deutschen Zentrumspartei zu den Reichstagswahlen, 14.3. 1924" in ibid., 428–430, quote on 430.
96. "Wahlaufruf der 'Germania,' 27.3. 1925" in ibid., 450–453; on the politics of the Center Party during the 1925 election of the Reich president, see Karsten Ruppert, *Im Dienst am Staat von Weimar: Das Zentrum als regierende Partei in der Weimarer Demokratie 1923–1930* (Düsseldorf, 1992), 109–130.
97. Regarding the Center Party's political theories about the state, see Detlef Junker, *Die Deutsche Zentrumspartei und Hitler 1932/ 33: Ein Beitrag zur Problematik des politischen Katholizismus in Deutschland* (Stuttgart, 1969), 127–155; Morsey, *Deutsche Zentrumspartei*, 236–242; on the connection between Social Democratic and Catholic republicans see Detlef Lehnert, "Von der politischkulturellen Fragmentierung zur demokratischen Sammlung: Der 'Volksblock' des 'Reichsbannerlagers' und die katholischen Republikaner" in Lehnert and Megerle, *Pluralismus als Verfassungs- und Gesellschaftsmodell*, 77–129.
98. Moritz Föllmer, "The Problem of National Solidarity in Interwar Germany," *German History* 23, no. 2 (2005): 202–231.
99. From the *Deutsche Mittelstandszeitung*, 1/1/1927, quoted in Föllmer, "Problem of National Solidarity," 216, who rightly noted that discord could hardly be smashed. Föllmer's observation could be taken further—the metaphor does not so much seek reconciliation but rather a violent production of enforced consensus.
100. Quoted in Heinrich August Winkler, *Von der Revolution zur Stabilisierung: Arbeiter und Arbeiterbewegung in der Weimarer Republik 1918 bis 1924* (Berlin: 1984), 436.
101. *Protokoll über die Verhandlungen des Parteitags der Sozialdemokratischen Partei Deutschlands, abgehalten in Görlitz vom 18. bis 24. September 1921* (Berlin, 1921), IIIf; on the discussion of the program, see Heinrich August Winkler, "Klassenbewegung oder Volkspartei? Zur Programmdiskussion in der Weimarer Sozialdemokratie 1920–1925," *Geschichte und Gesellschaft* 8 (1982): 9–54.
102. Quoted in Paul Nolte, *Die Ordnung der deutschen Gesellschaft: Selbstentwurf und Selbstbeschreibung im 20. Jahrhundertt* (Munich, 2000), 101. According to Nolte, an emphatic and naïve notion of the Volk played an important role for the SPD, generally speaking.
103. Winkler, "Klassenbewegung," 18.
104. Ibid., 28.
105. See Winkler, *Der Schein der Normalität: Arbeiter und Arbeiterbewegung in der Weimarer Republik 1924 bis 1930*, 2nd ed. (Berlin, 1988), especially 324, note 295.
106. Friedrich Ebert, *Schriften, Aufzeichnungen, Reden*, 2 vols. (Dresden, 1926), vol. 2, 159.
107. In a speech in Hamburg on 17 August 1922 Ebert said: "In the thought of German unity, in the idea of a German Reich itself that securely circumscribes our Volksgemeinschaft lie the roots not only of our cultural significance but also our economic strength and the possibility of free development." And in Kiel on 4 September 1922: "In this struggle to assert ourselves, we will need the cooperation of all our *Volksgenossen* (Volk comrades). Thus the thought of a firmly connected *Volksgemeinschaft* must increasingly become part of or flesh and blood." Ebert, *Schriften*, vol. 2, 253, 265; ibid. for more supporting documents.
108. See the vivid description in Franz Walter, *Nationale Romantik und revolutionärer Mythos: Politik und Lebensweisen im frühen Weimarer Jungsozialismus* (Berlin, 1986), 12–25; also Reinhard Lüpke, *Zwischen Marx und Wandervogel: Die Jungsozialisten in der Weimarer Republik 1919–1931* (Marburg, 1984), 35–40. At a meeting of young socialists at the Imperial Youth Conference in August 1920, they declared: "We are

beginning to recognize that the political and economic class struggle is not enough to make socialism a reality. We want to become new people, true socialists. A new world needs new people. But then we want to enliven the party with our spirit. We desire that [the party] becomes the party of the future. We demand from the party full freedom for our desire." Quoted in Winkler, *Schein der Normalität*, 265.

109. For elaboration see Lüpke, *Zwischen Marx und Wandervogel*, 52–56.
110. On the Hofgeismar Conference see Walter, *Nationale Romantik*, 40–48; Lüpke, *Zwischen Marx und Wandervogel*, 63–70; Franz Osterrath, "Der Hofgeismarkreis der Jungsozialisten," *Archiv für Sozialgeschichte* 4 (1964): 525–569; Winkler, *Schein der Normalität*, 367–369.
111. On Haubauch, now see Peter Zimmerman, *Theodor Haubach (1896–1945): Eine politische Biographie* (Hamburg, 2004), 123–150; on Mierendorff, see Richard Albrecht, *Der militante Sozialdemokrat: Carlo Mierendorff 1897–1943* (Berlin, 1987).
112. Hermann Heller, "Sozialismus und Nation (1925)," in *Gesammelte Schriften* (Leiden, 1971), vol. 1, 437–526, here 468.
113. Thus the *Illustrierte Reichsbannerzeitung* in October 1925 stated that the goal of the organization was "to forge an iron band of German togetherness and *Volksgemeinschaft*, above everything that was divisive and beyond classes and party-political world views." Quoted in Winkler, *Schein der Normalität*, 383. Regarding conflicts within the young socialists and the whereabouts of the members of the Hofgeismar Circle, see Winkler, *Schein der Normalität*, 376–378; Walter, *Nationale Romantik*, 169–177; Lüpke, *Zwischen Marx und Wandervogel*, 78–133, 145–152.
114. See the insightful comparative analysis of the National Socialist *Volksgemeinschaft* and the Social Democratic Volksheim in Sweden by Götz, *Ungleiche Geschwister*.
115. Martin H Geyer, *Verkehrte Welt: Revolution, Inflation und Moderne, München 1914–1924* (Göttingen, 1998), 391–397.
116. Wehler, *Gesellschaftsgeschichte*, vol. 4, 345.
117. Freytagh-Loringhoven, *Weimarer Verfassung*, 399f.
118. Quoted here in Adolf Hitler, *Sämtliche Aufzeichnungen 1905–1924*, ed. Eberhard Jäckel and Axel Kuhn (Stuttgart, 1980), 84–204. The speech was first printed in Reginald R. Phelps, "Hitlers 'grundlegende' Rede über den Antisemitismus," *Vierteljahrshefte für Zeitgeschichte* 16 (1968): 390–420; see the extensive interpretation of the speech by Klaus Holz, *Nationaler Antisemitismus* (Hamburg, 2001), 359–430.
119. Hitler, *Sämtliche Aufzeichnungen*, 184.
120. Ibid., 190.
121. Ibid., 200.
122. Ibid., 201. The call for "the removal of the Jews from our Volk" does not signify an anticipation of Auschwitz; in this regard I oppose Holz's interpretation of the speech, namely that the term *Entfernung* (removal) is the equivalent of killing. Holz, *Nationaler Antisemitismus*, 416–424. In 1920 the formulation "Entfernung der Juden aus unserem Volke" was directed more toward excluding them from the Reich. Hitler continued his sentence as follows: "... the removal of the Jews from our people [thunderous and persistent applause and hand clapping], not because we begrudge them their existence—we congratulate the rest of the world on their visit [much amusement]—but because the existence of our own Volk means a thousand times more to us than that of a foreign race [Bravo!]."
123. See Shulamit Volkov, "Das geschriebene und das gesprochene Wort: Über Kontinuität und Diskontinuität im deutschen Antisemitismus," in Shulamit Volkov, *Antisemitismus als kultureller Code: Zehn Essays*, exp. 2nd ed. (Munich, 2000), 54–75; see also Donald L. Niewyk, "Solving the 'Jewish Problem': Continuity and Change

in German Antisemitism, 1871–1945," *Leo Baeck Institute Yearbook* 35 (1990): 335–370, who like Volkov distinguishes between rhetorical anti-Semitism and the active, murderous anti-Semitism of the National Socialists.

124. Hitler, *Sämtliche Aufzeichnungen*, 201.

125. In a study on the widespread topos of the "Führer" in the Weimar Republic, Thomas Mergel notes that the "Führer" was expected to be "one of us," someone who would show us what "we have in us," and an outsider to the quotidian professional political enterprise of reaching compromises; he would be someone who breaks out of the routine and does the unexpected, someone surprising and "intuitive" who "instinctively" makes the right decisions and takes risks. After a number of disappointments in this regard, these expectations converged in a particular and evidently convincing way on Hitler. Thomas Mergel, "Führer, Volksgemeinschaft und Maschine: Politische Erwartungsstrukturen in der Weimarer Republik und dem Nationalsozialismus 1918–1936," in *Politische Kulturgeschichte der Zwischenkriegszeit 1918–1939*, ed. Wolfgang Hardtwig (Göttingen, 2005), 91–127.

2

Anti-Semitic Violence in the Weimar Republic

At the beginning of the First World War many German Jews hoped that by fulfilling their patriotic duty and exhibiting their national loyalty they would finally be accepted into the German *Volksgemeinschaft*. Their hopes were deceiving. The moment that the certainty of victory in 1914 evaporated and the war's hardships and deprivations were felt not only at the front but also in Germany, anti-Semitism quickly acquired a public resonance, particularly the allegations that "Jewish black marketers" and "war profiteers" were earning millions while "Germans" were forced to starve. The German army's notorious "Jewish census" of 1916 (the results of which were never published, thus further fueling wild speculations and suspicions) were an expression of the anti-Semitic resentment toward the Jews for supposedly "shirking."[1]

After sudden disillusionment set in following the unexpected admission by the Supreme Military Command that the war could no longer be won, "the Jews" were held responsible for the defeat. Revolutionaries with Jewish backgrounds like Rosa Luxemburg, Hugo Haase, and Eugen Leviné seemed to confirm the ant-Semitic worldview, namely that it was the Jews who stuck the "knife in the back" of the German Volk and now wanted the downfall. Victor Klemperer observed that, after the October Revolution in Russia, the bourgeois newspaper *Leipziger Neuesten Nachrichten* always referred to Leon Trotksy as "Trotski-Braunstein, the Talmudist" and loved anti-Semitic allusions. The archenemy was not merely Bolshevism but especially "international Jewry."[2]

After anti-Jewish pogroms with tens of thousands of fatalities in Poland, White Russia, and the Ukraine, anti-Semites also began threatening pogroms in Germany.[3] In October 1918 the Leipziger Heinrich Pudor distributed a leaflet that concluded with the words: "Pogroms in Germany! Either German or Jewish-English World Government! Paper and ink are now useless: anti-Semitism must finally be active, it must move from theory to praxis, it must become action!"[4] In February 1919, the Centralverein deutscher Staatsbürger jüdischen Glaubens (C.V.) warned that leaflets, rumors, etc. had caused such an overheated mood that one must "in all seriousness reckon with pogroms."[5] As reported in the newspaper *Neue Züricher Zeitung*, in November 1919 "the whole world, from the prime minister to the small district speaker, is talking about the German Volk's highly menacing mood for a pogrom."[6]

The Deutschvölkischer Schutz- und Trutz-Bund (German Nationalist Protection and Defiance Federation) soon emerged as the organizational center of the anti-Semitic campaign. Its membership rapidly grew from 5,000 members at its founding in 1919 to around 180,000 by the middle of 1922.[7] In 1920 the directors of the federation themselves produced almost 20 million leaflets and fliers, on top of which came the propaganda material from the numerous regional and local groups. In many instances, events held by the Deutschvölkischer Schutz- und Trutz-Bund led to beatings and violence, and to the plundering, mugging, and mistreatment of Jews.[8]

The hatred was directed above all toward Jewish refugees from Eastern Europe, the so-called *Ostjuden*. They were alleged to have brought Bolshevist propaganda to Germany and increased the Jewish population by immigrating and obtaining citizenship. Dramatic imagery lent emphasis to the anti-Semitic expulsion campaign, like the "threatening flood" or the "inundation of Germany with rootless elements from Galicia or the Russian border states, foreign in kind and foreign to the land."[9] At a mass gathering of farmers in Würzburg in April 1920, the leader of the Bavarian People's Party explained that the farmers would gladly deliver the demanded quota of foodstuffs, but they simultaneously demanded "that the 80,000 lousy *Ostjuden* [get] thrown out."[10] The newspaper article noted: "acclamations: beat them to death."[11]

Fall 1923

The severe excesses in November 1923 in the Berlin neighborhood Scheunenviertel, where numerous Eastern Jewish migrants and refugees lived, were no coincidence. As it was, the year 1923 marked the height of postwar turbulence. The occupation of the Rhineland by French and Belgian troops in January triggered a resistance—supported and financed by the government—that, shortly after it began, shook the political and economic foundations of the Republic. In the "struggle for national emancipation," radical anti-republican groups sought to gain members and believed that the time was ripe for the overthrow. In the fall, the Communists attempted to seize power through violence in Hamburg as part of the so-called German October plan; the National Socialists attempted likewise in November in Munich. The government's financing of the strikes in the Rhineland shattered the state's finances and drove inflation to dizzying heights. Savings melted away, while speculators amassed huge fortunes. "You cannot begin to imagine," wrote Betty Scholem at the end of October from Berlin to her son Gershom, who had recently immigrated to Palestine:

> Within three days, the dollar jumped as follows: 10 billion, 18 ½ billion, 40 billion. Bread 900 million, 2 ½ billion, 5 ½ billion. The collapse is complete. Looting flares up here and there, but it is not much; the distraught women are far too worn down, they put up with everything. *Until now* there has been no sign of disturbances, but for weeks one has expected them with every hour. One is simply amazed that they have not occurred. But at the slightest sign of a mob, the stores immediately roll down their blinds.[12]

Indeed, on 5 November it only took a spark to ignite severe looting and excesses in Berlin's Scheunenviertel. On this day, the price of bread rose to RM 140 billion, and at the same time rumors circulated that the employment office was not distributing any money. This initiated the spontaneous looting of bakeries and grocery stores—and by no means only those stores thought to be owned Jews. Anti-Semitic agitators felt that their time had come, and after becoming aware of the disturbances they moved into the Scheunenviertel and in their diatribes blamed the inflation and misery above all on the Jews. To be sure, the police quickly got involved, sealing off the Scheunenviertel and conducting raids, and in the following days they had the situation largely under control again. But the extent of the excesses was considerable. There was at least one death, and many people were injured, some of them severely. The director of the C.V. in Berlin, Steinthal, was badly abused after an agitator falsely accused him of a knife attack. According to police, over 200 stores—owned predominantly by non-Jews—were looted. Yet it was telling that store owners in the Scheunenviertel had tried to protect their stores with signs like "Christian business people."[13]

As with Walther Rathenau's murder the previous year, the outbreak of violence had a shocking effect on the Democrats. "Berlin had its Jewish pogrom," reported the 8 November edition of the Social Democratic *Vorwärts* in large letters on the first page. "Berlin has been disgraced. A dishonor for a Volk that counts itself among the civilized."[14] Beneath the headline "The hour of fate for German Judaism," the Zionistic weekly *Jüdische Rundschau* continued with its article:

> A Jewish pogrom took place in the streets of Berlin. Berlin was the stage for sad and shameful events, the kind of which, until now, have only been characteristic of less cultivated states. The fruit of seeds that have been systematically spread for five years has ripened! The anti-Semitism that has proliferated throughout Germany has now, after recently becoming an official government maxim, above all in Bavaria, also claimed its victims in Berlin.[15]

And even the levelheaded Betty Scholem described the situation to her son as follows: "There were no pogroms in Berlin. But the anti-Semitism has so thoroughly permeated and contaminated the Volk that one hears ranting about the Jews everywhere, quite openly and in such an unabashed manner like never before."[16]

The events in Berlin were not unique. There were reports of anti-Semitic excesses during the fall of 1923 from other localities in the Reich as well, especially from Upper Silesia, where the German-Polish border altercations had just subsided and residents were still caught up in an atmosphere of civil warfare. In Beuthen, where Upper Silesia's largest Jewish community resided, the regional chapter of the C.V. had already noted violent attacks on Jews in a letter to the Bürgermeister in the summer of 1922. The C.V. warned of the "increasingly threatening anti-Semitic movement" in the city, where significantly the ant-Semitic Deutschsoziale Partei (German Social Party) formed the second largest fraction in the city parliament, after the Catholic Center Party.[17] In September 1923, during disturbances caused by food shortages, organized gangs of mostly youths attacked and beat up pedestrians who supposedly looked Jewish—on 22 and 25 September, there were even grenade explosions. Then on 5 October, there was a full-blown pogrom. From about 6:00 p.m. until midnight, hundreds of young men went on a rampage in the town center of Beuthen, beating people with clubs so badly that they required hospitalization. Twenty victims suffered serious injuries. The C.V.-Zeitung reported that cries rang out like "beat the Jews to death" and "Hitler is here tomorrow, then we will buy everything for free."[18] Although the police pronounced an assembly ban, violent assaults continued to occur even during the next few days.[19] As the C.V.-*Zeitung* also determined, this was apparently not simply a case of spontaneous demonstrations, but rather of a prearranged pogrom carried out by anti-Semitic fighting groups.[20]

Things were similar in East Prussia. In Ortelsburg, according to reports by Kurt Sabatzky, director of the regional association of the C.V., "on Saturday, the 13th of October, large groups of rowdy elements passed by stores belonging to Jews and there looted clothing, shoes, and cigarettes."[21] The occasion for violence was provided by a demonstration against inflation by workers, who were politically riled up by right-wing radical anti-Semitic speakers. The police did absolutely nothing and simply watched the looting.[22] Likewise, violent assaults against Jews took place in neighboring Neidenburg. Here, too, at the end of September, the local chapter of the C.V. listed the numerous anti-Semitic incidents of bullying and assaults of the preceding month that emanated from the Deutschvölkischer Freiheitspartei (German People's Freedom Party) in Neidenburg. The party, with its swastikas, had been heating the atmosphere with a number of inflammatory rallies. Publicly in the marketplace, speakers stirred up hatred with calls like: "Just go to the Jew Lazarus, and take the millions for yourself, and smash [his] skull in for me, if you have the courage! Who are the blood-suckers? The Jews! Who provoked the war? The Jews!"[23] During the course of September, the aggression escalated into violence. Gangs mostly comprised of young people traversed the streets, threatening supporters of the Republic and denouncing them as "Jewish lackeys" and beating up Jewish citizens. Sabatzky also held Neidenburg's Deutschvölkischer Freiheitspartei responsible for the excesses in Ortelsburg, which was some 40 km away.[24]

In October 1923, National Socialist gangs hunted down Jewish businesspeople in Nuremberg. After two violent perpetrators were captured and convicted in November, around 200 National Socialists gathered for a campaign of revenge throughout the city, attacking the houses and businesses of Jews.[25] In Halberstadt in Saxony, the Bürgermeister reported an upsurge of anti-Semitic agitation by the Alldeutscher Verband (All-German Association), which resonated especially among young people. There were also attacks on Jews, which could have been stopped by the deployment of police.[26]

In most localities where excesses occurred, militant anti-Semitic groups had already been active in the previous months, drawn in part from the reservoir that remained of the Deutsch-Völkischer Schutz- und Trutz-Bund, which by now was banned. These combat brigades apparently formed the core of the perpetrators. They provided the initiative and were prepared to engage in criminal acts and seriously injure defenseless people. But it is also clear from the reports that these militant violent groups were not alone. The extremely precarious year of 1923 provided resonant space for agitators and groups primed for violence so that, as in Ortelsburg, even a workers' demonstration against inflation could be turned anti-Semitic and spurred on to violence. The fact that the reports speak time and time again of crowds that looted stores and engaged in violence indicates that perpetrators were not limited to clearly defined and organized violent gangs, but that there were co-perpetrators, inciters, and onlookers who gathered around this core, supporting the excesses and even enriching themselves in the looting.

What is striking in most of the reports is that the police rarely showed up to put an end to the violence and restore the rule of law. Whether this was because the law enforcement agencies were supposedly surprised by the outbreak of violence (thus adopting the trivializing reading of Neidenburg's district administrator, which hardly seems credible in light of the numerous prior incidents and the repeated warnings by the C.V.) or whether the police deliberately held back and more or less passively watched the activities cannot be definitively clarified. But when the police did get involved, the excesses quickly ceased. These were limited acts of violence, actions that were directed not toward a political overthrow but rather against a minority. Yet the significance of these "states of emergency from below"—these moments during which, albeit for a short duration and in a limited area, the legal and state order was abrogated and the protection of citizens could no longer be guaranteed—for the daily cohesion of the Weimar Republic should not be underestimated. The fact that during these postwar years the Republic could be so severely challenged and called into question in so many places revealed the fragility of the loyalty to the constitution and of the state's monopoly of violence.

But there was resistance as well. Directly after the excesses in Oldenburg, the Oberbürgermeister publicly declared it a disgrace to the town that such things had happened. These assaults involved rowdy anti-Semites of the worst kind, and the police were directed to take the strongest possible action against them.[27] In Berlin during the weeks after the pogrom, the SPD held no fewer than twelve rallies against anti-Semitism. The C.V., in a manner that was decidedly civically minded and self-consciously German, staged a protest assembly with the motto: "For reconstruction—against self-destruction [Selbstzerfleischung]"; it challenged "Jewish citizens in German regions to take a stand with all the strength they have available for the integrity of the Empire and the recovery from severe hardship of the prior florescence and greatness." The pogroms were blamed on a deluded minority, whereas the German Jews, despite centuries of persecution, would always loyally fight for Germany's salvation and renewal.[28] As Jacob Toury notes, instead of being conscious of crisis, Jews were still ostensibly only experiencing a crisis of consciousness in the fall of 1923. In C.V. circles, nobody was prepared to admit that the attacks were by no means directed only against "*Ostjuden*" but rather against Jews in general—that what had occurred was not an "*Ostjuden* pogrom" but a "Jewish pogrom."[29]

In contrast, the Zionist *Jüdische Rundschau* warned against concluding that the anti-Semitic movement was finished because the Hitler Putsch in Munich had failed:

> For the understanding which recognizes the sad and shameful facts can do little against the unbridled passions, the compulsive affects, which do not ask about truth or falsehood, that do not go mad even when things happen that should teach the masses to doubt the judgment of their previously blindly revered leaders. Anti-Semitism has eaten its way too deeply into the souls; it has become a Volk's disease against which apologetic arguments can accomplish little.[30]

And in the same edition, Arnold Zweig arrived at the clear-sighted analysis that the distinction between German Jews and *Ostjuden*, which was so carefully and often condescendingly drawn within the community of assimilated German Jews, would break down during the moment of action. They—the German Jews—"will then no longer, one would hope, be prepared to abandon the *Ostjuden* in order that they themselves can stand on the side of the righteous. Hopefully, they will then know that those who go along with the distinction are themselves infected with anti-Semitism, which like every affective disposition is always ready to spread to them infectiously."[31]

How clearly these differences were drawn even by liberals is shown by a resolution of the Berlin organization of the German Democratic Party. The resolution admittedly raised a "strong protest against the unchristian *völkisch* Jew-baiting that indiscriminately and inhumanely turns against our long-established Jewish fellow citizens"; but at the same time it blatantly ostracized the *Ostjuden*. And even the clear condemnation of the anti-Jewish acts of violence by Cardinal Faulhaber in Munich, who preached from the pulpit that the hatred of the Jews was not Christian, ended with the peculiar sentence: "every human life is precious, even that of an Israelite."[32] Finally, one also needs to note, however, that right-wing, anti-Semitic, and anti-republican violence also led to the creation of the Reichsbanner Schwarz-Rot-Gold in February 1924. With cautious optimism, Carl von Ossietzky wrote in mid September 1924: "Something has changed during these last months in Germany. People have become visible who want to defend the Republic."[33]

Violence in the Provinces

Despite the protests, the situation for the German Jews remained precarious. Thus at the beginning of June, the *Stürmer* picked up on an unsolved murder in Breslau, characterizing it as a "ritual murder." A short time later, in a leaflet circulating in the city, a Jewish household servant who had committed suicide was accused of "ritual murder." Local newspapers reprinted the leaflet and thus insured further distribution of this ludicrous charge. Even though the authorities immediately distanced themselves from the story and the local uproar appeared to subside, the allegations of ritual murder were now in the air and were repeatedly revisited by the *Stürmer* and other National Socialist newspapers.[34]

But could such threats against the Jews in Germany be more of an exception? What applied to one region did not necessarily apply to another. In the middle of 1927, the writer Georg Hermann raised the question in the *C.V.-Zeitung* as to whether the way of life for Jews in large cities was more isolated than in the countryside. In the large cities, the Jews lived on a "self-selected island" or were banished to this island, perhaps without even knowing it. In contrast, in the countryside (by which Hermann was referring mostly to southwest Germany—i.e., Baden and Württemberg) the "German Jew still lives entirely within the *Volksgemeinschaft*, speaks its language down to the last details, follows each hue of its dialect, and, apart from his religious practices, does not distinguish himself from it in any way worth mentioning. He also enjoys the same civic respect." However, this "close community with the *Volksganzen* [the whole of the Volk])" compels the Jews in the countryside to exercise stronger self-control. Hermann cites an acquaintance who reported on the constant fear of attracting attention within mainstream society:

> I grew up as the son of the only Jewish family in a small vineyard community along the Rhine. And thus many things were forbidden to me that without further ado would have been permitted to young Jewish people in a large city. My father adamantly insisted that none of us attract attention in any way, or that we would keep our distance from any kind of thing that would be somehow awkward for us. Even though we were well off, my mother was not allowed to wear any jewelry; and even though I had more intellectual interests, I was not allowed to exclude myself from any kind of

sports activities. Indeed I felt that I was living under double control, that of the community and that of my parents' home.[35]

The *C.V.-Zeitung* received so many responses to this article that in the following week it published some of these letters from readers, in which a folksy tone often prevailed that contrasted "unspoiled" rural life with the "uprooted" existence in the city. Complaints were made above all about the economic distress that was causing the Jews in the small towns and villages to suffer; boys, most of whom were indifferent to Judaism, were wandering off to the cities, where they were hoping to find greater earning potential and better living conditions; meanwhile, the elderly stayed behind. A doctor from Egelsbach near Darmstadt noted bitterly: "the Jewish community life in the village is in a shambles; the older generation no longer has the strength to clean it up, because the struggle for daily bread sucks up what little strength there is."[36]

Later reports based on memory often shared the harmonic perspective regarding the cohabitation of Christians and Jews in the provinces, and yet they still repeatedly revealed the difference that existed between "us" and "them."[37] Jacob Borut calls this barely recognizable yet always palpable boundary separating non-Jews from Jews an "invisible barrier."[38] Even before the war, many Jews had become members of gun clubs and gymnastic clubs, and the affluent were gladly looked upon as donors. But they were not allowed to become presidents of these associations. And while in large cities like Cologne and Düsseldorf it was possible for Jews to become members of carnival associations, this was not the case in the small localities of the Rhineland. The generation gap, which was typical in Jewish life in Germany at this time, also revealed itself here. Young Jews in particular were the ones who were either joining the sports associations that were rapidly multiplying in the countryside in the 1920s or founding their own sports associations.[39]

The National Socialists soon broke into the superficial provincial idyll. Josef Weil from Karlsruhe, who agreed in principle with Georg Hermann's harmonic point of view, reported at the same time in the *C.V.-Zeitung* on the National Socialist's agitation efforts in the region. Speakers came to the villages and staged anti-Semitic events in order to win over the rural population for the "*völkisch*" cause.[40] Indeed, because of its electoral success in the countryside, as of 1927 the NSDAP significantly shifted its focus to maintain a presence and demonstrate strength in small and mid-sized localities. To do so, regional SA units were brought together and then marched through the villages. As Peter Longerich writes, this kind of a military spectacle must in one sense have been a "welcome diversion" for the villagers, comparable to the annual fair, the presentation of a film, or the visit by a circus.[41] The stereotypical course of events, which repeatedly offered opportunities for the outbreak of violence, assured that the particular locality was quite literally occupied by the SA: the ceremony honoring the fallen at the local war memorial, the propagandistic march through the small town, the public rally, the concert by the SA band, the evening event at the hall, and finally the torchlight march and ceremonial tattoo at night.[42]

Thus on 6 March 1927, numerous Nazi brigades from Cologne, Coblenz, and Wiesbaden descended upon the small Hessian town of Nastätten because the Jewish farmer Hermann Henning had organized an assembly there on the subject of "the true face of National Socialism." The first conflicts with the four gendarmes in Nastätten had erupted by the afternoon. When the Nazis wanted to storm the hotel where the event was supposed to take place and where Henning was staying, it even came to a firefight with the police in which a National Socialist was killed.[43]

An incident like this may appear as a part of a straightforward continuation of ant-Semitic violence from the Weimar Republic to the National Socialist regime, but one can distinguish some important differences. Although they found themselves clearly outnumbered, the four police in Nastätten bravely attempted to defend the legal order. They even received support from the local firefighters. This behavior may have been motivated less by solidarity with the Jewish farmer Hermann Henning than by a desire to protect the peace of the town from an assault by a group of strangers. Even so, it is worth noting that quite a few residents of Nastätten courageously opposed the violent attacks of the National Socialists. Moreover, in February 1928 a local court in Wiesbaden sentenced eleven of the violent National Socialist perpetrators to six months in jail and, for a brief time, the local chapters of the NSDAP in Cologne, Coblenz, and Wiesbaden were banned.[44]

In the C.V.-Zeitung of 1 April 1927, the deputy director of the C.V., Alfred Wiener, listed the anti-Jewish assaults of the previous week and cited hateful anti-Semitic appeals from a number of National Socialist and völkisch papers. And at the end of his article, he asked:

Will the authorities now finally take serious action against the gross legal violations that the völkisch press dares to undertake daily against Jewish German citizens? Will the state governments and city administrations now keep themselves constantly informed about the dangerous and brutal objectives of National Socialism, and draw from this their conclusions, and in an appropriate manner intervene there where it is required, not for the good of the Jews, but for the good of the state?[45]

The C.V. tried to counteract the slogan "beat the Jews to death" with the motto "Humans, be humane!" But this could hardly be effective against the National Socialist fighting groups' declared intentions to perpetrate violence. With its acts of violence, the SA could effectively challenge the Weimar Republic on a daily basis, for the latter needed to protect the state's monopoly of violence and thus always found itself on the defensive. At the same time, violence made it possible to draw the boundary between "us" and the "enemy of the Volk" in a manner that was both sharp and irreconcilable. The more that the NSDAP managed to gain footing in localities by establishing local chapters and SA divisions, the more it tried (in keeping with the concept that Joseph Goebbels successfully demonstrated in Berlin) to terrorize political opponents with violence and to practice an "anti-Semitism of action."

During the party congress in Nuremberg at the beginning of August 1929, in which according to NSDAP figures 100,000 party members participated, some 25,000 SA members saw to an atmosphere charged with violence. SA gangs threatened pedestrians. They forced their way into the union office, compelling employees to take down the black-red-gold flag. And they attempted to storm the clubhouse of the Communist youth league. The town center was literally occupied by SA groups; it was a sign of general anarchy, noted the Nuremberg press in light of the events.[46] At the end of 1928, under the headline "National Socialistic terror! Countryside and small towns are being especially worked over," the C.V.-*Zeitung* dedicated numerous pages to the description of the violence against Jews in the German Reich, drawing particular attention not only to Bavaria, but also to the bordering Vogtland in Saxony, the Rhineland, Hanover, East Frisia, Greater Berlin, and East Prussia.[47]

In East Prussia, the NSDAP remained a marginal political force until 1928. There were German *völkisch* groups in the larger towns, and there is evidence of small National Socialist cells from the beginning of the 1920s in Königsberg, Elbing, and Allenstein. But not until March 1925 did a NSDAP local chapter form in Königsberg.[48] Other localities followed; in February 1926 Joseph Goebbels spoke in Königsberg for the first time, and there was violent conflict with Communists. But the expansion of the party organization remained minimal. The incumbent Gauleiter, Bruno Scherwitz from Königsberg, was therefore thrown out, and Erich Koch from the Ruhr region was brought in. Koch reorganized the party apparatus, started new local chapters and built up the SS, and he published a National Socialist newspaper—the *Ostdeutscher Beobachter*—which by the end of 1930 had increased its circulation to 7,000 copies. As a police report recorded in May 1929, the newspaper focused especially on the "philistines' craving for sensation."[49]

Like Goebbels in Berlin, Koch sought to mobilize the party with a policy of violent action and to terrorize political opponents, Communists,
Social Democrats, and Jews. Reporting about East Prussia in November
1928, the *C.V.-Zeitung* noted that processions often took place in the
evening, during which there were repeated confrontations with pedestrians. In smaller localities, National Socialist gangs suddenly appeared
on bicycles and harassed not only the Jewish population but also those
with other political ideas; they gave open-air speeches and then just as
suddenly disappeared again.[50] Koch publicly threatened Kurt Sabatzky,
saying that he would "chasten him with his riding crop," and a second
time, saying that after the National Socialists assumed power, the C.V.
syndic would be the first to "hang." Sabatzky was assaulted a number of
times, and in 1931 his female colleague Else Ascher was seriously injured
in an assassination attempt using explosives at an event held by the Social Democratic Reichsbanner.[51]

Caesura 1930

The results of the Reichstag elections on 14 September were a shock for
many observers, even though there were advance indications for the National Socialists' political success in the earlier Landtag (state parliament)
elections. The SPD admittedly lost votes in September 1930, but with
24.5 percent it still remained the strongest fraction in the Reichstag; the
KPD increased its part from 10.6 to 13.1 percent. In contrast, the bourgeois camp suffered dramatic losses, whereas the success of the National
Socialists exceeded all expectations,[52] its votes climbing from just over
800,000 to over 6.4 million. And with that, the NSDAP straightaway
became the second strongest party in the Reichstag—a political landslide
the likes of which had never been seen before in the Weimar Republic.[53]

In contrast to the other parties, the NSDAP managed to distinguish
itself as a "*Volkspartei*" that represented an electable alternative for all
social strata. Although the breakthrough with the Catholic electorate
would first occur in 1933 and the Social Democratic and Communist-ori-
ented workers remained resistant to National Socialism, the NSDAP also
attained significant success in electoral districts with a high percentage of
workers. This was because, unlike the bourgeois German Nationals, the
NSDAP represented an electoral alternative for workers with nationalist
attitudes. For people in the middle strata, who felt themselves extremely
threatened by the economic and social conditions, the NSDAP served
as a party of cumulative protest. On the basis of his experience of the

National Socialists' success, the sociologist Theodor Geiger coined the catchphrase "panic in the middle class."[54]

Yet despite the unmistakable caesura, some voices still believed in the unswerving nature of the world's course. The commentator for *Abend* took refuge in the metaphor of the ebb and flow of the tides; accordingly, the present National Socialist success would drain away just like that of the anti-Semites during the Kaiserreich.[55] Similarly, Leopold Schwarzschild's *Tagebuch* stated that all of the panic reigning in Germany was unwarranted. What had happened amounted to nothing more than a return to the situation in the Reichstag as it was in May 1924, except for the minor difference that the German Nationals had been replaced by the National Socialists.[56]

Meanwhile, the *Jüdische Rundschau* had already subjected the NSDAP's electoral victory in Thuringia in January 1930 to a clear-sighted analysis. The votes for the NSDAP were increasing from election to election; in many town and state parliaments, they had become an important factor. And with the growing strength of the National Socialists, an increasingly larger section of the bourgeoisie would ally itself with the new power against Communists and also the Jews. People should not be deceived: "The anti-Semitism of the National Socialists will not represent a reason for the broadest strata of the German Volk to reject cooperation with and support for the National Socialists." Thus it was no longer sufficient on the part of the Jews to denounce the National Socialists as "reactionary, bloodthirsty, medieval, fascistic, and Jew-baiting." For "whether we Jews like it or not, there must indeed be something about the National Socialist party that meets the actual needs of broad sectors of the German Volk."[57]

For the C.V. Board of Directors, writes Avraham Barkai, the Reichstag election was a traumatic experience.[58] After the success of the National Socialists in the state parliamentary elections in Baden in October 1929, the C.V. still believed it could demonstrate that the percentage of votes for the NSDAP in places with Jewish populations was lower than in places where Jews did not live.[59] Ludwig Hollander still continued to emphasize that anti-Jewish motivations did not provide the deciding factor in the electoral decision, but the "instillation of anti-Jewish thought patterns" nonetheless signified a great danger. Even so, it could not be the task of the Centralverein to combat National Socialism as an overall manifestation. That needed to be done by the political parties. The C.V. needed in the first instance to grapple with the "anti-Jewish views and excesses of this party, and with the *völkisch* body of thought in general." Meanwhile, the German Jews—preferably by word of mouth and "tactfully in every form"—should seek to enlighten the German members of the population by establishing relations with them.[60]

There were two voices within the C.V. urging for a policy of total defense against National Socialism that expressly included the new methods of mass propaganda. One was Hans Reichmann; the other was Alfred Wiener, who was Reichmann's colleague, superior, and elder by fifteen years as well as a longtime syndic of the C.V. The C.V. met the propagandistic flood of anti-Jewish brochures, leaflets, pamphlets, and books with its own informative literature, like the handbook *Anti-Nazi*, first published in 1930. A camouflaged organization, which was simply called Büro Wilhelmstraße (Wilhelmstraße Office) and was directed by Walter Gyßling, provided information (some of which came directly from the Nazis themselves) to government agencies, parliamentarians, editors, high school teachers, and clergy.[61]

On the part of the National Socialists, the violent "propaganda of action" only really got going after the electoral success in 1930. The National Socialists proceeded on the opening day of the Reichstag, 13 October, in their own fashion. Gangs of young men traversed the town center engaging in vandalism, smashing the display windows of the Wertheim department store on the Kurfürstendamm and other stores in the town center with purportedly Jewish owners.[62]

What the *C.V.-Zeitung* apostrophized as "stupid youthful escapades" was deliberate strategy. Activism, battle, and violence as "*Gemeinschaftserlebnis*" (community experience) constituted an integral part of daily life in the SA at the end of the 1920s and beginning of the 1930s. Brutal brawls between the SA and its political opponents, especially Communists; marches through the proletarian quarter of Berlin; hate-filled anti-Semitic attacks against the vice president of the Berlin police, Bernhard Weiß: this was all supposed to break the left-wing hegemony and assert the SA's own claim to power. At the same time, violence as "the experience of battle" consolidated the internal cohesion of the SA groups and openly demonstrated the fascist order's claim of superiority. Violence, writes Sven Reichardt, imparted "an image of the strength, discipline, inevitability, and intransigence of fascism."[63]

Far more than two-thirds of SA members were under thirty years old;[64] in the violent political actions researched by Dirk Schumann, which occurred in Saxony from 1930 to 1932, over two-thirds of the almost exclusively male actors were born after 1900.[65] What distinguished the SA in large cities like Berlin was precisely its youth and its high number of unemployed. The SA offered young men "a feeling of not being superfluous. The non-stop fascist activism suggested the potential for actively shaping a society, the socio-economic changes of which had left young men passive and helpless." In the process, "the images of violence and or-der, of national salvation and comradely manliness [appeared] as a viable way out. The radicalism of the slogans and the possibility for the violent expression of frustrations, on the one hand, and the desire to be taken up into the national *Volksgemeinschaft*, on the other hand, were what made the fascistic fighting groups attractive."[66]

For SA platoons (Stürme) in Berlin, it was usual on a Sunday to travel to the Kurfürstendamm in order to harass and beat up pedestrians. Walk-ing alongside the columns of SA were plainclothes SA men chosen for their strength; they were called "*Watte*" (wadding) and both protected the flanks and selectively jostled and beat up pedestrians. A contempo-rary National Socialist text described such a deployment as follows:

> From Kaiserplatz in Wilmersdorf all the way to Wittenbergplatz, the "*Watte*" is extremely unfriendly to each Jew that it encounters. The uniformed SA in the middle of the street does not even look. That is not its concern. It carries the flag and Adolf Hitler's idea through West Berlin, which is called the Jewish west. In this moment, it is to be nothing more than the great threat of the Führer.[67]

Thus on the evening of the Jewish New Year, 12 September 1931, it came to bloody excesses on the Kurfürstendamm. According to findings by the court, about 1,000 SA men were deployed, shouting slogans like "Germa-ny awake, Judah die" (*Deutschland erwache, Juda verrecke*) and "beat the Jews to death," and during the march they assaulted and beat pedestri-ans.[68] In October the NSDAP organized a "meeting in central Germany" in Braunschweig; around 100,000 men traveled to the town, which itself had only 150,000 residents, and in a certain sense they fully occupied the place. SA platoons traversed the streets, smashing windows, destroying stores, shooting up houses. The authority of the state was replaced by the violent power of the SA, which realized its own notions of political order—of "cleaning up." The police were completely overburdened, and the military did not get involved, largely because the National Socialists were backed up by the fact that the interior minister and thus the police commander for the state of Braunschweig was already a National Social-ist. The upshot of the two-day meeting: two dead workers and sixty-two seriously injured.[69]

In Würzburg, a guest performance was scheduled in the city theater on the evening of 19 November 1930 by Habima, a Hebrew theater group founded in Moscow that by then had taken up residence in Palestine. During the Reichstag election, the NSDAP in Würzburg had gained over 5,000 votes compared to local elections nine months earlier and thus had almost caught up to the SPD and left all other parties behind, with the exception of the Bavarian Volkspartei. As early as the morning of the performance, National Socialist students distributed leaflets calling for a protest against this "cultural disgrace." Word for word, the leaflet stated among other things:

> Würzburgers, the Jew thus does not shrink from denigrating the city the-
> ater, which is maintained with your tax pennies, as a showplace for an
> advertisement of his culture, which is not one.... Würzburgers! Students!
> Protest against this cultural disgrace! Join the Defense Front of Awakening
> Germany! Against the bolshevization of the theater! For German ways and
> culture![70]

In front of the theater, National Socialist groups ranted and jeered, trying to disturb the event, but the deployment of police, who cleared the streets, allowed the performance to take place undisrupted. Yet when the patrons left the theater, there were fierce excesses. A dozen people were abused, beaten, slapped, and kicked. An engineer from Nuremberg was beaten up by a group of youths after a female demonstrator had called out: "That is a Jew, beat him to death!" The Oberbürgermeister of Würz-burg, who late in the evening wanted to look after the matter himself, was denounced by the demonstrators as a "Jew Bürgermeister." A female Jewish theater patron reported later: "How I made it home, I no longer know, just that it was one or two o'clock in the morning and the fear did not leave me for days."[71] At a protest assembly of the Jewish community and the C.V. a few days later, there were bitter complaints that during the excesses no police were on hand to intervene. Thus the recommendation to create a Jewish self-defense league met with broad approval at the as-sembly.[72]

In Prussia, territorially the largest state in the German Reich, the po-lice registered 579 violent confrontations at political events for the year 1929. In the following year that number quickly leapt to 2,494; it re-mained around that same level with 2,904 incidents in 1931; and then it almost doubled again in the year 1932, with 5,296 registered confron-tations in Prussia alone.[73] By the Reichstag election in July 1932, Prus-sia alone counted 101 dead, among them 40 National Socialists and 46 Communists. Political violence, according to Richard Bessel, became a ubiquitous phenomenon in the German Reich.[74]

After the Reichstag election in July 1932, which despite the NSDAP's extraordinary showing still disappointed lofty expectations, the SA let its hatred run free in a series of assaults, attacks, and assassinations. The scope of the outbreak of violence becomes apparent when one considers

East Prussia as a regional example. In the night of 31 July/1 August, Nazi gangs in Königsberg attacked private homes, set gas stations ablaze, threw a bomb at the headquarters of the SPD, and destroyed Jewish stores. In the process, one Communist city councillor was murdered and other Social Democratic and liberal politicians were shot and seriously wounded. Attempts to murder the Communist Reichstag representative Schütz and the C.V. Director Sabatzky failed only because neither was in his own home.[75] In the following days, terror gripped all of East Prussia. Workers were killed in Norgau, Tilsit, and Lötzen; in Elbing, the SA assaulted the working-class neighborhood, and in southern East Prussia, stores belonging to Jewish citizens were the target of anti-Semitic attacks. Besides Bialla and Ortelsburg, an attack also occurred in Osterode, and a bomb was placed in front of the Lonky department store, which fortunately, however, did not explode.[76]

In December of the same year, fourteen perpetrators, all members of the Osterode SA, stood as defendants before a special court in Allenstein. They testified that prior to the action, at an SA leadership meeting, the directive was given to "stick it to" (*eins auswischen*) the Jews and the Communists. The court came to the conclusion that a violation of the explosives act did not occur, but only "gross misconduct," theft, and willful damage to property. Four defendants were acquitted; the rest were sentenced to prison terms of between six weeks and two and a half years.[77]

Assault on the Constitutional State

Political violence in the Weimar Republic was organized violence, exercised either by secret commandos who attempted to murder republican and Jewish politicians, by military associations, or by paramilitary militias like the Communist Red Front Fighters' League and the National Socialist SA. The objective was in each case clear: the destruction of the democratic constitutional order and the overthrow of the Republic.

The dilemma for the Weimar Republic lay in the fact that it possessed neither the loyalty of its citizens nor a loyal military power that could successfully meet an armed challenge. As early as the Kapp Putsch in 1922, the government discovered that it could no longer depend on the military, which had taken a position of benevolent neutrality vis-à-vis the instigators of the putsch. It was only the general strike that saved the Republic. In contrast, the military was always fully prepared to crush left-wing uprisings. Yet while the Republic managed, with difficulty but ultimately successfully, to defend itself from open attempts to stage a coup, it was largely defenseless against street violence. The police force was often insufficient to effectively and permanently suppress the violent battles in the streets and halls. And the political leadership was afraid to prohibit the creation of armed militia.

Thus the Republic was constantly challenged in a matter that was of central importance to the state—namely the preservation of its monopoly of violence—without possessing sufficient means to meet this challenge successfully. At the same time, each street battle between left-wing and right-wing militias shook the confidence in the Republic's capacity to uphold the law and ensure security, and to defend the state's monopoly of violence. For the respective political parties, their violent militias opened up a political arena beyond the constitution—indeed, in opposition to the constitution—an arena that by its very existence seriously brought into question the constitutional state. Superiority over political opponents was no longer measured only by the number of ballots but rather by dominance in street violence. It was not only the constitutional order that determined the meaning of the political parties but rather more their "clout" during conflicts. Hannah Arendt has emphatically indicated that each political order must be supported by power, that is, by the capability of the citizens to join with one another and to deal with one another on the basis of mutual understanding. "When we say of somebody that he is 'in power' we actually refer to his being empowered by a certain number of people to act in their name."[78] Violence, in contrast, can only be deployed instrumentally, and as a means of coercion. The most effective command always comes from the barrel of a gun, and it can count on prompt and uncontradicted obedience, but what can never come from the barrel of a gun, insists Hannah Arendt, is power. "Power and violence are opposites; where the one rules absolutely, the other is absent. Violence appears where power is in jeopardy, but left to its own course it ends in power's disappearance."[79]

The organized violence, which dramatically increased during the final phase of the Weimar Republic, caused—according to the meaning of Hannah Arendt—the disappearance of power. More precisely, it caused the disappearance of democratic, republican power. The Republic's strength to master the challenge of violence had already waned prior to January 1933. The backroom politics of the Reich president that led to the appointment of Hitler as Reich chancellor mirrored the political condition of the Republic. In previous years, the violent militias of the KPD and the NSDAP had already successfully demonstrated the weakness of the Republic. But the violence of the SA went still one decisive step further, for it did not merely challenge and seek to weaken the constitutional Weimar state and political opponents but proceeded just as brutally against the Jews, an unarmed defenseless minority who neither presented a violent threat nor for their part possessed an equal paramilitary defensive association.

The asymmetrical violence went beyond a battle against an opponent who was recognized as an equal. The violent attacks of the SA against Jews sought the elimination of the Jewish minority in Germany, who, humiliated and frightened, were supposed to be driven out of Germany by terror. Even in the years prior to 1933, the NSDAP and the SA attempted to draw the anti-Semitic boundaries of the *Volksgemeinschaft* through German society, and to exclude through violent means those who from their perspective did not posses the right to exist in Germany.[80]

The violence of the SA turned anti-Semitism into a political practice wholly independent from considerations of electoral tactics. While election campaign slogans sought to propagate the *Volksgemeinschaft* by virtue of inclusion, the violent practice of the National Socialists at the same time made the exclusion of those who were not supposed to belong to the *Volksgemeinschaft* brutally apparent. The violent actions against the Jewish minority in Germany were not a battle against an opponent with the intent of overpowering him. Rather, they were acts of exclusionary violence that sought expulsion and disappearance. The Communists were to be vanquished; the Jews were to be destroyed.

For the moment there was resistance. What characterized the Weimar Republic as a constitutional state was the fact that the democratic forces were able to withdraw from the complicity that is achieved by violence when one allows it to occur and does not oppose it. Social Democrats and Liberals organized demonstrations against the denunciation of a "Jewish" republic. A free press reported on the violent assaults and the criminal acts of the National Socialists. In particular the C.V.—after recognizing, albeit late, the danger of the National Socialist movement—made efforts to educate and mobilize opposing forces. Significantly, the C.V. had access to the legal process and the opportunity to file complaints against ant-Semitic perpetrators in the courts. Thus far the constitutional state was still sufficiently intact that courts exercised independent judgment, even though the handling of the cases and the judgments that were rendered already made visible the erosion of the constitutional order. Consequently, legal counseling formed a large part of the C.V.'s activity.

For this reason, despite many continuities, the transfer of power to Adolf Hitler on 30 January 1933 marked an undeniable break, for it decisively changed the context of political violence. Henceforth, the SA, SS, and NSDAP groups were no longer acting as organizations that tried to assert themselves with violence against political opponents and ultimately still measured their success according to electoral results; rather, they acted as organs of the regime, which in the name and with the support of the state moved violently against members of the political opposition, who were initially persecuted as enemies of the state but above all as *Volksfeinde*—enemies of the people.

Notes

1. Werner Jochmann, "Die Ausbreitung des Antisemitismus in Deutschland 1914–1923," in *Gesellschaftskrise und Judenfeindschaft in Deutschland 1870–1945* (Hamburg, 1988), 99–170.
2. Victor Klemperer, *Curriculum Vitae*, 2 vols. (Berlin, 1996), vol. 2, 607; and the chapter "Revolution und Antisemitismus," in Avraham Barkai, *"Wehr Dich!"* (Munich, 2002).
3. On new reports about the pogroms, see Burkhard Asmus, *Republik ohne Chance* (Berlin, 1994), 166f., 172f., 182, 206f.
4. Quoted in Dirk Walter, *Antisemitische Kriminalität und Gewalt* (Bonn, 1999), 28; Walter describes the years immediately after the war as the "offensive of pogrom-anti-Semitism."
5. Quoted in Cornelia Hecht, *Deutsche Juden und Antisemitismus in der Weimarer Republik* (Bonn, 2003), 106; for further evidence of the anxieties about pogroms, ibid., 101–119. In this connection, it is significant that at this particular moment, Hitler spoke out against pogrom anti-Semitism in a programmatic letter to Adolf Gemlich on 16 September 1919: "Anti-Semitism based purely in emotions will find its final expression in the form of pogroms. The anti-Semitism of reason, however, must lead to the methodical legal fight against and abolishment of the prerogatives of the Jew that he possesses in contrast to the other foreigners living among us (foreigner legislation). Its final objective, however, must be the actual removal of the Jews." Hitler, *Sämtliche Aufzeichnungen*, 88–90.
6. Quoted in Walter, *Antisemitische Kriminalität*, 35f.
7. According to an assessment in November 1922 by the Imperial Commission for the Supervision of Public Order, the Deutschvölkischer Schutz- und Trutz-Bund was "the largest, most active and most influential anti-Semitic association in Germany." Quoted in Uwe Lohalm, *Völkischer Radikalismus: Die Geschichte des Deutschvölkischen Schutz- und Trutz-Bundes 1919 1923* (Hamburg, 1970), 11; Lohalm also provides details about the organization and praxis of the association. After the murder of Walther Rathenau in June 1922, the association was banned due to its undisguised calls for violence.
8. See Lohalm, *Völkischer Radikalismus*, 123.
9. On the history and persecution of the *Ostjuden* in Germany, see Trude Maurer, *Ostjuden in Deutschland 1918–1933* (Hamburg, 1986); Jack Wertheimer, *Unwelcome Strangers: East European Jews in Imperial Germany* (New York, 1991); Steven E. Aschheim, *Brothers and Strangers: The East European Jews in German and German Jewish Consciousness, 1800/1923* (Madison, 1999).
10. Quoted in Walter, *Antisemitische Kriminalität*, 61; numerous other examples in Maurer, *Ostjuden in Deutschland*, 104–160.
11. Maurer, *Ostjuden in Deutschland*, 327. On the Bavarian politics of expulsion and internment against *Ostjuden*, see Walter, *Antisemitische Kriminalität*, 52–79.
12. Gershom Scholem and Betty Scholem, *Scholem, Betty—Gershom Scholem, Mutter und Sohn im Briefwechsel 1917–1946*, ed. Itta Shedletzky (Munich, 1989), 88 (23

October 1923). Gershom (Gerhard) Scholem, born in 1897 to a respected Jewish family in Berlin, took an early interest in Jewish studies, earned a doctorate studying the Kabbalah, and immigrated to Palestine in 1923. In 1925 he became a lecturer on mysticism at the Hebrew University in Jerusalem and worked there as an internationally esteemed scholar until his retirement in 1965. Scholem died in 1982 in Jerusalem.

13. Walter, *Antisemitische Kriminalität*, 153–155; Maurer, *Ostjuden in Deutschland*, 329–344; Hecht, *Deutsche Juden und Antisemitismus*, 177–186; David Clay Large, "'Out with the Ostjuden': The Scheunenviertel Riots in Berlin, November 1923," in *Exclusionary Violence: Antisemitic Riots in Modern History*, ed. Christhard Hoffmann, Werner Bergmann, and Helmut Walser Smith (Ann Arbor, 2002) 123–140. Large argues that the excesses were not the work of right-wing agitators but broke out spontaneously and, moreover, that the looters were to be found not so much in the right-wing but in the left-wing milieu. But Large does not provide any empirical evidence for his thesis and above all overlooks the fact that the violence was distinguished between a more spontaneous phase during the day and a subsequent phase in the evening and night that was fomented by agitators. For the background in Berlin, see Andrea Lefèvre, "Lebensmittelunruhen in Berlin 1920–1923," in *Der Kampf um das tägliche Brot: Nahrungsmangel, Versorgungspolitik und Protest 1770–1990*, ed. Manfred Gailus and Heinrich Volkmann (Opladen, 1994), 346–360; and in particular, Thomas Lindenberger, *Straßenpolitik*.

14. Quoted in Walter, *Antisemitische Kriminalität*, 151.

15. *Jüdische Rundschau*, 9 November 1923, 1. On the reaction to the unrest in the daily newspapers (some of which, like the *Berliner Lokal-Anzeiger*, did not shy away from openly anti-Semitic reporting), see Burkhard Asmus, *Republik ohne Chance*, 549–551.

16. Scholem, *Briefwechsel*, 95 (11/20/1923).

17. Letter from the C.V. local chapter of Beuthen to the mayor, 8 July 1922; quoted in Hecht, *Deutsche Juden und Antisemitismus*, 166f.

18. "Die Ausschreitungen in Beuthen," CVZ, 11 October 1923. Cornelia Hecht incorrectly read: "Morgen ist Hitler da, dann taufen [i.e., instead of 'kaufen', that is, 'baptize' instead of 'buy' —trans.] wir alle umsonst." Hecht, *Deutsche Juden und Antisemitismus*, 169.

19. Hecht, *Deutsche Juden und Antisemitismus*, 168f.

20. "Die Ausschreitungen in Beuthen," CVZ, 11 October 1923.

21. Kurt Sabatzky, "Die Ausschreitungen in Ostpreußen," CVZ, 27 October 1923; and Stefanie Schüler-Springorum, *Die jüdische Minderheit in Königsberg/ Preußen 1871–1945* (Göttingen, 1996).

22. C.V., regional association of East Prussia, Notiz über den Bericht zweier Kaufleute aus Ortelsburg, 18 October 1923, CAHJP Jerusalem, HM2/8718, fol. 647–649 (Special Archive Moscow, 721-1-1101). According to information provided by District Administrator v. Throata, the police were completely surprised by the incidents and thus were not in a position to intervene. Sabatzky to the C.V. Berlin, 25 November 1923, ibid. fol. 641f.; on Ortelsburg, see Andreas Kossert, "Die jüdische Gemeinde Ortelsburg: Ein Beitrag zur Geschichte der Juden in Masuren," in *Zur Geschichte und Kultur der Juden in Ost- und Westpreußen*, ed. Michael Brocke, Margret Heitmann, and Harald Lordick (Hildesheim, 2000), 87–124—however, Kossert does not deal with the excesses in the fall of 1923.

23. Report on a rally held by the Deutschvölkische Kampfgewerkschaft on 15 August 1923 from the "Denkschrift über das Treiben der völkischen Kampfgewerkschaft

und der Deutschvölkischen Freiheitsparteiin Neidenburg," written by the C.V. local chapter of Neidenburg, 27 September 1923, CAHJP Jerusalem, HM2/8762, fol.
562–568 (Special Archive Moscow, 721-1-2375).

24. C.V. Neidenburg, "Denkschrift." Later in a lower court in Neidenburg, a number of
perpetrators were assessed fines for disturbing the peace and causing bodily harm.
"Neidenburger Idyll. Deutschvölkische Radauhelden vor Gericht," CVZ, 31 January
1924. I thank Dr. Jacob Borut, Yad Vashem Archives, Jerusalem, for numerous references to the events in Neidenburg.

25. Report from the C.V. local chapter Nuremberg to the C.V. headquarters in Berlin, 14
November 1923, Special Archive Moscow, 721-1-2375, 341f.

26. Walter, Antisemitische Kriminalität, 115–117; Hecht, Deutsche Juden und Antisemitismus, 175–177.

27. "Antisemitische Exzesse in Deutschland: Die Judenausschreitungen in Oldenburg,"
Jüdische Rundschau, 6 November 1923.

28. See the extensive reports about the rallies in Berlin in the CVZ, 30 November
1923.

29. Jacob Toury, "Gab es ein Krisenbewußtsein unter den Juden während der 'guten
Jahre' der Weimarer Republik 1924–1929," Tel Aviver Jahrbuch für deutsche Geschichte
17 (1988): 145–168, here 150; see also Martin Liepach, "Das Krisenbewusstsein des
jüdischen Bürgertums in den Goldenen Zwanzigern," in Juden, Bürger, Deutsche:
Zur Geschichte von Vielfalt und Differenz 1800–1933, ed. Andreas Gotzmann, Rainer
Liedtke, and Till van Rahden (Tübingen, 2001), 395–417; and the nuanced analysis of reports based on memories, Werner Bergmann and Juliane Wetzel, "'Der Miterlebende weiß nichts': Alltagsantisemitismus als zeitgenössische Erfahrung und
spätere Erinnerung (1919–1933)," in Jüdisches Leben in der Weimarer Republik/Jews in
Weimar Republic, ed. Wolfgang Benz, Arnold Paucker, and Peter Pulzer (Tübingen,
1998), 173–196.

30. "Die judenfeindliche Welle in Deutschland," Jüdische Rundschau, 20 November
1923.

31. Arnold Zweig, "Die Summe," in ibid.

32. Jüdische Rundschau, 18 December 1923.

33. Quoted in Walter, Antisemitische Kriminalität, 154.

34. See Walter, Antisemitische Kriminalität, 177–192; see also more generally Susanna
Buttaroni and Stanislaw Musial, eds., Ritualmordlegenden in der europäischen Geschich-
te (Vienna, 2002); Rainer Erb, ed., Die Legende vom Ritualmord: Zur Geschichte der
Blutbeschuldigung gegen Juden. Berlin, 1996.

35. Georg Hermann, "Großstadt oder Kleinstadt," CVZ, 3 June 1927

36. "Großstadt, Kleinstadt, Dorf. Eine Aussprache," CVZ, 1 July 1927 and 22 July 1927.
See also Hecht, Deutsche Juden und Antisemitismus, 291f.

37. See also Bergmann and Wetzel, "'Der Miterlebende weiß nichts'"; for an instructive
regional study, see Ulrich Baumann, Zerstörte Nachbarschaften: Christen und Juden in
badischen Landgemeinden 1862–1940 (Hamburg, 2000).

38. Jacob Borut, "'Bin Ich doch ein Israelit, ehre Ich auch den Bischof mit'—Village
and Small-Town Jews within the Social Spheres in Western Germany Communities
during the Weimar Republic," in Benz et al., Jüdisches Leben in der Weimarer Republik,
117–133.

39. Ibid., 120. On the fierce disputes regarding the "authenticity" of German Jews, see
Michael Brenner, Jüdische Kultur in der Weimarer Republik (Munich, 2000).

40. Josef Weil, "Von völkischer Arbeit in Baden. Sie wollen das Land 'erobern,'" CVZ, 2
September 1927; see also "Die völkische Gefahr am Rhein," CVZ, 8 April 1927.

41. Peter Longerich, *Die braunen Bataillone: Geschichte der SA* (Munich, 1989), 72–77; see also Johnpeter Horst Grill, "The Nazi Party's Rural Propaganda Before 1928," *Central European History* 15 (1982): 149–185, particularly 130–133.

42. Sven Reichardt, *Faschistische Kampfbünde: Gewalt und Gemeinschaft im italienischen Squadrismus und in der deutschen SA* (Cologne, 2002), 104.

43. Walter, *Antisemitische Kriminalität*, 206f. In his essay on violent anti-Semitism, Jacob Borut investigates further cases in the Rhineland. Jacob Borut, "Gewalttätiger Antisemitismus im Rheinland und in Westfalen in der Zeit der Weimarer Republik," *Geschichte im Westen* 22 (2007): 9–40.

44. A few days after the incident in Nastätten, there also were excesses in Cologne in front of the synagogue on Roonstraße, in which two Jewish persons suffered stab wounds. Walter, *Antisemitische Kriminalität*, 200. In January in Breslau, groups of National Socialist thugs went on the hunt at night for persons that they felt looked like Jews and beat them up; the same occurred in Chemnitz, where some forty National Socialists traversed the streets in broad daylight on a Sunday chanting, "throw them out of our Fatherland, beat them to death, the entire band of Jews, Ugh! Jew Republic!" and assaulting a Jewish merchant. Hecht, *Deutsche Juden und Antisemitismus*, 194.

45. Alfred Wiener, "Soll das so weiter gehen?" CVZ, 1 April 1927; on Alfred Wiener, see the brief portrait in Barkai, "*Wehr Dich!*" 162f.

46. Hans-Gerd Jaschke and Martin Loiperdinger, "Gewalt und NSDAP vor 1933: Ästhetische Okkupation und physischer Terror," in *Faszination der Gewalt: Politische Strategie und Alltagserfahrung*, ed. Rainer Steinweg (Frankfurt am Main, 1983), 133–140.

47. CVZ, 16 November 1928.

48. Gerhard Reifferscheid, "Die NSDAP in Ostpreußen: Besonderheiten ihrer Ausbreitung und Tätigkeit," *Zeitschrift für die Geschichte und Altertumskunde Ermlands* 39 (1978), 61–85; on Königsberg, see Schüler-Springorum, *Die jüdische Minderheit*, 212f.

49. Christian Tilitzki, *Alltag in Ostpreußen 1940–1945: Die geheimen Lageberichte der Königsberger Justiz 1940–1945* (Leer, 1991), 13.

50. "Nationalsozialistischer Vormarsch! Flaches Land und Kleinstadt werden besonders bearbeitet," CVZ, 16 November 1928.

51. From Sabatzky's unpublished manuscript, "Meine Erinnerungen an den Nationalsozialismus," (ca. 1941), quoted in Schüler-Springorum, *Die jüdische Minderheit*, 227.

52. Whereas the Deutsche Demokratische Partei (1930 Deutsche Staatspartei), the Deutsche Volkspartei, and the Deutschnationale Volkspartei had won 27.8 percent in May 1928, now they only had a little more than half of that, namely 15.5 percent, whereby the DNVP suffered especially heavy losses.

53. Eberhard Kolb, *Die Weimarer Republik*, vol 16: *Oldenbourg Grundriß der Geschichte*, 6th ed. (Munich, 2002), 127. The metaphor of a landslide is also found in Winkler, *Weimar*, 388, and in Hans Mommsen, who emphasizes in particular the modern, wide-ranging propagandistic electoral campaign. Hans Mommsen, *Verspielte Freiheit*, 319, 341–344.

54. Theodor Geiger, "Die Panik im Mittelstand," *Die Arbeit* 7 (1930): 637–654; above all Jürgen W. Falter, *Hitlers Wähler* (Munich, 1991)

55. See Hans-Helmuth Knütter, "Die Linksparteien," in *Entscheidungsjahr 1932: Zur Judenfrage in der Endphase der Weimare Republik*, ed. Werner E. Mosse and Arnold Paucker (Tübingen, 1966), 332.

56. Markus Behmer, *Von der Schwierigkeit, gegen Illusionen zu kämpfen: Der Publizist Leopold Schwarzschild—Leben und Werk vom Kaiserreich bis zur Flucht aus Europa* (Münster, 1997), 282.

57. M.W., "Zwangsläufige Entwicklung. Zur Lage der Juden in Deutschland," *Jüdische Rundschau*, no. 7, 24 January 1930. According to information from Avraham Barkai, to whom I am thankful for his friendly help, the initials "M.W." presumably refer to Moses Waldmann, who was the editor of the *Jüdische Rundschau* at the time.

58. Barkai, *"Wehr Dich!"* 201.

59. An assumption, however, that does not withstand critical examination. Martin Liepach, "Zwischen Abwehrkampf und Wählermobilisierung: Juden und die Landtagswahl in Baden 1929," in Benz et al., *Jüdisches Leben in der Weimarer Republik*, 9–23.

60. Quoted in Barkai, *"Wehr Dich!"* 201–204; on the reaction in the Jewish press, see also Chaim Seeligmann and Givat Brenner, "Die Reichstagswahlen des 14. September 1930 im Spiegel der jüdischen Presse in Deutschland," *Tel Aviver Jahrbuch für deutsche Geschichte* 17 (1988): 169–192.

61. Arnold Paucker, *Der jüdische Abwehrkampf gegen Antisemitismus und Nationalsozialismus*, 31f., 48f.; see also Barkai, *"Wehr Dich!"* 185–191. On Büro Wilhelmstrasse, see especially Leonidas E. Hill, " Walter Gyssling, the Centralverein and the Büro Wilhelmstrasse, 1929–1933," *Leo Baeck Institute Yearbook* 38 (1993): 193–208; see also Walter Gyßling, *Mein Leben in Deutschland vor und nach 1933 und Der Anti-Nazi: Handbuch im Kampf gegen die NSDAP*, ed. with an introduction by Leonidas E. Hill (Bremen, 2003).

62. "Zertrümmerte Fensterscheiben: zu den Ausschreitungen in der Berliner Innenstadt," *CVZ*, 17 October 1930.

63. Reichardt, *Faschistische Kampfbünde*, 119; see also Thomas Balistier, *Gewalt und Ordnung: Kalkül und Faszination der SA* (Münster, 1989).

64. Mathilde Jamin, *Zwischen den Klassen: Zur Sozialstruktur des SA Führerschaft* (Wuppertal, 1984), 87–89; Conan Fischer, *Stormtroopers: A Social, Economic, and Ideological Analysis, 1929–1935* (London, 1983), 48–50; Reichardt, *Faschistische Kampfbünde*, 348.

65. Dirk Schumann, *Politische Gewalt in der Weimarer Republik 1918–1933: Kampf um die Straße und Furcht vor dem Bürgerkrieg* (Essen, 2001), 330.

66. Reichardt, *Faschistische Kampfbünde*, 388; see also by the same author, "Gewalt, Körper, Politik: Paradoxien in der deutschen Kulturgeschichte der Zwischenkriegszeit," in *Politische Kulturgeschichte der Zwischenkriegszeit 1918–1939*, ed. Wolfgang Hardtwig, vol. 21 of *Geschichte und Gesellschaft Sonderhefte* (Göttingen, 2005), 205–239.

67. Quoted in Balistier, *Gewalt und Ordnung*, 155.

68. The court sentenced twenty-seven SA men to prison sentences from nine months to a year and nine months. The leaders of the action, Graf Helldorf and his adjutant Ernst, were acquitted on appeal of charges of leading the riots and disturbing the peace. For details on the trials, see Walter, *Antisemitische Kriminalität*, 211–221.

69. Jaschke and Loiperdinger, "Gewalt und NSDAP vor 1933," 140–143; on the occupation of cities as a form of violence, see Reichardt, *Faschistische Kampfbünde*, 110–113.

70. Quoted in Hecht, *Deutsche Juden und Antisemitismus*, 222.

71. Quoted in Roland Flade, *Juden in Würzburg 1918–1933* (Würzburg, 1985), 345.

72. In the court proceedings in February 1931 against ten young men and a 20-year-old woman, the sentences were less severe than the incarceration demanded by the state attorney for violating the public peace and committing bodily harm. Three of the accused went unpunished for "lack of evidence." Ibid., 347f.

73. Figures according to Reichardt, *Faschistische Kampfbünde*, 63; Reichardt maintains that the "explosive-like growth" for the year 1930 cannot be explained by a correla-

tion with growing membership figures, for the growth of the SA did not advance in 1930 and it was only in 1931 that its strength exceeded 100,000 men; in contrast, for 1932 one can determine a clear connection between the quantitative growth of the SA and an increase in violence. On the escalation of SA violence during the last three years of the Weimar Republic, see also Balistier, *Gewalt und Ordnung*, 157–160; and Pamela E. Swett, *Neighbors and Enemies: The Culture of Radicalism in Berlin 1929–1933* (Cambridge, 2004).

74. Richard Bessel, *Political Violence and the Rise of Nazism: The Storm Troopers in Eastern Germany 1925–1934* (London, 1984), 76. Schumann, too, speaks of a "ubiquitous character of political violence" from 1930 onward. Schumann, *Politische Gewalt in der Weimarer Republik*, 317.

75. Schüler-Springorum, *Die jüdische Minderheit*, 228; Bessel, *Political Violence and the Rise of Nazism*, 87–89. Of twenty-six anti-Semitic attacks in the first half of August 1932, twelve took place in East Prussia alone. Reichardt, *Faschistische Kampfbünde*, 73.

76. Tilitzki, *Alltag in Ostpreußen*, 24. In Bialla, the bomb was supposed to explode in the bedroom of the Jewish merchant Lampel, but it missed its target and went of at the wall of the house. *Vossische Zeitung*, no. 262, 15 August 1932, Yad Vashem Archives, JM/10511, fol. 1. The investigation proceedings by the senior state attorney produced no results and were closed on 29 March 1933. In Ortelsburg, the proceedings against four identified perpetrators were closed by December 1932.

77. CVZ, 30 December 1932.

78. Hanna Arendt, *On Violence* (New York: 1970), 40.

79. Ibid., 56. See Jan Philipp Reemtsma, "Die Gewalt spricht nicht: Zum Verhältnis von Macht und Gewalt," in Jan Philipp Reemtsma, *Die Gewalt spricht nicht: Drei Reden* (Stuttgart, 2002), 7–46.

80. For this reason, the discussion among historians as to whether the National Socialists sought to obtain their political objectives with anti-Semitic slogans or if instead one can recognize the public decline of explicitly anti-Semitic positions in election campaigns between 1930 and 1933 does not do the problem justice. See Gerhard Paul, *Aufstand der Bilder: Die NS-Propaganda vor 1933* (Bonn, 1990); Ian Kershaw, "Antisemitismus und die NS-Bewegung vor 1933," in *Vorurteil und Rassenhaß: Antisemitismus in den faschistischen Bewegungen Europas*, ed. Hermann Graml, Angelika Königseder, and Juliane Wetzel (Berlin, 2001). "Work and bread" was the election campaign slogan of the Nazis, and undoubtedly most of the NSDAP voters hoped that Hitler would provide them with employment and secure social and political conditions. Nonetheless, the anti-Semitism of the party—even if one assumes that the voters had decided for the NSDAP not because of but rather despite its anti-Semitic positions—did not disappear—Oded Heilbronner, "The Role of Nazi Antisemitism in the Nazi Party's Activity and Propaganda: A Regional Historiographical Study," *Leo Baeck Institute Yearbook* 35 (1990). According to Heinrich August Winkler, anti-Semitism may not have been in the foreground with respect to the mobilization of voters; but for the internal integration of the National Socialist movement itself it was indeed decisive. Heinrich August Winkler, "Die deutsche Gesellschaft der Weimarer Republik und der Antisemitismus: Juden als 'Blitzableiter,'" in *Antisemitismus: Erscheinungsformen der Judenfeindschaft gestern und heute*, ed. Günther B. Ginzel (Bielefeld, 1991); likewise see Reichardt, *Faschistische Kampfbünde*.

3

1933

"They won't do anything to us—after all, we're Germans"

"Ice-cold shock," noted the 25-year-old Sebastian Haffner on 30 January 1933 as he read the first newspaper reports about the appointment of Hitler as Reich chancellor:

> Then I shook it off, tried to laugh, tried to think, and indeed found many reasons for reassurance. In the evening I discussed the prospects of the new regime with my father and we agreed that, to be sure, it had a chance to wreak a pretty large amount of harm, but hardly a chance to rule for long.[1]

For Luise Solmitz from Hamburg, born in 1889, former teacher and wife of a retired officer, this day signified the beginning of a new hope. "And what a cabinet!!!" she wrote in her diary. "The likes we would never have dared dreamed of in July. Hitler, Hugenberg, Seldte, Papen!!! A large part of my German hope depends on each. National Socialist drive, German National reason, the apolitical Stahlhelm and Papen, who for us is unforgotten…. Giant torchlight procession in front of Hindenburg and Hitler by National Socialists and Stahlhelm, who are finally, finally going together again. That is a memorable 30 January!"[2]

A few days later, a commensurate torchlight procession moved through Hamburg, which Luise Solmitz enthusiastically described as a "wonderful uplifting experience for us all." Admittedly there were also cries of "Judah, die" and songs sung about Jewish blood squirting under knives, but, as she added after the war: "Who at the time took that seriously?"[3] But the reality looked different. On the same night of 30 January in Lübeck, the editor-in-chief of the *Lübecker Volksboten* and Social Democratic Reichstag representative Julius Leber was assaulted and stabbed with a knife.[4]

While the C.V. did not deceive itself about the seriousness of the situation, it called upon people to quietly wait and see at first.[5] Ludwig Holländer wrote in the lead article of the *C.V.-Zeitung* on 2 February 1933: "Even in these times, the German Jews will not lose their calm, which is given to them by the consciousness of the inseparable bond with all *real* Germans."[6] Kurt Jakob Ball-Kaduri reported on a gathering of Jewish tradesmen on the evening of 30 January at Café Leon on the Kurfürstendamm in Berlin. The first speaker, a liberal, did not even address the change of power; the second, a Zionist, made emphatic warnings about this change in light of the historical turn that had now occurred, but nobody wanted to listen to him. The audience considered his words to be overly pessimistic.[7] "They won't do anything to us—after all, we're Germans," said a Jewish butcher from a village in Rhine-Hesse, voicing an opinion that was characteristic of many.[8] As Wolfgang Benz notes, the self-calming assurance of the German Jews that Reich Chancellor Hitler would not be able to make real what the party leader Hitler had propagated[9] was based above all on the continued existence of the constitution and the ability of Hitler's conservative administrative partners to constrain him. Both hopes were bitterly disappointed.[10]

Was 30 January 1933 the beginning of a "totalitarian revolution," as Hans-Ulrich Wehler suggests, following up on the earlier studies by Karl Dietrich Bracher?[11] For the moment, it was a victory for the German Right, which, by including the National Socialists, now formed the government with a broad coalition. The general strike announced by the KPD in case the NSDAP assumed power ruefully failed to materialize, and the remaining opponents waited instead to see whether the new authorities would follow up their militant proclamations with actions. But Hitler himself left no room for doubt that he did not conceive of the new regime as part of a continuum that included the line of cabinets during the Weimar Republic. Three days after his appointment as Reich chancellor, he unmistakably declared to the commanders of the army and the navy: "Complete reversal of the present internal political situation in Germany. No tolerance for activities of any kind of ethos that opposes the objective (Pacifism!). Those who will not let themselves be converted must be made to bend. Extermination of Marxism, root and branch."[12] In this respect, the German Right was unified. Vice-Chancellor von Papen had spoken already during the cabinet session on 31 January about how the upcoming Reichstag election in March 1933 had to be the last election in Germany, stating that a return to the parliamentary system was to be forever avoided.[13]

The new elections—forced by Hitler because he hoped that a clear plebiscitary vote would turn the Reichstag into a pliable instrument—already offered plenty of opportunities to take terrorist action against the Left, now also with the help of the state's means of violence. On 17 February Göring instructed the police to support national propaganda with all of its powers; in contrast, it was to "oppose the operations of subversive [*staatsfeindlich*] organizations with the sharpest methods" and "when necessary, ruthlessly make use of firearms." A few days later he deployed 50,000 members of the SA, SS, and Stahlhelm as auxiliary police.[14]

But coincidence also came to the aid of the new authorities, for the arson attack on the Reichstag by Marinus van der Lubbe on 27 February—immediately portrayed by the National Socialists as an attempted Communist uprising—provided the opportunity the next day to suspend the Weimar constitution with the Decree of the Reich President for the Protection of the People and the State.[15] The arrests, carried out according to prepared lists, began promptly on the morning of 28 February; in the following weeks, thousands were arrested by police or dragged into "wild" camps, where with whips, iron rods, and leather belts they were beaten, tortured, or even murdered.[16]

Despite this terror, the National Socialists did not manage, as they had hoped, to obtain the absolute majority during the Reichstag election on 5 March; for the time being they still needed the German Nationals to create a government.[17] Nonetheless, a phase of the takeover began in the states and municipalities right after the election. Within only a few days, Reich commissioners were deployed in Hamburg, Bremen, Hesse, Baden, Wurttemberg, Saxony, Bavaria, and other states, after the SA in each respective locality first threatened a takeover and thus created the situation that legitimated the imperial regime's intervention and forced the creation of state administrations under National Socialist leadership.[18] This teamwork—this mutually strengthening and radicalizing reciprocity in which the "power from below" was used by the NS leadership "above" in order to push through more radical political measures in opposition to state administrations—would be the model for National Socialist actions in the following years.

But this brought into question a central criterion of state order, namely the monopoly of violence.[19] The National Socialists were set on the use of violence as a political means from the outset; for them, violence was an inseparable part of their political conception and praxis. Yet now that they had obtained state power, they were by no means in a position or prepared to think in "state-like" terms. A result of belittling the state in their political thought—in *Mein Kampf* Hitler wrote unmistakably "that the highest purposes of a person's being is not the preservation of the state or even a regime but the preservation of his kind"[20]—was a misconception of the meaning of the state's monopoly of violence.

Naturally, the NS leadership was warily anxious to keep the supreme commanding authority for the application of violence in its own hands. But at the same time, the NS regime witnessed the creation of new agents of violence like the concentration camps and the secret state police, which were purposely detached from the administrative context of the existing state and thus also detached from the state's monopoly of violence. By shooting to death SA leaders, generals, and conservative opponents, the regime leadership itself provided evidence of its intention to unscrupulously and arbitrarily eliminate opponents by murdering them. Although the NS leadership maintained the centrality of the authority to exercise violence, it also promoted the proliferation of violent powers and the diffusion of violence. And by no means did the local NSDAP and SA groups understand "their" seizure of power merely as a change in political parties within the continuity of the Republic. Rather, they understood it as the beginning of a radical transformation, during the course of which violence, as always, would be the central political instrument. During the first weeks of the new regime, the violent furor of the SA and the NSDAP, which now saw themselves as history's victors, first and foremost brutally struck political opponents—above all Communists and Social Democrats, but also Jewish Germans.

Reporting from Gersfeld in Hesse, the *C.V.-Zeitung* noted that only a few days after Hitler's appointment as Reich chancellor, on Saturday 4 February, the leader of the local NSDAP called for the Jewish residents to be taken from their homes. Thereupon a crowd moved to the house of a respected merchant named Bachrach; three National Socialists violently broke in the house and injured the unsuspecting man, who was sitting with his family, hitting and kicking him so severely that he collapsed and required medical treatment. "The barbarous attack," noted the C.V. report, "is all the more incomprehensible since Bachrach had never come forward politically and both personally and professionally generally enjoyed great popularity."[21]

On the Kurfürstendamm in Berlin, one day after the Reichstag election in March, there were anti-Jewish excesses that escalated into bloody pursuits. The German correspondent for the *Manchester Guardian* reported on 10 March: "many Jews were beaten by the Brown Shirts until their heads and faced flowed with blood. Many collapsed helplessly and were left lying in the streets until they were picked up by friends and pedestrians and brought to the hospital."[22] In Königsberg on 7 March, there was an arson attack on the old synagogue; two days later there were a number of arson attacks on Jewish stores. Six days later, SA men in Königsberg carried off the former film theater manager Max Neumann and abused him so badly that he later died of his injuries in the hospital. A baker named Rubinstein, whose store had been the target of one of the arson attacks, also suffered serious injuries, as did Arthur Cohn, the chairperson of the East Prussian Synagogue Association. At the same time, SA people murdered the Communist representative Schütz, who had been able to escape an attempt on his life a year earlier. The fact that Kurt Sabatzky, the director of the C.V. in East Prussia, was not a victim of violence is probably only thanks to Königsberg's police commissioner, who earnestly recommended that Sabatzky leave town, for he could no longer assure his safety.[23] The wave of terror so intimidated the Jewish communities in East Prussia that the Königsberg C.V. requested a new syndic from headquarters in Berlin. It explained that "as a result of the psychological disposition of our fellow believers in the province, the activity of Herr Sabatzky has essentially been paralyzed, because they are afraid of somehow being seen with him."[24]

In Breslau, on Saturday morning 11 March, SA gangs forced Jewish business and department stores to close. Even though the police got involved and "calmly" pressured them to leave, the stores of Jewish proprietors remained closed "voluntarily" until Monday.[25] At the same time, the SA assaulted the Breslau district and regional courthouse to drive out Jewish lawyers, state attorneys, and judges. The *Frankfurter Zeitung* reported on the violent actions: "With calls of 'Jews out!' all of the offices and conference rooms were opened and the Jewish lawyers, judges, and state attorneys were forced to leave the building immediately. In the corridors and halls, heated scenarios played themselves out. The lawyers' room was emptied within a few minutes, and the Jewish lawyers left the justice building, some without taking their coats. Numerous judicial proceedings had to be interrupted."[26] The SA occupied the courthouse for three days, denying entrance to Jewish magistrates and lawyers, and in doing so forced a so-called *justitium*—a standstill in the administration of justice. Even when the courts resumed work, the president of the higher regional court had decreed that only seventeen Jewish lawyers would now be admitted to the Breslau courts.[27] Jewish lawyers and judges were likewise denied access in other courts in the Reich.[28]

As a young assessor, Sebastian Haffner experienced a similar action on 31 March in the Berlin Superior Court:

I went to the library as if this were a day like any other—I did not have a meeting—and situated myself at the long work table with a file.... Outside in the corridors there was a clatter, a long series of rough footsteps climbing the stairs, then a distant inextricable tangle of blustering, shouting, door slamming. A couple of people stood up and went to the door, opened it, peeked out, and came back. A couple of people went to the constable and spoke with him, still in a hush—in this room one was only allowed to speak in a hush. Outside the noise grew louder. Someone spoke into the persistent silence: "SA." Thereupon another said, with a voice that was not especially loud: "They are throwing out the Jews," at which two or three people laughed. In that moment, this laughter was more frightening than the process itself: in a flash, it brought to mind that, of course, Nazis were sitting even in this room, how strange.... Shortly thereafter someone appeared in the entrance, perhaps a kind of senior constable, and called loudly: "The SA are in the building. Jewish gentlemen would do well to leave the building for today." At the same time, one heard shouting, as if to illustrate: "Jews out!" A voice answered: "They are already out," and again I heard the two or three people who earlier had laughed briefly chuckle, gleefully. I now saw that they were interns, like me.... The door was torn open, brown uniforms poured in, and one, apparently the leader, called in a resounding and rigid stentorian voice: "Non-Aryans are to leave the premises immediately!" ... My heart was beating. What could be done, how could one's composure be maintained? By ignoring it, don't let yourself be disturbed! I immersed myself in my file. I read some sentences, mechanically: "The claim of the accused is incorrect, but also immaterial..." Take no notice! As a brown uniform came toward me and confronted me: "Are you Aryan?" Before I could think, I had answered: "Yes." A scrutinizing look at my nose—and he retreated. But the blood flowed to my face. A moment too late, I felt the shame, the defeat. I had said "yes"! Well, yes, I was an "Aryan," in God's name. I did not lie. Only I had let much worse things happen. What a humiliation, to promptly declare upon the question of an unauthorized person that I am Aryan—on which, incidentally, I placed no value. What a disgrace, to pay this price so that I would be left in peace here behind my file! Taken by surprise even now! Failed during the first test! I should have let myself get slapped.—As I left the superior court, it stood there as always, grey, cool, and unperturbed, elegantly set back from the street behind its park trees. Looking at it, one could not tell that it had just collapsed as an institution.[29]

Looking back while exiled in London in 1939, Haffner commented on his own behavioral uncertainty during the maelstrom of events:

Yes, I seethed and blustered during this March in 1933. Yes, I frightened my family with wild suggestions: quitting the civil service; emigrating; making a show of converting to Judaism. But speaking these intentions was as far as it went. Drawing upon a wealth of experience from a life that had transpired from 1870 to 1933 (though it certainly did not cover these new developments), my father placated me, calmed me down, tried softly to defuse my pathos with irony. I let it happen.... And so, uncertain, waiting, going about my daily routine, swallowing the anger and the horror or, quite unproductively and quite comically, letting it burst forth in streams at the dining table at home—getting on with life, disengaged, like millions of others, I let the things affect me.[30]

During the Reichstag elections of 5 March, the majority of Germans did not vote National Socialist. Beyond the widespread approval, there was also hesitation, skepticism, all the way to firm rejection. But like Luise Solmitz, many Germans hoped for an end to the "party quarrels" and political "bickering." Thus above all, people expected the regime to create order, overcome the economic crisis, and transcend political divisions. The newspapers that had not yet been brought into line with the NSDAP still correctly referred to Hitler as the Reichskanzler; but National Socialist propaganda systematically built him up as the "*Volkskanzler.*" On his forty-fourth birthday, 20 April 1933, the *Völkischer Beobachter* wrote: "The nation honors the Führer. The whole German Volk is engaged in the dignified and unostentatious celebration of Adolf Hitler's birthday. All towns and villages adorned with flags as never seen before—religious services, torchlight processions, parades. Countless proofs of loyalty for the *Volkskanzler....*"[31] Despite electoral results that were by no means unified, the readiness to throw the republican constitutional state overboard in favor of the new political order was apparently high. There was, wrote Sebastian Haffner, "a very wide-spread feeling of having been rescued and freed from democracy. What does a democracy do when the majority of the people no longer want it?"[32]

Without the willing cooperation of many Germans in administrations, associations, parties, universities, and companies, the so-called "*Gleichschaltung*" (synchronization)—a concept whose technological overtones mask the dedicated practice that was involved—would never have been realized in such a short amount of time. The members of the Poetic Arts Department in the Prussian Academy of the Arts obediently permitted the exclusion of Heinrich Mann, Alfred Döblin, Jakob Wassermann, and others—with the notable exception of Ricarda Huch, who thereupon announced her resignation.[33]

Munich—the "City of Wagner"—loudly expressed its indignation in April about an allegedly disparaging lecture on Richard Wagner by Thomas Mann, which he had delivered in Amsterdam and Brussels.[34] At Easter in 1933, the well-known Protestant bishop of Berlin Otto Dibelius, who later became an active and persecuted member of the Confessional Church, wrote a confidential circular to the pastors in his region. He explained that "we do not only understand, but are also full of sympathy" for the motives that had given rise to the *völkisch* movement. "Despite the nasty tone that the word has in many cases acquired, I have always considered myself an anti-Semite. One cannot fail to recognize that in all of the corrosive manifestations of modern civilization, Judaism played a leading role."[35]

The NS leadership settled on a double strategy of promise and terror, the offer of integration and the violence of ostracism, of inclusion and exclusion. On the one hand, the National Socialists annihilated the opposition with pitiless and public terror and dissolved independent organizations like parties and unions;[36] on the other hand, they sought above all to win over non-Jewish Germans with symbolic politics. Thus the regime leadership staged the opening of the Reichstag on 21 March—without the Social Democratic and Communist representatives—in the Potsdam Garrison Church as a festival of national unity, with a festive religious service, rifle salutes, and parades by the Reichswehr, SA, and SS.[37] On the same day it proclaimed both an amnesty law for crimes committed "in the struggle for the national rising of the German Volk" and an ordinance for the "defense against insidious acts," according to which those who made claims that could damage the "well-being of the Reich or a state or the reputation of the Reich regime or a state regime or the parties and associations standing behind these regimes" could be imprisoned for up to two years.[38] Two days later, on 23 March, the Reichstag passed—albeit in opposition to the votes of the SPD—the so-called enabling act, which gave the regime the right to create laws and thus disempowered the parliament.[39]

The first of May was renamed the "Day of National Labor," and for the first time in German history declared a holiday. With a large propagandistic effort, and under the motto "Honor labor and heed the worker!" the National Socialists held May Day celebrations all over, featuring speakers who proclaimed the transcendence of class divisions and cheered the *Volksgemeinschaft*—only on the next day to occupy union offices with the SA, arrest union functionaries, and dissolve the organizations. In their place, they installed the German Labor Front (Deutsche Arbeitsfront), which appropriated the confiscated union property and became the single compulsory organization for both companies and workers.[40] While the regime leadership in Berlin staged the unity of the Volk, the party organizations in the local communities made unmistakably clear who in any case would not be included in the national *Volksgemeinschaft*.

April Boycott

Two days after the Reichstag elections, a boycott campaign against Jewish stores got underway in the Ruhr region, namely in Essen, Bottrop, and Mülheim. "In the morning in the streets of the Essen shopping district," reported the *Jüdische Rundschau* on 10 March 1933, "a colorful life prevailed. A crowd of people had gathered at the gates and entrances to numerous Jewish stores—the Karstadt department store Althoff, on which flew a Swastika flag, and the EPA and Woolworth standard-price stores." SA sentries prevented potential customers from entering the stores, which were subsequently closed. The police tolerated the behavior of the SA and euphemistically declared that the action was a protest rally. The NSDAP officially denied that it had instigated the closing of the stores. Instead, according the report of the *Jüdische Rundschau*, it attributed the demonstration to the fact that "the nationally-minded population is apparently no longer willing to accept the continued existence of Jewish department stores and large Jewish businesses and accordingly demands the closing of the businesses."[41]

The boycotts quickly spread throughout the Reich as the National Socialist press reported intensively on the actions in order to help them gain momentum.[42] In central Germany, Mecklenburg, and likewise in southwestern German towns, the local SA and party groups organized campaigns against Jewish stores, demonstrating loudly with slogans and standing as sentries bearing signs like "Don't buy from Jews!" and other such slogans. The actions were always accompanied by violence. In Duisburg during the second half of March, wild raids by SA gangs of Jewish stores and private homes, abuses, and devastations are recorded for almost every single day. The Jewish proprietor of a furniture store, who was beaten by an SA man and, covered with blood, sought the help of police, had to listen them explain that they were powerless to do anything against such violence.[43]

There was also courageous resistance. In Wesel, situated in the Rhineland, a Jewish businessman, wearing the uniform of his old regiment, stood next to the SA sentry in the entrance of his store and distributed leaflets of his own, which stated: "We consider this action, which in this city goes hand in hand with slanderous claims, as an attack on our honor and as a desecration of the reputation of 12,000 German front-line solders of Jewish faith."[44] The C.V. reported that during the time that followed, "the ladies and gentlemen of decent bourgeois circles in Wesel, the wives of former officers of the Wesel regiment, etc., that is to say, mainly people on the political right" made a demonstrative point of visiting this store.[45]

The NS regime made an effort to gain control over these "individual actions" (*Einzelaktionen*), as they were referred to in NS terminology. Appealing to party and SA members on 10 March in the *Völkischer Beobachter*, Hitler called for "highest discipline" and turned matters around, blaming the violence on "unscrupulous subjects, mainly Communist spies."[46] The national regime held the executive authority in its hands and "the further implementation of the national rising" should be "one that is directed from above, according to plan"; meantime, "the harassment of individual persons, obstruction of cars and disturbance of business life must basically stop." Accordingly, an edict from the Reich Interior Ministry of 13 March 1933 expressly warned against "closures of and threats against retail stores." [47]

Admittedly, the actions ebbed after this, but by no means did they stop.[48] Just a few days after Hitler's appeal, the Industry and Trade Conference reported to both the Reich chancellor and Göring that anti-Jewish actions were persisting.[49] In Würzburg on 11 March 1933, for example, a mass of people led by the local NSDAP leader forced Jewish stores to close, and in the process violence broke out.[50] On the same day in Rostock, a so-called EPA standard-price store was forced to close, and its owner by the name of Lowenstein and an employee were badly beaten—whereupon the police declared that they were powerless to do anything against these kinds of incidents, which were also occurring in Schwerin and other places.[51] In Pirmasens on the night of 20 March, unknown perpetrators smashed the windows of Jewish stores and in one store even started a fire that destroyed a large amount of the store's inventory and caused tens of thousands of Reichsmarks' worth of damages.[52] On the same day in Dortmund, SA and SS gangs drove the Jewish butcher Julius Rosenfeld and his son through the city to a brickyard, where they stood them up against a wall and threatened them with firearms. They were beaten and compelled to sing the "Horst-Wessel" song, and the son was forced to burn off his father's beard with a burning newspaper.[53]

In Duisburg on 24 March, SS members forced their way into the apartment of the director of the Jewish community, Mordechei Bereisch, who was of eastern Jewish decent and held a Polish passport. They dragged him on a march through the city, accompanied by a large crowd. Bereisch was draped in a black-red-gold flag—the symbol of the Weimar Republic—which two other Jews were forced to carry behind him like a train. As the procession approached the city theater, the crowd had grown to about 1,000 people, police reported. Fortunately, Bereisch managed to escape into the Jewish community center, where he was taken into protective custody by police. On the same day he applied for a visa to flee to Belgium.[54]

In Hersfeld in Hesse, SA and SS men brought Jewish citizens from apartments and dragged them to the SA's favorite pub. There the local SS leader gave a speech, following which the Jews were forced on a procession through the city with signs that called for the boycott of Jewish stores in Hersfeld. Finally at the market place, they had to make a "voluntary statement" denouncing "World Jewry" before they were eventually released from the grip of the perpetrators.[55]

Apparently the pressure from below was still strong enough that the NS leadership in Berlin was searching for an opportunity to accommodate the party base's readiness for action in the hope that it could be controlled. The decision for a nationwide boycott, publicly legitimated as a defense against international "Jewish scaremongering [*Greuelpropaganda*]" was made on 26 March in Berchtesgarden during a conversation between Hitler and Goebbels, who immediately composed an appeal for a boycott against the German Jews.[56]

In actuality, the appeal, which appeared in the press on Monday, 27 March, reinvigorated the local campaigns, which had just begun to ebb. On that same evening in Witten, the windows of thirty businesses and residences were smashed; as determined later by the Imperial Economic Court, the perpetrators were groups of young people who emerged out of the crowd and perpetrated the excesses "without fear of the public, in plain view of the gathered people." Thereupon to prevent further violence, the police sealed off the entire town center of Witten.[57]

Similar incidents occurred the following day in Göttingen, where jeering SS men dragged a number of Jews through the street in a cattle car.[58] In Dortmund on the afternoon of 28 March—one week after the violence against Julius Rosenfeld and his son—the SA took around 100 Jewish citizens, including numerous doctors, lawyers, and merchants, into "protective custody." According to a police report, about 2,000 people gathered on the Steinplatz in front of the police building to watch the spectacle. Apparently this produced such a crowd that the police had to clear the square repeatedly, sometimes by using their clubs.[59] On the same day in Oberhausen, SA gangs forced Jewish stores to close, and in the afternoon a number of Jewish citizens, including the rabbi of Oberhausen, were led through the streets with signs.[60]

On 28 March the NS regime published its appeal for all party groups to build action committees for the boycott on 1 April so that the action could be implemented "promptly"—the boycott must be "brought right into the smallest farming village, in order to target in particular the Jewish merchants in the countryside."[61] But three days later, it was apparently trying once again to keep this readiness for action contained. According to the central boycott committee, standard-price stores, department stores, and large subsidiary operations that belonged to Germans—that is, not to Jews—were not to be boycotted. Likewise, Goebbels published a declaration that the boycott would only be in effect on 1 April, and, if necessary, it would be resumed the following Wednesday if the "scaremongering [Greuelhetze] from foreign lands" did not cease.[62]

In its official directive on 31 March to NSDAP groups, the boycott committee again indicated that there was to be no application of any kind of violence, and placards "with provocative content" were forbidden.[63] This did not prevent Julius Streicher, the director of the committee, in his central appeal published on 31 March in the Völkischer Beobachter, from fomenting the action with anti-Semitic hatred and even imagining his own position as akin to that of Martin Luther against the Catholic Church:

Millions of Germans have waited longingly for this day on which the German Volk in its entirety would be awakened, on which it finally recognizes in the Jew the World Enemy.... All-of-Judah [Alljuda] has sought this battle; it shall have it! It shall have it for as long as it takes for it to know that the Germany of the brown battalion is not a Germany of cowardice and surrender. All-of-Judah shall have the battle for as long as it takes until the victory is ours! National Socialists! Defeat the World Enemy! And if the world were full of devils, we must still be successful![64]

Sebastian Haffner observed that "a certain murmuring of disapproval, suppressed but audible" coursed throughout the land, something that moved the NS leadership after 1 April to drop part of these measures.

Of course, what was strange and discouraging is that—after the initial fright—this initial generous demonstration of a new murderous attitude unleashed a flood of conversation and discussion—not about the anti-Semitism question, but rather about the "Jewish question." ... Everyone suddenly felt himself obligated and entitled to have his own opinion about the Jews and to express it. One made fine distinctions between "decent" Jews and others; when some, as if to exonerate the Jews (why exonerate? from what?) made mention of their scientific, artistic, medical contributions, others would reproach them for precisely the same reasons: they had "foreignized" [überfremdet] science, art, medicine. Indeed it quickly became generally common and popular to describe the practice of decent and intellectually valuable professions by the Jews as crimes or at least as indiscretions. With a frown, the fact that the Jews, in a highly reprehensible manner, comprised such and such a percentage of doctors, lawyers, reporters, etc. would be held against the defenders of the Jews. Indeed, one quite enjoyed deciding the "Jewish question" by calculating percentages.[65]

Emden

In Emden, home to the largest Jewish community in northern Germany,[66] the National Socialist *Ostfriesische Tageszeitung* made ready for the boycott day by reporting on 29 March that the day before "members and sympathizers of the NSDAP" had gathered in front of Jewish stores and called for boycotts. An outcome of this gathering was that the display windows in the Valk department store and the Watermann store were smashed, as was the window in the door to the store belonging to a cobbler named de Jonge.[67] As was the case everywhere else in the German Reich, SS and SA columns were deployed on Saturday morning and posted sentries in front of stores with Jewish proprietors. The police were directed to get involved only in cases of "obvious acts of violence against life and property," but otherwise not to impede the action.[68] "Lively activity prevails in the town," reported the *Emder Zeitung*, a *völkisch*-nationalistic newspaper. "The public is voicing its approval of the action from all sides."[69] After the action concluded, the NSDAP held yet another rally at the Neuer Markt, during which the NSDAP district leader gave a short speech. The speech deserves to be cited at length, for it makes the purpose and course of the boycott action unmistakably clear:

German *Volksgenossen*! This day was the prelude to the counter-attack of the NSDAP against the scaremongering of foreign Judaism. We have not yet launched a general attack, but even so the enemy will have noticed that when the holy German wrath erupts, his fate is sealed. Our Führer wants to give the world's Judaism the opportunity to cease with the cowardly ambush attacks and has ordered a suspension of the boycott until 10 o'clock Wednesday. If by then the scaremongering in foreign lands is not completely stopped, we will again resume the defensive battle with twice the intensity and pursue it persistently and ruthlessly until German Judaism is finally destroyed. We will never let the hilt be taken from our hand by such a cowardly and dirty opponent as is Judaism. Our struggle is pure and animated by an honest and ardent will to steer the German Volk toward a better future and to free it for all time from the realm of parasites, namely the exploitative, usurious and unproductive Jews. Under our leadership the Jews will not be able to poison the German spirit, disgrace German culture, drag German heroism through the dirt. We will again awaken the powers that slumber in the German Volk and again create for Germany the place in the sun that it deserves. Everything for the German Volk, for Germany's greatness and future. In this holy struggle we cannot let ourselves be led astray by sentimental and comfortable philistinism. We will ruthlessly continue with the struggle to save the German Volk until the victorious end, unburdened by inappropriate softness. Our purpose, our great objective, sanctifies the means. He who cannot follow us can no longer think German and only shows that he is already infected by the Jewish pacifistic poison and is no longer vitally alive. He who continues to buy from Jews shows that he does not want to help with the German reconstruction. We National Socialists in the town administrations and everywhere will work toward defending German labor and German business. We challenge all German-thinking citizens henceforth to stop buying from Jews, once and for all; and to now only consider German medium-sized [companies] and tradespeople. He who wants to stand up for the Jews may have the same experience as did many of Emden's Communists, who must pay for their fanatical struggle for Judaism—for [this and] nothing else lurks behind Communism—with their freedom.[70]

Many of Emden's Jews understood the threat. Jacob Leufgen, born in Emden in 1920, was a "half-Jew" according to NS terminology, for his mother was Jewish but his father, a baker, was not. He directly experienced the change in mood. Immediately after the SA also stood sentry at his parents' bakery, in the first days of April more than ninety customers canceled their bread-rolls, which the boy would deliver in the mornings. "You no longer need come for now. We want to see what is going to happen. Then we'll order more."[71] Ruth Ascher remembered after the war how everyday life permanently changed after the boycott: "One could suddenly and clearly feel that we were excluded from the Christians. We no doubt held ourselves back, for the Emdeners were no longer allowed to buy in Jewish shops. That was terrible, one can hardly imagine this today: suddenly the customers were no longer able to go to their merchant, someone whom they sometimes did not even know that he was a Jew."[72]

Edwin Landau, born in 1890, was the proprietor of a plumbing shop in Deutsch-Krone in West Prussia, a man with German nationalist leanings, a war veteran and founder of the local chapter of the Reichsbund jüdischer Frontsoldaten (Imperial Association of Jewish Frontline Soldiers). On 1 April his world collapsed:

In front of our business as well, two young Nazis posted themselves and prevented customers from entering. The whole thing appeared incomprehensible to me. It did not make sense to me that such a thing could even be possible in the 20th century, for such things had at most occurred in the Middle Ages. And yet the bitter truth was that outside in front of the door stood two boys in brown shirts, the executive organs of Hitler. And for this Volk, we young Jews had once stood in the trenches in the cold and rain and spilled our blood in order to protect the land from the enemy. Were there no longer any comrades from this time who were disgusted by this activity? ... I took my war decorations and put them on, went into the street and visited Jewish shops, where I was also stopped at first. But I was boiling inside, and I wanted nothing more than to scream my hatred into the face of these barbarians. Hatred, hatred—since when had this element grabbed a hold in me?—Within only a few hours, a transformation had occurred in me. This land, this Volk, that I previously loved and treasured, had suddenly become my enemy. So I was no longer a German, or I was no longer supposed to be one. Naturally, this is not something that can be settled within a few hours. But one thing I experienced right away: I was ashamed that I belonged to this Volk. I was ashamed because of the confidence I granted to so many who were now unmasked as my enemies. Suddenly the street also appeared strange; indeed the whole city had become strange to me.[73]

Germany as a place of culture and civilization, far away from barbaric places and barbaric times, which now had been overtaken by barbarity in a manner as frightening as it was incomprehensible—this was a prevailing theme in the descriptions by German Jews. The boycott evoked similar images for Victor Klemperer: "I have also truly felt myself to be German. And I have always imagined: the twentieth century in central Europe is something different from the fourteenth century in Rumania. Mistake."[74] Hans Reichmann, syndic for the Centralverein deutscher Staatsbürger jüdischen Glaubens, was taken to the Sachsenhausen KZ after the 1938 November pogrom and emigrated to England in the spring of 1939. Immediately after fleeing, he wrote a detailed report about the events of the last years that ended with the passage: "When, for the first time after the World War, I saw a French memorial tablet that spoke about the struggle of humanity against barbarism, I was moved to embarrassment. Today I myself would like to be a chronicler of the misdeeds and to light a beacon that will help burn out the barbarism."[75]

In the First World War, the awareness of belonging to a civilized nation was still intact. All of the warring parties projected the same self-image of defending civilization against barbarian enemies—the talk about the German "Huns" was equally as widespread among the allies as the German phantasm of fighting against Russia's Asiatic barbarism. The reciprocity of imputing civilization and barbarism might lead to being "moved to embarrassment," but it did not shake one's firm belief in one's own civilization. Rather it placed this belief in a certain kind of balance. But now barbarism had erupted in one's own land. Foreign barbarians had not invaded Germany from abroad; rather, the barbaric forces unmistakably derived from German society itself. That self-confidence of belonging to a civilized nation, which found expression vis-à-vis the French memorial in the feeling of embarrassment, was destroyed with a single blow; the self-perception was revealed as a deception. What from one's own perspective had been arduously and persistently assembled over the centuries into a civilization could apparently be literally swept away over night. Horrified, Edwin Landau, Victor Klemperer, and Hans Reichmann believed they recognized how thin the cultural sheen really was—so thin that it might collapse at any time and barbarism again take hold. It was a disturbing—indeed, destructive—experience of a deep rift in one's own biography, the collapse of a feeling of security and the previously self-evident certainty that one was living in a civilized society.

In an 4 April 1933 article in the *Jüdische Rundschau*, one that would later be cited repeatedly, the chief editor Robert Weltsch tried to turn persecution and dishonor into pride. Under the headline "Wear it with Pride, the Yellow Patch," he wrote:

> On April 1, German Judaism received a lesson that reaches far deeper than even its embittered and today triumphant opponents suppose.... On Saturday, many Jews had a difficult experience. Not because of their inner faith, not because of their loyalty to their own community, not out of pride for a great past ... rather it was because of the imprint on a red note and a yellow patch that they were suddenly standing there as Jews. The troops went from house to house, pasting over stores and signs, painting windows, for 24 hours straight the German Jews were in a certain sense made to stand in the pillory. Apart from other signs and inscriptions, in the display windows one often saw a large Magen David, the shield of King David. This was supposed to be a dishonor. Jews, pick it up, the Shield of David, and carry it with honor![76]

There were indeed confrontations in front of Jewish stores between SA sentries and customers who wanted to gain entrance.[77] It was the Bürgertum in particular that reacted with indignant disapproval to the "rowdiness" of the action, and certainly many others also feared that this kind of campaign would compromise Germany's economic recovery. A courageous lawyer from Bremen, Dr. Wilhelm Cramer, a member of the NSDAP since 1931, protested in a letter to the Bürgermeister against the April boycott:

> I joined the party years ago because the renewal of our legal order was a part of your program. This lofty and important goal, which necessarily lies in the elaboration and development of an idea of law, can only be reached if the ruling party bases all of its measures and ordinances on the maxims of justice. But this principle has been damaged by the boycott against Jewish stores! Even if it were true—something for which there is still no conclusive proof—that the anti-German propaganda can be traced back to Jewish elements in foreign countries (and not, as I suppose, to political

opponents), holding the Jews who reside in this land responsible for this would still not be justified.[78]

But such voices were few and not publicly heard. To be sure, according to David Bankier, foreign observers registered a rejection of the boycott among the people, but nobody noted any public statements *in favor* of the Jews.[79]

Internationally, the April boycott was a discredit to the regime. During the last days of March, representatives of Jewish organizations in Great Britain and the United States pointed out that the demonstrations in New York against the Nazi boycott, for example, were a double-edged sword, for they also provided the NS leadership with arguments for supposed "scaremongering" abroad. But the international outrage due to the anti-Jewish policies persisted and was directed toward the regime.[80] As late as June, Foreign Minister von Neurath complained in a report that the "Jewish question" was still being "used" against Germany at the World Economic Conference in London and the counterstatements made by German diplomats were not being met with "understanding."[81] In any case, there was enough insight within the regime's leadership about Germany's dependence on international trade relations to assure that the boycott was no longer centrally driven.

Added to that was the fact that the boycott affected non-Jews as well. Thus, for example, the "Christian employees and workers" of Jewish stores in Aachen took a public stance in opposition to the April boycott because it harmed not only the Jewish owners but also threatened the jobs of employees.[82] After Goebbels proclaimed on 31 March—even before the official start of the boycott—that the "scaremongering abroad is on the decline," the central boycott committee declared on Sunday 2 April that the boycott was suspended until Wednesday and all placards, posters, and the like were to be removed.[83] On Tuesday Goebbels informed the Reich cabinet that a continuation of the boycott did not seem necessary and that he would see to an appropriate press communiqué.[84] The next day the *Völkischer Beobachter* reported that the Reich administration had noted with "satisfaction" that the boycott had not failed in its effect and therefore did not need to be resumed. Nonetheless, the applicable NSDAP organization would remain in place so that "the defensive campaign could be established again in case of a revival of the badgering."[85]

Despite this official retreat, on the one hand the NS leadership had clearly revealed that, along with all of the legal possibilities offered by the approval of the enabling act of 23 March, it would also implement illegal measures like the boycott to persecute the German Jews. On the other hand, despite the attempt to contain the revolutionary violence "from below" and bring it under control, the pressure from the party base and the SA was apparently strong enough for the NS leadership to decide to implement a centrally directed nationwide action for 1 April, thus channeling the readiness for action and allowing it expression for a limited time.[86] To be sure, reports everywhere in the National Socialist press emphasized that the boycott was "disciplined" and took place without incident. But as indicated above, there were actually numerous acts of violence. And in any case, the organization of a nationwide boycott, approved and supported by the state leadership, was a massive assault on economic freedom and in many places amounted to the criminal act of coercion. The state had broken the law.

Dual State

The use of violence to overcome administrative obstacles and intimidate possible opponents was something that the NS leadership had practiced from the outset, and this power tactic would remain an essential part of its political praxis, even in the coming years. Thus at the beginning of April 1933 localized actions helped push through the anti-Semitic laws that forced Jews out of public service, severely restricted the activities of Jewish medical doctors and lawyers, and limited the number of Jewish students at universities. After the war, Vice-Chancellor Franz von Papen justified his opportunism as follows: "In order to prevent the over-heated cauldron from exploding, we conservative members [of the imperial regime—M.W.] found that it might be practical to absorb the entire revolutionary wave with a basic moderate law."[87]

Violence remained a constant problem for National Socialist rule. From the perspective of the regime leadership, violent actions at the grassroots level had above all a mobilizing function that was supposed to keep members in a constant state of watchful preparedness and put pressure on the state bureaucracy. Yet the assumption on the part of headquarters that local violent action could in a certain sense be engaged on command and then, when politically expedient, disengaged again proved shortsighted. It demonstrated how little National Socialists, who saw themselves as a movement against the bourgeois constitutional state order, understood about that state order. The NS leadership believed it could abandon the basis of the state—namely the monopoly of the use of physical force—in favor of a regime that governed by command. Headquarters was supposed to have the supreme command authority, and at the same time its actual agents were supposed to extend far beyond the traditional instruments of state power, namely the military and police. With their anti-statist political thought, which only made reference to the Volk, the National Socialists wiped away the carefully articulated web of legal and administrative controls of state violence in a constitutional state. But they were not in a position to create the totalitarian government-by-command that they had in mind.

The resulting duality of statehood was something that Ernst Fraenkel analyzed early on. Fraenkel, a lawyer who stemmed from a Jewish family, made a name for himself during the Weimar Republic as a Social Democratic legal theoretician and was forced to leave Germany in September 1938. Exiled in the United States, he published an analysis of the NS regime entitled *The Dual State*.[88] The concept of the "dual state" was supposed to signify the coexistence of a "normative state," which in general respects its own laws, and a "prerogative state," which does not respect those same laws. By "prerogative state" Fraenkel meant a "governmental system which exercises unlimited arbitrariness and violence unchecked by any legal guarantees"; by "normative state" he meant an "administrative body endowed with elaborate powers for safeguarding the legal order as expressed in statutes, decisions of courts, and activities of the administrative agencies."[89]

Fraenkel expressly emphasized that he did not refer "to the coexistence of the state bureaucracy and the party bureaucracy" but rather wanted to take into consideration

> the entire bureaucratic and public machine.... Both the party and the state in its narrower sense function within the scope of the Normative State and the Prerogative State. Preoccupation with the superficial distinction between party and state tends to efface the more significant distinction between the Normative State and the Prerogative State.[90]

In contrast, the SS and police apparatus, which clearly belonged to the prerogative state, demonstrated the connection between the statist police and the National Socialist organization.

> Endowed with all the powers required by the state of siege, the National-Socialists were able to transform the constitutional and temporary dictatorship (intended to restore public order) into an unconstitutional and permanent dictatorship and to provide the framework of the National-Socialist state with unlimited powers. The National-Socialist coup d'état resulted from the arbitrary application of the Emergency Decree of February 28, 1933, which made a mandatory dictatorship absolute. The extension and maintenance of the absolute dictatorship is the task of the Prerogative State.[91]

The difference between a "provisional" and "sovereign" dictatorship went back to Carl Schmitt and his text *Die Diktatur*, published in 1921. The "sovereign" dictatorship, according to Schmitt, "does not suspend an existing constitution by virtue of a law based therein, that is, a constitutional law. Rather, it tries to create a situation to make possible a constitution that it sees as a genuine constitution. Thus it refers not to an existing constitution but to one that is to be brought about."[92] Ernst Fraenkel picked up this idea in order to characterize the actual National Socialist transformation of the constitutional state. A few pages later Fraenkel again emphasized that Schmitt's doctrine of a state of emergency—a suspension of rights with an authority that was in principle limitless and free from any kind of normative strictures—was adopted by the Gestapo.[93]

Fraenkel repeatedly made reference to Schmitt as a mastermind of National Socialist legal theory. Schmitt's 1934 publication *On the Three Types of Juristic Thought* considered not only normativism as a way of thinking about laws and regulations, and decisionism, by which law was thought about in terms of decisions rendered by judges, but also called for a doctrine of concrete order that referred to concrete *Gemeinschaften* (communities) within the Volk. "For the doctrine of concrete order," wrote Schmitt, "'order' is also juristically not in the first instance a regulation or a sum of regulations, but rather, the other way around—the regulation is only a part of and a means for order."[94]

Not that Schmitt was interested in allowing concrete *Gemeinschaften* to be comparable sources of law for concrete orders as soon as they simply comprised an ordered whole. Only in connection with the National Socialist conception of the *Gemeinschaft* did the concept first obtain its decisionistic element, for the only groups recognized as agents of concrete order were those that were accepted as a "*Gemeinschaft*" in the National Socialist meaning of the term.[95] The doctrine of concrete order legitimated the arrangement of different *Gemeinschaften* into racial hierarchies. While the German *Volksgemeinschaft* was to live in relative legal security, other groups, above all the Jews and beyond them all so-called "*Fremdvölkische*" (alien *völkisch* elements) and "*Gemeinschaftsfremde*" (elements alien to the community) were pushed beyond the protection of the law and persecuted without limitations. Jews were excluded from "German law"; from the National Socialist perspective, they were now only objects of political measures.

In local political praxis, the objective was to create social distance between Jews and "*Volksgenossen*" and to stigmatize any solidarity and sympathy with the persecuted in order to isolate Jewish neighbors and declare them without rights—indeed, free game. National Socialist *Volksgemeinschaft* politics meant, for one, the terroristic repression of political opponents and the merciless exclusion of Jews from German society. And for another, it meant offering symbolic inclusion to all non-Jewish Germans, those who, if they did not already belong to the supporters of the "new Germany," were still supposed to be won over to a position of neutral goodwill toward National Socialism. The aim was to transform the preexisting political and cultural orders into the order of a racist *Volksgemeinschaft.*

Anti-Jewish politics corresponded with the anti-Semitic worldview of the National Socialists; it also simultaneously provided the decisive medium with which to fundamentally change German society, to transform the existing "fine" boundaries between Jewish and non-Jewish Germans into unbridgeable trenches, to isolate the Jews and exclude them from society. And for this kind of politics, violence was a suitable instrument, since the bureaucratic methods of the old state allowed the racist homogenization of German society to be accomplished only slowly and with limitations. Moreover, violence was a suitable form of action in order to produce the *Volksgemeinschaft* beyond the bounds of constitutional statehood. The political concepts of the National Socialists were based on violence, and in the violent actions against Jews, one can recognize the contours of the National Socialist order—one in which law becomes *Volksrecht*, police becomes *Volkspolizei*, and the *Führerstaat* becomes a *Volksdiktatur.*

Notes

1. Haffner, *Geschichte eines Deutschen*, 104 (quotation translated by Bernard Heise).
2. Diary of Luise Solmitz, entry for 30 January 1933, in *Nationalsozialismus und Revolution: Ursprung und Geschichte der NSDAP in Hamburg 1922–1933: Dokumente*, ed. Werner Jochmann (Frankfurt am Main, 1963), 421. In terms of ministerial positions, the NSDAP found itself in a minority in the new cabinet. Apart from Hitler, the former Reich Chancellor and now Vice Chancellor Franz von Papen, the leader of the German Nationals Alfred Hugenberg, who took over the economic portfolio, and Franz Seldte, the leader of the right-wing nationalist paramilitary order Stahlhelm, who became the imperial employment minister, were considered to be the leading figures in the administration—wrongly, as would soon become apparent. Hans Mommsen, *Verspielte Freiheit*, 443–533; Ian Kershaw, *Hitler*, 2 vols. (Stuttgart, 1998–2000), vol. 1, 547–566.
3. Diary of Luise Solmitz, entry for 30 January 1933, *Nationalsozialismus und Revolution*, 421. Luise Solmitz was married to a Jew, who as a flight officer was personally acquainted with Göring. But by the time the family later found itself facing the regulations of the Nuremberg laws, and the daughter had to leave school, etc., the early enthusiasm for the new government had already faded away.
4. Reichsbanner people defended him and fatally wounded an SA man in a brawl. Leber and a Reichsbanner man were thereupon taken into captivity. Dorothea Beck, *Julius Leber: Sozialdemokrat zwischen Reform und Widerstand* (Berlin, 1983), 129f. On

further murders of Social Democrats and Communists see Heinrich August Winkler, *Der Weg in die Katastrophe: Arbeiter und Arbeiterbewegung in der Weimarer Republik 1930 bis 1933* (Berlin, 1987), 877–879.

5. The Declaration of the C.V. Presidium dated 30 January 1933 read: "Naturally, we have great mistrust vis-à-vis an administration in which National Socialists occupy the most important position, even though for us in the given situation there is nothing else to do but to wait and see what it does. We look upon the Reich president, in whose sense of justice and constitutional loyalty we trust, as a calming influence in this course of events. But even apart from that, we are convinced that no one will dare touch our constitutional rights. Every negative attempt will find us at our post in a decisive defense. For the rest, the slogan that applies especially today is: 'quietly wait and see!'" CVZ, 2 February 1933; see also Barkai, "*Wehr Dich!*" 270–278.

6. CVZ, 2 February 1933 (emphasis in the original). See Saul Friedländer, *Nazi Germany and the Jews*, vol. 1, 14f.

7. Kurt Jakob Ball-Kaduri, *Vor der Katastrophe: Juden in Deutschland 1934–1939* (Tel Aviv, 1967) 34; on the mood among the Jews in Germany during these months, see Leni Yahil, *Die Shoah: Überlebenskampf und Vernichtung der europäischen Juden* (Munich, 1998), 62–66.

8. Quoted in Bergmann and Wetzel, "'Der Miterlebende weiß nichts,'" 180.

9. Wolfgang Benz, "Prolog: Der 30. Januar 1933," in *Die Juden in Deutschland 1933–1945: Leben unter nationalsozialistischer Herrschaft*, ed. Wolfgang Benz (Munich, 1988), 16.

10. According to Joachim Fest in his bitingly critical portrait of Papen, the readiness with which conservative nationalism put itself at the disposal of the National Socialist seizure of power revealed "how inept and burnt-out to the core it was. When put to a practical test as demanded by the times, no other social group failed to a similar degree." Joachim Fest, "Franz von Papen und die Konservative Kollaboration," in *Das Gesicht des Dritten Reiches: Profile einer totalitären Herrschaft* (Munich, 1993), 222.

11. Wehler, *Gesellschaftsgeschichte*, vol. 3, 601.

12. Notes of General Lieutenant Liebmann, in Thilo Vogelsang, "Neue Dokumente zur Geschichte der Reichswehr 1930–1933," *Vierteljahrshefte für Zeitgeschichte* 2 (1954): 397–436; here 434f.; see also now the recently discovered notes of General Hammerstein in Reinhard Müller, "Hitlers Rede vor der Reichswehrführung 1933: Eine neue Moskauer Überlieferung," *Mittelweg* 36 11, no. 1 (2001): 73–90.

13. Institut für Zeitgeschichte, ed., *Akten der Partei-Kanzlei der NSDAP: Rekonstruktion eines verlorengegangenen Bestandes* (Munich, 1983), part I, vol. 1, 6.

14. MBliV, 1933 I, 169; see Martin Broszat, *Der Staat Hitlers: Grundlegung und Entwicklung seiner inneren Verfassung* (Munich, 1969), 93. In the beginning of March, Göring declared in a speech in Frankfurt am Main: "I am not even thinking about conducting only a defensive battle in a bourgeois manner and with bourgeois diffidence. No, I am giving the signal to go over to the offensive all along the line. *Volksgenossen*, my measures will not be debilitated by any kind of bureaucracy. Here I do not have to exercise justice, here I only need to destroy and exterminate, nothing else!" Quoted in Josef Becker and Ruth Becker, eds., *Hitlers Machtergreifung 1933: Vom Machtantritt Hitlers 30. Januar 1933 bis zur Besiegelung des Einparteienstaates 14. Juli 1933* (Munich, 1992), 117.

15. Verordnung des Reichspräsidenten zum Schutz von Volk und Staat, 28 February 1933, *RGBl* I, 83; see Thomas Raithel and Irene Strenge, "Die Reichstagsbrandverordnung: Grundlegung der Diktatur mit den Instrumenten des Weimarer Aus-

nahmezustandes," *Vierteljahrshefte für Zeitgeschichte* 48 (2000): 413–460. Regarding the ongoing controversy about the principals behind the arson attack, see the sober evaluation provided by Hermann Graml, "Zur Debatte über den Reichstagsbrand," in *Der Reichstagsbrand und der Prozess vor dem Reichsgericht*, ed. Dieter Dieseroth (Berlin, 2006), 27–34.

16. In the summer of 1933, 26,000 people were imprisoned in concentration camps. Wolfgang Benz and Barbara Distel, eds., *Terror ohne System: Die ersten Konzentrationslager im Nationalsozialismus 1933–1935*, vol. 1: *Geschichte der Konzentrationslager, 1933–1945* (Berlin, 2001), 8.

17. The NSDAP obtained 43.9 percent of the votes and thus only managed to obtain a majority in the new Reichstag with the help of the German Nationals.

18. Still fundamental in this regard, see Karl Dietrich Bracher, Wolfgang Sauer, and Gerhard Schulz, *Die nationalsozialistischen Machtergreifung: Studien zur Errichtung des totalitären Herrschaftssystems in Deutschland 1933/34*, 2nd ed. (Cologne, 1962).

19. See Max Weber's well-known definition: "The state is that human community which within a specific area … claims for itself (successfully) the monopoly of legitimate physical violence." Max Weber, *Wirtschaft und Gesellschaft: Grundriß der verstehen den Soziologie*, 5th ed. (Tübingen, 1980), 822 (quote translated by Bernard Heise); see also Dieter Grimm, "Das staatliche Gewaltmonopol," in *Herausforderungen des staatlichen Gewaltmonopols: Recht und politisch motivierte Gewalt am Ende des 20. Jahrhunderts*, ed. Freia Anders and Ingrid Gilcher-Holtey (Frankfurt am Main, 2006), 18–38.

20. Adolf Hitler, *Mein Kampf*, 349th–351st printing (Munich, 1938), 104.

21. CVZ, 9 February 1933. Also in February: in Breslau, a Jewish Reichsbanner member named Walter Steinfeld was stabbed to death after a rally held by the republican "Iron Front"; in Hamburg, a Jewish merchant was assaulted and seriously injured by uniformed National Socialists after a service in the synagogue. *Jüdisches Wochenblatt*, 17 February 1933, in Wieland Eschenhagen, *Die "Machtergreifung": Tagebuch einer Wende nach Presseberichten vom 1. Januar bis 6. März 1933* (Darmstadt, 1982), 190.

22. On the anti-Semitic violence in the first months of the NS regime, see Comité des Delegations Juives, ed., *Das Schwarzbuch: Tatsachen und Dokumente: Die Lage der Juden in Deutschland 1933* (Paris, 1934), 495–499; the quote from the *Manchester Guardian* is on 499; Friedländer, *Years of Persecution*, 18f.; Longerich, *Politik der Vernichtung*, 26–30.

23. See Schüler-Springorum, *Die jüdische Minderheit*, 297f.

24. C.V. Königsberg to the headquarters in Berlin, 24 March 1933, quoted in ibid., 298. Sabatzky took an assignment in Leipzig, where he became the director of the central German regional association; in 1939 he emigrated to England. In his place, Dr. Max Angerthal took over the office of syndic of the regional association in East Prussia. In 1939, after the C.V. was banned, Angerthal went to Berlin and worked for the Reich's Association of the Jews in Germany. In 1943 he was deported to a death camp and murdered.

25. Preußische Politische Polizei, Bericht, Berlin 11 March 1933, Kulka and Jäckel, *Die Juden in den geheimen NS-Stimmungsberichten 1933–1945*, 45. In any event, the police commissioner was SA Obergruppenführer Edmund Heines, who one year later would be a victim of the Rohm murders.

26. *Frankfurter Zeitung*, 12 March 1933, quoted in Comité des Delegations Juives, *Schwarzbuch*, 94. See also the report based on the memory of Ludwig Foerder, "Der erste Pogrom auf eine deutsches Gericht (Erinnerungen eines Augenzeugen)," The

Wiener Library P.II.b. no. 174, Yad Vashem Archives, Jerusalem, 02./130; see also the descriptions in Walter Tausk, *Breslauer Tagebuch 1933–1940* (Berlin, 1988), 34–41.

27. See Comité des Delegations Juives, *Schwarzbuch*, 94–191; Adam, *Judenpolitik im Dritten Reich*, 47f. On the situation of the Jews in Breslau under the Weimar Republic and under National Socialism see Tausk, *Breslauer Tagebuch*; Willy Cohn, *Verwehte Spuren: Erinnerungen an das Breslauer Judentum vor seinem Untergang*, ed. Norbert Cohns (Cologne, 1995); Horst Kühnel, *Juden in Breslau 1850–1945: Beiträge zu einer Ausstellung* (Munich, 1993); Leszek Ziątkowski, *Die Geschichte der Juden in Breslau* (Wrocław, 2000). On the Jews in Breslau more generally, see Manfred Hettling, Andreas Reinke, and Norbert Conrads, eds., *In Breslau zu Hause? Juden in einer mitteleuropäischen Metropole der Neuzeit* (Hamburg, 2003); Till van Rahden, *Juden and andere Breslauer: Die Beziehungen zwischen Juden, Protestanten und Katholiken in einer deutschen Großstadt von 1860 bis 1925* (Göttingen, 2000).

28. See Kurt Pätzold, *Faschismus, Rassenwahn, Judenverfolgung: Eine Studie zur politischen Strategie und Taktik des faschistischen deutschen Imperialismus (1933–1935)* (East Berlin, 1975). For cases in Gleiwitz, Görlitz, Frankfurt am Main, Hamburg, Stuttgart, Berlin, Chemnitz, and other cities see Comité des Delegations Juives, *Schwarzbuch*, 101–109. For Prussia, on 31 March 1933 the Reich commissioner for the Prussian judiciary ordered that all Jewish judges and Jewish lawyers were to be forced to take leave and were no longer allowed to enter courthouses. Walk, *Das Sonderrecht für die Juden im NS-Staat*, vol. 1, 22.

29. Haffner, *Geschichte eines Deutschen*, 144–148 (quotation translated by Bernard Heise).

30. Ibid., 135 (quotation translated by Bernard Heise).

31. Quoted in Ian Kershaw, *Der Hitler-Mythos: Führerkult und Volksmeinung* (Stuttgart, 1999), 78.

32. Sebastian Haffner, *Von Bismarck zu Hitler: Ein Rückblick* (Munich, 1987), 219.

33. Inge Jens, *Dichter zwischen rechts und links: die Geschichte der Sektion Dichtkunst an der Preußischen Akademie der Künste*, 2nd ed. (Leipzig, 1994); Claudia Bruns, "Ricarda Huch und die Konservative Revolution," in *WerkstattGeschichte* 25 (2000): 5–33.

34. A detailed discussion of the controversy can be found in Hans Rudolf Vaget, *Im Schatten Wagners: Thomas Mann über Richard Wagner* (Frankfurt am Main, 1999), 229–261.

35. Quoted in Friedländer, *Years of Persecution*, 42; on the position of the Church in 1933, see Klaus Scholder, *Die Kirchen und das Dritte Reich*, (Berlin, 1977), vol. 1, 277–700.

36. On the widespread reporting in the German papers about the concentration camps, which naturally did not describe the brutal reality in the camps but rather an ideological image of hard but salutary work so that the inmates learned discipline and later could return to the *Volksgemeinschaft*, see Gellately, *Hingeschaut und Weggesehen*, 77–88.

37. See Bracher, Sauer, and Schulz, *Nationalsozialistischen Machtergreifung*, 150–152. A description of the theatrical event is found in André François-Poncet, *Als Botschafter in Berlin 1931–1938* (Mainz, 1949), 106–109; on the festive religious service with Bishop Dibelius, see Günter Brakelmann, "Hoffnungen und Illusionen evangelischer Prediger zu Beginn des 'Dritten Reiches': gottesdienstliche Feiern aus politischen Anlässen," in *Die Reihen fast geschlossen: Beiträge zur Geschichte des Alltags unterm Nationalsozialismus*, ed. Detlev Peukert and Jürgen Reulecke (Wuppertal, 1981), 141–146; on the events of 21 March, see also Hans Rudolf Vaget, "Wagner-Kult und nationalsozialistische Herrschaft: Hitler, Wagner, Thomas Mann und die 'nationale

Erhebung,'" in *Richard Wagner im Dritten Reich*, ed. Saul Friedländer and Jörn Rüsen (Munich, 2000), 265–271.

38. See Bernward Dörner, *"Heimtücke": Das Gesetz als Waffe: Kontrolle, Abschreckung und Verfolgung in Deutschland 1933–1945* (Paderborn, 1998). After that there were so many denunciations that even the police expressed criticism. Kershaw, *Hitler*, vol. 1, 587.

39. See *Das "Ermächtigungsgesetz" vom 24. März 1933: Quellen zur Geschichte und Interpretation des "Gesetzes zur Behebung der Not von Volk und Reich,"* ed. Rudolf Morsey (Düsseldorf 1992).

40. Michael Schneider, *Unterm Hakenkreuz: Arbeiter und Arbeiterbewegung 1933 bis 1939* (Bonn, 1999).

41. *Jüdische Rundschau*, 10 March 1933, 1. The newly appointed higher police leader west (Höhere Polizeiführer im Westen) later issued instructions to the police stations under his command to safeguard the opening of the stores.

42. Longerich, *"Davon haben wir nichts gewusst!"* 59. On 16 March, the *Israelitische Familienblatt* related that during the previous week there had been reports from throughout the Reich about boycott actions, the closings of Jewish stores, and the abuse of their owners. Günter Plum, "Wirtschaft und Erwerbsleben," in Benz, *Die Juden in Deutschland*, 274.

43. Ingrid Buchloh, *Die nationalsozialistischen Machtergreifung in Duisburg: Eine Fallstudie* (Duisburg, 1980), 113.

44. Quoted in Longerich, *Politik der Vernichtung*, 27.

45. Ibid.

46. Adolf Hitler, *Hitler: Reden und Proklamationen 1932–1945*, part 1: *Triumph*, vol. 1: *1932–1934*, ed. Max Domarus (Leonberg, 1988), 219. Similar appeals were also made in the different states. Heinrich Himmler, police president commissioner in Munich, expressly declared to press representatives that he was prepared to protect all state citizens, and that he considered states citizens of Jewish faith to be state citizens just like those of non-Jewish faith. CVZ, 16 March 1933.

47. Longerich, *Politik der Vernichtung*, 28.

48. I do not share Longerich's impression that after 13 March the actions against Jewish stores were essentially stopped. According to his evaluation, the initiative for the boycott actions grew "strongly from the grass roots"; in any event, the fact that the actions for the most part ceased during the second half of March demonstrated "that the party leadership possessed a considerable amount of authority and that it did not need to organize a boycott (as a concession to the party base) in order to take control of the anti-Semitic movement that had gotten underway." I feel that this evaluation is too simple. It is clear that Hitler's appeal was not without effect. But this did not suppress the persistent desire for anti-Semitic action in the local party groups. The boycott throughout the Reich is thus clearly to be understood as an attempt by the party leadership to contain this energy within a controllable framework. Longerich's conclusion that the "party base admittedly worked independently but always within the parameters set by the regime" must therefore be inverted. Actually it was the constant transgressions of the established parameters that always provided the party leadership with the opportunity and legitimation to radicalize its politics of persecution. Quotes from ibid., 31. See also Nolzen, "The Nazi Party and Its Violence against Jews," 249–253.

49. Pätzold, *Faschismus, Rassenwahn, Judenverfolgung*, 48.

50. Flade, *Juden in Würzburg*, 355.

51. Notice, C.V. Berlin 11 March 1933, Special Archive Moscow, 721-1-2321, fol. 51.

52. *Frankfurter Zeitung Handelsblatt*, 21 March 1933, Special Archive Moscow, 721-1-2321, fol. 163.
53. After five hours the father was set free under the extortive condition that, within the next two hours, he would provide a slaughtered ox as ransom for his son. Ulrich Knipping, *Die Geschichte der Juden in Dortmund während der Zeit des Dritten Reiches* (Dortmund, 1977), 25; see also Barkai, *Vom Boykott zur "Entjudung,"* 24.
54. Buchloh, *Nationalsozialistischen Machtergreifung*, 133f.; Günter von Roden et al. *Geschichte der Duisburger Juden* (Duisburg, 1986), 797f. This forced march was only one out of a total of four "Jewish processions" in Duisburg in March 1933. See Roden et al., which also deals with more cases of violence and assaults against Duisburg Jews in February and March 1933.
55. Otto Abbes, *Hersfelds jüdische Geschichte 1330 bis 1970* (Bad Hersfeld, 2002), 108f.
56. Joseph Goebbels, *Die Tagebücher von Joseph Goebbels, im Auftrag des Instituts für Zeitgeschichte und mit Unterstützung des Staatlichen Archivdienstes Rußlands*, part I: *Aufzeichnungen 1923–1941*, ed. Elke Fröhlich (Munich, 2000–2004), 156.
57. Judgment of the First Senate of Imperial Economic Court regarding the determination of damages, 4 December 1933 (Special Archive Moscow, 721-1-2501), 73–76.
58. Longerich, *Politik der Vernichtung*, 36.
59. Der Höhere Polizeiführer im Westen/Sonderkommissar des Ministers des Innern, report dated 27–28 March 1933, Kulka and Jäckel, *NS-Stimmungsberichten*, 47; Knipping, *Die Geschichte der Juden in Dortmund*, 27.
60. Der Höhere Polizeiführer im Westen, report dated 27–28 March 1933; Kulka and Jäckel, *NS-Stimmungsberichten*, 47. According to reports from the Reichsbank subsidiaries, on 1 April there were also boycotts, among other places, in Amberg, Aplerbeck, Essen, Glogau, Halberstadt, Hamborn, Herne, Liegnitz, Ludwigshafen, Mannheim, Mülheim/Ruhr, and Wittenberg. Similar reports are also available for Altona, Emden, Bad Freienwalde, Eberswalde, Görlitz, Göttingen, Kiel, Lüneburg, Münster, Oranienburg, Prenzlau, Schwedt an der Oder, Stettin, Stolp, Wernigerode, and Zittau. Pätzold, *Faschismus, Rassenwahn, Judenverfolgung*, 65; reports in the *Vossischen Zeitung*, 29 March 1933 and *Deutsche Allgemeine Zeitung* 30 March 1933, both in Comité des Delegations Juives, *Schwarzbuch*, 299; see also the many reports about the boycott actions throughout the German Reich in March that were gathered into a file by C.V. headquarters, Special Archive Moscow, 721-1-2321.
61. *Völkischer Beobachter*, 29 March 1933.
62. Hitler made similar arguments at the ministerial conference on the same day. Konrad Repgen and Hans Booms, eds., *Akten der Reichskanzlei: Regierung Hitler 1933–1938*, part 1: *1933/34*, vol. 1: *30. Januar bis 31. August 1933*, comp. Karl-Heinz Minuth (Boppard am Rhein, 1983), 277.
63. Directives of the boycott committee of 31 March 1933, printed in *IMG*, vol. 29, 266–268.
64. Streicher's Appeal, "Schlagt den Weltfeind," *Völkischer Beobachter*, 31 March 1933, printed in *IMG*, vol. 29, 264–266.
65. Haffner, *Geschichte eines Deutschen*, 138f. (quotation translated by Bernard Heise).
66. Emden was once a major citadel for the Calvinist reformation—the famous theologian and state law specialist Johannes Althusius (1557–1638) was active here for over thirty years. It had an old Jewish community that reached back to the expulsion of Portuguese and Spanish Jews at the end of the fifteenth century. In 1925 the town had about 27,000 residents, including 24,000 Protestants, more than 1,600 Catholics, and around 700 Jews. See the entry for Emden in Obenaus, *Historisches Handbuch*, vol. 1, 533–569.

67. Facsimile of the article in Marianne Claudi and Reinhard Claudi, *Goldene und andere Zeiten: Emden – Stadt in Ostfriesland* (Emden, 1982), 70.
68. Radio announcement by the Prussian Interior Ministry, 31 March 1933, in Longerich, *Politik der Vernichtung*, 37. Yet there was violence nonetheless. During the boycott of Jewish businesses on 1 April 1933 in Kiel, the son of a Jewish merchant shot an SS man during a conflict, turned himself in to the police, and was arrested. An angry crowd forced its way to the jail and lynched him. Dieter Hauschildt, "Vom Judenboykott zum Judenmord. Der 1. April 1933 in Kiel," in *"Wir bauen das Reich": Aufstieg und erste Herrschaftsjahre des Nationalsozialismus in Schleswig-Holstein*, ed. Erich Hoffmann and Peter Wulf (Neumünster, 1981), 335–360.
69. Facsimile of the article in Claudi and Claudi, *Goldene und andere Zeiten*, 70.
70. *Emder Zeitung*, 3 April 1933, printed in Claudi and Claudi, *Goldene und andere Zeiten*, 71.
71. Marianne Claudi and Reinhard Claudi, eds., *Die wir verloren haben: Lebensgeschichten Emder Juden* (Aurich, 1988), Interview 28.06f.
72. Ibid., Interview 7.05.
73. Edwin Landau, "Mein Leben vor und nach Hitler," in *Jüdisches Leben in Deutschland: Selbstzeugnisse zur Sozialgeschichte*, vol. 3: *1918–1945*, ed. Monika Richarz (Stuttgart, 1982), 104. In November 1934 Landau moved with his family to Palestine and opened a new plumbing business in Ramat Gan.
74. Victor Klemperer, *Ich will Zeugnis ablegen bis zum letzten: Tagebücher 1933–1945*, vol. 1, ed. Walter Nowojski in collaboration with Hadwig Klemperer (Berlin, 1995), 15.
75. Hans Reichmann, *Deutscher Bürger und verfolgter Jude: Novemberpogrom und KZ Sachsenhausen 1937 bis 1939*, ed. and with introduction by Michael Wildt (Munich, 1998), 281.
76. Robert Weltsch, "Tragt ihn mit Stolz, den gelben Fleck," *Jüdische Rundschau*, 4 April 1933. This edition, wrote Weltsch on 22 April 1933 to Martin Buber, has found an "unprecedented echo." John V. H. Dippel, *Die große Illusion: Warum deutsche Juden ihre Heimat nicht verlassen wollten* (Berlin, 1997), 193f. Hans Reichmann also (according to Weltsch) told him that, despite all the differences in opinion, he had spoken for the entire German Jewish community, Robert Weltsch, "Looking Back Over Sixty Years," *Year Book of the Leo Baeck Institute* 27 (1982): 388. Weltsch fled to London after the 1938 November pogrom, and when the war was over he directed the Leo-Baeck Institute for many years.
77. Friedländer, *Years of Persecution*, 22; David Bankier, *The Germans and The Final Solution: Public Opinion under Nazism* (Oxford, 1992), 69; Marion Kaplan, *Between Dignity and Despair: Jewish Life in Nazi Germany* (New York, 1998), 22–24.
78. See Marcus Meyer, "Ein schwieriger Patient: Ein Bremer Rechtsanwalt und der 'Judenboykott' im April 1933," in *Arbeiterbewegung und Sozialgeschichte: Zeitschrift für die Regionalgeschichte Bremens im 19. und 20. Jahrhundert* 11 (2003): 16–29. As the son of the president of Bremen's cotton exchange, Cramer was a member of Bremen's traditional Bürgertum. After writing this letter, he was ejected from the NSDAP, brought to a psychiatric clinic, and declared incompetent. Because of this declaration, officials of the Federal Republic of Germany refused to either compensate him or reinstate him as a lawyer.
79. Bankier, *The Germans and the Final Solution*, 69. Peter Longerich noted two critical comments in the *Deutsche Allgemeinen Zeitung* and the *Frankfurter Zeitung*: Longerich, *"Davon haben wir nichts gewusst!"* 62. In any event, a few days later both newspapers supported the anti-Semitic laws prohibiting Jews from practicing their professions

because of "the greater tendency toward fairness and practicality." Longerich, *"Davon haben wir nichts gewusst!"* 64.

80. See Helmut Genschel, *Die Verdrängung der Juden aus der Wirtschaft im Dritten Reich* (Göttingen, 1966), 76–78.

81. Neurath to Reich President von Hindenburg, 19 June 1933, printed in *IMG*, vol. 40, 465–468.

82. Elmar Gasten, *Aachen in der Zeit der nationalsozialistischen Herrschaft 1933–1944* (Frankfurt am Main, 1993), 143.

83. Genschel, *Die Verdrängung der Juden*, 54; Friedländer, *Years of Persecution*, 19–25.

84. Repgen and Booms, *Akten der Reichskanzlei*, part 1, vol. 1, 286, note 1.

85. *Völkischer Beobachter*, 04/05/1933.

86. Older research still understood the 1 April boycott as a consciously implemented manipulative initiative of the NS leadership in order to push through the anti-Jewish laws that subsequently followed. In contrast, newer research emphasizes the pressure from the party base that forced the leadership to act. Longerich, *Politik der Vernichtung*, 30. Nolzen stresses that the NSDAP was interested above all in mobilizing the population and that the boycott is not to be evaluated only with reference to the goals of the state leadership. Nolzen, "The Nazi Party and Its Violence against Jews," 235.

87. Franz von Papen, *Der Wahrheit eine Gasse* (Munich, 1952), 321.

88. Ernst Fraenkel, *The Dual State: A Contribution to the Theory of Dictatorship* (New York, 1941). Fraenkel returned to Germany after the war. As of 1953 he was a professor for political science at the Freien Universität Berlin. He died in March 1975. A German edition of his book appeared shortly before his death.

89. Fraenkel, *The Dual State*, xiii.

90. Ibid., xv.

91. Ibid., 5.

92. Carl Schmitt, *Die Diktatur: Von den Anfängen des modernen Souveränitätsgedankens bis zum proletarischen Klassenkampf* [1921] (Berlin, 1994), 134 (quotation translated by Bernard Heise).

93. Fraenkel, *The Dual State*, 25; see Michael Wildt, "Ernst Fraenkel und Carl Schmitt: Eine ungleiche Beziehung," in *Geschichte als Experiment: Studien zu Politik, Kultur und Alltag im 19. und 20. Jahrhundert: Festschrift für Adelheid von Saldern*, ed. Daniela Münkel and Jutta Schwarzkopf (Frankfurt am Main, 2004), 35–48.

94. Carl Schmitt, *Über die drei Arten des rechtswissenschaftlichen Denkens* (Hamburg, 1934), 13 (quotation translated by Bernard Heise).

95. Ibid., 14f.

4

THE BOYCOTT AS A POLITICAL ARENA

The photographs all look more or less the same. A large banner stretches across a grey village street: "The Jews are our Misfortune!" Or SA troopers stand in front of nondescript storefronts with homemade placards in their hands: "Germans! The World Jew seeks your Destruction! Defend Yourselves!" Only with difficulty does our eye sense the predominance of these provocations, for today, even in the smallest villages, we are accustomed to seeing colorful and spacious display windows crammed with advertisements and marketing exhibits: brand-name products spelled out in garish, glowing letters on the walls, large billboards from which advertisements assault the eye. In the 1930s the village streets were grey and nondescript, colorfully decorated only for village festivals or religious holidays. Back then, the anti-Semitic banners or placards dominated the scene. There was no chance of avoiding them. People walking through the streets, running errands, going shopping, or chatting with neighbors were met with the provocation to hate the Jews: "The Jews are our Misfortune"; "Those who buy from Jews are traitors to their people"; "The food you get from the Jew will kill you." These are just a few of the anti-Semitic slogans seen in the Lower Saxony town of Hameln in April 1934, as noted by the regional chapter of the Central Association of German Citizens of Jewish Faith (Centralverein deutscher Staatsbürger jüdischen Glaubens).[1]

In July 1934 a letter arrived at the C.V. in Berlin from the small town of Sandersleben in Anhalt. Situated in the eastern Harz Forest, Sandersleben had some 3,000 inhabitants in the 1930s, including a small Jewish community that dated from the seventeenth century but now only consisted of four families.[2] The letter was written by Adolf Adler, son of the merchant Herman Adler:

Today, for the first time, I turn to you as a member, for I do not know whether the "Reich's Deputation of the German Jews" is responsible for this matter, and also I do not know its address. I have been a member for a number of years (and not only since the upheaval), and this gives me reason to hope that you will protect my interests in the following matter. On the night of June 23–24, the windows of my father's store were completely pasted over with large red notices—included are two of the posters, which were torn off elsewhere. The two enclosed photos will also give you a "vivid" impression of what happened. The following Sunday, we covered our display window and on Monday morning we immediately informed the police of what had occurred and filed a report, and I personally went to the Bürgermeister, as the local police authority, and lodged a complaint. Meanwhile on Sunday morning I had taken a photo of the display window, which someone must have seen, for it caused me great problems. More about that forthwith.

Early Tuesday around 8:30, I was forced out of bed and arrested; and I was told that if I turned over the camera and the photograph, the matter would be resolved. But I was no longer able to do so, for I had sent the film to my brother, who was staying with relatives while vacationing in northern Germany—I had already done so on Monday. When I explained this to the police officer, he searched the house and then immediately took me to the Bürgermeister. There, however, I could only recount this same story, whereupon I was released. The film was later confiscated by the local police in Blumenthal (Unterweser), where my brother was staying.

Now for the second part. On the night of July 3–4, 1934, our windows—and this time the three showcases as well—were daubed over a second time, and in an even more vulgar manner. Clearly, this time there weren't enough large notices, so the scoundrels (for they can be described no other way) took small notices and, using brown oil paint, smeared the word "Jew" on the windows and a large swastika. They even went so far as to dump the paint can over in the entry way, right on the stoop. In the end they must have thought that the swastika might indicate who did it, and so they painted the swastika enclosed in the form of a rectangle. ...

So immediately on the morning of that same day I went to the police, that is, to the Bürgermeister, and let him know that this time I would photograph the windows and lodge my complaint at a higher level, and that we would by no means remove the paint. At the same time, I told the Bürgermeister that I came on behalf of the Israeli community, because vandalism had also occurred a second time at another Jewish shop, and at the same time on behalf of my father. The other Jewish shopkeeper is 79 years old and can no longer lodge complaints on his own, and my father has a heart condition and gets so upset about such things that he authorized me. A police report was filed for this second incident as well. And now comes the main point: on the night of July 5–6, a window grating on the local Synagogue was torn off and three of the window panes were smashed, and on the other side a grating was damaged (that is, a hole was made) and likewise a window was broken with a fist-sized stone. When this was discovered early Friday, my father himself, in his capacity as the director of the local "Israeli Religious Community," went to the Bürgermeister and lodged a complaint and also filed a report. ...

On the occasion of my father's visit to the Bürgermeister, the latter came back to the smearing of the windows and recommended that we, *in our own interests*, clean the panes, and we did this, too, on Friday—I guess I do not need to describe to you the great degree of difficulty involved if I reiterate for you that the smeared mess was "*oil* paint." It took us hours to do so … and early Saturday again there was a small notice on it. Hence, even though the Bürgermeister had promised us relief.

My father's business suffered incredibly because of the boycott that time— as indeed did the other small Jewish businesses here on the square—and these new attacks are bringing us ever closer to ruin. Where you are, you could *hardly understand* the effect that something like this has on a small square.

And now to the main reason for my letter today: I have purposely reported in a somewhat rambling and extensive manner so that you might be able to form a precise image of what has happened here. You can believe me, I would have preferred coming there at some point and making a report to you in person, but unfortunately I do not have the money, because I myself am also barely managing to feed myself by means of a small agency and would die if I could not at least eat and sleep at home. By the way, I am 26 years old.

I am asking you now, with regard to the attempted break-in and the damage to the synagogue, to possibly make it public in your "*C.V.-Zeitung*" so that the greater public gets to learn about what is actually going on.

With respect to the painting of the window, I ask you possibly to intervene for us with a higher authority. But please make only the "most discreet" use of the pictures.

I would greatly appreciate hearing from you at some point about what you have done and accomplished for us in this matter.

I greet you with a Jewish greeting

Respectfully

Adolf Adler.[3]

The C.V. headquarters in Berlin passed the letter along to the central German regional association, whose business manager, Kurt Sabatzky, immediately drove to Sandersleben, confirmed all of the details, and spoke with the Jewish families in the town. It appeared that the identities of the perpetrators who vandalized both the stores of Goldstein and Adler and also damaged the synagogue were known. But the Jews of Sandersleben, meanwhile, no longer dared to make themselves available as witnesses for the criminal prosecution.[4] Just one week earlier in the *Sanderslebener Zeitung*, the Jewish community had published an advertisement promising a reward of ten RM for anyone who "who verifies for us the nefarious perpetrators who on the night from Thursday to Friday tore off the window grating from our House of God and smashed in the windows."[5]

On the same day that Adolf Adler's letter arrived, the C.V. turned to both the Reich Economics Ministry and the Gestapo in Dessau with the request that they intervene in Sandersleben.[6] There were no replies. Sabatzky, who visited Sandersleben again at the beginning of August, reported instead that the display windows of Hermann Adler's store had been smeared with paint again and that recently a group had even appeared in front of the store, chanting slanderous slogans and calling for a boycott. At the same time, Hermann Adler heard from the state attorney in Bernburg that the proceedings had been closed because, despite a detailed inquiry, the search for the perpetrators had been unsuccessful.[7]

His son's business license was confiscated by police in connection with the police investigation into the photographs and never returned. The Sandersleben police reported to their superiors that they had "constantly monitored the activities of Adler," but they had not been able to determine anything suspicious. Nonetheless, when the local police stations were requested by the Gestapo in Anhalt to report by 1 October 1934 "cases in which Jewish elements were established to be agents of substantive work in the Communist party," the police in Sandersleben were quick to report that "here the Jew Adolf Adler is under suspicion of Marxist activities. The evidence required to initiate criminal proceedings could thus far not be obtained." Even so, Adler did not get his business license back, and a passport for which he had applied was also denied.[8]

Adolf Adler continued to be targeted by police. In September 1935 he was denounced by an SA Oberscharführer visiting Sandersleben from Bad Soden, who alleged that Adler had given letters and photos to a passenger on the steamship *Europa* that had traveled from Bremen to New York. Almost at the same time, a report arrived from the Dessau constabulary that Adolf Adler had allegedly infected a prostitute in Aschersleben with venereal disease. Thereupon Adler was arrested and transferred to the court prison in Bernburg. The allegations proved baseless; weeks later Adler was released from custody and left Sandersleben. In 1937 he was supposedly still active as a salesman in Berlin, after which his trail vanishes.[9]

The impression that the boycott of 1 April lasted only a day is deceptive. While this may have been true in the large cities, where party organizations and police had opportunities to exercise control, this by no means applied to the provinces. There the boycott actions continued beyond April, for they offered local party organizations an ideal arena in which to win local hegemony after they had acquired power.[10] With the appointment of National Socialist Bürgermeisters, the exclusion of Communists and Social Democratic fractions from the town councils, the persecution and terrorization of the opposition, and the *Gleichschaltung* of previously independent clubs and associations, the National Socialists had crushed the organizations of their opponents. But they were no closer to achieving their most important goal, namely the production of the *Volksgemeinschaft*. Even though they held the control centers and positions of authority, they had not won the sympathies of those who viewed them with skepticism or opposition, nor had the political and cultural order actually been transformed. Without directly attacking the local dignitaries and the local establishment, the anti-Semitic actions against Jewish citizens within the community created opportunities to dismember previously established relationships and reputations, and stigmatize Jewish neighbors, thereby sharpening existing local boundaries and making them unbridgeable. The National Socialists sought the exclusion of Jewish neighbors from the village community—and insofar as they increasingly achieved this absolute exclusion, they created the *Volksgemeinschaft* they were looking for—not merely a loyal community of all *Volksgenossen* that, hardworking, obedient, and self-satisfied, drank its beer and settled down within Germany, but rather a racist *Volksgemeinschaft* that was aggressively prepared to wage war and conquer "Lebensraum."

Tradition of Boycotts

Boycotts against Jewish businesses were by no means an invention of the National Socialists. Leaflets calling for people not to buy "from Jews" date back to the nineteenth century.[11] After the First World War, the anti-Semitic Deutschvölkischer Schutz- und Trutz-Bund supported the boycott of Jewish merchants; even after it was banned, appeals for boycotts continued during the Weimar Republic.[12] But it was the National Socialists who first systematically deployed the boycott as a political weapon for their movement. The boycotts were promoted not only by the party itself but also by a variety of other groups affiliated with the National Socialists, like the Kampfgemeinschaft gegen Warenhaus und Konsumverein (Battle Community Against Department Stores and Cooperatives) in Upper Bavaria, and above all the Kampfbund des gewerblichen Mittelstands (Battle Group of Small and Mid-sized Businesses), which was led by National Socialists. Between 1925 and 1929, the "quiet boycott," as it was referred to in the C.V.- Zeitung, increasingly gained ground.

In the state parliaments, the National Socialist fractions called for the cancellation (albeit without success) of all contracts with companies whose proprietors were of "non-German origins" as soon as possible. The Hessian interior minister responded in opposition to such a request by the NSDAP fraction at the end of December 1932, noting

> that the currently widespread agitation against Jewish business people, which mostly amounts to using leaflets to call upon the population to avoid businesses with Jewish proprietors and only to purchase from Christians, has already led to the first disturbances of the public order. Last Sunday in Gießen and Mainz, tear gas and stink bombs were thrown into a number of department stores of the type mentioned, which considerably alarmed the visitors of these businesses. Thus in the interest of maintaining public order, I have given instructions to determinedly prevent this agitation that is threatening the public order.[13]

At the local level as well, NSDAP chapters tried to implement the boycott of Jewish businesses as a political instrument even before the takeover of power. Thus for example the National Socialist majority in the town council of Neustadt an der Aisch in Bavaria resolved in October 1932 that Jewish companies should no longer receive public contracts. However, after the C.V. protested, this resolution was rescinded by higher authorities as illegal.[14] SA and SS men stood sentry in front of Jewish businesses and took notes about those customers who still dared to shop there. The Nazis were already threatening to publish the names of the customers, as was being done in Altenburg in Thuringia.[15] Activists tried above all to evoke anti-Jewish passions during Christmas. In 1927 the NSDAP began their "enlightenment campaigns" against department stores. In November 1928 the *Völkischer Beobachter* announced: "Christmas is coming! Tens of thousands, yes, millions are bringing their money to Jewish department stores, thereby destroying the small to medium-sized businesses and contributing to the plundering of wide circles and strata of our Volk."[16] The National Socialist boycott campaigns spread quickly from the large cities into the provinces. On the occasion of the coming Christmas season, National Socialist calls for boycotts were made with "tremendous force." Urgent requests for advice and aid were arriving almost daily from individual members and local chapters, wrote the C.V.'s main administration center to the subordinate C.V organizations in December 1930.[17] With an emergency proclamation on 8 December 1931 to "secure the Christmas peace," the imperial regime prohibited the distribution or display of political leaflets, placards, etc. with political content in public byways and squares. As the Berlin headquarters of the C.V. noted in a circular sent to all regional associations, this included the distribution of leaflets calling for boycotts of Jewish businesses.[18]

Thereupon the NSDAP actions in the large cities evidently ebbed, but the boycott actions in the small towns and communities remained virulent.[19] Beneath the headline "Christmas—A Celebration for Germans or a Profitable Killing for the Jews?" the local NSDAP in Elbing, West Prussia, agitated for boycotts in December 1932 as follows:

> German *Volksgenosse*! It is true, you have duties vis-à-vis your family, but you have even greater duties vis-à-vis your Volk. You love your son and your daughter and you want to make them happy. But you should also love your German brother and not let him starve. Look at him, your German brother. Look at him, the small merchant and tradesman. He was once one of the most steadfast pillars of the state, the small business and trades person [*kleiner Mittelstand*]. Today he has been proletarianized. He has been ruined by the unfair pricing competition of the department stores. And who helped bring about his ruin? You! His German brother.... Maybe you would still have work today, if you had not supported the Jews instead of the German brother and if everyone else had also done the same.... Why do you care about the dirty Jew? He does not belong in your Fatherland. Disdain him and do not let him earn anything, then he will disappear on his own and your German brother can live again.... Have you ever heard about the "stab in the back?" In 1918, villains with Galician names stabbed the German Front in the back. You have spoken out with outrage about this stab in the back. But you yourself are such a backstabber, if you betray the German *Volksgemeinschaft* by bringing your money to the Jew. Ger-

man *Volksgenosse*, think about it! Do not buy from Jews, but rather from Germans![20]

In neighboring Riesenburg in December 1932, the Protestant pastor Kuptsch, who was known as a National Socialist, encouraged the representatives of the church congregations to protest the fact

> that the Jews in our town, who have nothing in common with Christendom, advertise for their businesses with Christian symbols and customs in their display windows prior to major Christian festivals and before the confirmation of our Christian youth. The united church-congregational bodies raise a sharp protest against these Jewish business practices which demeaningly use Christian symbols and customs as a means for Jewish business advertisements, and request that our local officials take the necessary steps to forbid Jews from using these business advertisements which deeply wound Christian sensibilities.[21]

The *C.V.-Zeitung* reported in April 1932 on the fervid boycott actions in Ortelsburg, Goldap, and Lyck.[22]

As the C.V. emphasized, the boycott actions prior to 1932 differed from one region to the next. Northern Germany was hit stronger than Baden or the Ruhr region, for example. Along with East Prussia and the Vogtland, Pomerania was a core region for boycott actions—the C.V. went so far as to say that there was a "state of emergency" in Pomerania because the economic existence of Jewish merchants was seriously threatened.[23] The same applied to Schleswig-Holstein, where an increase in anti-Semitic incidents resulted in serious consequences for Jewish businesses.[24] To mobilize increased economic solidarity, in 1932 the Prussian regional association of Jewish communities began a month of advertising under the motto "our right to work." At the same time, the development of a Jewish cooperative credit union was supposed to help small merchants, tradespeople, and middle-class circles through financial crisis. But the resources made available could naturally only mitigate distress—by no means could they resolve it completely.

For the time being, the C.V. could still reach its goals by filing complaints against illegal boycotts in the German courts.[25] Thus in Königsberg the Kiewe department store, together with a local co-op, won a case against the NSDAP, which had denounced them as a "mortal enemy of all honest producers." In 1925 the calls for a boycott by an anti-Semitic association of shoe merchants were countered when, upon request by the C.V., non-Jewish merchants and manufacturers rallied around their Jewish business colleagues. And in 1929 a group of Jewish merchants successfully filed a complaint against the National Socialist *Ostdeutscher Beobachter*.

But two years later, Kurt Sabatzky, who at this time was still the business manager of the East Prussian regional association, was unable to gain the solidarity of non-Jewish livestock traders in East Prussia. Sabatzky and the C.V. filed complaints against NSDAP Gauleiter Erich Koch and other leading National Socialists for defamation, incitement to class hatred, and the disruption of assemblies. Although these complaints led to fines, they were often reduced upon appeal or revoked altogether.[26]

In Beuthen in December 1932, the district court granted an injunction against the National Socialist daily newspaper *Deutsche Ostfront* and prohibited the paper from publishing appeals for anti-Jewish boycotts. In the subsequent court proceedings, the judges Neumann, Swarzenski, and Dr. Braun courageously decided that calling upon people not to buy from Jews was a violation of the Civil Code, particularly since the *Deutsche Ostfront* distinguished Jewish businesses not from Christian but from German businesses. "This difference may be in accordance with the program of the National Socialist Workers' Party of Germany, but it does not correspond to the content of the current constitution. According to the latter, everyone possessing German Reich or German state citizenship is to be regarded as German."[27]

By contrast, the complaints by Jewish businesspeople in Danzig against the boycott appeals in the National Socialist newspaper the *Vorposten* failed. In March 1932 the district court ruled that while advertisements that called for the boycott of specifically identified businesses violated moral standards, within the context of "the general racial struggle which is not prohibited by law per se," the newspaper's headline, which said not to buy "from Jews," was not objectionable. Such appeals "from anti-Semitic circles in the population" had arisen in earlier times and did not contain any discernible forbidden boycott methods. The *Vorposten* was simply making use of its right of freedom of expression.[28]

This constitutional protection upon which German Jews could place their confidence disappeared when the National Socialists seized power—and at the same time, the violent pressure for boycotts by local NSDAP, SA, and HJ increased. In the beginning of July 1933, for example, the C.V. regional association of central Germany compiled a list of anti-Semitic incidents for the month of June. Apart from arrests and job dismissals, they included a resolution by the town of Plauen to prohibit Jews from visiting the town's swimming pools; an order from the district court president of Chemnitz prohibiting his subordinate officials, workers, and staff from patronizing "Jewish, Marxist, and subversive companies"; and a continuous boycott against Jewish businesses in Quedlinburg, where noncompliant housewives were threatened with being listed as "un-German" in the local paper in a section entitled "In the Stocks."[29]

Likewise for Pomerania, the C.V. reported in October 1933 that in many places the boycott of Jewish businesses continued in full force. The deputy leader of the NSDAP chapter in Gollnow near Stettin issued an appeal in the local newspaper at the end of August 1933 that stated: "The struggle against Judaism continues to be led with National Socialist energy. For the last time, I draw attention to the fact that no *Parteigenosse* may enter a Jewish business in order to make purchases there." On a number of days during September in Schivelbein, according the C.V. in Pomerania, troops of up to fifty individuals—mostly schoolchildren—led by SS had moved through the streets and forced customers out of Jewish stores.[30] On 24 March 1934, the Saturday before Palm Sunday, local groups of the NS trade organization arranged a nationwide boycott against the businesses of Jewish merchants in order to put a stop to shopping prior to the holiday. This boycott action, which Armin Nolzen has characterized as one of the most intense, took place even though it had been explicitly forbidden by Hitler.[31]

Resentment

On 16 April 1934, the director of the state police in Kassel, Friedrich Pfeffer von Salomon, reported to the secret state police office in Berlin that the hatred against the Jews had made itself felt in numerous excesses since the beginning of the year. On 3 January in Baumbach—and likewise at the end of March and the beginning of April in Gensungen, Felsberg, Eschwege, Korbach, and Gelnhausen—numerous windows were shattered in homes of Jewish families and in the synagogue; at the end of February a farmer was badly mistreated by SA people because he employed Jewish farm laborers; at the beginning of March at the Kassel Dye Works AG, the Jewish boss was beaten up by a subordinate, the synagogues in Tann and Korbach were broken into and robbed, and in Gelnhausen a meeting of the Jewish community was attacked when large stones were thrown through the windows into the conference room.[32]

These acts of anti-Semitic violence, of which the incidents in Kassel represent only a small sample, took place in the context of a vulnerable moment for the NS regime in spring 1934. Resentment prevailed in the middle-class business world. Sales had rapidly receded, reported Social Democratic informants from all parts of Germany to the SPD committee-in-exile in Prague. As a result of low wages, workers could only buy the cheapest of goods. People were ranting and raving and voicing their disappointments during meetings of the National Socialist Organization of Crafts, Commerce and Industry (NS HAGO).[33] The Social Democratic reporters registered dissatisfaction even among workers, above all because of the drastic reduction in wages. Within the span of a year, wages in the porcelain and glass industry in the Upper Palatinate declined in some instances by around 50 percent compared to 1932; likewise in the metal industry in Saxony.[34] To be sure, the fear of unemployment remained too great for the resentment to be transformed into public protest—after all, in 1934 there were still over 2.7 million unemployed. But the performance of the National Socialist Factory Cell Organization (NSBO) during the elections for the *Vertrauensräte* (Councils of Trust) in March and April 1934 was evidently so poor that the regime did not publish the results.[35]

The mood was miserable among farmers as well. Eggs, butter, and lard now had to be delivered to central buying offices, but the system did not work. According to a report from eastern Germany, the entire operation seemed as if it had only been contrived to satisfy NS office-seekers.[36] Previously there had been two stages between producers and consumers; now there were four or five, which had also impacted prices. Housewives, according to Pfeffer in his report, were outraged by the price of eggs at the weekly markets. In some areas of the district, urbanites were driving into the countryside to forage for eggs as they had done during the war. Moreover, complained the Gestapo in Kassel, Jewish merchants had become involved in the wholesale egg market. Only with difficulty was the SA restrained from destroying all 65,000 eggs belonging to both a Jewish wholesaler and the egg collection center that had sold them to him.[37]

The SPD's *Deutschland-Berichte* determined that while Hitler continued to be held in high regard by the population, there was rising indignation due to the discrepancy between promises and performance. The SPD informants were able to report on twenty-two cases of corruption that had come to light within only five weeks.[38] "While confidence in the Führer is unshakeable everywhere," reported the Kassel Gestapo at the beginning of June in 1934, "in many instances, the criticism of the lower organs and especially of local conditions is equally strong. Among the old *Parteigenossen*, the discussion is about the often excessive expenditure for representation, the acquisition of vehicles, horses by the SA (riding promenades!) etc."[39]

Indeed, during these months the SA was the focus of criticism. Thus with the murderous purge on 30 June 1934, Hitler not only destroyed the SA leadership's hope of becoming the "Volk's army" of the Third Reich, but he was also able to strengthen his aura by securing order with a firm hand.[40] Approval of the murders was reported from all parts of Germany. Reports from Hanover maintained that Hitler's reputation and popularity had "never [been] greater"; reports from the Ruhr region stated that the "energetic, radical, and courageous performance by the Führer ... was wholly approved of by the overwhelming majority of the population."[41] Even Kassel reported that the general mood had improved. The reason was "in the first instance the quick and ruthless suppression of the Röhm revolt. The bond between the Volk and the Führer has only become closer." Now people were hoping that the party would be cleansed right down to the lowest units.[42] The SPD's *Deutschland-Berichte* summed up the impact of the events on the loyalty of the population as follows:

> 1. The broad masses did not understand the political significance of the events; 2. large—apparently very large—parts of the Volk are actually celebrating Hitler because of his ruthless decisiveness and only a small part has started to become reflective or even outraged, 3. large parts of the workforce have also succumbed to the uncritical veneration of Hitler.[43]

The intensification of anti-Semitic politics also took place in the context of the regime's reinvigorated agitation against "reactionaries" and the Catholic Church. Internal enemies were supposed to be held responsible for the economic difficulties, and here the "fight against Judaism" acquired central significance.[44] On 11 May in the Berlin Sportpalast, Propaganda Minister Goebbels inaugurated the "struggle against state vermin," against "killjoys," "complainers," and "quibblers":

> There are people who cannot stand themselves, and they already get annoyed when they look at a mirror. They find something to complain about with everything. They vex not only their own lives but also the lives of others. One cannot speak with them about great things because their hearts are too weak and too lacking in passion in order to grasp great things.... For some time we have not engaged with these people; now they will get to know us! We will not do it, the way we very well could, with state power; rather we appeal to our allies, the Volk.

The struggle for enlightenment was to be waged throughout the entire land and brought into the most distant village, and at the same time, the alleged creators of the difficulties were to be identified: the Jews.

> But since the Jews abroad are boycotting us, I cannot retract the Jewish legislation domestically. Instead, we simply need to withstand this crisis. The Jews perhaps intend to do their Jewish fellow citizens a service. But they are doing the worst thing they possibly can, for they should not believe that if they actually push the boycott so far that it really represents a serious threat to our economic situation, that we will therefore let the Jews leave freely.... We have protected the Jews. But if they think, they may thus step onto German stages in order to present art to the German

Volk; if they think, they may thus show up again in the editorial offices to write German newspapers; if they stroll again across the Kurfürstendamm as if nothing had happened, let these words serve as a final warning. They are to comport themselves in Germany in a manner that is appropriate for guests.[45]

Goebbels' speech was distributed in the National Socialist provincial press and understood as the anacrusis for a new anti-Semitic campaign.[46] The Kassel Gestapo also noticed this trend. "The hatred against the Jews," stated a report from April 1934, "is increasing more and more." It noted "that the activists of the movement give vent to their hatred of Judaism through excesses and material damages. Within the movement there is no understanding for the fact that, on the one hand, the exclusion of the Jews from trade and commerce is demanded at educational evenings and party events of all kinds, while on the other hand, the economic strength of Judaism increases more and more and official and semi-official bodies conduct business with the Jews."[47] At all of the movement's events, reported the Kassel Gestapo one month later, "propaganda is being fiercely made against the Jews in accordance with the party program. At the moment this can especially be observed in the operation against complainers and killjoys."[48]

This conflict between the political pressure of the local organizations of the NSDAP and the state authorities during these months can be clearly observed. The entire Jewish question, stated the Kassel Gestapo director Pfeffer, was suffering from the contradiction between the Jewish policies of the Ministry of Economics and the NS movement. While on the one side there were attacks against the Jews, on the other side the state was declaring the economic equality of the Jews and demanding that steps be taken against such violations. The "simple fighter" did not understand why he was being taken to task for operations that grew out of the movement's propaganda. Apart from that, highly esteemed members of the NS trades and commerce organizations were coming under suspicion of initiating SA and HJ anti-Jewish actions only in order to shut down competition.[49]

Boycott Actions in Hesse

In the 1930s the administrative region of Kassel still had a rural character. As one might expect, in Kassel and Hanau the proportion of those employed in industry and trade was high, and Marburg was shaped by its university. But the percentage of those employed in agriculture and forestry in the districts of Hünfeld and Frankenberg, for example, was far above 50 percent.[50] Of the circa 1,400 communities, over 1,300 did not have more than 2,000 residents.[51] In 1933, over 80 percent of the approximately 1.1 million people in the Kassel administrative region were Lutheran and 17 percent were Catholic. While the Catholics were concentrated in the Episcopal town of Fulda and its surroundings, Catholic communities could also be found in the districts of Hünfeld, Fritzlar, Schlüchtern, and Wolfhagen. In the Kassel administrative district, the 1933 census registered slightly more than 13,000 people as so-called religious Jews, which corresponded to a proportion of 1.2 percent.[52]

Until 1930 the Reichslandbund (Imperial Rural League) was by far the strongest political party in the rural communities of Hesse. It was only after this point that the National Socialists established a footing. During the agrarian crisis of the late years of the Weimar Republic, the NSDAP presented itself as a forceful party representing farmers. To be sure, the causes for the crisis were to be found in agrarian politics at the national level as well as in worldwide overproduction. But it stood to reason that the farmers saw themselves primarily as the victims of policies determined by external forces and tried to draw attention to their plight with numerous meetings, rallies, and demonstrations. With their anti-Semitic agitation, which blamed "Jewish usurers" for the agrarian crisis, the National-ist Socialists quickly gained support in Hesse.[53]

In the Reichstag elections of 1928, during a period of apparent economic stability, the Right had noticeably continued to lose ground. The German Nationals were at almost 14 percent, the NSDAP had almost 3 percent, whereas the Social Democrats recovered to 35 percent and the Communists took over 7 percent of the votes. Two years later, in the middle of the worldwide economic crisis, the picture had completely changed. The Social Democrats were at 28 percent, the Communists at almost 10 percent; the small farmers' parties were at 12 percent; and while the Liberals and Conservatives no longer played a role, the NSDAP had emerged as a new power and taken second place with 22 percent of the votes. With respect to support for the NSDAP, districts like Ziegenhain, Marburg, and the town of Wolfhagen were above average, while Catholic regions like Fulda and Gelnhausen and places with Communist leanings like Schmalkalden and Hanau were clearly below the average. Then, in the July 1932 elections, the NSDAP became the strongest political power in the administrative region of Kassel, with almost 47 percent of the votes—in sixteen of twenty-eight electoral districts, it even managed to make it over the 50 percent mark. Admittedly, in the November election of the same year the Hessian NSDAP had to register a slight loss in votes, but with just over 45 percent it remained by far the strongest party. In the election of March 1933, the party then secured an absolute majority with 53 percent of the vote—something that it had hoped to accomplish in the Reich as a whole, but in vain.[54]

Schlüchtern

With over 300 persons, the Jewish population in Schlüchtern still comprised some 10 percent of the town's residents at the beginning of the 1930s. Most of them were tradespeople and merchants, many of whom were involved in livestock and textiles. The leather trader Jakob Hirsch Rothschild was a Liberal Democratic town representative for a decade prior to the First World War and even after that until 1924. As late as March 1933, the merchant Siegmund Neuhof was elected to the town representative assembly by virtue of the independent bourgeois list of candidates, but in August he was forced to leave the committee because of National Socialist pressure. And there was also the three-towered soap factory in Schlüchtern that belonged to the Wolf family, whose Sephardic roots in Hesse could be traced back to the seventeenth century. Even so, the Wolf family and their factory were repeatedly the target of anti-Semitic hatred on the part of the *völkisch* movement.[55]

Max Wolf was also the ombudsman for the local chapter of the C.V., which had existed since the First World War. At the beginning of the 1920s it had seventy-six members and developed a brisk activity.[56] Thus, for example, the syndic of the Frankfurt chapter, Dr. Marx, spoke in November 1926 about "the invisible swastika." And one month later his colleague, Schweriner, gave a lecture about "the serious and the cheerful in C.V. work" to more than 220 listeners that "captivated the audience and provided for a pleasant and successful meeting for the chapter."[57] It was the best meeting of the C.V. in Schlüchtern since its founding. Nonetheless, though the difference between Jews and non-Jews may at times have been invisible, by no means did it ever go away. When in 1907 the daughter of the soap factory owner Viktor Wolf wanted to become a member of the tennis club (a high-society association in Schlüchtern), she was informed that the club did not allow Jews. Her father grew so angry that he wrote a letter to the chairperson of the tennis club, a district court judge named Dr. Hengsberger. In the letter he accused Hengsberger of lying because the latter had earlier declared that he kept his distance from any sort of anti-Semitism, which was why Wolf had expressly supported Hengsberger's candidacy as a Reich representative. Thereupon Hengsberger filed a legal grievance for slander that was upheld in court because, according to the judges, one could very well disapprove of political anti-

Semitism but nonetheless oppose convivial togetherness with Jews in a social setting.[58]

In contrast to what people often like to say today, namely that prior to the assumption of power by the National Socialists in 1933 Jews and "Germans" (as if German Jews were not Germans) lived together in a peaceful and good-neighborly manner, this example reveals the ever-tangible boundary between Jews and non-Jews in Germany. Even those who publicly condemned anti-Semitism prevented the Jews from gaining equal access to cultural institutions, clubs, and associations in which social distinction was a fundamental principle. Among German students, the demand for the exclusion of Jewish fellow students was vehemently represented. The Deutsche Hochschulring (German University Circle), a collection of *völkisch* student associations, was the strongest political student association during the Weimar Republic, and it was expressly committed to "German *Volkstum*" and the "German *Volksgemeinschaft*." Jews could belong to neither since "Jewish kind [was] not German kind."[59] With respect to associations in the German provinces, Jacob Borut has also shown just how subtly yet inflexibly the dividing line was drawn vis-à-vis Jewish "neighbors."[60]

The local NSDAP chapter in Schlüchtern was founded relatively late in the early 1930s. Its founders included Heinrich Lecher, a postal inspector who would be the Ortsgruppenleiter for many years; Eckart Fritz, a textile engineer; and Georg Schöner, a teacher who would emerge as a propaganda speaker. The SA Sturm in Fulda also boasted about having played a decisive role in founding the NSDAP chapter in Schlüchtern.[61] The chapter's late founding, however, did not impede the electoral successes of the NSDAP in Schlüchtern. During the new election for the Reichstag in September 1930, the proportion of votes for the NSDAP increased sevenfold compared to 1928. Its portion of 19.2 percent was surpassed only by the Catholic Center Party (24.3 percent) and the SPD (21.9 percent).[62] In the Reichstag elections of March 1933 the National Socialists in Schlüchtern obtained 1,300 votes, thereby leaving the Social Democrats—who were in second place with 450 votes—far behind, along with all the other parties.[63] The NSDAP district leader Johannes Puh became the town's Bürgermeister. Right after the election, SA men burned the black-red-gold flag of the Weimar Republic during a public parade. Ortsgruppenleiter Lecher and the local leader of the German Nationals, the estate owner Richard Wegmann, gave victory speeches. House searches of Communists and Social Democrats had already occurred in February; and one month later, around twenty people were arrested and put in prison in Schwarzenfels.[64]

The hatred of the SA groups also erupted against the Jews. During the boycott of 1 April, conflict broke out with Jewish merchants who wanted to remove the boycott placards from their stores and were temporarily arrested.[65] And as if there was some kind of accumulated need for anti-Semitic expression, the National Socialist press in the summer of 1933 stated: "Because of its thorough Jewification and the proximity of the black [that is, Catholic—M.W.] district of Fulda, for a long time the Schlüchtern district was a political no-man's land." At a rally in April 1934 at the town gym in Schlüchtern, a Hamburg Gauschulungsleiter named Werner stirred up hatred: "I did not say that you should beat the Jews to death. If tomorrow it says in the newspaper that it has happened, then I cannot do anything about it anyway. I will drink a couple more glasses of apple wine."[66] The Gestapo, too, reinforced the anti-Semitic tone in its reports: "One cannot forget that, particularly in Electoral Hesse, Judaism has played a significant role for over 100 years and plundered the population in an exemplary fashion."[67]

Synagogues were badly damaged in Tann in the district of Fulda, Hüttengesäß in the regional district of Hanau, and in Melsungen and Korbach. In the Schlüchtern district, destruction was visited upon a Jewish cemetery. As early as February 1934, windows were smashed at night and shot at in Sterbfritz.[68] At the end of March the Darmstadt attorney Reis, acting on behalf of the C.V., turned to the state police in Hesse in order to warn them of excesses on the occasion of the Jewish Passover festival—probably, too, in light of the pogrom that had taken place a few days earlier in Gunzenhausen.[69] Reis reported on a series of communities in Upper Hesse: violence in Alsfeld; a reported explosion in Ortenberg; the breaking of windows in private Jewish homes, the destruction of a synagogue, and the erection of signs stating "We do not need any Jews" in Altenstedt, Gedern, Rohrbach, and Büdingen. In his letter Reis wrote that "the Jewish residents are of the opinion that they have tried to exercise the greatest possible restraint so that the actions of the perpetrators cannot be traced back to their behavior."[70]

In Schlüchtern, too, in April and May 1934, the windows of homes and businesses were shattered and, directly at the town entrance, a banner was strung over the road that led from the train station to the town center. On one side the banner stated, "The Jews are Germany's misfortune"; on the other, "Tell me whom you buy from, and I will tell you who you are."[71] In September 1934 a group led by the painter Ludwig Kohlenbusch, who had previously been the NSDAP Ortsgruppenleiter in Schlüchtern, forced the Jewish manufacturer Leo Stern on a march through the town because he allegedly had a relationship with a non-Jewish woman. Kohlenbusch had large signs made up for this procession that read: "This sow-Jew disgraced a Christian girl in the Hessischer Hof in Fulda." A witness deposition taken in 1947 states the following about this procession:

> During this action, Leo Stern was kicked in an inhumane manner, beaten, slapped, and so brutally abused that, because of such abuse, great upset and anger was demonstrated in all circles of the population in the town. It was a scandalous parade. At the fore, the HJ blew fanfares; then came Kohlen-busch, standing in a car, ordering "Halt!" in front of every Jewish house. There Stern had to turn so that the signs on his chest and back could be read. The youth glared, the streets were black with people.... Later one heard that, due to such severe abuse, Leo Stern became very ill and died soon thereafter.[72]

Two months later in Volkmarsen in the district of Wolfhagen, near Kassel, an Ortsgruppenleiter had a girl led through the streets with a sign around her neck because of an alleged relationship with a Jewish man.[73] The NSDAP's anti-Jewish propaganda in rural communities had become "livelier" again, reported the Kassel Gestapo in October 1934. At the en-trances to numerous communities and inns were signs that read: "No ac-cess for Jews!" and "Jews are not wanted here!" To be sure, the state police had previously always taken action against these signs, but recently they were being erected in such great number on village streets and at commu-nity entrances at the instigation of local NSDAP groups that the Gestapo was allowing the party groups to do so.[74] In December the Kassel state police complained that even though it had made its opposition unequivo-cally clear, local groups always continued to erect such signs. As a result, those communities and rural districts where such signs were frequently found were being held up as examples worth emulating. The authorities, who took action against them because of central directives, were then "often accused of friendliness toward Jews and an un–National Socialist attitude." Likewise, efforts to implement the Reich Economics Ministry's edicts against the boycott of Jewish businesses repeatedly faced difficulties as well. "Often for fear of the party," the local police authorities were "not sufficiently cracking down against excesses, like those in particular which had occurred before Christmas."[75]

Gelnhausen

Not far from Schlüchtern, and also within the administrative region of Kassel, lies Gelnhausen, a town that looks back on a long history. Holy Roman Emperor Frederick I von Hohenstaufen, named Barbarossa, constructed an imperial palace here at the end of the twelfth century.[76] And the Jewish community figures among the oldest in Germany. The mention of Jews in the city dates back as far as the early thirteenth century.[77]

Since the beginning of the twentieth century, many Jewish families had left Gelnhausen's Judengasse (Jewish Alley), as the street was called that led from the lower market to one of the town gates, and settled in other neighborhoods. Meanwhile, non-Jewish families had since moved into the Judengasse, which was consequently renamed Brentanostrasse in 1906. Nonetheless, the synagogue remained—it dated back to the seventeenth century and had been expanded and renovated a number of times since then. In May 1933, 162 Jewish people still lived in Gelnhausen; three years later there were still 130. But after that many Jews left the town—in March 1937, only 55 remained, and on 1 November 1938, a few days before the nationwide pogrom, the last Jewish family departed.[78]

Apart from the medical practitioner Dr. Max Schwarzschild, the dentist Dr. Leo Wisnia, and the legal attorney Dr. Elkan Sondheimer, the Gelnhausen Jews mostly operated businesses like the Max Stern department store, Arthur Meyer's colonial wholesale trade, the shoe stores of Betty Bergen, Leo Loeser, and Siegfried Strauss, and the automotive garage of Josef Blumenbach; they also worked as tradespeople, like the seamstress Selma Scheuer and the baker Simon Ullmann in the Langgasse. There were five Jewish livestock traders, a banking business belonging to the Lorsch brothers, and Marcus Linick's printing company and publishing house, which published an edition of the *Gelnhäuser Nachrichten* every fourteen days—until right after the National Socialists took power, when Linick was forced to transfer his newspaper by 1 April 1933 to a "Christian firm," as was stated in an advertisement by Marcus Linick in the last edition he supervised.[79]

Manfred Meyer, born in 1905 and one of three children of the wholesaler Arthur Meyer and his wife Gitella, recounted that his childhood had been carefree and lighthearted. Later in school, however, he and his fellow Jewish students were often abused and insulted in the street, "but we usually ignored it or ran away."[80] Gelnhausen was admittedly an administrative town "but had always been somewhat touched by anti-Semitism. Many were members of the German National Party and of the German Volk's Party. So there arose a certain societal anti-Semitism."[81] This anti-Semitism was indeed noticeable to the children as well, who as a rule were left to themselves and played with other Jewish children. Nonetheless, they also had other contact, like in the local soccer club. Arnold Hess was among the best players, as was Manfred Meyer's cousin Ernst, who played for the youth team. After finishing school, Manfred Meyer began an apprenticeship at a colonial goods wholesaler in Frankfurt, where he remained until the company was "Aryanized" in 1936. On Saturdays he drove home to spend the Sabbath with his parents—"particularly during the Hitler period I did not want to leave them alone. It was bad enough, living in Gelnhausen during this time. It is impossible for me to describe all of the misdeeds."[82]

As early as 1932, on the three Sundays before Christmas, SA and NSDAP members stood as boycott sentries in front of all the Jewish businesses to prevent customers from entering.[83] A few months later the NSDAP also issued an appeal in Gelnhausen to boycott all Jewish businesses, doctors, and lawyers starting 1 April 1933.[84] At ten o'clock sharp, according to the report in the *Gelnhäuser Tageblatt*, amidst the participation of "a large and curious crowd," SA and SS men took up sentry positions in front of the Jewish businesses, of which, however, only very few were open. Most of the Jewish merchants had closed their stores on this day in order to avoid confrontations.

The NSDAP particularly gave itself credit in Gelnhausen because this action had been carried out with absolute discipline:

> The great care taken by local party leadership to avoid incidents can be seen from the fact that it had company signs which were smeared up by provocateurs cleaned again. The local leadership of the NSDAP places value on the message that it naturally opposes such machinations and severely condemns them. The population is asked to notify police authorities of any kind of observations that might lead to the identification of perpetrators.[85]

But this by no means kept party members from taking violent action against Jews. Richard Scheuer was the brother of Heinrich Scheuer, who was the last director of the Jewish community in Gelnhausen. Looking back, Richard Scheuer described the town in the years 1934/35 as a "stronghold of strident anti-Semitism."[86]

As mentioned above, at the end of March 1934 a conference between the representatives of the Provincial Association for Jewish Welfare Services and Vocational Retraining and the board of the Israelite community was attacked when large stones were thrown through the windows of the conference room. In the night leading to 14 April, the widow Heilmann had three windows broken by thrown rocks. In his report for August and September 1934, the administrator of the district of Gelnhausen mentioned more broken windows and also threats against individual Jews. In one case it came to such "severe unrest in the population" that two Jews had to be taken into "protective custody."[87] At the end of October 1934 a large rally of the German Labor Front took place in Gelnhausen. During the rally, as reported by the local chapter of the C.V., the district administrator Löser from Hanau said that it would be a shame if Germans today were still to bring their money to the Jews, and such people should be punished with scorn. He said that if Jews had financial claims against a *Volksgenosse*, they should be shown the door and paid off in fifty-cent increments, for Jews came last.[88]

After the seizure of power, bullying and beatings were not uncommon. Richard Scheuer later remembered how in 1938 he and others had to carry the coffin of a deceased Gelnhausen Jewess through the streets because they were not allowed to use a hearse. "It was a party for the youth, who insulted the pallbearers and the few people who followed the coffin. Upon reaching the cemetery we said certain prayers for the dead according to ancient Jewish customs. The person assigned this task and the few congregational members had stones thrown at them from all sides."[89]

Just a few years earlier, one could still discern some patterns of behavior that opposed the radicalization of violence and adhered to the state's structural order. Thus in the Jewish cemetery in Altengronau in the district of Schlüchtern, on the morning of 1 May 1934, more than thirty gravestones were discovered to have been knocked over and partially demolished. According to the report by the Jewish cemetery association in Altengronau, the cemetery presented a sorry picture. In any event, the Gestapo appeared as early as the next day and together with the local police initiated an investigation. Within a very brief time, the perpetrators had been identified: four schoolchildren between the ages of seven and twelve who confessed to having done the deed on Sunday, 29 April. According to the Altengronau Jews, the parents of the children took responsibility for paying for the damages, and thus the grave markers were largely restored. The state attorney closed the proceedings against the boys, who were still juveniles.[90] Yet such cases—in which the police identified the perpetrators and the parents also took responsibility for the misdeeds of their children—appear only rarely in the files of the C.V. And they appear only during the early years of the NS regime.

Political Arena

Despite their conquest of the state's power apparatus, the dissolution of the parties, the *Gleichschaltung* of associations and the terror against the political opposition, and despite concentration camps, torture, and murder, the National Socialists faced the problem at the local level of establishing a permanent political hegemony. The production of the *Volksgemeinschaft* was the central task, particularly in the provinces—the villages and smaller communities. The persecution of the German Jews as *Volks-*

feinde, as "racial opponents of the German Volk" was simultaneously the most important method and an essential objective of National Socialist politics. It was a means by which racial boundaries could be drawn within local societies and by which the existing civil order could be radically transformed, and together with the expulsion of the Jews it enabled the localities themselves to become "Jew free." Therefore, the "politics of the *Volksgemeinschaft*" meant above all politics against the Jews.

The boycott actions opened up a political arena that offered many possibilities for radicalization. Naturally, intentionally interfering with a business operation was illegal, and in times of the constitutional state such attacks against commercial freedom could be countered—this is shown by the fact that the C.V. and Jewish merchants were able to obtain administrative decrees from the democratic state governments of the Weimar Republic and legal judgments from the courts.

But insofar as the NSDAP interpreted boycott actions as demonstrations—as free expressions of political opinion—it was already possible during the Weimar period to wield the boycott as a political and social weapon. These kinds of considerations fell away after the seizure of power. The legal restrictions were not actually lifted, but the institutions that were responsible for implementing them grew increasingly weaker and less willing to stand up for the normative state.

The Reich Economics Ministry saw the commercial freedom of Jewish businesses not from the perspective of protecting civil freedoms, but rather mostly from that of utility. As long as enterprises with Jewish proprietors were useful for the Volk's economy, it was desirable to condone them. The interests of the Gestapo and local police were directed in the first instance toward maintaining control and not toward propping up the constitutional state. The conflict faced by police in a situation where they were breaking up boycotts and decried as "servants of the Jews" was thereby preordained and—as will be more closely illustrated below—led to vehement pressure by police for legal measures that codified Jews as citizens with inferior rights.

The local NSDAP groups, whose leaders were often Bürgermeisters, quickly recognized the potential of boycott actions for shaping politics. Far more effective than mere demonstrations, boycotts could directly harm local Jewish families and socially isolate them. At the same time these actions made it possible to intimidate those *Volksgenossen* who, despite all threats, still shopped in Jewish businesses. The boycotts turned with all their hatred against Jewish businesspeople and against their non-Jewish customers.

The radicalization of the argumentation can be read in the Elbing NSDAP's leaflet of October 1934. First, it reminds readers of the "duty" that everyone has not only to their family but also to their Volk. Then it appeals to the "solidarity" that binds everyone to their German "brother," who was ruined not through his own fault but rather by the competing "Jewish" department stores, and who must be restored by one's shopping. And finally it threatens that everyone who still buys from a Jewish business is "stabbing" the *Volksgemeinschaft* in the back and thereby becomes a "traitor." Instead of economically rational behavior, which is indifferent to *völkisch* notions and whereby goods are purchased where they appear to be the least expensive, the leaflet called for a different morality, one that was supposed to align itself with the well-being of the *Volksgemeinschaft* and also, if necessary, demanded sacrifice. The cherished principle of "common good before self-interest," which in a certain sense represents the basic economic creed of the *Volksgemeinschaft*, always implies an antiliberal invective that targets economic rationality.

Last but not least, the boycott actions could be arbitrarily intensified and radicalized. Placards and banners could be supplemented with sentries placed in front of businesses, which considerably heightened the deterrence of customers. Additionally, the sentries could photograph the customers or use violence to prevent them from entering the stores. At night the display windows could be pasted over, smeared up, and later smashed, and finally homes and their owners could be violently assaulted.

Jewish proprietors attempted to react to the increasing threat and intensified danger with courage and self-assertion. The decision to close a store when SA or HJ stood as sentries out front was obviously difficult, even if customers could no longer be expected that day. Together with the C.V., they intervened with Bürgermeisters, district administrators, the Reich Economics Ministry, and even the Gestapo in order to protest against the attack on commercial freedoms that were guaranteed by the Reich regime. But success was minimal—the ministry in Berlin was much too far away and its power was too exclusively dependent on the executive organs of the police and municipal authorities for such intervention to have ever been effective.

For the local chapters of the NSDAP, the persecution of Jewish political opponents, the boycott of Jewish businesses, and the denunciation of so-called *Rasseschandefälle* (cases of racial defilement) offered promising political fields in which to make practical the policies of the *Volksgemeinschaft* at the local level. In the same way that violent actions were inseparable from National Socialist politics prior to 1933 in order to intimidate political opponents and literally demonstrate corporal strength, such actions continued to be part of politics after the seizure of power. Violence did not merely represent a means or an instrument that, after the conquest of state power, would be relinquished in favor of available statist means of coercion, like the police and the judiciary. National Socialist politics was violence, it operated through violence, and it was through violence that these politics found expression.

Notes

1. C.V. Hanover to District President Hanover, 23 September 1935, Special Archive Moscow, 721-1-2338, fol. 108.
2. Peter Puschendorf, "Sandersleben," in *Wegweiser durch das jüdische Sachsen-Anhalt*, ed. Jutta Dick and Marina Sassenberg (Potsdam, 1998), 174–180.
3. Adolf Adler to C.V. Berlin, 9 July 1934, Special Archive Moscow, 721-1-2397, fol. 104f. In 1931, the Adler family moved from Hettstedt to Sandersleben, where the father had purchased the fabric and menswear store from Salomon Goldstein. Adolf Adler, born in 1908, was active in the Sandersleben chapter of the Reichsbanner Schwarz-Rot-Gold until 1933 as a secretary and in the chapter of the Workers-Samaritan Association as a treasurer. He thus had already caught the eye of local police as a "Marxist agitator." Bernd G. Ulrich, *Nationalsozialismus und Antisemitismus in Anhalt: Skizzen zu den Jahren 1932 bis 1942* (Dessau, 2005), 32.
4. C.V. regional association of central Germany to Berlin headquarters, 19 July 1934, Special Archive Moscow, 721-1-2397, fol. 76.
5. A newspaper clipping with this advertisement from *Sandersleutener Zeitung* dated 7 July 1934 is included in the file: Special Archive Moscow, 721-1-2397, fol. 106.
6. C.V. Berlin to Reich Economics Ministry and to the Gestapo Dessau, both dated 11 July 1934, Special Archive Moscow, 721-1-2397, fol. 97f. Hans Reichmann sent copies of both letters, together with a letter that described the actions undertaken by the C.V., to Adolf Adler.
7. C.V. regional association of central Germany to Berlin headquarters, 9 August and 27 August 1934, Special Archive Moscow, 721-1-2397, fol. 73f.
8. Ulrich, *Nationalsozialismus und Antisemitismus*, 34.
9. Ibid., 35
10. Nolzen makes a similar argument. Nolzen, "The Nazi Party and Its Violence against Jews," 256.
11. Henry Wassermann and Eckhart G. Franz, "'Kauft nicht beim Juden': Der politische Antisemitismus des späten 19. Jahrhunderts," in *Juden als Darmstädter Bürger*, ed. Eckhart G. Franz (Darmstadt, 1984), 123–136.
12. Sibylle Morgenthaler, "Countering the Pre-1933 Nazi Boycott against Jews," *Leo Baeck Institute Year Book* 36 (1991): 127–149.
13. Quoted in CVZ, 19 January 1933.
14. Quoted in Morgenthaler, "Countering the Pre-1933 Nazi Boycott against Jews," 130.
15. Ibid., 133.
16. *Völkischer Beobachter*, 30 November 1928, cited in Heinrich Uhlig, *Die Warenhäuser im Dritten Reich* (Cologne, 1956), 35.
17. C.V. central administration to all regional associations, officers, and local chapters of the C.V., 10 December 1930, printed in Paucker, *Jüdische Abwehrkampf*, 196.
18. C.V. Berlin, signed by Dr. Ludwig Holländer, to all regional associations and officers of the C.V., 11 December 1931, CAHJP, HM2/8714, fol. 1795 (Special Archive Moscow, 721-1-887).

19. Uhlig, *Die Warenhäuser im Dritten Reich*, 37; Morgenthaler, "Countering the Pre-1933 Nazi Boycott against Jews," 134. Peter Longerich concludes that the NSDAP party newspapers seized on anti-Jewish themes with renewed vigor around the New Year of 1932/33. Longerich, *"Davon haben wir nichts gewusst!"* 59.
20. Leaflet from the NSDAP, Elbing, 10 October 1932, appendix to a letter by the C.V., regional association East Prussia to Berlin headquarters, 14 December 1932, CAHJP, HM2/ 8768, fol. 1991 (Special Archive Moscow, 721-1-2549).
21. Quoted in C.V. regional association East Prussia to Berlin headquarters, 21 December 1932, CAHJP, HM2/8768, fol. 1979 (Special Archive Moscow, 721-1-2549). Sabatzky noted in his letter that because of the attitude of the Riesenburg town administration, this resolution had no practical consequences.
22. Kurt Sabatzky, Masuren, CVZ, 15 April 1932.
23. Morgenthaler, "Countering the Pre-1933 Nazi Boycott against Jews," 134f.
24. Ibid., 135.
25. See Udo Beer, *Die Juden, das Recht und die Republik: Verbandswesen und Rechtsschutz 1919–1933* (Frankfurt am Main, 1986), 74–77.
26. Schüler-Springorum, *Die jüdische Minderheit*, 287. However, in an investigation of 321 court rulings regarding boycott cases, Donald Niewyk came to the conclusion that only 32 judgments, most of them in East Prussia, Bavaria, and Lower Silesia, could be characterized as "too lenient." Morgenthaler, "Countering the Pre-1933 Nazi Boycott against Jews," 145f.
27. Antrag auf Erlaß einer einstweiligen Verfügung, 16 December 1932; Beschluß des Landgerichts Beuthen, 17 December 1932; Urteil des Landgerichts Beuthen, 10 January 1933, CAHJP, HM2/8766, fols. 710–715, 728–736 (Special Archive Moscow, 721-1-2472).
28. Urteil Landgericht Danzig, 15 March 1932, CAHJP, HM2/8766, fols. 222–231 (Special Archive Moscow, 721-1-2457).
29. C.V. regional association central Germany to Berlin headquarters, 6 July 1933, Special Archive, Moscow, 7221-1-261, fols. 266–270.
30. C.V. regional association Pomerania to Berlin headquarters, Berlin, 26 October 1933, CAHJP, HM2/ 8797, fols. 1027–1030 (Special Archive Moscow, 721-1-3019).
31. Nolzen, "The Nazi Party and Its Violence against Jews," 256.
32. Kassel Gestapo to Berlin Gestapo, 16 April 1934, printed in Thomas Klein, ed., *Die Lageberichte der Geheimen Staatspolizei über die Provinz Hessen-Nassau 1933–1936* (Cologne, 1986), vol. 1, 80f.
33. Klaus Behnken, ed., *Deutschlandberichte der Sozialdemokratischen Partei Deutschland (Sopade) 1934 bis 1940*, reprint (Frankfurt am Main, 1980), April/Mai 1934, 46–48; on the creation and editing of the reports, see Longerich, *"Davon haben wir nichts gewusst!"* 28–32.
34. Behnken, *Deutschlandberichte*, April/Mai 1934, 33f.; see Ludwig Eiber, *Arbeiter unter der NS-Herrschaft: Textil- und Porzellanarbeiter im nordöstlichen Oberfranken 1933–1939* (Munich, 1979), 95–98. A table representing gross workers' earnings in the German Reich from 1918 to 1944 can be found in Tilla Siegel, "Lohnpolitik im nationalsozialistischen Deutschland," in *Angst, Belohnung, Zucht und Ordnung: Herrschaftsmechanismen im Nationalsozialismus*, ed. Carola Sachse et al. (Opladen, 1982), 104.
35. See Broszat, *Staat Hitlers*, 204.
36. Behnken, *Deutschlandberichte*, April/Mai 1934, 53.
37. Kassel Gestapo report dated April 1934, 4 May 1934, in Klein, *Lageberichte der Geheimen Staatspolizei*, vol. 1, 89, 07f.
38. Behnken, *Deutschlandberichte*, April/Mai 1934, 54–58.

39. Kassel Gestapo report dated April 1934, 1 June 1934, in Klein, *Lageberichte der Geheimen Staatspolizei*, vol. 1, 102; more generally see Frank Bajohr, *Parvenüs und Profiteure: Korruption in der NS-Zeit* (Frankfurt am Main, 2001).

40. See Kershaw, *Hitler*, vol. 1, 627–662; on the reaction to the murders within the populace, see Kershaw, *Der Hitler-Mythos*, 109–121.

41. Quoted in Kershaw, *Der Hitler-Mythos*, 111.

42. Kassel Gestapo report dated April 1934, 4 August 1934, in Klein, *Lageberichte der Geheimen Staatspolizei*, vol. 1, 126.

43. Behnken, *Deutschlandberichte*, Juni/Juli 1934, 197.

44. Longerich, *"Davon haben wir nichts gewusst!"* 76f.; Nolzen, "The Nazi Party and Its Violence against Jews," 257.

45. Quoted in the *Völkischer Beobachter*, 13–14 May 1934, 1.

46. Longerich, *"Davon haben wir nichts gewusst!"* 257.

47. Kassel Gestapo report for April 1934, 4 May 1934, in Klein, *Lageberichte der Geheimen Staatspolizei*, vol. 1, 88.

48. Kassel Gestapo report for May 1934, 1 June 1934, in Klein, *Lageberichte der Geheimen Staatspolizei*, vol. 1, 111. In mid August the NSDAP party headquarters issued a declaration that prohibited all party members from representing Jews in any respect, speaking for Jews at state offices or other places, receiving party donations from Jews, issuing them permits of any kind, or associating with them in public or in establishments. StdF, decree dated 16 August 1934, signed Heß, in Institut für Zeitgeschichte, *Akten der Partei-Kanzlei der NSDAP*, part I, microfiche no. 101 07626f.

49. Kassel Gestapo report for May 1934, 1 June 1934, in Klein, *Lageberichte der Geheimen Staatspolizei*, vol. 1, 111.

50. Thomas Klein, ed., *Der Regierungsbezirk Kassel 1933–1936: Die Berichte des Regierungspräsidenten und der Landräte* (Darmstadt, 1985), vol. 1, xxiv.

51. Ibid., xxiii.

52. Ibid., xxiiif.

53. Around the turn of the century, Hesse was under the sphere of influence of Otto Böckel (1859–1923), a folk song collector with a doctorate in German studies and one of the most successful anti-Semitic agitators of the Kaiserreich. In 1887 in the electoral district of Marburg-Kirchhain-Frankenberg-Vöhl, he managed to win himself a position as a Reichstag representative. To be sure, Böckel's political star later fell, but as late as 1912 an anti-Semitic candidate from the German Social Party won a seat in the electoral district of Marburg. See Hansjörg Pötzsch, *Antisemitismus in der Region: Antisemitische Erscheinungsformen in Sachsen, Hessen, Hessen-Nassau und Braunschweig 1870–1914* (Wiesbaden, 2000), in particular 199–213.

54. Election results in Klein, *Regierungsbezirk Kassel*, vol. 1, cxvi.

55. On the history of the Jews in Schlüchtern, see Paul Arnsberg, *Die jüdischen Gemeinden in Hessen: Anfang, Untergang, Neubeginn*, 2 vols. (Frankfurt am Main, 1971), vol. 2, 273–279; Lucia Krucker, "Zur Geschichte der Jüdischen Gemeinde in Schlüchtern." *Unsere Heimat* 4 (1988): 31–68.

56. C.V. regional association Hesse to Berlin headquarters, 30 May 1920, CAHJP, HM2/8722, fol. 1845 (Special Archive Moscow, 721-1-1342).

57. C.V. regional association Hesse to Berlin headquarters, 20 December 1926, CAHJP, HM2/8722, fol. 1796 (Special Archive Moscow, 721-1-1342).

58. Mitteilungen aus dem Verein zur Abwehr des Antisemitismus, 27 November 1907; *Allgemeine Zeitung des Judentums*, 3 January 1908, Yad Vashem Archives, Pinkas Kehillot Schlüchtern.

59. Quoted in Michael H. Kater, *Studentenschaft und Rechtsradikalismus in Deutschland 1918–1933: Eine sozialgeschichtliche Studie zur Bildungskrise in der Weimarer Republik* (Hamburg, 1975), 22.
60. Borut, "'Bin Ich doch ein Israelit,'"; see also Menahem Kaufman, "The Daily Life of the Village and Country Jews in Hessen from Hitler's Ascent to Power to November 1938," *Yad Vashem Studies* 22 (1992): 147–198.
61. Klaus Schönekäs, "'Christenkreuz über Hakenkreuz und Sowjetstern': Die NSDAP im Raum Fulda," in *Hessen unterm Hakenkreuz: Studien zur Durchsetzung der NSDAP in Hessen*, ed. Eike Henning et al. (Frankfurt am Main, 1983), 135.
62. The German Nationals (5.3 percent), the Communists (6.1 percent) and the Landvolkpartei (9.9 percent) had already been left far behind and defeated. Hans Möller, *Geschichte und Geschichten aus Schlüchtern: Ausschnitte aus 1250 Jahre Stadtgeschichte* (Hanau, 1994), 121.
63. Christine Wittrock, *Das Unrecht geht einher mit sicherem Schritt Notizen über den Nationalsozialismus in Langensebold und Schlüchtern* (Hanau,1999), 78. The Battle Front (Kampffront) Black-White-Red received 146 votes, the Center Party 121 votes; the Deutsche Staatspartei 96 votes; the KPD 78 votes, and the DVP 69 votes.
64. Wittrock, *Das Unrecht geht einher mit sicherem Schritt*, 79; Möller, *Geschichte und Geschichten aus Schlüchtern*, 121.
65. Krucker, "Zur Geschichte der Jüdischen Gemeinde in Schlüchtern," 42.
66. Quoted in ibid., 43.
67. Kassel Gestapo report for April 1934, 4 May 1934, in Klein, *Lageberichte der Geheimen Staatspolizei*, vol. 1, 88.
68. C.V. regional association Hesse to Berlin headquarters, 17 May 1934, CAHJP, HM2/8808, fols. 680–683 (Special Archive Moscow, 721-1-3182); Kassel Gestapo report for April 1934, 4 May 1934, in Klein, *Lageberichte der Geheimen Staatspolizei*, vol. 1, 88.
69. On Palm Sunday, 26 March 1934 in Gunzenhausen in Franconia, the local SA leader Kurt Bär gave an inflammatory anti-Semitic speech, whereupon a number of Gunzenhausen residents went to the homes of their Jewish neighbors and with brutal violence dragged thirty people to prison, where they were seriously abused. In the process, two Jewish residents died. During the next weeks the anti-Semitic mood in Gunzenhausen remained so virulent that the police reinforcements that had been deployed could only be recalled at the beginning of May. In July 1934 Kurt Bär, who had been found guilty of breaching the peace by the district court in Ansbach, shot down the Jewish innkeeper Strauss and his son, evidently for revenge. Soon thereafter Strauss died of his injuries. See Kershaw, "Antisemitismus," 295f.
70. Reis to the Hessian Gestapo, Darmstadt, 29 March 1934, CAHJP, HM2/8796, fol. 1072f. (Special Archive Moscow, 721-1-3002).
71. C.V. regional association Hesse to headquarters in Berlin, 17 May 1934, CAHJP, HM2/8808, fol. 680f.
72. Quoted in Wittrock, *Das Unrecht geht einher mit sicherem Schritt*, 88.
73. Kassel Gestapo report for November 1934, 5 December 1934, in Klein, *Lageberichte der Geheimen Staatspolizei*, vol. 1, 196.
74. Kassel Gestapo report for October 1934, 5 November 1934, in ibid., vol. 1, 196.
75. Kassel Gestapo report for December 1934, 5 January 1935, in ibid., vol. 1, 211.
76. Karl Schreiber, "800 Jahre Stadtrechte Gelnhausen," in *Gelnhausen, die Barbarossastadt: 800 Jahre Stadtrechte*, published for the Stadtverwaltung Gelnhausen (Bad Homburg, 1970), 47–54.

77. Although the Jews were under the protection of the captain of the Barbarossa castle, they were victims of Jewish persecutions during the year of the plague in 1348. All the Gelnhausen Jews were rounded up and publicly burnt in front of the town. Arnsberg, *Die jüdischen Gemeinden in Hessen*, 240.

78. "Hauptdaten zur Geschichte der israelitischen Kultusgemeinde," in *Festschrift Ehemalige Synagoge Gelnhausen*, ed. the Magistrat der Barbarossastadt Gelnhausen, comp. the Geschichtsverein Gelnhausen (Gelnhausen, 1986), 108.

79. Elfriede Kaiser, "Handel und Gewerbe bei den Gelnhäuser Juden," in *Festschrift Ehemalige Synagoge Gelnhausen*, 67–74.

80. Manfred Meyer, "Jüdisches Leben in Gelnhausen," in *Gelnhäuser Heimat-Jahrbuch: Jahreskalender für Familie und Heim in Stadt und Land zwischen Vogelsberg und Spessart* (n.p., 1988), 63.

81. Ibid.

82. Ibid., 65. Arnold Hess was murdered together with his whole family—wife and children. Ernst Meyer managed to escape, but his parents were killed in the death camps.

83. Richard Scheuer, "Das Ende der israelitischen Kultusgemeinde in der ehemals freien Reichsstadt Gelnhausen," in *Festschrift Ehemalige Synagoge Gelnhausen*, 75–82.

84. The corresponding appeal in the *Gelnhäuser Tageblatt* is printed as a facsimile in *Zur Geschichte der Juden in Gelnhausen während der nationalsozialistischen Vergangenheit: Ein Stadtrundgang*, ed. the Gelnhäuser Historischen Gesellschaft e.V. (Gelnhausen, 1996), 7.

85. Quoted in ibid., 9.

86. Scheuer, "Das Ende der israelitischen Kultusgemeinde," 77.

87. Report of the administrator of the district of Gelnhausen, 29 August 1934 and 29 September 1934, in Klein, *Lageberichte der Geheimen Staatspolizei*, vol. 1, 196.

88. C.V. regional association of Hesse to Berlin headquarters, 12 November 1834, Special Archive Moscow, 721-1-2345, fol. 72.

89. C.V. regional association of Hesse to Berlin headquarters, 12 November 1934, Special Archive Moscow, 721-1-2345, fol. 72.

90. C.V. regional association of Hesse to Berlin headquarters, 2, 5, and 15 May 1934, CAHJP, HM2/8808, fols. 688, 693, 695 (Special Archive Moscow, 721-1-3182).

5

The Crowd as an Actor

The year 1935 began with a success in foreign policy for the NS regime. The Treaty of Versailles had stipulated that the people in the Saarland—which was under the administration of the League of Nations but was in fact economically integrated with France—were to decide fifteen years after the treaty settlement whether they were to rejoin the German Reich, belong to France, or maintain the status quo. Hitler's opponents tried to turn the plebiscite into a vote against the NS regime—and they suffered a bitter defeat. Ninety-one percent of the Saarlanders voted on 13 January for reunification with Germany.[1] "The mood of the population was influenced in the best of ways by the overwhelming result," noted the Kassel state police in its interpretation of the outcome. "General confidence has grown and become firm because of the continued developments in domestic and foreign policies. Participation at the festivities on 30 January was generally very lively. All in all one can speak of an improvement in attitude."[2]

Hitler used the political success of the Saarland plebiscite for a decisive step. On 16 March he announced to foreign ambassadors that, in violation of its commitment in the Treaty of Versailles, Germany would reintroduce general military service and increase the strength of the armed forces fivefold to over 500,000 men.[3] Hitler's visit the next day in Munich turned into a triumphant procession. "All of Munich is on its feet," wrote a Social Democratic observer. "One can force a Volk to sing, but one cannot force it to sing with such enthusiasm. I have experienced the days of 1914 and can only say that the declaration of war did not make the same impression on me as did the reception of Hitler on 17 March."[4]

Naturally, the Saarland plebiscite also made an impression on German Jews. All those who had hoped for the victory of Hitler's opponents reacted with dismay. Others believed—with the support of the C.V., no less, which had appealed to the Saarland Jews not to emigrate but to integrate themselves "into the *Gemeinschaft* of German Jews"[5]—that they could demonstrate their membership in the *Volksgemeinschaft* with a public display of German nationalism. The situation reports by the Gestapo and district presidents indicated lively meetings of Jewish associations for the first weeks of 1935. Within the German nationalist Imperial Association of Jewish Frontline Soldiers (Reichsbund jüdischer Frontsoldaten), Hitler's announcement of the implementation of general military service even encouraged members (particularly former officers) to voluntarily make themselves available to the Wehrmacht.[6] Apparently many German Jews—like their non-Jewish neighbors—had also hung black-white-red flags from their windows. Thereupon the Gestapo head office in Berlin declared a flag prohibition, for "according to National Socialist principles, Jews do not count as part of the German *Volksgemeinschaft*" and they were therefore not allowed to display black-white-red flags. All Gestapo agencies in the Reich were informed accordingly.[7]

The flag prohibition shocked those affected. The Düsseldorf Gestapo reported that the Gestapo decree had "caused great dismay in Jewish circles. They cannot understand in these circles that Jewish war veterans, officers, etc. are even being prohibited from raising the black-white-red flag."[8] In Stettin a Jewish merchant was taken into "protective custody" because, according to the Gestapo, he "was being threatened by an excited crowd for displaying a black-white-red flag."[9] The flag decree, according to the Königsberg Gestapo, has "made a very special impression on the Jews. They see with renewed clarity that they are not viewed as belonging to the German *Volksgemeinschaft*."[10]

But the regime's victories in foreign policy could not hide the continuing economic difficulties and the population's unsatisfactory material living conditions. There still were high unemployment and low wages, a steep increase in the cost of living on the one hand and constrictions in the provision of foodstuffs on the other.[11] For these months, the *Deutschland-Berichte* by the exiled SPD make mention of indifference and dissatisfaction. In addition to the economic difficulties there were

two big mass-psychological operations by the regime that provided relief: the Saarland plebiscite and the introduction of general military duty. Not that the delirium of nationalistic enthusiasm, which was evoked by these two operations, had a lasting effect. The enthusiasm in both instances quickly gave way to renewed disillusionment. But what remained was a basic pessimistic feeling: Hitler is indeed successful at everything; he pushes through whatever he wants.[12]

Discord prevailed within the SA as well, for after the bloody purge of the SA leadership in June 1934 the organization's significance steeply declined and expectations for a "second revolution" were disappointed.[13] As stated in an SA report from the end of 1934, after the Saarland plebiscite expectations increased that "the drive against Jews, political Catholicism and first and foremost the masters of the economy will begin."[14] The Cologne Gestapo reported in January 1935:

> In a few small circles of strongly revolutionary National Socialists, whom one can also predominantly describe as constantly dissatisfied, the idea was floating around that the second revolution they were longing for would come after 01/13/1935. What was supposed to happen was paraphrased with the words "night of long knives," "Bartholomew's Day Massacre," and "Reich week of murder." Even in larger SA circles, there was the notion that the order would now be given.[15]

The dissatisfaction of middle-class NS activists and the SA provided an essential driving force for the resumption of anti-Jewish actions at the beginning of 1935. In a circular on 19 February to the party organization, Rudolf Heß himself criticized the increasing bureaucratization within the party and called for a "living frontline spirit," which local chapters could only understand as an appeal for more activity.[16] At the beginning of May, the Rhineland Gauleiter Grohé blatantly wrote that "clearer propaganda against shopping in Jewish stores will not only correspond with our basic principles, but it will also relieve the somewhat depressed mood in middle-class circles."[17]

Complaints that German "Volksgenossen," bureaucrats and even NSDAP members were still shopping in Jewish stores can be found throughout the situation reports by the Gestapo, district presidents, and district administrators. According to the state police in rural areas, even the livestock trade remained in Jewish hands. Farmers concluded transactions with Jewish livestock traders because they paid higher prices and non-Jewish traders had neither the personnel nor the organizations to enable them to replace the Jewish traders.[18] The report by the Cologne Gestapo for March 1935 stated:

The boycott measures against department stores and Jewish businesses that are currently being demanded by the party once more, on the one hand, and the propagation of retail trade, on the other hand, by no means had the attention or success that one had expected of them. One discovers repeatedly that the bourgeois and the person of little means prefers to find a department store and also does not inquire as to whether he is shopping at a Jewish or Christian company. People apparently want to shop at those places where they believe they will get the best price. This position emerges clearly, particularly from conversations among women in both these and worker's circles.[19]

And in April the Trier Gestapo noticed:

Members of the movement attempted to boycott the Jewish business people. In the reported month, the display windows and doors of a number of Jewish stores and also the sidewalks in front of these [stores] were painted with inscriptions [like] "Jew," etc. in oil paint. This kind of propaganda is extremely ineffective. The larger part of the public barely takes notice of it. The fact that Christian employees of these Jewish businesses must remove such paint repeatedly gives rise to an especially ill humor.[20]

The party and the state had apparently not advanced very far in one of the most important areas of National Socialist politics, namely the anti-Semitic orientation of German society. There were even examples of admirable moral courage. In Hildesheim, for example, it had become customary to make public the names of familiar citizens who shopped in Jewish businesses at meetings of the party and its organizations. When the city museum director Dr. Schöndorf was confronted, he defended himself, saying that as long as his superiors did not expressly prohibit him, he was free to shop in Jewish stores. Also named was Lieutenant Colonel (retired) Niemann, who despite public attacks continued to maintain his relationships with Jews.[21] In Bückeburg in Westphalia, the wife and daughter of Bürgermeister Wiehe, who was also a former German National representative in the state parliament, were observed in the Weihl department store, which belonged to a Jewish businessman. Thereupon an article appeared in the Schaumburg-Lippische Landeszeitung under the headline "Provocation," in which the family was insulted. This in turn led Bürgermeister Wiehe to file charges against the newspaper's editor. In June, Frau Wiehe was once again denounced in the newspaper for shopping at a Jewish business. And on the same day a procession of demonstrators formed in the town carrying placards that stated: "Who buys from Jews? The Bürgermeister!" and "Must I then go out to town?" (Muß I denn zum Städele hinaus—a German folksong). According to the report by the Bückeburg Gestapo, the procession moved through the street while singing. Now and then a single voice called out: "Who buys from Jews?" whereupon the crowd responded in unison: "The Bürgermeister! Fie!" The procession of demonstrators stopped in front of the Bürgermeister's residence and shouted out its denunciating slogans. After marching a little further, the procession dissolved; but naturally this action was the talk of the town and so discomfited the place that the next day the Bürgermeister was placed on leave effective immediately by the administrator of the Bückeburg district.[22]

Hans Mommsen and Dieter Obst have still maintained that the actions during 1935 were "more compensatory operations as opposed to ideologically consistent behavior,"[23] but the incident shows otherwise. Rather, they were directly intended to resume the offensive in anti-Semitic politics, to carry out the social isolation of the German Jews and above all to destroy whatever contact still remained between the non-Jewish and Jewish populations. Peter Longerich rightly maintains that, after successfully driving the Jews from public service in 1933/34, it was now a matter of segregating the Jewish minority as completely as possible.[24]

Gelnhausen

The vigorous anti-Jewish excesses of the year 1935 did not begin first in early summer; nor did they predominantly take place in the large cities.[25] Manfred Meyer, the son of the merchant Arthur Meyer, was a young man almost thirty years old at that time. In a report fifty years later he recalled a violent action in Gelnhausen in Hesse in January 1935, one that he had vividly preserved in his memory.

> Almost every evening, the window panes in our house, Barbarossastrasse 6, were broken. So one day my parents furnished the outside of the windows with a wooden screen. This worked well for weeks and months. One Friday afternoon, the Nazi Gauleiter Sprenger drove along Barbarossastrasse and asked what was the meaning of the boards in front of the windows. He then was told: "Jewish people live here, and every night the windows were broken." One Friday evening, as we men were in the synagogue, a police officer thereupon advised my mother to remove the boards. My mother told him, it was Saturday, the men are in the synagogue, he could come back again at around 9 o'clock. Truth be told, this police officer actually spoke to my father again around 9 o'clock. My father explained to him that we were strictly orthodox and did not do any kind of work on Saturdays, but he promised when Saturday had passed, at quarter past eight, the next minute the boards would be removed, as desired. The police officer reckoned

that he could only warn us. After that, my brother and I heard noise on the street. Mostly adolescents and pre-adolescents were ranting and screaming that they would come back again in an hour; if the boards had not been removed, they would come into our house and remove them themselves.[26] … Thus I said to my brother: "We cannot allow that this mob forces its way into our house and even takes our father into custody." Even if our religion forbids work on a Saturday, in this case we had to obey the order of the horde. So my brother Robert and I removed the wooden screens.[27]

The contemporary written records provided by the C.V. files, which agree with Meyer's portrayal, do not confirm whether there really was a police officer who warned the Meyer family. But even if we presume that it was important for Manfred Meyer to anchor a "good German" in this story, the story loses none of its expressive force, for otherwise the family's isolation, its existential abandonment, would hardly be bearable.[28]

This incident led the board of the C.V. in Gelnhausen to speak to the Bürgermeister. But even though he agreed to identify the perpetrators,[29] the incidents continued. The shoe merchant Siegfried Strauss in the Langgasse also had his windows smashed. At the beginning of February an apparent provocateur tried to get at least three Jewish merchants to sell him merchandise after business hours. Thereupon a detailed article appeared in the Gelnhäuser Anzeiger on 7 February about "the nocturnal dealings of Jewish business people" and how "the Jew" cannot be bothered with the laws regarding business hours:

True to his Talmud, he rather avoids them where he can and defrauds his hosts. In Gelnhausen we have by lucky chance received three examples of this on the editorial desk. Since, understandably, Jewish businesses are being increasingly avoided, a number of Jews are taking to selling their wares after the onset of darkness. They reckon thereby with a throng of those sad elements that are always prepared to betray the interests of their Volk…. In our opinion, there is no longer any room in our state for these kinds of business people and business practices. Anyone who is such an unreliable guest that he does not even honor our laws must be banned. Businesses that only live by violating the law no longer have the right to exist. Moreover, we are of the conviction that the German business people in Gelnhausen are in a position to thoroughly meet the entire needs of the population by seven o'clock in the evening.[30]

On the very same evening a group of people gathered in front of the stores of Keip and Strauß in the Langgasse; they made a loud fuss, shouted, and kicked the closed shutters. During the night, Strauß was assaulted and beaten so badly that his wounds required stitches.[31] Two days later another anti-Semitic article appeared in the *Gelnhäuser Anzeiger* in which Max Moritz was attacked by name. Subsequently on the same evening, a crowd of people broke through the door of Moritz's residence in the Langgasse, forced its way into the home, cut the electric cable, destroyed furniture, and threatened to come again in an hour. As stated in the C.V. report, Max Moritz's family was deathly afraid, particularly since a four-year-old child lay sick in bed. Indeed, the crowd returned and continued being boisterous until Moritz was taken into "protective custody" in the early morning.[32]

These same events read quite differently in the report by the district administrator of Gelnhausen, who allows the perpetrators' perspective—written into these state reports—to become apparent:

> In recent times, a number of Jewish residents have evoked indignation in the German population because of their provocative behavior. Thus on the evening of 9 February 35 a number of people gathered in front of the house of the merchant Moritz on the Langgasse in Gelnhausen and demanded the proper payment of employees by Moritz. These and other irregularities of the aforementioned Jew had been denounced in publications of the press and had caused agitation in the population. In order to restore public peace and order and to protect his own person, Moritz was taken into preventative detention and the released again the next day.... Criminal complaints had to be filed with the senior prosecutor against three Jewish merchants because the persons concerned employed their personnel beyond the stipulated work period and, respectively, did not comply with business hours.[33]

Thereupon Dr. Matzdorff from the Kassel C.V. established contact with the state police agency in Kassel. In a conversation, the Gestapo spokesman, Hütteroth, D. Jur.—an "exemplar of the dashing SS lawyer" (Thomas Klein)—offered assurances that violations of the penal code would under no circumstances be tolerated and that Gestapo agents were currently en route to a number of different places in order to, as Hütteroth put it, make things right.[34] But only ten days after this discussion, Matzdorff reported to the Kassel Gestapo that nocturnal attacks in Gelnhausen had taken place again. Julius Strauß was on his way to the train station to pick up his wife when he was attacked and hit on the head with a club; David Heß fled from his pursuers into a house and from there informed the police, who then brought him home; likewise Alfred Buxbaum, coming home from the train station, had to seek refuge in a house and allow himself to be escorted home by a police officer.[35] Also in the nights that followed, the number of attacks in which windows were broken and stores were damaged did not decline.[36]

In March 1935, after the medical practitioner Dr. Schwarzschild likewise had a number of windows smashed with large stones, he decided to file a complaint against persons unknown with the state attorney's office in Hanau: "Considering the fact that for about a half a year hardly a week goes by without windows being broken or other property damaged on houses which belong to Jews or are lived in by Jews, to my knowledge without the perpetrators being investigated or punished, I urgently request that the investigation be carried out."[37] But hopes for state protection and justice were in vain, for soon thereafter Schwarzschild received notice from the Hanau state attorney that the perpetrators were unknown and that the investigation had therefore been closed. At the end of April, his wife was attacked by five people while taking a walk through town, although fortunately she was able to flee with her companion into a car that just happened to be passing by. This time Schwarzschild did not bother filing another complaint, even though the perpetrators were known.[38]

In June Schwarzschild addressed a petition to both the district president and the state police agency in Kassel. He reported that while on his way to deliver a baby one night, he was attacked and beaten by two young men. On his return home he was escorted by the father and brother of the new mother, which was why the young men, who were apparently lying in wait, did not launch another attack. "The Jewish residents here feel completely without protection; hardly anyone still dares to leave the house after the onset of dusk."[39] The Gelnhausen Bürgermeister, whom Schwarzschild had already visited twice, declared that the police force was not in a position to stop the excesses or to identify the perpetrators, even though Schwarzschild had recognized one of the thugs as a Jungvolk leader named Heinz Schmidt. "I have been practicing medicine here for over thirty years, was in the war for four years, and now it has reached the point where I can no longer dare leaving my home at night for emergencies."[40] Instead, on the day after the attack Schwarzschild was picked up by two police officers and brought through the city to the town hall, where he was accused of referring to the three men that night as "criminals." Schwarzschild made it clear that it was not him but one of his escorts who had used the term, whereupon he was released, but then the father and brother of the new mother were taken into "protective custody."[41]

The report by the Kassel district president, in turn, portrayed these events from a significantly different perspective: "A regrettable incident occurred in recent days in Gelnhausen, where a Jewish doctor, on his way to a difficult delivery, was stopped by two people and beaten. There were no damages, for the doctor was still able to reach the patient on time."[42] The district president's cynical concluding sentence drew the unmistakable boundaries of the *Volksgemeinschaft*. The fact that it was Dr. Schwarzschild who suffered damages was no longer relevant in the world of the Kassel district president's report. Jewish Germans, even though they were still legally state citizens with a right to protection from attacks and violence, disappeared from view and no longer existed as legal persons.

The incidents in Gelnhausen reveal the erosion of both legal consciousness and the legal order within just two years of the National Socialists' takeover of power. Even though the violent attacks clearly amounted to the crime of inflicting intentional bodily harm, and even though the perpetrators had, at least in part, been recognized by the victim, the competent state attorney's office reported that the perpetrators were unknown and the investigation was closed. Even if the assurances of Gestapo spokesman Hütteroth, namely that violations against the penal code would by no means be tolerated, were perhaps less duplicitous than one might be prepared to assume today, they had no impact whatsoever on the actual practices of the Kassel state police agency.

For the victims, this took away the ground on which they thought they stood as citizens of a constitutional state. With respect to Schwarzschild himself, the rupture is clearly visible. At the beginning of the year, the nocturnal breaking of windows was self-evidently a reason to file charges against unknown persons. But the succinct message by the Hanau state attorney, namely that it did not want to punish crimes against Jews, must have been so discouraging and disheartening that Schwarzschild just a short time later declined to file a new complaint, even though this time his wife was actually physically threatened. And as if he had to experience the lawlessness and helplessness literally in his own flesh, not only did he himself become the victim of a violent attack, but he was even declared to be a perpetrator, taken into custody, and publicly led through the streets of Gelnhausen as a delinquent.

One cannot overestimate the gravity of this experience—and only two years after Hitler seized power. The fact that Germany was being ruled by an anti-Jewish party was obvious. And the political actions of local National Socialists and their supporters, and the everyday harassment and discrimination were also plain to see. The fact that this regime was promulgating anti-Semitic laws and ordinances that drastically limited the legal status of Jews and violated the civil right to equality before the law was likewise an everyday experience. But the fact that the police, judiciary, and courts were no longer willing to enforce the valid legal code or to punish crimes of physical assault when perpetrated against Jewish persons must have had a devastating effect.

Intensification of Violence

The *Stürmer* in particular mobilized anti-Semitic hate propaganda in 1935. So-called *Stürmer-Kästen*—large display cases over one meter wide, painted bright red and decorated with anti-Semitic slogans like "The Jews are our misfortune" and "The father of the Jews is the Devil"—were set up everywhere in the communities of the German Reich. They not only displayed the latest edition of the *Stürmer* but also denounced those *Volksgenossen*—often with full names and addresses—who still shopped at Jewish businesses:

National Socialist German Worker's Party, Local Chapter Haren (Ems)

Warning

The following are still buying meat from Jews:

1) The cartwright Joh. Wolbers, who delivers wheelbarrows to the work service camps.

2) Motor vessel skipper Franz Held, who received a subsidy to build a residential home.[43]

The business manager of the C.V.'s regional association of East Prussia reported in August 1935: "The '*Stürmer*'-*Kästen* are constantly besieged. The inscriptions and pictures have a strong effect on the public so that the old clientele, completely anxious, won't dare to enter the stores."[44] During the first months of 1935, the situation reports of the Gestapo, district presidents, and district administrators noted that *Stürmer-Kästen* were being set up in more and more places and that anti-Semitic propaganda was getting stronger. "Enlightenment of the racial question is taking hold in the district population inasmuch as the *Stürmer* is becoming increasingly wide-spread. Contributing to this enlightenment are the *Stürmer-Kästen*, which have been erected in a number of different rural communities in the district. With this, it is to be hoped that Jewish trade will suffer losses."[45] In Saxony, NSDAP Gauleiter Mutschmann instructed each local chapter to display the *Stürmer* in a "good visible location." In order to supervise the implementation of the order, local chapters were supposed to send a photo of their *Stürmer* display to the district leadership by the middle of June.[46]

One can easily imagine the kind of social pressure that resulted from such notices, particularly in smaller communities. Anyone publicly denounced by their full name could count on both concrete economic disadvantages and social ostracism. Indeed, who would want to have anything to do with a "friend of Jews" when the powers that be in the community made a point of demanding that Jewish neighbors should be avoided? When both material security and membership in the village community were important? Those who remained opposed to the social ostracism of the Jews still had some support from the policies of the Reich Economics Ministry, which for utilitarian reasons was not ready to restrict the economic activity of the Jews. In conflicts with local party activists, citizens like the Hildesheim museum director could appeal to the fact that none of his superior state authorities had forbidden him as a bureaucrat from buying from Jews. But the social pressure to distance oneself from Jewish neighbors was incredibly strong, and only a few were able to withstand it.

The excesses in Gelnhausen were no coincidence. In January and February reports from Bremen, Aachen, Cologne, and Coblenz also indicated that the anti-Jewish boycott movement was regaining momentum.[47] The state police in Coblenz, Cologne, and Hanover reported violence in January and February, as did the district president in Aschaffenburg, the superior president in Pomerania, and the district administrator in Fulda.[48] Reports from the districts of Aachen, Lower Franconia, and Friedberg also mentioned pistol shots taken at Jewish residences.[49] And the gendarmerie in Biblis reported that numerous display windows of a Jewish store had been shattered with an explosive.[50]

Time and again the reports mention not only activist groups but also crowds of people who accompanied the actions. In Stettin, a Jewess who was considered wealthy was accused in the press of donating tattered shoes to the winter humanitarian aid program. Thereupon, on the following Sunday, her shoes—the state and police reports say nothing about whether the accusations were justified or whether the shoes presented by the demonstrators even belonged to the woman from Stettin—were returned to her by a parade of demonstrators. The crowd was carrying a banner that said: "Rosa Rosenbaum gets back her donation to winter welfare." Since the woman was not in her apartment, the shoes were hung in a window, whereupon the procession dissolved.[51]

The demonstration a few days later was more threatening. Again, it was the press that incited the action by labeling the dismissal of a non-Jewish employee by the Jewish proprietor of a shoe store in Stettin as an assault against the German *Volksgemeinschaft*. The dismissal was apparently due to the economic difficulties caused by continuing boycotts, for the reports mention the store's "closing sale" and the owner's anger at the "closing sale vultures" who were only buying from him because prices had now been reduced. Again a crowd of people gathered (according to reports by the superior president and the Gestapo, it numbered over 5,000) and pulled the owner, Fritz Lindner, out of the store. The decorator at the time, Rudolf Voß, witnessed the event. He later reported that a "jeering mass of people, beating both of them with sticks" had dragged Lindner and his wife through the streets until the police finally stepped in and literally took them into "protective custody." A large part of the crowd— the C.V. report mentions 700 to 1,000 people—moved on to a Jewish clothing store and demanded the removal a black-white-red flag that was displayed in the window for the occasion of the next day's celebration of the Saarland plebiscite. In addition, the man was accused of having a relationship with a non-Jewish woman. Again, the mob pulled their victim from the store and beat him. The man was only freed from the crowd by the actions of the police, who took him into "protective custody" as well.[52]

The C.V. immediately appeared the next day before the Stettin police president and the Gestapo in order to secure the release of the three prisoners. With respect to Frau Lindner and the owner of the clothing store, Werner Blochert, they were successful. But Fritz Lindner himself remained under arrest. Although the examining magistrate later let him return home, after only a few hours he was arrested again by Gestapo officers. Not until five days later did the Berlin C.V. note that Fritz Lindner had now also been released from "protective custody."[53]

Official statements regarding the number of people who participated in such actions are certainly only to be used with caution, for it could very well have been in the interests of state authorities to emphasize the population's readiness to take action against the Jews by citing high numbers for their regions. Likewise, mentioning a large crowd could also emphasize the ability of the police to retain control of critical situations with few personnel, or it could draw attention to the necessity of supplying the police with more personnel and equipment. In contrast, such interests, which might have influenced the numbers cited in state reports, did not obtain with respect to the C.V. Rather, one can assume that its reports to Berlin headquarters sought to represent a realistic portrayal of the situations. While keeping in mind the fundamental difficulty of quantitatively estimating the size of crowds, the C.V. statements about the crowds of people can thus be believed.

Moreover, the reports give no indication as to whether the crowds included uniformed members of NS organizations, party members, or civilian Nazi supporters, or participants, curious individuals, or pedestrians. But even if one can rightly assume that a large part of these crowds was made up of members of NS organizations, the level of mobilization is in each case considerable, for the crowd of 700 to 1,000 people who participated in the excesses against Fritz Lindner far exceeds the core of activists who initiated such an action. Participating in these actions were also people who otherwise might not be considered National Socialist activists—people who in these situations became interested enough to participate in these actions or, if they were simply passing by, to allow themselves to be drawn in.

In May the anti-Semitic transgressions momentarily reached a high point. Almost forty incidents were reported by police and state authorities during this month. Both the Gestapo in Arnsberg and the state police authorities in Berlin and Cologne spoke of an increase of the "anti-Semitic wave," and in the administrative region of Aachen, strict instructions by NSDAP Gauleiter Grohé were apparently necessary to roll back the violence. Nonetheless, excesses occurred even afterward in the districts of Erkelenz and Düren.[54] Reports from state authorities in provincial Bavaria also registered a clear increase in anti-Semitic activities. Thus the district president of Swabia reported that at the beginning of May signboards had been erected (often by local HJ) in the towns and most of the rural communities with inscriptions like "Jews are not welcome here!" or "*Volksgenossen!* Caution! Jewish stores in the square! Avoid them!" The superior president of Upper Bavaria likewise reported that placards and signs with anti-Jewish slogans had been set up in many places. On some streets there were statements painted in red oil paint such as "We recognize the Jew as the biggest scoundrel throughout the land" ("*Als größter Lump im ganzen Land ist uns der Jud bekannt*") or "Oh Lord, send them Moses so that he leads them to Jerusalem."[55]

Likewise in the large cities of Munich and Berlin, which have received considerable attention in the historical literature, these weeks witnessed a number of serious incidents. In Munich the police had noticed a growth in the anti-Jewish boycott movement at the end of March. By April the display windows of Jewish businesses were increasingly being smeared with anti-Semitic slogans like "Jew," "sow-Jew," "get the Jews out," and similar messages. According to police, they were apparently dealing with a small, well-organized group that, having carefully observed the street patrols of the patrol officers, would at night, during an unguarded moment, write on the display windows with caustic silicic acid. Since the beginning of May, however, the perpetrators were no longer satisfied with

slogans; rather, they had taken to smashing the display windows with cob-
blestones. On 18 May the first open clashes in broad daylight occurred;
first directed against a street gathering of the Catholic Caritas organization, they subsequently grew into a demonstration in front of a number of
Jewish businesses.

One week later, on the afternoon of 25 May, crowds of people gathered
first in front of the Uhlfelder and EPA department stores in Rosental, and
then in front of almost all of the Jewish stores in Munich, whereupon,
as the police wrote, they "promptly" took action against the stores. The
perpetrators forced their way into the stores, threw out the customers, and
forced the proprietors to close the stores; in a number of cases they also
mistreated the non-Jewish employees. A larger crowd near Bahnhofplatz
was apparently so agitated that it attempted to storm the guardroom at
the main railway station because some demonstrators were allegedly being
detained there. Thereupon Austrian SS members from the Schleißheim
barracks got involved, even physically assaulting individual policemen.
In the evening, thugs in civilian clothes also attacked the Catholic journeymen's center on Schommerstrasse. Once again, those involved were
apparently SS people, who were taken into custody by SS Gruppenführer
Schmauser, who happened to be there at the time, and brought to the
Herzog-Wilhelm barracks.[56] On this day alone, the daily report by the
Munich police directorate recorded thirty arrests.[57]

In another location, a larger group of young people gathered in front of
a tobacco store on Hohenzollernstrasse and threateningly demanded that
the proprietress close her store. Police officers from the competent precinct intervened and took one of the demonstrators to the station. Thereupon the crowd also moved to the station and tried to drive the police
officers away and free the arrested demonstrator. The insults were strident: "darlings of the Jews," "black sow-dogs," "sow-scoundrels," "blood-
hounds," "the station will be also taken down!" The crowd was dispersed
only with the help of reinforcements and an additional riot squad.[58]

The Bavarian Interior Ministry later determined that the incidents
were not isolated actions but rather an "organized course of action by the
demonstrators directed from a single position." At first it was assumed
that the instigators were promoters from the *Stürmer* publishing house,
but then it was determined that the people involved were members of the
NSDAP, particularly the SS, and members of Austrian SA barracks on
Franziskanerstrasse. Even though the interior minister had an in-depth
discussion about the excesses with SS Gruppenführer Schmauser and a
number of other SA leaders, it could not be determined who was ultimately responsible. But the interior minister requested that the party for-
mations conduct a careful investigation and impose severe disciplinary

punishments on everyone who participated in the action. He instructed the police that all men who had been captured by police were to remain under arrest. "I made the seriousness of my order on the evening of 25 May exceptionally clear to the assembled SA and SS leaders, whereby in case of any attacks the police were to make use not of their bayonets but of their firearms."[59]

The physical assault against the police officers had clearly transgressed a sensitive boundary for the regime. On the one hand, party groups in many places had previously broken the state's monopoly of violence and resorted to violent "self-help," and they had been assured that the party leadership would provide political cover. On the other hand, the excesses in Munich revealed to the NS leadership the dangerous potential of violence for blurring boundaries that, left unchecked, could escalate into attacks against police. Local violence also concealed danger for the regime, first because it undermined the central claim of a monopoly of violence, and second because open brutality might provoke members of the population to disassociate themselves from the regime.

The clear intentions of the police president and the interior minister in Munich not to tolerate any attacks against the police and to severely punish the perpetrators draws attention to both the boundary in the spring of 1935 and the urgent need for state regulations with respect to the German Jews. On the one hand, state organs like the police supported the regime's anti-Jewish policies; on the other hand they had to make sure that state instructions were obeyed—and, if necessary, they also had to protect Jewish citizens against the attacks of the party, HJ, and SA. The state organs desperately wanted to be freed from this dilemma. Time and again, state police authorities like the Cologne Gestapo demanded a consistent policy: "The events in the last months have shown that in the future clear instructions from the central government authorities are absolutely necessary about *what is permissible within the framework of the wave of anti-Jewish propaganda and what is not permissible*, for otherwise the police executive officer, who ultimately bears the entire burden of responsibility, either does not have the necessary support during an intervention or does not let himself be seen in the vicinity of critical situations. In both cases, however, ultimately it is *state authority* that suffers."[60]

In June the actions eased slightly. Over thirty local violent actions were mentioned in both police and state reports and also in the C.V. documents. Additionally, the Gestapo in Aachen and Coblenz reported a number of unspecified incidents in their districts. While the regions of Hanover, Cologne, and Magdeburg registered a decline of anti-Semitic propaganda, other districts like Kassel, Arnsberg, Bad Kreuznach, and Königsberg still reported that boycott actions continued. Thus the Gestapo in Kassel noted: "the anti-Semitism in the Volk remains fresh and active. As a result, the fact that it vents itself in excesses against the Jews cannot be avoided, especially if the latter behave so arrogantly and provocatively. So during the reported month there were numerous incidents again."[61]

Despite the obvious efforts by both the government authorities and also the NSDAP Gauleitung to reduce the violence, in July and August the number of actions shot up drastically. Hardly any of the 200 extant situation reports for these months fail to mention "individual actions" and excesses. A new "large wave of propaganda" against the Jews could be observed; in many places anti-Semitic processions and demonstrations were organized in which thousands of people participated. In Osnabrück, a town with about 95,000 residents at the time, there was a rally on 20 August with 25,000 participants, during which NSDAP district leader Münzer spoke on the subject "Osnabrück and the Jewish Question." According to police reports, he stated the following:

> What is happening in Osnabrück today is not anti-Semitism in the usual sense. It is not a struggle against the Jew as such but is a struggle for the German soul, that is, a kind of pro-Germanism. The Führer desires that every German, in recognizing the Jewish danger, little by little comes to reflect completely on his Germanness, that he accepts that any compromise with the Jews must harm the German Volk and thus ultimately himself. In Osnabrück, nothing has happened to any Jew, we have not prevented anybody from entering a Jewish business. The only thing is that those Germans who came out of Jewish stores were photographed in order to show them that they have not yet recognized the great German mission. As a warning to themselves and other Volksgenossen, the pictures are hanging in the cases. It is indeed correct that in the struggle for the complete salvation of our German Volk that all—and that means all—Volksgenossen must stick together; and it is also correct when it is said here and there that anyone who buys from Jews is a traitor to the Volk. For he supports the Jews in their efforts to rule the world and damages the German Volk in its defense and thus in its struggle for its own existence. The current action is a question of the education of the German human being who for decades has been contaminated by Jewish poison and is now to be freed from this poison by a radical treatment.[62]

With respect to the regions of Hanover and Braunschweig—namely from the communities of Einbeck, Northeim, Seesen, Höxter, Bodenfelde, and Holzminden—the northwest German regional association of the C.V. reported to Berlin as follows: "the conditions [can] hardly be described and the situation of our friends is almost untenable. Apart from heavy attacks, especially the destruction of all display windows in the most diverse localities, the business life of Jewish enterprises has come to an almost complete halt."[63] The demands of the perpetrators did not merely extend to the boycott of Jewish businesses but now were increasingly concerned with making the Jews disappear altogether. In the community of Elsoff in Siegerland on a late afternoon in July, a formation from the Labor Service numbering 100 men stood at the homes of the two Jewish families living in the community and chanted: "If Germany is to live, the Jews must die." Then upon command the houses were bombarded with rocks.[64] Meanwhile leaflets were circulating in Mainz: "Jews! We demand you! Disappear from Mainz!"[65] In Dormagen in the Rhineland, banners that were hung at Jewish apartment buildings read: "If you Jew do not give way soon, we will walk over your corpses" ("*Wenn Du Jud nicht bald tust weichen, gehen wir über Deine Leichen*").[66] These were not merely words. A rally in Dormagen demanded that a locally known person named Bernhard Katz leave the town. The effect was apparently threatening enough that Katz fled to Düsseldorf, where the Gestapo took him into "protective custody." According to the police report, "the Jew's return would evoke great agitation in the population."[67]

The three Jewish families in Harpstedt near Bremen were no longer able to buy foodstuffs in the village, so they had to drive to Bremen for their daily bread. Likewise, Jews in Lichenrod in Hesse were not allowed to enter the bakery, and the baker, who had until then served both Jewish families and the Arbeitsfront, was now faced with the choice of serving either the Jews or the Arbeitsfront. Apart from bread, it was just as impossible to obtain milk, either from the dairy or from the farmers. Reporting from Dormagen, the C.V. noted that Jewish families were no longer being provided with milk for their small children.[68] Similar reports can be found in C.V. documents that pertain to other places in the Reich as well—from Rastede in Lower Saxony to Stavenhagen in Mecklenburg; from Preußisch-Holland in East Prussia to Dessau in Saxony and Pyritz in Pomerania. The message of these actions to Jewish families was unequivocal: disappear or we will let you starve!

East Prussia

At the beginning of February 1935, the business manager of the C.V. in East Prussia, Dr. Max Angerthal, had offered encouragement to the sixty or so delegates at a regional C.V. conference in Elbing. The Gestapo report about the conference represented Angerthal's position as if it were unambiguous and perhaps purposely downplayed the ambivalence of the speech. According to the report, the C.V. business manager had emphasized the importance of supporting and maintaining even the most minimal Jewish existence in East Prussia. The current laws and ordinances once again offered the Jews an existence and a means to live. Even though access to the trades or academic careers was temporarily prohibited to Jews, the Jewish merchant was still guaranteed the freedom to operate in economic terms. It was the primary obligation of every Jew in Germany to support his fellow believers in every regard; Jewish knowledge and Jewish culture had to be carefully maintained—this according to the Gestapo in its report.[69]

As early as April 1935, an alleged ritual murder in Tauroggen in Lithuania caused a sensation. Although the Lithuanian Interior Ministry immediately dismissed such rumors as an incitement to hatred, this did not prevent the *Tilsiter Zeitung*, the *Preußische Zeitung*, and *Der Gesellige*, published in Schneidemühl, from writing about the supposed ritual murder under headlines like "12-Year-Old Girl Slaughtered by Jews" and "Unbelievable Jewish Government in Lithuania." Naturally, the April edition of the *Stürmer* also appeared with the headline "Ritual Murder in Lithuania."[70] Thereupon in Christburg near Marienburg—a town with at least 3,000 residents, of whom about 130 were Jews who had already suffered for years from the boycott campaigns and violent actions—a sign erected on the busiest street read:

> The time of the Jewish Passover feast is approaching. In which Jews require Christian blood for their superstitious customs. In Lithuania, in the town of Turongu, a 12-year-old girl was slaughtered for this purpose. The fact that this custom also exists in Germany has been shown by the cases in Lonitz [it must have meant Konitiz—M.W.] and Marienburg, 1917, among others. Children and adolescents are especially at risk and are hereby warned.[71]

The text was signed by NSDAP Ortsgruppenleiter Schulz. Although Angerthal—the business manager of the C.V. in East Prussia—immediately turned to the Gestapo in Königsberg, he received very little information. Days later the sign was still standing in Christburg. "A removal of the sign did not take place," the state police determined internally, "because public peace and security have not been disturbed by it, and a disturbance was also not to be feared."[72] The C.V. group in Schneidemühl reported that a respectable Jewish trader was thrown out by a Christian customer who remarked that he did not want to do business with people belonging to circles in which ritual murder was practiced.[73]

In this atmosphere of suspicion and hatred, violence again erupted during the spring in East Prussia. On 23 April, according to police statements, around 500 to 600 people gathered in front of the parental home of a young Jewish man in Marienburg because he had allegedly harassed two girls from the BDM. The crowd was so threatening that the police, as they themselves stated, took two Jews into "protective custody" in order to prevent excesses.[74] Two days later in the *Weichsel-Wacht*, under the headline "Marienburg Jew Gets Impertinent," one could read the following:

> The times in which the Jew was able to insult German *Volksgenossen* in his impertinent manner on the highways and byways are finally over. In the new Germany he is only a tolerated guest and should always feel and behave as such. Thus the population is all the more perturbed and disgusted when it hears that Jews, through impertinent and provocative behavior, have abused this right of a guest, as did the Jewish boy Felix R. from Marienburg on this recent Easter Sunday. On the morning of this day, when together with two other Jews he encountered a local BDM leader and her friend in the town park, he felt himself compelled to provoke them in an insolent manner and utter insulting statements about the BDM. On the same day, R. continued with his insolent comments about the girls at the train station. We are not about to silently turn a blind eye to this kind of behavior.[75]

At the beginning of May, a Jewish trader took down his booth at the annual market in Marienburg for fear of attacks after party activists had erected a sign in front of it that read: "Jews are our misfortune."[76] A little later the target was a war invalid named Sally Goldstrom. There had been legal proceedings against him at the beginning of June—allegedly, there was a danger that he would become delinquent in his support payments for a child born out of wedlock during a relationship many years back. But since Goldstrom had met his obligations, he was pronounced innocent. Nonetheless the local newspaper reported in such a slanderous way that on 21 June he was taken from his home by some young people. They hung a sign around his neck that read "girl-violator, Jew" and forced him to wander around the Marienburg market. Meanwhile a crowd of around 200 people had gathered, emitting cries like "girl-violator of Marienburg." According to the police who were called to the scene, there was a danger that the demonstrators would violently attack Sally Goldstrom, so they took him into "protective custody" and released him again the following morning.[77] In August the C.V. reported to Berlin headquarters that over twenty windows in the synagogue had been smashed, and that, while many people were inside, stones were thrown through the windows. For some time already, the synagogue's back wall had been painted with slogans like "House of the racial violators! You Jews are found out, get out of this land!" ("*Haus der Rasseschänder! Ihr Juden seid erkannt, raus aus diesem Land!*")[78]

In Liebstadt, a small town just over thirty kilometers northwest of Allenstein, where only about forty Jews resided, the boycott actions had had a profound effect. Angerthal had already reported in June 1933 that customers who had shopped in Jewish stores had been photographed and the photos had been publicly displayed in the window of the NSDAP's local propaganda director. Two years later a notice was posted proclaiming that Jews were prohibited from accessing the town's swimming facilities, the taverns hung up signs saying that Jews would not be served, and retirees had received anonymous letters stating that their pensions would revoked if they bought "from Jews."[79]

Then in July the actions against the Jews in Liebstadt became unbearable. Now there was a *Stürmer-Kasten* at the town hall, on which was written: "Without a solution to the Jewish question, no salvation for the German Volk" and "Anyone who buys from Jews is a traitor to his Volk." On the morning of 10 July, the Jewish merchants discovered that their windows had been smeared with the words: "Jews out!" In the night prior to 14 July, the sidewalks in front their stores had been painted with statements like "Heed the *Stürmer*, Jews out!" The police determined that the perpetrators were two journeymen apprentices. On market days, every Tuesday and Wednesday, activists with cameras appeared in front of the Jewish stores and photographed the customers. On 20 July, it was a whole group of adolescents that was taking pictures. And during the night, the sidewalks were again painted with anti-Semitic slogans.[80]

On Sunday morning, 14 July, in Bischofsstein near Rastenburg, about 100 people gathered in front of the business and residence of a Jewish merchant, chanting for a long time: "Hang them up, the Jews! Beat them to death, the Jews! Germany awake—Judah die!"[81] In Goldap, where in 1935 there remained but a single Jewish store whose windows were repeatedly smashed, the mayor—who was also the NSDAP district leader—explained verbatim to the C.V. syndic that he had taken it upon himself to see to the destruction of this store, and that this would be accomplished. This was admittedly not an order from the government, but a matter for the party.[82] In Christburg, where the "ritual murder" sign had been erected, a customer who had purchased a jacket in a Jewish store was stopped. Someone held his bicycle while others yanked him from the bike. They took him to task and brought him into a side street where numerous people were gathering. The police only managed to free the man with difficulty, making it possible for him to leave the town.[83]

On 22 July Max Angerthal described for the Berlin headquarters a case from the West Prussian town of Osterode, about which he had just learned by telephone:

> On Saturday morning, 07/20/35, aside from the taking of photographs, larger groups of eight- to ten-year-old children approached the stores. They covered over all of the display windows with notices: "you are a slave to the Jews [*Judenknecht*]." Mostly they tore off the corner of the notice with the syllable "*knecht*," so that the text stated: "you are a Jew." The leather trader Wittenberg ran after the boys simply in order to take them to task. Thereupon he was accused of having beaten one of the boys. At first an older HJ member appeared in front of W.'s store threatening that he would be stabbed and beaten to death, [for] he had assaulted a German boy. The boy also pulled out a dagger. Then a number of likewise older HJ members appeared. The boys overpowered W. in his store, threw him to the ground and shouted [that] they wanted to beat him to death.[84]

At first the boys disappeared from the store, but then they besieged Wittenberg's house; he considered the situation so dangerous that he wanted to leave Osterode for the time being. But the HJ boys followed him to the train station and saw to it that he could not buy a railway ticket. Even the train station supervisor, who had initially objected, submitted to the adolescent violence.

Wittenberg returned home, but in the afternoon another group of HJ boys appeared, led by an SA man. They dragged him from the house, hung a sign around his neck that read: "This dirty Jew has beaten a German boy!" And beating and kicking him, they forced him to march through the town. While doing so the adolescents called out: "Judah die!" "The Jews must get out of Germany!" and other anti-Semitic slogans. After an hour, as the procession approached the district hospital, Wittenberg could barely walk. Only at this point did a police officer intervene, saying that Wittenberg would be taken into protective custody. But this had little influence on the adolescent perpetrators, and they continued to proceed with Wittenberg through the streets of Osterode. Finally, at the market square, four police officers showed up and managed to free Wittenberg from the crowd and bring him to the station. In the evening he was released for the time being.

But the crowd, Angerthal continued in his report, also went to other houses and businesses that belonged to Jews, laying waste to the office of a mill operation and likewise leading the Jewish mill director Kallmann through the streets until arriving at the police station, where he was taken into protective custody as well.[85]

The C.V. reports make it apparent that adolescents increasingly played a prominent role as actors in the boycott actions. Whereas in 1933/34 it was still SA and SS men who stood sentry in front of Jewish stores, took photographs, and harassed pedestrians, increasingly the reports make mention of HJ members, little boys, schoolchildren, and adolescents in general who showed up at the stores, shouting slogans and trying to prevent customers from shopping. Certainly, ordinary everyday factors cannot be overlooked: young people, especially schoolchildren, were easy to mobilize and could also be deployed during the day, whereas their older brothers and fathers were once again employed and therefore could only be drawn into the planning for non-business hours and weekends.

But one should also consider that these boys—for the most part these were male adolescents, even though a few C.V. reports also mentioned BDM groups that participated in boycott actions—had for two years been growing up in a public space poisoned by the NS regime's anti-Semitism. From the very outset, violence was an essential component of socialization within the HJ.[86] Moreover, they possessed far fewer social relationships with the Jewish merchants, whom older people had patronized in previous years and known for a long time.

It is also telling that those who were supposed to protect the law and prevent criminal action intervened only late or not at all. Instead of stepping in at the onset of violence, the police allowed it to continue for a number of hours before bringing it to a halt. In Osterode the police initially accepted the fact that the adolescent perpetrators ignored the police officer's demands and continued to drive the Jewish leather trader Wittenberg through the town before, finally, four police officers then enforced their own demands. And even then the police did not take action against the violent adolescent perpetrators, who had, after all, violated the criminal code. Rather, they took the Jewish victim into custody and closed his store. The adolescent actors could evidently rest assured that they more or less had the approval of the adults—even those who, because of their official duties, were responsible for maintaining public order. The problem was not that the transgression of boundaries and the disrespect of predominant everyday rules were part of a standard repertoire of pubertal behavior, but rather that adults were no longer defending such boundaries and rules. According to the experience of these adolescents, Jews could be insulted, mistreated, and even beaten without adults or law enforcement officials getting involved. Furthermore, these adolescents could also imagine themselves in a heroic role, bravely and fearlessly carrying out actions that the adults did not dare but secretly wanted to do.

Collective Violence

The groups that are mentioned in the C.V. reports were summoned together. They did not originate spontaneously, but neither were they organized beforehand. Within such groups there would undoubtedly be a core of National Socialist activists, but numerous other people would join—those who either heard about the action or read a corresponding appeal in a newspaper. Evidently a local newspaper report about a Jew was often sufficient to give the signal for an action against him. Media and communication are indispensable for the initiation of collective violence. Thus Stanley Tambiah, in his investigation into violent excesses between Hindus and Muslims in India and Sri Lanka in the 1980s and 1990s, emphasized the significance of rumors that were largely based on unsubstantiated horror stories about the murders of pregnant women and children, poisoned wells, or defiled shrines, which in turn built on traditional and familiar stories that were always renewed by repeated telling. Rumors cause anger and hatred, and they are produced by anger and hatred; they are often deliberately seeded by "riot captains" and spread quickly and widely through the media.[87] Similarly Helmut Walser Smith, in his study about the anti-Semitic excesses in Konitz in West Prussia in the spring of 1900, underscores the significance of rumors and circulating accusations for the outbreak of collective violence.[88]

The C.V. reports also indicate that crowds increasingly accompanied the boycott actions, demonstrations, and violence. It is often impossible to precisely discern from the sources how the individual members of such crowds were involved in the events—whether as active perpetrators, cheering participants, observers who approved and legitimated the legal violations, or merely curious passers-by, who by virtue of their own passivity made the violence possible—never mind the parts of the population that saw what was happening but looked away and continued on in order not to become involved. In order to produce the "*Volksgemeinschaft*," the "politics from below"—i.e., the more or less secret complicity at the local level by which the valid legal order was effectively suspended for the Jews, who were denied protection—was just as necessary as the decrees, laws, and measures instituted from "above." In the moment when laws could be violated with impunity against a group, a boundary was drawn within which the *Volksgenossen* were constituted as a *Volksgemeinschaft*, and beyond which the Jews and other "*Fremdvölkische*" (alien *völkisch* elements) were excluded as "*Gemeinschaftsfremde*" (elements alien to the community).

The case studies indicate that it would be a mistake to focus only on the actively engaged actors. Just as the perpetrators were by no means merely recipients of orders who carried out instructions but rather people who decided upon the violent acts themselves, so too did the observers, passers-by, and bystanders play an equal constitutive role as people who granted tolerance or approval—as accomplices. Even the victims, by virtue of their personal humiliation and degradation and by their public disempowerment, were enjoined to affirm the empowerment of the *Volksgenossen*.

The violence was public—it was supposed to make a spectacle of the victim's helplessness and the perpetrator's power. The victim's visible humiliation was a constitutive component of the action, not just as a picture in the *Stürmer-Kasten* but rather in the flesh at the marketplace or in front of the town hall, in a community's central place, where everybody passed and everyone could see the publicly humiliated person being exposed to abuse. Wittenberg, who defended himself against a malicious assault on his economic existence and also against property damage as defined by the legal code, had to acquiesce to a complete reinterpretation of the facts. The adolescent boys were the masters of the situation. They interpreted the event, and not merely clandestinely amongst themselves and vis-à-vis their victim. By marching Wittenberg through the town with a sign around his neck that read "This dirty Jew has beaten a German boy," they claimed the power of public interpretation, which could have been effectively refuted only by an equally public objection. The excessive violence of the perpetrators stood opposite the complete and humiliating helplessness of the victim, which extinguished his dignity as a person.

Neither did this situational complicity simply disappear when people more or less secretly repudiated the actions, a fact that did not escape the Gestapo. In its report for July 1935, the Königsberg Gestapo noted

> that, especially in the countryside, there still needs be extensive educational work. The sense of Judaism's harmfulness is absent from both the simple rural population and also frequently the urban population. The reason for this is, above all, that the population is accustomed to always finding obligingness, credit, and an undifferentiated friendliness in Jewish businesses, whereas, by contrast, the feeling of status, indifference, and pecuniary correctitude often found with Aryan merchants angers the simple people.[89]

The Gestapo in the district of Arnsberg in Westphalia assessed the mood of the population similarly:

> Unfortunately, the boycott of Jewish businesses in many cases also took on unpleasant shapes. It did not always limit itself to the avoidance of Jewish businesses, but rather many times resulted in assaults against Jewish businesses whose display windows were smeared up or broken. Often the cus-

tomers were also photographed and publicly pilloried in other ways. These assaults were generally disapproved of, especially since people suspect that the NS HAGO is behind these actions and they therefore suspect that the real reason is envy of the competition.[90]

This perception—namely that it was primarily self-serving economic motives that lurked behind the anti-Semitic actions—was also reported by other state police agencies. Based on his investigation of a diverse array of situation reports by the Gestapo and government authorities, David Bankier has concluded that the anti-Semitic propaganda was unsuccessful. Only "hooligans and the young" had been won over by the violent attacks, while "ordinary Germans" behaved as passive onlookers who were more likely to bemoan the resulting damages and fear losing face for Germany abroad. In any event, however, National Socialist anti-Semitism was not rejected because of ethical considerations or moral indignation. Save for a few courageous exceptions, there was no solidarity with the persecuted; rather, indifference prevailed. "Whereas anti-Semitism played an integrative role for the party and its followers, it did not have the same function in spurring the general population to action."[91]

In my judgment this argument essentializes the "population," transforming it into a collective subject and forgoing the possibility of considering the different behavioral possibilities and levels of participation. As the examples show, this "passivity"—this watching—was itself an indispensable component of these actions. Even the passer-by was a part of the public performance. All the people who followed the event—laughing, smirking, being curious, clapping, urging, or even showing skepticism and reservation—took part in the actions. Setting up a polarity between the activists on the one hand and the population on the other distorts from the outset the situation being investigated. In contrast, the complex of motives, intentions, and participations—the dynamic of the systems that made the radicalization of politics possible—becomes apparent within the different practices.

Evidently there was still reluctance and hesitation within the population about supporting the violent boycott actions because they were practiced by party organizations like the SA, HJ, and SS and not by "legitimate" state organs. As a result the actions were perceived as a breach of order. Everyone within the population who had rejected the brutal violent actions of the summer of 1935 could thus be satisfied with the "restoration of law and order" resulting from the Nuremburg laws, even though in reality the violence "from below" contributed significantly to the creation of racial laws that themselves signified a clear intensification of the political and legal persecution of the German Jews. Thus the behavior cannot always be unequivocally and succinctly divided into participation, complicity, and indifference—as would appear to be the case in some historical controversies.[92] Rather, a variety of behaviors were possible in different situations and constellations of violence—all of which were nonetheless always directed against the Jews.

What from one perspective appeared as a conservative insistence on the state's monopoly of violence revealed itself from another perspective within the National Socialist state as a way to accept the illegal policy of violence if it was ostensibly practiced by the police and other state organs—even when these themselves had since become part of a comprehensive regime of violence and the constitutional state's traditional monopoly of violence had been dissolved.

The fact that the policy of violence at the local level nonetheless managed to obtain its objective and achieve an effect was reported in the SPD's *Deutschland-Berichte*: "Imperceptibly, the race propaganda nonetheless leaves its traces. The people are losing their impartiality vis-à-vis the Jews and many tell themselves: the Nazis actually are right in their struggle against the Jews; but people are against the excesses of this struggle."[93] In January 1936, the *Deutschland-Berichte* stated that anti-Semitism had "without a doubt established roots in wide circles of the Volk," and even Social Democrats, while "firm opponents of the excesses," were "in favor of breaking Jewish hegemony once and for all and of assigning to the Jews a specific field of activity."[94]

Notes

1. See Patrik von zur Mühlen, *"Schlagt Hitler an der Saar!"*: *Abstimmungskampf, Emigration und Widerstand im Saargebiet 1933–1935*, 2nd revised ed. (Bonn, 1981); Gerhard Paul, *"Deutsche Mutter – heim zu Dir!" Warum es mißlang, Hitler an der Saar zu schlagen: Der Saarkampf 1933–1935* (Cologne, 1984); and now Ludwig Linsmayer, ed., *Der 13. Januar: Die Saar im Brennpunkt der Geschichte* (Saarbrücken, 2005).
2. Kassel Gestapo report for January 1935, 5 February 1935, in Klein, *Lageberichte der Geheimen Staatspolizei*, vol. 2, 216.
3. Kershaw, *Hitler*, vol. 1, 693.
4. Behnken, *Deutschlandberichte*, March 1935, 279. The report continued: "Our comrades believe that war is inevitable and that the social revolution could then come as long as everything does not collapse. Eight days after the proclamation the mood of the population [has] receded again. Once [the] initial high of enthusiasm had passed, one saw many worried faces. There are more than a few who believe that Germany could be attacked; fear of war can be discerned everywhere, especially among older people. The confidence in the political talent and honest intentions of Hitler is always increasing, just as Hitler has again gained extraordinary ground among the Volk. He is loved by all."
5. CVZ, 20 December 1934; see Barkai, *"Wehr Dich!"* 338.

6. According to the report of the Gestapo in Saxony for March 1935, Kulka and Jäckel, *NS-Stimmungsberichte*, CD-ROM, doc. no. 714; similarly the report for February and March 1935 by the district president for Upper and Middle Franconia, ibid., doc. no. 732. The report of the Aachen Gestapo for February 1935 stated: "Above all, it is the Centralverein deutscher Staatsbürger jüdischen Glaubens which in all of its meetings thus far has propagated for remaining in Germany, and insisted that the hundred-year residence of the Jews in Germany also gives them a right to live here.... In turn, the *Jewish frontline fighters* [Reichsbund jüdischer Frontsoldaten—M.W.] base their claim for their right to live in Germany on the fact that thousands of Jewish soldiers had shed their blood for Germany." Ibid., doc. no. 610. The Reich's Deputation of the German Jews, for its part, reacted by requesting associated organizations to withhold information about the number, form, and subject matter of the meetings. See Otto Dov Kulka, ed., *Deutsches Judentum unter dem Nationalsozialismus*, vol. 1, *Dokumente zur Geschichte der Reichsvertretung der deutschen Juden 1933–1939* (Tübingen, 1997), 190.
7. Geheimes Staatspolizeiamt II 1 B 2, "Lagebericht Juden," 19 February 1935, Special Archive Moscow, 501-1-18, fols. 63–69, excerpts printed in Kulka and Jäckel, *NS-Stimmungsberichte*, 115–117, quote on 116. In April 1935 the Reich Interior Ministry retroactively sanctioned these orders by the Gestapo; in September 1935, the Reich Flag Law (which was part of the Nuremberg laws) finalized the prohibition. Adam, *Judenpolitik im Dritten Reich*, 118.
8. Düsseldorf Gestapo report for February 1935, in Kulka and Jäckel, *NS-Stimmungsberichte*, CD-ROM, doc. no. 621; likewise Coblenz Gestapo report for February 1935, ibid., doc. no. 62; Erfurt Gestapo report for March 1935, ibid., doc. no. 698; Magdeburg Gestapo report for March 1935, ibid., doc. no. 708; Saxony Gestapo report for March 1935, ibid., doc. no. 714; Breslau district president report for March 1935, ibid., doc. no. 723; Province of Lower Silesia chief president report for February and March 1935, ibid., doc. no. 730.
9. Stettin Gestapo report for February 1935, ibid., doc. no. 648.
10. Königsberg Gestapo report for March 1935, ibid., doc. no. 704. The Armed Services Law, which was decreed in May and excluded Jews from military service, made the exclusionary intentions of the regime unmistakable. The CVZ displayed a commentary in bold on its title page: "May 21, 1935, the day on which the law went into effect, is historically the opposite pole of another date, 4 September 1814. Deeply moved, today we are remembering that day on which, with the expressed repeal of the 'previous older laws regarding the supplementation of the army,' it was determined for the Prussian Jews that 'immediately upon completion of his twentieth year of life, every native is obligated to defend the fatherland.'" CVZ, 23 May 1935; see Barkai, *"Wehr Dich!"* 351.
11. For more detail on the "crisis of mood" during the first months of 1935, see Longerich, *Politik der Vernichtung*, 70–73.
12. Behnken, *Deutschlandberichte*, April 1935, 504f.
13. See Longerich, *Die braunen Bataillone*, 227f.
14. Quoted in Bankier, *The Germans and the Final Solution*, 50. Similar evaluations can be found in the reports by the district presidents of Würzburg and Cologne; ibid.
15. Quoted in ibid.
16. Circular by Hess regarding the appeal for maintaining a "living frontline spirit," 19 February 1935, Institut für Zeitgeschichte, Akten der Partei-Kanzlei der NSDAP, part III, microfiche no. 30389.

17. Cologne-Aachen Gauleitung report for February 1935, Kulka and Jäckel, *NS-Stimmungsberichte*, CD-ROM, doc. no. 678; see also Marlis Steinert, *Hitlers Krieg und die Deutschen* (Düsseldorf, 1970), 57; and Longerich, *Politik der Vernichtung*, 72.

18. See Falk Wiesemann, "Juden auf dem Lande: die wirtschaftliche Ausgrenzung der jüdischen Viehhändler in Bayern," in *Die Reihen fast geschlossen: Beiträge zur Geschichte des Alltags unterm Nationalsozialismus*, ed. Detlef Peukert and Jürgen Reulecke (Wuppertal, 1981), 381–396; Werner Teuber, *Jüdische Viehhändler in Ostfriesland und im nördlichen Emsland 1871–1942: Eine vergleichende Studie zu einer jüdischen Berufsgruppe in zwei wirtschaftlich und konfessionell unterschiedlichen Regionen* (Cloppenburg, 1995); on Hesse, see Kaufman, "The Daily Life of the Village and Country Jews in Hessen," 168–171.

19. Cologne Gestapo report for March 1935, Kulka and Jäckel, *NS-Stimmungsberichte*, CD-ROM, doc. no. 703.

20. Trier Gestapo report for April 1935, ibid. doc. no. 789. At the end of March 1935, the Berlin Gestapo also stated: "Boycott of Jewish businesses in an exaggerated measure often had the opposite effect and led to a strong increase of visits to Jewish businesses." Geheimes Staatspolizeiamt II 1 B 2, report dated 25 March 1935, Special Archive Moscow, 501-1-18, fols. 85–94; also Kulka and Jäckel, *NS-Stimmungsberichte*, CD-ROM, doc. no. 687, although here the report is mistakenly ascribed to the SD-Hauptamt, Abt. J I/6. Already during the previous month, it had noticed that the boycott measures were "mostly ineffective" and resulted rather in "damage to the reputations of the authorities who had to implement the decrees of the Reich Economics Ministry [naturally this referred primarily to the Gestapo itself—M.W.] and produced conflicts between the state and the movement." Thus the NSDAP leadership was requested to issue a decree to the party organization to prohibit "dealings with Jews" and in particular shopping in Jewish stores. Geheimes Staatspolizeiamt II 1 B 2, "Lagebericht Juden," 19 February 1935, Special Archive Moscow, 501-1-18, fols. 63–69; also Kulka and Jäckel, *NS-Stimmungsberichte*, CD-ROM, doc. no. 551; printed in part in Kulka and Jäckel, *NS-Stimmungsberichte*, 116.

21. District President Hildesheim report for April/May, 1935, Kulka and Jäckel, *NS-Stimmungsberichte*, CD-ROM, doc. no. 893. The district president described these events as "typical examples for the lack of comprehension and blindness to reality of certain parts of the Bürgertum!"

22. Minden Gestapo report for April/May 1935, Kulka and Jäckel, *NS-Stimmungsberichte*, CD-ROM, doc. no. 948. The Bückeburg NSDAP insisted that Wiehe be relieved from duty and gained the approval of the Reich Interior Ministry for moving Wiehe into retirement. Gerd Steinwascher, *Judenverfolgung in Schaumburg 1933–1945* (Bückeburg, 1988), 14.

23. Hans Mommsen and Dieter Obst, "Die Reaktion der deutschen Bevölkerung auf die Verfolgung der Juden," in *Herrschaftsalltag im Dritten Reich*, ed. Hans Mommsen and Susanne Willems (Düsseldorf, 1988), 381.

24. Longerich, *Politik der Vernichtung*, 75.

25. As still maintained by Friedländer, *Years of Persecution*, 137f.

26. The report by the C.V. local chapter mentions a group of forty to fifty people who called out: "We will not be provoked! Remove the boards!" Note regarding Gelnhausen attached to the letter by the C.V. regional association Hesse to Berlin headquarters, 17 January 1935, Special Archive Moscow, 721-1-2345, fol. 66.

27. Meyer, "Jüdisches Leben in Gelnhausen," 65.

28. Examples of such help in everyday life are described in Kaplan, *Between Dignity and Despair*, 39.

29. C.V. regional association Hesse to Berlin headquarters, 17 January 1935, Special Archive Moscow, 721-1-2345, fol. 68.
30. Quoted in C.V. report on Gelnhausen, undated [1935], Special Archive Moscow, 721-1-2345, fols. 61–64.
31. Ibid.
32. Ibid.
33. District administrator Gelnhausen report for January and February 1935, Kulka and Jäckel, *NS-Stimmungsberichte*, CD-ROM, doc. no. 676.
34. Matzdorff to the C.V. Berlin, 12 February 1935, Special Archive Moscow, 721-1-2345, fol. 54; on the young SS lawyers, see Michael Wildt, *An Uncompromising Generation. The Nazi Leadership of the Reich Security Main Office* (Madison, WI, 2010).
35. Matzdorff to Kassel Gestapo, 22 February 1935, Special Archive Moscow, 721-1-2345, fol. 50.
36. Matzdorff to Kassel Gestapo, 05 March 1935, ibid., fols. 44–45.
37. Schwarzschild to Hanau state attorney's office, 25 March 1935, ibid., fol. 37.
38. Matzdorff to C.V. Berlin, 30 April 1935, ibid., fol. 34.
39. Petition by Dr. Schwarzschild to the district president and the Kassel Gestapo, 26 June 1935, appendix to the letter from C.V. regional association Hesse to C.V. Berlin, ibid., fols. 23–24.
40. Ibid.
41. Ibid.
42. Kassel district president, report for May and June 1935, Kulka and Jäckel, *NS-Stimmungsberichte*, CD-ROM, doc. no. 962.
43. Copied in the file: Special Archive Moscow, 721-1-2338, fol. 255.
44. Angerthal, C.V. regional association East Prussia to Berlin headquarters 25 June 1935, Special Archive Moscow, 721-1-2335, fol. 38.
45. District administrator Marburg, report for May and June 1935, Kulka and Jäckel, *NS-Stimmungsberichte*, CD-ROM, doc. no. 991.
46. "Sachsen voran! Martin Mutschmann und sein Gaubefehl," *Der Stürmer*, no. 25, June 1935.
47. See the reports from the Gestapo agents in Aachen for March 1935, Bremen for February 1935, Cologne for January and February 1935, Coblenz for December 1934, and January 1935. Kulka and Jäckel, *NS-Stimmungsberichte*, CD-ROM, doc. nos. 562, 585, 618, 628, 690.
48. Coblenz Gestapo report for December 1934 and January 1935, ibid., doc. no. 585; Cologne Gestapo report for February 1935, ibid., doc. no. 628; Hanover Gestapo report for February, ibid., doc. no. 624; district president Lower Franconia/Aschaffenburg report for January 1935, ibid., doc. no. 594; superior president Pomerania, report for January and February, ibid., doc. no. 657.
49. Aachen Gestapo report for March 1935, ibid., doc. no. 690; district president Lower Franconia/Aschaffenburg, report for January 1935, ibid., doc. no. 594; district office Friedberg, report for January 1935, ibid., doc. no. 604.
50. Gendarmerie Biblis, report for 12 January 1935, ibid., doc. no. 601.
51. A similar case appears in the *Stürmer*, which reprinted an article from the *Lübecker Generalanzeiger* dated 16 December 1934 in which the Jewish proprietors of a department store in Bad Segeberg were denounced for allegedly having donated dirty and torn clothing to winter welfare. There, too, the items were returned by a crowd in an aggressive demonstration. "Juden verhöhnen das Winterhilfswerk," *Der Stürmer*, no. 5, January 1935. The same action is reported again from Stuttgart, where the rabbi of the Jewish community allegedly donated dirty and torn clothing. "Der Hohn des

Rabbiners," *Der Stürmer*, no. 9, February 1935. The accumulation of cases leads to the assumption that these cases involved intentional provocations in which winter welfare packets labeled with false names of senders were donated in order to foment an anti-Jewish mood.

52. Stettin Gestapo report for February 1935, Kulka and Jäckel, *NS-Stimmungsberichte*, CD-ROM, doc. no. 648; district president Stettin, report for 28 February 1935, ibid., doc. no. 659; superior president province of Pomerania, report for January and February 1935, ibid., doc. no.657; statement by Rudolf Voß, quoted in Robert Thovez, *Die Geheime Staatspolizei in den preußischen Ostprovinzen 1934–1936: Pommern 1934/35 im Spiegel von Gestapo-Lageberichten und Sachakten* (Cologne, 1974), vol. 1, 177; district president Stettin, express letter to the Prussian minister president, 1 March 1935, in ibid., vol. 2, 413; C.V. regional association Pomerania to Berlin headquarters, 1 March and 3 March 1935, CAHJP, HM2/8797, fols. 970–975 (Special Archive Moscow, 721-1-3019); see also Bogdan Frankiewicz, "Das Schicksal der Juden in Pommern nach 1933," in *Der faschistische Pogrom vom 9./19. November 1938 – Zur Geschichte der Juden in Pommern: Kolloqium der Sektionen Geschichtswissenschaft und Theologie der Ernst-Moritz-Arndt-Universität Greifswald am 2. November 1938* (Greifswald, 1989), 43.

53. C.V. regional association Pomerania to Berlin headquarters, 3 March 1935; C.V. Berlin, Notiz, 8 March 1935, CAHJP HM2/8797, fols. 964, 970–972 (Special Archive Moscow, 721-1-3019).

54. Arnsberg Gestapo report for May 1935, Kulka and Jäckel, *NS-Stimmungsberichte*, CD-ROM, doc. no. 838; Berlin Gestapo report for May 1935, ibid., doc. no. 841; Cologne state police report, ibid., doc. no. 853; Aachen Gestapo report for May 1935, ibid., doc. no. 837; see also the printed reports in Kulka and Jäckel, *NS-Stimmungsberichte*, 129–158.

55. District president Swabia, situation report, 7 June 1935; district president Upper Bavaria, report for May 1935, quoted in Martin Broszat, Elke Fröhlich and Falk Wiesemann, eds., *Bayern in der NS-Zeit: Soziale Lage und politisches Verhalten der Bevölkerung im Spiegel vertraulicher Berichte*, vol. 1 (Munich, 1977).

56. Munich police directorate, report for March, April, and May 1935, Kulka and Jäckel, *NS-Stimmungsberichte*, CD-ROM, doc. no. 862; Munich constabulary, police district 2, 2nd watch, daily report for 25 May 1935, ibid., doc. no. 992.

57. Munich police directorate, daily reports for 25–26 and 27 May 1935, ibid., doc. no. 863 (also printed in Kulka and Jäckel, *NS-Stimmungsberichte*, 137f.), no. 898.

58. Munich police directorate, police district 11, precinct I, report for 25 May 1935, Kulka and Jäckel, *NS-Stimmungsberichte*, CD-ROM, doc. no. 923.

59. Bavarian State Interior Ministry, report on the events of 25 and 28 May 1935, ibid., doc. no. 881.

60. Cologne Gestapo report for June 1935, ibid., doc. no. 942 (also printed in Kulka and Jäckel, *NS-Stimmungsberichte*, 143), emphasis in the original.

61. Kassel Gestapo report for June 1935, Kulka and Jäckel, *NS-Stimmungsberichte*, CD-ROM, doc. no. 940.

62. Osnabrück Gestapo report for August 1935, ibid., doc. no. 1109.

63. C.V. regional association northwest Germany to Berlin headquarters, 12 August 1935, CAHJP, HM2/8797, fol. 70f. (Special Archive Moscow, 721-1-3012).

64. C.V. regional association Rhineland-Westphalia to Berlin headquarters, 24 July 1935, Special Archive Moscow, 721-1-2914, fol. 414f.

65. C.V. regional association Hesse to Berlin headquarters, 22 August 1935, Special Archive Moscow, 721-1-2969, fol. 21.

66. C.V. regional association Rhineland-Westphalia to the Düsseldorf Gestapo, 9 July 1935, CAHJP, HM2/8790, fols. 457–459 (Special Archive Moscow, 721-1-2914).
67. Düsseldorf Gestapo report for July 1935, Kulka and Jäckel, *NS-Stimmungsberichte*, CD-ROM, doc. no. 1008.
68. C.V. regional association northwest Germany to Berlin headquarters, 12 August 1935, Special Archive Moscow, 721-1-2338, fol. 196; C.V. regional association Hesse to Berlin headquarters, 26 September 1935, CAHJP, HM2/8699, fol. 2274 (Special Archive Moscow, 721-1-236); C.V. regional association Rhineland-Westphalia, file note, 12 July 1935, CAHJP, HM2/8790, fol. 455f. (Special Archive Moscow, 721-1-2914).
69. Königsberg Gestapo report for February 1935, Kulka and Jäckel, *NS-Stimmungsberichte*, CD-ROM, doc. no. 629.
70. *Der Stürmer*, no. 16, April 1935.
71. C.V. regional association East Prussia to Berlin headquarters, 6 April 1935, CAHJP, HM2/ 8758, fol. 2457f. (Special Archive Moscow, 721-1-2293). In its report for April, the Königsberg Gestapo also mentioned the incident and cited the placard's text. Königsberg report for April 1935, Kulka and Jäckel, *NS-Stimmungsberichte*, 132.
72. Königsberg report for April 1935, Kulka and Jäckel, *NS-Stimmungsberichte*, 132.
73. C.V. Schneidemühl to Berlin headquarters, 15 April 1935, CAHJP, HM2/8758, fol. 2446f. (Special Archive Moscow, 721-1-2293).
74. Königsberg Gestapo report for April 1935, Kulka and Jäckel, *NS-Stimmungsberichte*, CD-ROM, doc. no. 771. The two people in custody were released the following day.
75. Transcription of the article as an appendix to the report by the C.V. regional association East Prussia regarding the "Marienburg incident" to Berlin headquarters, 2 May 1935, CAHJP, HM2/8760, fols. 1716–1718 (Special Archive Moscow, 721-1-2335).
76. Königsberg Gestapo report for May 1935, Kulka and Jäckel, *NS-Stimmungsberichte*, CD-ROM, doc. no. 854.
77. C.V. regional association East Prussia to Berlin headquarters, 4 July 1935, CAHJP, HM2/8760, fol. 1709f. (Special Archive Moscow, 721-1-2335); Königsberg Gestapo report for June 1935, Kulka and Jäckel, *NS-Stimmungsberichte*, CD-ROM, doc. no. 943.
78. C.V. regional association East Prussia to Berlin headquarters, 20 August 1935, Special Archive Moscow, 721-1-2335, fol. 273.
79. C.V. regional association East Prussia to Berlin headquarters, 9 June 1933, CAHJP, HM2/ 8778, fols. 1056–1057 (Special Archive Moscow, 721-1-2672); C.V. regional association East Prussia to Berlin headquarters, 8 July 1935, CAHJP, HM2/8760, fol. 1614 (Special Archive Moscow, 721-1-2335).
80. C.V. regional association East Prussia to Berlin headquarters, 16–21 July 1935, CAHJP, HM2/8760, fols. 1610–1613 (Special Archive Moscow, 721-1-2335).
81. C.V. regional association East Prussia to Berlin headquarters, 23 July 1935, CAHJP, HM2/ 8783, fol. 1733 (Special Archive Moscow, 721-1-2804).
82. C.V. regional association East Prussia to Berlin headquarters, 5 July 1935, CAHJP, HM2/ 8783, fol. 2061 (Special Archive Moscow, 721-1-2804).
83. C.V. regional association to Berlin headquarters, 15 July 1935, Special Archive Moscow, 721-1-172, fols. 90–95.
84. C.V. regional association East Prussia to Berlin headquarters 22 July 1935, CAHJP, HM2/ 8784, fols. 721–723 (Special Archive Moscow, 721-1-2808).
85. A similar case also took place in Schivelbein in Pomerania in August. Here a coal dealer named Kronheim chased away a group of little boys who were harassing his

customers in front of his store, telling them to "get out of here!" Thereupon a short time later some forty of the boys' relatives returned, forced their way into the store, and compelled Kronheim to walk through the streets with a sign that read: "Jew Kronheim wanted to beat a little boy." They made sure that all of the Jewish stores in Schivelbein were closed for the day. The police took Kronheim into protective custody, but in the evening a large assembly took place in "protest against the Jew Kronheim, who wanted to beat a little boy." And during the night, the windows were smashed in the houses where Schivelbein's Jews resided. Report by the C.V. regional association Pomerania to Berlin headquarters16 August 1935, CAHJP, HM2/8797, fol. 822f. (Special Archive Moscow, 721-1-3019). Kronheim became so ill while under arrest that a few days later he was taken to a hospital in Bad Polzin. His store remained closed at first, but with the intervention of the C.V. it was opened again a week later.

86. See Michael Buddrus, *Totale Erziehung für den totalen Staat: Hitlerjugend und nationalsozialistischen Jugendpolitik*, 2 vols. (Munich, 2003); Michael H. Kater, *Hitler-Jugend* (Darmstadt, 2005); an increased participation by the Hitler Youth in anti-Semitic actions is also maintained in Nolzen, "The Nazi Party and Its Violence against Jews," 268f.

87. Stanley J. Tambiah, *Leveling Crowds: Ethnonationalist Conflicts and Collective Violence in South Asia* (Berkeley, 1996), 236–239; similarly see anti-Jewish pogroms from the end of the nineteenth century and beginning of the twentieth century in John D. Klier and Shlomo Lambroza, eds., *Pogroms: Anti-Jewish Violence in Modern Russian History* (Cambridge, 1992).

88. Helmut Walser Smith, *The Butcher's tale: Murder and Anti-Semitism in a German Town* (New York, 2002).

89. Königsberg Gestapo report for July 1935, Kulka and Jäckel, *NS-Stimmungsberichte*, CD-ROM, doc. no. 1015; David Bankier also emphasized that the anti-Jewish violence in the summer of 1935 was rather reluctantly received by the population. Bankier, *The Germans and the Final Solution*, 70–76.

90. Arnsberg Gestapo report for August 1935, Kulka and Jäckel, *NS-Stimmungsberichte*, CD-ROM, doc. no. 1087.

91. Bankier, *The Germans and the Final Solution*, 70.

92. While Ian Kershaw supported the position that the German population behaved rather indifferently to the persecution of the Jews, Otto Dov Kulka characterized the position of the Germans as passive complicity. Ian Kershaw, "The Persecution of the Jews and German Popular Opinion in the Third Reich," *Leo Baeck Institute Yearbook* 26 (1981): 261–289; Otto Dov Kulka, "Die Nürnberger Rassegesetze und die deutsche Bevölkerung im Lichte geheimer NS Lage- und Stimmungsberichte," *Vierteljahrshefte für Zeitgeschichte* 32 (1984): 582–624; see also Sarah Gordon, *Hitler, Germans, and the "Jewish Question"* (Princeton, 1984), 171–174; Bankier, *The Germans and the Final Solution*, 76–80.

93. Behnken, *Deutschlandberichte*, August 1935, 922 (report from Bavaria).

94. Behnken, *Deutschlandberichte*, January 1936, 24 (report from Saxony); see also Bernd Stöver, *Volksgemeinschaft im Dritten Reich: Die Konsensbereitschaft der Deutschen aus der Sicht sozialistischer Exilberichte* (Düsseldorf, 1993), 246–261.

6

"RACIAL DEFILEMENT"
Honor, Gender, and Volk's Justice

The fear of "mixing blood" and "racial defilement" has existed ever since the biological racial model gained popularity and Europeans began to define themselves as "white" in opposition to "black," "red," "brown," and "yellow" people.[1] In particular, it was colonial rule by European states in Africa and Asia that raised questions regarding the permissibility or prohibition of "racial mixing." At the same time, the conception of "racial purity" was closely linked to the anti-Semitic construction of an "impure Jewish body."[2] In 1905 the colonial administration in German Southwest Africa—today's Namibia—prohibited "mixed racial marriage"; the German colonies in German East Africa and Samoa followed. However, as emphasized by a representative of the Catholic Center Party during the 1912 Reichstag debate regarding marriage prohibitions, this meant encouraging extramarital relationships. More out of fear for the institution of marriage than from an anti-racist position, the majority in the Reichstag supported an SPD resolution that both legalized "mixed marriages" and also made fathers responsible for supporting children born out of wedlock. Accordingly, the imperial colonial office stipulated the registration "mixed children," but at the same time also allowed the police to intervene against extramarital relationships between German men and African women in cases where these created a "public nuisance." Thirty years later, Heinrich Krieger, an employee of the NSDAP's racial policy office, wrote that this ordinance made it fully permissible to "pillory racial defilers."[3]

The ambivalence of the Reichstag debate is unmistakable. Supporters of marriage prohibitions like the state secretary of the imperial colonial office, Wilhelm Solf, warned that "our race [will become] bastardized." Others wanted to use the prohibition to strengthen "racial sensibility."[4] The debate concerning "mixed marriages" in the colonies reveals how even before the First World War racial positions were influencing the political public, and how sexuality—especially when concerning members of different races—became politics. And the question of gender played a decisive role. During the Kaiserreich the cultural irritant was the relationship between German men and African women. But twenty years later, during the post–World War I occupation of the Rhineland by French troops, which included units from North Africa, the concern was with relationships between "colored" soldiers and German women. Now, apart from questions of racial purity, concubinage, and alleged moral decay, the discussion proceeded in a much sharper tone about "honor" and "defilement." The subject of the discussion was referred to as the "Schwarze Schmach" (black disgrace).[5]

The Deutschnationale Volkspartei expressed its indignation in April 1920 in a question put to the imperial government: "Our youth in the Palatinate and the Rhineland is being defiled, our Volk contaminated, the honor of the German and the white race crushed under foot." And the representatives of all parties in the National Assembly—except for the USPD—spoke in a common resolution about the "inextinguishable disgrace" incurred because of the stationing of "colored" soldiers in Germany and the fact that "these savages" represented a "gruesome danger" for German women and children.[6] Even Reich President Ebert, a member of the SPD, complained "that the use of colored troops from the lowest cultural level as supervisors of a population with the elevated spiritual and economic significance of the Rhinelanders [is] a provocating violation of the laws of European civilization."[7] As in Dresden, where the Housewife Association (Hausfrauenverband) called for a rally in June 1921, public rallies and demonstrations also took place in other cities in order to protest against the "black disgrace."[8]

First, as Gisela Lebzelter has emphasized in her study, there was a noticeable dramatic intensification of the conflict. It became a question of either/or: the survival or downfall of the white race. In 1927, the state of Bavaria considered whether so-called "Rhineland bastards" should be forcibly sterilized, a project that the National Socialists made real.[9] Second—this is something that Cornelia Essner draws attention to—the idea of the contamination of the white race due to mixing with foreign races took hold.[10] Theoretically, it was possible, as Eugen Fischer did, for example, to put forward the idea that the "crossing" of different races would ennoble the "lower" races or optimize their best characteristics. But instead, it was the theories of contagion and anti-Semitism that gained plausibility within the social discussion, according to which any sexual contact with a "lower race," especially the Jews, would incurably poison the "higher race."

The racial theorist Houston Stewart Chamberlain was married to Richard Wagner's daughter, Eva von Bülow, and lived in Bayreuth where he enjoyed considerable respect within *völkisch* circles.[11] Known for his work *The Foundations of the Nineteenth Century*, he especially emphasized the "purity requirement," claiming in a customary anti-Semitic manner that the Jewish Volk itself made masterful use of the "law of blood" to expand its rule, allowing not a single drop of blood in and infecting the Indo-Europeans with their blood. "If this were to persist in this manner for a few centuries," stated Chamberlain, "in all of Europe there would only be a single racially pure Volk, that of the Jews—all the rest would be a herd of pseudo-Hebraic mestizos and thus an undoubtedly physically, spiritually, and morally degenerated Volk."[12]

This racist, apocalyptic phantasm of "blood contamination" was very widely spread by Alfred Dinter's *The Sin against the Blood*, a novel published in 1917 that within a very short period was reprinted several times and reached an estimated 1.5 million readers. Dinter's novel contributed significantly to the spread of the radically anti-Semitic contagionist notion that a single act of sexual contact with a Jewish man was sufficient to forever contaminate the children of an "Aryan" woman, even if those children were from a "racially pure" man.[13] The phantasm of the "preeminent potency of Jewish blood" and a Jewish plan of "racial poisoning"—the connection between sexuality and anti-Semitism—had always dominated National Socialist propaganda, especially that of the *Stürmer*. Dinter himself, who joined the National Socialists early on and for a brief period, from 1925 to 1928, was the Thuringian NSDAP Gauleiter, demanded in his book that marriages between "Germans and Jews" be prohibited and that every Jew who "defiled a German girl" be punished.[14]

Persecution of "Racial Defilement" after the Seizure of Power

As early as March 1930, Wilhelm Frick, who was the interior minister for Thuringia, brought to the Reichstag a "law for the protection of the German nation," according to which those "who contribute or threaten to contribute to the deterioration and disintegration of the German Volk by mixing with members of the Jewish blood community [*Blutsgemeinschaft*] or colored races" would be guilty of "racial treason" and punished with imprisonment and stripped out their civil rights.[15] Achim Gehrke was the director of the NSDAP's office for genealogy, established in 1931, and after the seizure of power was the "specialist for racial studies" in the Reich Interior Ministry. In 1933 in a number of influential memoranda he promoted the prohibition of "mixed marriages" and the deprivation of German citizenship for Jews. Similarly, within the Interior Ministry in April 1933 there was also a "draft for a law regulating the position of the Jews," but because of the "law for the restoration of the professional civil service" of 7 April, it proceeded no further.[16]

In September 1933 the Prussian justice ministry published a memo-randum entitled "National Socialist Criminal Justice," largely written by State Secretary Roland Freisler. Under the section entitled "Protection of the Race and Volk traditions," it stated that there should be a "stop to the racial mixing that has taken place in Germany over the course of centu-ries." The first step necessary in order to privilege "northern blood"—the so-called *Aufnordung*—was to ensure that "henceforth no Jews, negroes, and other coloreds are accepted into German blood." In any event, the memorandum met with intense misgivings within the country, particu-larly from the Churches. As a result, subsequent meetings of the criminal law commission determined that, while including "racial protection" in the criminal code was in principle desirable, it was hardly possible for the foreseeable future.[17]

But the condemnation of "racial defilement" did not merely take place in government departments officially working on juridical regulations and laws. Rather, such condemnations were apparently also informing the ini-tiatives of the National Socialist movement. Threats were already being made prior to 1933. In December 1930, the *C.V.-Zeitung* cited the Ingol-stadt newspaper *Donauboten*, in which a woman was publicly denounced wholly in terms of Arthur Dinter's jargon for having a relationship with a Jew:

It is known that the Jew has an inborn lust for the blonde woman. While the like-blooded Jewess assures the propagation of his race, the Jew seeks out more the highly natured Aryan woman to service his Asiatic drives.... It is a fact that an unspoiled German woman has an instinctive disinclina-tion towards the Jews. The only women who have nothing against hav-ing relationships with Jews are those who have acquired perverse impulses because of modern literature and trendy madness. On the basis of this un-derstanding, we have already threatened once in the *Donauboten* to pub-licly pillory those women who trespass against the *Vollblutgemeinschaft* [full-blooded or thoroughbred community] and deal with Jews. In Ingolstadt it is a certain Thea D. who apparently considers it an honor to be the first one mentioned. We warned her in her own interest, for the result is usually disgrace. Only in consideration of her very decent parents, for whom the mentioning of her name would be a misfortune, are we refraining this time from revealing her identity. If she is seen with the Jew again, she will be stigmatized. We request all racially conscious Germans to keep watch for Christians who serve the Jews and to provide us with their addresses and those of the Jews, including the facts of the case. Ingolstadt must be cleansed of Jewish cultural defilement.

As the *C.V.-Zeitung* reported, this matter was not confined to the newspaper article. The Ortsgruppenleiter of the Ingolstadt NSDAP also sent a threatening letter in the name of the party to the parents of the denounced woman.[18]

After the National Socialist seizure of power, such threats could become practice. The procession that took place in Marburg in August 1933, described in this book's introduction, was by no means an exception. In Würzburg in the summer of 1933, a 29-year-old Jewish wine merchant was denounced to the NSDAP for "racial defilement" after a neighborhood dispute. Thereupon SS men took him from his home and forced him through the town with a sign hanging around his neck that read: "I lived with a German woman in concubinage." Afterward the police took him into "protective custody," releasing him a week later with instructions to leave Würzburg.[19]

In Nuremburg, also in the summer of 1933, a Jewish merchant and his girlfriend on an excursion were picked up by forestry officials and then turned over to the SS. The SS first marched the couple through a nearby village and then drove with them to Nuremburg. In a statement to the state attorney's office, the man noted the following:

> Arriving in Nuremberg, a wild commotion erupted. In order to draw people's attention to us, there was loud jeering, shouting, whistling, and honking. We had to leave the car and were then dragged through the crowd of people to the music podium, where the leader of the drive gave an inflammatory, wild speech against us to the beer drinking public. This went on for hours from one beer garden to the next. We were pushed, spat upon, beaten, and berated by the incited crowd, and in so doing the females in the crowd quite especially played an exceptional part.[20]

The man was subsequently taken into "protective custody" and later brought to the Dachau concentration camp. After a two-year imprisonment he was able to emigrate to South Africa. The woman was released, only to be detained again in order to publicly shear her hair. Such en-

croachments are also documented for 1934, like the public abuse of the
Jewish manufacturer Leo Stern in September 1934 in Schlüchtern in
Hesse and a "racial defilement" procession in Oberbieber in Westphalia.[21]
But it was not until 1935 that the "racial defilement" actions crystallized
as the central focus of local Nazi groups.[22]

Political support was provided at the beginning of the year by the Gestapo, which wanted to implement the prohibition of marriages between
people stemming from Jewish and non-Jewish families, called "German-
Jewish mixed marriages" according to the terminology colored by contemporary anti-Semitism. In December 1934 the SS Race and Settlement Office participated in a conference on racial policy held at NSDAP
headquarters—the so-called "Brown House" in Munich—during which
the "final and complete exclusion of the Jews from the German *Lebensge-
meinschaft*" was criticized as insufficient and marriage and sexual prohibitions were requested anew.[23] The Gestapo supported this tendency in its
reports and henceforth noted "dissatisfaction" in the population with the
regime's racist policies. In February 1935 the Berlin state police reported
that cases in which alleged "Jewish business managers were sexually abusing their German personnel" were proliferating and characterized these as
"occurrences that evoke the revulsion of the *Volksgenossen* to the utmost
and repeatedly give occasion for the most indignant denunciations. For
the Volk, which is thinking more and more in racist terms, it is utterly
incomprehensible that these goings-on are not brought to a halt with dra-
conian measures by the state."[24]

Similarly, the Coblenz Gestapo wrote in the same month that "fortunately" the signs were increasing "that the sensibility in the population
for the great importance of maintaining the purity of the race is growing."[25] At the same time the state police reported about a demonstration
in Simmern in the Rhineland at the end of February that was directed
against the Jewish livestock trader Max Israel, who was accused of having
"approached an Aryan young girl in an immoral manner," as the Gestapo
put it. "Regretfully," noted the Gestapo tersely, "this demonstration had
as a consequence that considerable damage was caused to a number of
Jewish homes by the breaking of windowpanes."[26]

A female apprentice in a department store in Simmern had, in fact,
denounced Max Israel to an acquaintance, whereupon the action got underway. A number of years after the war, Max Israel's son described what
happened on that evening. He was thirteen years old at the time.

> On February 23, 1935, a Christian acquaintance of my parents came to my
> parents at 3 o'clock on Saturday afternoon to inform them that the Nazis
> would come to our house on the same evening at 8 o'clock in order to ar-

rest my father.... The brother of my father, Joseph Israel, his grown family, and a number of Jews came together to discuss what my father should do. It was decided that he should leave Simmern immediately.... We did not know where he went. My mother and I and a few relatives afterwards suggested taking a walk through the town to find out perhaps whether there was really anything to this warning. We found the town completely normal and everyone went back home. Meanwhile it had grown dark, and my sister and I sat in our pajamas at dinner. Precisely at 8 o'clock we heard a lot of racket outside and someone banged very hard on our entry door. My mother opened the door and the leader of this crowd of young scoundrels asked to see my father. My mother answered that he was not home and she did not know where he was staying. They did not believe her and stormed through the whole house and could not find him. The entire Mühlengasse was full of members of the Nazi party. We later found out that these people belonged to the SA but were not in uniform.... As they heard outside that my father was not to be found, they became like animals.... Outside there was plenty of shouting and they took the window shutters on the ground floor off their hinges and threw them through the window in our living room, took apart a wall of our manure pile across from our house and bombarded us with the stones. We had hidden ourselves in all the corners of the kitchen, which was on the ground floor, to protect ourselves from being stoned. The situation became worse by the minute, for they smashed all of the windows in the house. By now it was already 10 o'clock, and a few of these scoundrels came into the kitchen and tried to bombard us with their stones. Suddenly I saw my mother crawl out of the corner. She ran to our entry door and shouted with all of her strength, could they stop for a minute with the bombarding so that she could take her children up to the first floor.

As if on command, it was quiet for a half a minute, and our mother brought us up into the bedroom. With incredible force, she shoved a heavy piece of furniture in front of the door in order to barricade it. From this moment on it became worse. Many of those who were outside had burning torches and threw them through all of the windows in the ground floor, and it started to burn. We were very frightened that we would become victims of the flames. By now it was already 11 o'clock, and suddenly someone knocked on our door and we heard a voice, that they were the police and they wanted to take us into protective custody.[27]

Indeed, the police took Sybilla Israel and both of her children into custody and released them the next morning. A few months later the family went to Rotterdam, where they met Max Israel, who for weeks had hidden in a relative's coal shed in Düsseldorf before he could escape to Holland. From the Netherlands, the family emigrated to Palestine in December 1935.[28]

Blind destructive rage erupted when it became clear that Max Israel was not going to be taken. The breaking of windows turned into a bombardment of stones that was increasingly meant not to merely destroy things but also to hit people. In this situation of immediate danger to life and limb, the mother showed her presence of mind, managing to momentarily interrupt the crowd, which was like an animal that briefly pauses when it is yelled at; fortunately, it was enough for her to find refuge for herself and the children in the bedroom and barricade the room. Just a few seconds later the stunned and surprised crowd erupted into an even more intense hatred and no longer shied away from setting the house ablaze and possibly burning alive the woman with her two children, were it not for appearance of the police—who arrived just in time yet still three horrifying hours too late and interrupted the violent fury by taking the family into custody.

In Lohra in Hesse, a group of young men had apparently arranged to attack the residences of Jewish families during the night of 13–14 August. Stones were thrown and windows were demolished.[29] But in particular, they were after Moritz Levi, who was allegedly having a relationship with a married woman. A witness from the neighboring community later described the chase:

I lived, as already mentioned, in Sachsenhausen, on the other side of the Salzböge in Wiesengrund. The noise from a wild pursuit resounded from the village and came over to us, as a pack of determined guys chased a person. The footsteps of the person running for his life resounded far into the quiet of the night. The person fleeing still had to some extent a head start on his pursuers, who chased him, bellowing loudly like a pack of dogs. We could literally feel his fear as the pursued man ran for his life. From the bellowing of the pursuers, we heard snippets of words now and then: "beat him to death, the sow-Jew, beat him to death, the sow-Jew!"

The pursued man ran towards the Eselsmühle [literally: donkey's mill] and then the loud clatter of his running fell silent. In the courtyard of the Eselsmühle it was quiet. However, the pack of pursuers could not be stopped and also stormed into the mill's courtyard, where they then halted for they had indeed lost the trail. "Where is the sow-Jew? Where did he go? He must be here somewhere. We are going to get him yet!" Thus we heard the agitated discussion of the pursuers who no longer knew just what they should do, since simply forcing their way into a building of the Eselsmühle was something they apparently did not dare.

We heard as the house door of the residence in the Eselsmühle was opened and someone on the stairs addressed those gathered in the courtyard. It soon became clear that it was the proprietor of the mill, Herr F., who asked in a certain tone: "So, what is going on here? What is the meaning of this noise at night?" "We are looking for a Jew whom we have pursued, whom we want to hold to account. He disappeared here in the courtyard." "There is no one here," said the *Esel*-miller, "go home and go to bed. There is nobody here in our courtyard and there will be no more searching for anybody here." At first this did not satisfy the pursuers and they had all kinds of objections. But the *Esel*-miller remained firm and did not allow himself to become engaged in a discussion. Mr. F. was a respected person and he did not let himself get easily intimidated by the pursuers. As we could hear, his words were now somewhat louder and more determined and he demanded that the men now disappear from his courtyard. There arose an incomprehensible murmuring among the pursuers, and then they moved away, back again towards Lohra.[30]

In fact, the proprietor of the Eselsmühle had hidden Moritz Levi, who ran further during the night to the train station in Friedelshausen and in the morning fled to Holland by train. Later he was able to emigrate to Chile. The non-Jewish woman was arrested and interrogated; twelve of the violent perpetrators appeared in court and in September 1935 were convicted of disturbing the peace. They were fined and, in part, sentenced to a number of months in prison.[31]

Pillory Processions 1935

The Breslau SA proceeded systematically. At the end of January 1935 the *Stürmer* published an incendiary article on its title page, laid out large, about "racial defilement in Breslau."[32] A little later, following the example of the *Stürmer*, the *Schlesische Tageszeitung* began publishing a series of articles dealing with the theme "at the pillory," in which non-Jewish women who allegedly had intimate relations with Jews were denounced by name and address. In conjunction with that, the SA regularly organized propaganda processions on every Sunday around midday during which the names of these women were loudly announced. A list with these names was put up on the old pillory and guarded by SA people so that nobody could remove it.

The reaction within the Breslau population was apparently cautious and even negative. While the Gestapo wrote in its report that the action had "by and large" been welcomed, the district president reported that the population's posture "vis-à-vis these measures [was] in part dismissive,"[33] which hardly seems surprising since the action targeted non-Jewish girls and young women and exposed them in front of the *Volksgemeinschaft*. In a letter to the Breslau police president, a businessman voiced his indignation:

> During an automobile trip through Germany I roamed in Silesia and on this occasion also Breslau. On Sunday I also had the opportunity to be allowed to visit in your town the pillory in Breslau. Pardon me when I tell you that I felt as if I had been set back at least a century. I am expressly noting that I am a full Aryan and in no way have anything in common with Jews, but precisely for a full Aryan it is shameful to see something like that.[34]

A non-Jewish woman even filed a complaint about having been publicly denounced during the SA's Sunday "pillory procession" and indicated that she did not maintain an intimate relationship with Jews. The Breslau district court, however, did not support the woman's claim, reasoning that the concept of "racial defilement" referred not only to the "sexual union of an Aryan female with a non-Jewish male and the other way around" but "also [to] every other friendly interaction insofar as it extends beyond the framework of pure business."[35]

Apparently these Sunday processions were also the object of derisive shouting, which in turn increased the irritability of the SA and repeatedly led to fears of excesses.[36] The Breslau Gestapo, however, maintained its position "that the population is learning to see more racially and the aversion towards Judaism is increasing, supported by the fact that individual NSDAP local chapters are openly displaying the '*Stürmer*' in the town districts."[37] Then in June the Gestapo had some twenty people—Jewish men and non-Jewish women—arrested; a month later another twenty were arrested because of alleged "racial defilement." At the same time, corresponding articles published in the press spread information about the sex lives of those who had been arrested. At this point the mood in the town turned against the victims. At the end of July, when the forty men and women who had been arrested were supposed to be brought to a concentration camp, thousands of curious onlookers gathered on the street in order to follow the transport. According to the Gestapo, the population was indignant because there was no deviation from procedure and the prisoners were brought to the train station in a closed vehicle. A few thousand people had gathered there in order to chant insults at the prisoners.[38]

Norden

On Saturday, 20 July 1935, the *Ostfriesische Tageszeitung* published a 32-page supplement entitled "The Jews Are Our Misfortune" in which, in the style of the *Stürmer*, Jews were libeled, ridiculed, and insulted; at the same time all businesses with Jewish proprietors were listed, together with the usual appeal for a boycott, and additionally this edition contained a detailed article about "Iwan Rooseboom, the racial defiler of East Frisia." Two days later, on Monday morning, the two highest-ranking SA leaders in Norden, Hermann Schöttler and Arthur Jäger, went to the police station, filed charges against Christine Neemann and Julius Wolff for "racial defilement," and requested that both be taken immediately into protective custody. When the constable on duty, named Limbach, tried to play down the issue, advising both men to go to the district president or state police agency, the two SA leaders left the station. But around noon they made it know by telephone that they would lead both victims through the streets during the afternoon.[39]

Christine Neemann was born in Norden in 1902, as was her Jewish fiancé Julius Wolff, the son of a merchant. After the war in her indemnification claim she described the day as follows: "In the beginning of July 1935 I was taken by six SA men from my mother's apartment because I was engaged to a Jew, Julius Wolff. We were led through the streets, each of us with a sign around our neck: *Rassenschänder* [racial defiler]. In the open street, I was beaten and had my hair torn from my head, and we were then brought to the prison."[40] According to police reports, Christine Neemann still defended herself, tapping her finger on her forehead to indicate that she viewed the whole thing as madness—according to the report, this further agitated the crowd of around 200 to 300 people who were accompanying the procession.

After the police had arrested Christine Neemann and Julius Wolff, the crowd searched for another couple: the 31-year old Elisa Extra and her Jewish fiancé Richard Cossen. However, the crowd was able to find only Elisa, who was at her mother's, so she was marched alone through the streets of Norden with a sign: "I am a German girl and allowed myself to be defiled by a Jew." The druggist in Norden, an NSDAP and SA member, was given the assignment to document the action, and he subsequently also displayed his photographs in his shop window. The photos all show the participating crowd: common citizens—male and female, adolescents and children, even laughing young women keeping just ahead of the procession.

The next day the *Ostfriesische Tageszeitung* described the action as an expression of spontaneous *Volkszorn* (people's anger), which was due to the "outrageous carryings-on" of Norden's Jews and to which the SA had simply yielded. Max Klein was accused of continuing to work in his shop after business hours; Christine Neemann and Julius Wolff had made a public show of their relationship of many years, as had Richard Cossen and Elisa Extra, even though both women had been made aware numerous times "of their carryings-on." After Neemann and Wolff were taken from their apartments, groups of people engaged in lively discussion formed everywhere. "From all sides, chanting groups and shouts demanded that these two, who by virtue of their behavior had excluded themselves from the Volksgemeinschaft, be led through the town. The SA yielded to the will of the population and both were furnished with corresponding placards and led through the town. Everywhere the population loudly applauded and expressed its indignation through strong cries of fie!"[41]

The fact that this second procession also took place draws attention to the emotions that were involved—the passions that had not yet been sated and thus wanted the public humiliation to continue. On the same day, the crowd proceeded to the house of Max Klein and demanded his arrest until the police quickly came and also took him into "protective custody." Later they took Levi Altgenug into protective custody as well. In the end, apart from Christine Neemann and Elisa Extra, seven more people were taken into "protective custody" on that 22 July.[42]

Christine Neemann was taken from the prison in Aurich to the Moringen concentration camp and released at the end of August. Her employer in Norden, for whom she had worked for ten years, fired her. In 1936 she was imprisoned again because someone denounced her for saying that the Gestapo had mistreated her. In 1942 she married a train conductor. However, as she wrote in her indemnification claim after the war, with the wedding "the whole matter was dug up again. The Nazi mob would not leave me in peace." Julius Wolff was able to flee to America. The legal proceedings conducted in 1949 for the persecution of Christine Neemann and Julius Wolff resulted in the sentencing of six defendants to prison terms of between three and seven months. SA Sturmführer Jäger and a police officer were acquitted because of lack of evidence.

Elisa Extra was brought with Christine Neemann to the Moringen concentration camp and released at the end of August 1935. She also lost her job at the post office. She fled to Amsterdam and found a position as a maid with a Jewish family. Later she took care of the household of a man whose wife had been admitted to a psychiatric clinic. Her fiancé Richard Cossen was able to flee to Amsterdam in 1936 and from there to Argentina. After the war and legal proceedings that lasted more than ten years, Elisa Extra received a one-time payment for damages of DM 150 for her loss of earnings due to her KZ imprisonment. The coercion, unlawful detention, and physical injuries of Elisa Extra and Richard Cossen were not legally prosecuted.

Media

Without the numerous denunciations coming from the population, the Gestapo would not have been able to pursue cases of alleged "racial defilement." According to Robert Gellately's investigation of the Würzburg Gestapo, in 54 percent of the cases, accusations from the population comprised by far the most important reason that the police prosecuted "racial defilement."[43] In 1936, the year after the "racial defilement" actions and the Nuremburg laws, the number of denunciations rapidly shot up and remained at a high level until 1938, after which they again declined. The number of denunciations because of "friendship with Jews" also clearly rose in 1936 compared to 1935 and held steady until the deportations began in 1941.[44] Indicative of the emotions motivating the denunciations is the fact that large numbers of the accusations were classified by the Gestapo as false or unfounded.

Media, especially newspapers like the *Stürmer* that had already been mobilized at the beginning of the year, likewise played an important role. There was hardly an edition that failed to open on the first page with an incendiary article about a "racial defiler" or "girl defiler," always with full names and places of residence. With respect to the district court proceedings in mid June against the Jewish director of a trade school in Magdeburg because of alleged "racial defilement," the *Stürmer* published a special edition that, according to the Gestapo, sold exceptionally well in Magdeburg.[45] In July the Gestapo in Saxony registered anti-Jewish demonstrations in Dresden, Leipzig, Freital, and Radebeul and thirty-four arrests of Jews and non-Jews for alleged "racial defilement" during this month alone. This "public stigmatization of Jewish racial defilers and their objects as well as their unforgiving prosecution by the political police," according to the Gestapo, has "found approval everywhere.... By the publication of names in the daily press, the broad public was made aware of the danger of racial defilement, which was evidenced by countless numbers of complaints."[46]

Like the Breslau Gestapo, other state police agencies also reported that the display and sale of the *Stürmer* greatly contributed to an aggressive anti-Semitic mood. Time and again, one can observe a direct relationship between a public denunciation in the *Stürmer* and local activities. Thus in its May edition the *Stürmer* reviled an Austrian Jew living in Düsseldorf by name as a "racial defiler," and on the same day a large crowd gathered in front of his business and became so threatening that the police ultimately stepped in and dispersed the crowd.[47]

During the summer months in the district of Minden the *Stürmer* managed, with the support of the SA and SS, to increase its subscriptions by around 50 percent. According to the Gestapo, there was hardly a village of any significance that did not have a *Stürmer-Kasten*. Above all, it was the special edition about the Magdeburg proceedings that reached record sales figures. Newspaper dealers had to reorder the edition numerous times in order to satisfy the demand. "Undoubtedly," determined the Gestapo, "the population has become thoroughly activated in the Jewish question, and the attitude in the population towards the Jews is not friendly."[48]

Regional newspapers further fueled the anti-Semitic mood in the summer of 1935. On an almost daily basis in July and August the *Westdeutscher Beobachter* published articles directed against the Jews. The paper declared its outrage over "Jewish girl defilers" in Vienna and "Jewish fraud-banks" in Amsterdam, and reported with satisfaction about "Jew-free baths" in Mönchen-Gladbach and Rheydt. At the beginning of August the newspaper demanded the "identification of Jewish businesses."[49] Likewise, for example, the *Braunschweiger Tageszeitung* published an anti-Semitic article almost daily during these months. The *Miesbacher Anzeiger* reported about actions, demonstrations, and tumults against a "Jew-hotel"—the Park Hotel in Bad Tölz, which shortly thereafter was closed by the authorities. Then on 8 August the headline read: "Bad Tölz reports: cleansed of Jews!"[50]

But other methods of communication were used as well. Thus the alleged rape of a girl in Hessian Oldendorf resonated especially well in other districts of Lower Saxony because anonymous anti-Semitic leaflets were distributed—for example, in Bückeburg and the district of Rinteln—holding the Jews responsible for the sex crime. In July in Minden, red placards were pasted up at numerous locations during the night, especially on Jewish businesses, public buildings, and the Stahlhelm's display cases. The placards' headline stated: "Unheard-of racial defilement in the house of the Jew Löwenstein in Hessian Oldendorf."[51] The unrest in the neighborhood, particularly in Hameln, wrote the regional C.V. to headquarters in Berlin, was very great, and anxieties about possible excesses ran high.[52]

In Hessian Oldendorf itself there were nightly excesses in August, which motivated Jewish families to temporarily leave the place.[53] The Lutheran pastor Korff pasted the leaflet into the chronicle of his church and wrote:

The "cucumber time" in 1935 again brought much agitation and unrest to our town. I will keep it short, for that which is to be reported is actually very shameful for our homeland. The accusations of the red placard are based for the most part on untruths, according to the decision of the state attorney. The Jew Mannheimer was not brought to the gallows but rather was set free. "The German girl"—confirmand 1935—who, for a long time already, has a bad reputation, lied. Instead of exercising restraint vis-à-vis the Jews, one night a riotous assembly occurred, in which married men and women participated and undertook a campaign against the Jews who had in no way behaved provokingly. Windows were smashed. Houses were forced-into. Destruction inflicted. The Jews [were] forced to depart. Outbreaks of brutality![54]

Newspapers, leaflets, and rumors played a major role in the actions against "racial defilement," for not only did they make known the names of victims; rather, they also created the initial pogrom-prone mood that then led to actual excesses. In Pomerania it was the *Pommersche Zeitung* that in the summer of 1935 agitated more strongly against the Jewish population, reporting on cases of so-called racial defilement and unabashedly encouraging readers to engage in violence. Mid August witnessed the publication of a special edition entitled "the Jewish Mirror," which denounced the district's Jewish citizens by name.[55] Thus *Volksgenossen* demonstrated on 13 July in Stargard and the next day in Stralsund after the local Stralsund section of the *Pommersche Zeitung* fueled an anti-Semitic mood on the occasion of the wedding of the Jewish merchant Hein Cohn and the non-Jewish Lucie Grenzen. On the following day there were anti-Semitic demonstrations in Plathe and ten days later in Altdamm and in Wangerin. On 24 July in the Baltic beach town of Misdroy, a rally took place, featuring signs that read: "Jews! We are giving you another 24 hours' time!" The crowd proceeded to a Jewish children's home, which sheltered about ninety children, and extorted an agreement from the director to empty the home the next day.[56]

On 2 August Stettin itself witnessed a large anti-Jewish demonstration with supposedly 30,000 participants, summoned by the NSDAP after the town's Jewish businesspeople had complained in a telegram to the Reich Ministry of Economics about the ongoing boycott actions.[57] "The public pillorying in the *Stürmer* of German women who have relationships with Jews or of Germans who buy from Jews has found imitators everywhere," determined the district president of Stettin:

> The organization of the NSDAP is eagerly promoting the *Stürmer* by distributing it free of charge and by setting up display cases in which, apart from the *Stürmer*, local pillorying of *Volksgenossen* is made public. Naturally, these methods do not merely have a deterrent effect, but rather often also provide the occasion for a violent operation against the stigmatized *Volks-*

genossen.... In many cases, police officers or gendarmes have to take Jews or German girls in relationships with Jews into custody for the own security in order to prevent acts of violence. A means of coercion used frequently even in my district was leading these women through the town. Property damage such as the smashing of display windows, the destruction of business or occupational signs, and the like has been reported repeatedly.[58]

In Pölitz in Pomerania, a town with a small Jewish community in the administrative district of Stettin, the Bürgermeister watched in the early evening of 30 August as a group of about 400 people gathered at the market, reported the Stettin state police. The procession had been organized by the local chapter of the NSDAP, which, as is shown by an appeal now found in the Stettin archive, had secretly informed its members: "For verbal notification to all *Parteigenossen*. On Friday of this week around 6:30 in the afternoon, all of the *Parteigenossen* are asked to linger at the market place. Civilian clothes without party insignia. After taking note, this text is to be immediately destroyed."[59] Flyers that were distributed at the marketplace read:

> To the population of Pölitz!
>
> The racially defiling activities of the Jew ... are slapping national principles in the face; he is living with an Aryan woman in a dubious relationship, which the entire population of Pölitz finds offensive. Under the disguised name [...] the Jew [...] (for that is his Jewish name in actuality) is operating his businesses in Pölitz. The population demands the immediate removal of the Jew [...] from our town.

At the same time, slogans had been printed on the flyer for the crowds to chant:

Who lives in Pölitz under a disguised name?	The Jew [...] !
What is his name?	[...]
Who in Pölitz engages in racial defilement?	The Jew [...] !
With whom does he engage in racial defilement?	With the Aryan girl [...] from Bredow, born in Stolzenhagen!
Who is defrauding the town of taxes?	The Jew [...]!
What does the population of Pölitz demand?	That the Jew leaves Pölitz!

As he described in his report, the Bürgermeister subsequently enlisted the help of two police officers in order to put a stop to the activities, but when the men came to the marketplace the crowd had already gone to the Jewish victim's business, torn the man from his store, and led him through the town. With the help of the two police officers, the Bürgermeister was eventually able to take the Jewish businessman into "protective custody," but only after the crowd—which had grown to about 1,000 people—had arrived at the town hall. Even as the Bürgermeister was reporting by telephone to the district administrator, the crowd had moved out again to take hold of another Jewish citizen and lead him through the town. Again, the police intervened only when the procession arrived at the town hall.[60]

In Wolgast near Greifswald, a few hundred people gathered in front of the house of the Jewish businessman Georg R., accusing his son of having a relationship with a non-Jewish employee named Paula Z. The couple was dragged from the house, signs were hung around their necks—Arnold R.'s stated "I am a racial defiler," while Paula Z.'s stated "I am a Jew-whore"—and they were both forced through the town, harassed, insulted, and beaten. Finally they were locked in the town hall basement.[61] This pillory procession was linked with a second demonstration on the same day against the SA member Hermann Heiden from Wolgast, who two days earlier had been absent during an SA roll call and was instead found at a drinking party with, among others, a Jewish merchant. Heiden was immediately expelled from the SA, but on 15 August SA people and others met in front of his house to berate him. They might have even taken him from the house except for the fact that he had already fled to Stettin.[62]

It can also be shown in other cases that during these months the pillory processions started targeting non-Jewish persons. In Stettin at the end of July a crowd of about 1,000 people—mostly youth—demonstrated in front of the house of the Catholic provost because on Sunday he had ejected four uniformed Hitler Youth from the Church. The demonstrators chanted in groups and sang songs, and a few attempted to force their way into the house, although this was prevented by the police.[63] As early as January 1935, in Hilders near Fulda, two workers were taken from their building site and led through the community after a brawl with a KdF (Kraft durch Freude) group that was led by a local SA leader. The procession had even been announced with the community bell, and the victims had to carry a sign that stated: "I have insulted the SA and am the biggest pig-dog in the place." They were abused and forced to recite verses mocking themselves to a laughing crowd.[64] In Pasewalk, a National Socialist—a "proven, old party comrade," as the strict president emphasized in his report—was denounced by a fired worker and thereupon led around through the town with a sign of shame around his neck and berated and abused until he was taken into "protective custody."[65] Similarly, an employee reproached a worker for the being laziest person in the entire company, whereupon the latter complained to the German Labor Front in Stargard; on the evening of that very same day, the employee was taken from his home by a crowd, led through the village to the house of the worker and forced to apologize on his knees.[66] In Finkenwalde a crowd of around 250 people, summoned by the local renters association, moved from one house to the next belonging to allegedly anti-social homeowners, trying to force their way into the houses and drag out their owners; however, this was prevented by the three gendarmes on duty.[67]

Honor and Shame

The "pillory" is recorded throughout Europe since the twelfth century as the most common form of honor punishment of the Middle Ages.[68] It probably had its origins in Church penance, by which the sinner, often wearing a hair shirt, publicly performed penance with the framework of the Holy Thursday liturgy and thereby asked for forgiveness.[69] In contrast to the gallows, which stood outside the town walls, the pillar of shame—made out of wood and stone, and occasionally artfully finished, as in Breslau—stood in the middle of the town, at the market or in front of the town hall, open to all. As a punitive instrument for high justice, the pillory was a conspicuous sign of government authority that was directed predominantly against the "little people"—peasants and simple town citizens—while the higher estates could settle penalties with a fine.[70] In 1750 the Bavarian *Codex iuris Bavarici criminalis* expressly forbade enforcing pillory punishments on nobility, for the public dishonoring could possibly put the hierarchy of the estates at risk.[71]

A characteristic of punishment by pillory is that apart from being used to punish theft, perjury, and blasphemy, it was also used especially to punish all forms of violating sexual norms, chiefly adultery but also bigamy, incest, procuration, and fornication.[72] The public humiliation—putting the "shame" on display—was clearly the "just" punishment for the violations of norms that occurred in private.[73]

Honor, which is usually interpreted as a cultural code, i.e., a specific and changeable system of norms, signs, and practices—as Pierre Bourdieu wrote, as a complex dialectic of a challenge and response to that challenge[74]—was always closely linked with physical violence. What honor could be, according to Valentin Groebner, was always defined with violence, whereby one can distinguish three different fields of "honor" in the premodern period: first, that of men, for whom honor lay in not being physically overpowered; second, that of women, whose sexual purity needed to be defended; and third, that of mercantile honor, which amounted to trust and faith when concluding contracts—to "honorable" behavior.[75]

The public revocation of honor was inextricably linked with violent practice. The repertoire of medieval and early modern honor punishments included cutting off ears, branding, standing at the pillory, various kinds of shameful processions like carrying stones around the market while accompanied by a drumming town servant, the so-called donkey of shame, which was a wooden saw-horse construction with a sharp upper edge, and the so-called violin punishment, by which a two-part board was secured around the neck and wrists of the delinquent. Likewise, old sources mention the shearing of hair, and it was common to hang tablets around the convicts indicating their names and crimes.[76] Thus in early modern Lübeck, the hair of so-called licentious women was cut off and either attached to the pillory pole or, as was common in France, burned beside it.

Publicity was constitutive for honor punishments. In the early sources one finds all of the forms of public spectacle that we encounter in the 1930s. The town masses participate insofar as they accompany the delinquent's path to the pillory pole, often with music, and both at the pole and along the way they mock they defenseless victims, spit on them, or even literally attack them by throwing eggs, dung, or stones. On many illustrations of pillory scenes, even children are reaching for stones. As late as the early nineteenth century in Rügen, schoolchildren were still gathered under the direction of the rector when someone was brought to pillory.[77]

The public nature of the punishment disguised an ambivalent moment for the authorities, for the pillory as an instrument of rule could in a certain sense escape the hands of the punishing authorities and publicly be turned into the opposite if the crowd took the victim's side. When a Rostock town citizen and his lover were taken to the pillory in 1527, he accused the dignitaries in a loud voice of likewise making children with their serving maids, and thus transformed the public event into a medium by which to accuse the judges.[78] Daniel Defoe, who himself was forced to stand at the pillory, described his own experience as follows: "The people, one thought, would treat me badly. But things were different. Quite the opposite, they were on my side, wished that my judges stood beside me, and as I was taken down they expressed their sympathy with loud thanks and applause."[79] Thus the practice of public honor justice contained a constant and inevitable ambivalence that could transform the purpose of the punishment into its opposite, for the honor punishment imposed by the authorities was effective only if the "people's" understanding of honor corresponded with their own. If the two different conceptions of honor diverged, then the public space provided an arena in which they contested each other.

Honor punishments were thus also a part of traditional justice as practiced by the people. We are familiar with the Charivari or *Haberfeldtreiben*, by which people undertook a procession, usually at night, accompanied by deafening noise on improvised instruments, to a neighbor's house to draw attention to his or her shame.[80] As of the fifteenth century, the sources record instances where windows and doors were smashed, fires in hearths and ovens extinguished, furniture ruined, roofs dismantled, and even houses destroyed. Natalie Zemon Davis writes that in the towns of France—as in all of Europe—masquerades, Charivaris, farces, parades, and processions took place in order to publicly accuse members of the community of shamefulness. They were used to punish violations against moral norms—against "honor"—and the perpetrators were publicly mocked and humiliated: husbands who were beaten by their wives, adulterers, couples whose age or social disparity appeared offensive. Davis also draws attention to the fact that it was above all young men who organized such shaming practices, as their chances for marriage sank if widows or widowers, for example, "shamefully" married men and women who were very much younger.[81]

These processions could indeed be quite violent. But in contrast to the town carnival, which possessed a political dimension, they were generally not rebellious but rather served instead to sustain the existing normative order of the village, which had been challenged by an inappropriate "indecent" marriage, adultery, or behavior that called into question the patriarchal hierarchy of marriage (when, for example, wives beat their husbands). Excessive violence, however, breached the order and could in turn lead to the condemnation and punishment of the perpetrators.

E. P. Thompson also argued that the occasion for "rough music" was provided above all by the violation of patriarchal sexual norms.[82] The victims were predominantly women who had contravened the norms of a patriarchal society: the quarrelsome and angry woman, the wife who beat her husband. But cuckolded or beaten husbands could also be punished, since from the perspective of the community they were unable to assert the patriarchal order. Hiding behind these questions of honor, however, according to Thompson, were very tangible economic conflicts and rivalries. And even though the violence could become excessive, the ritual itself must be seen as a moment that controlled and channeled the violence.

Certainly, Thompson wanted to protect the punishment practices of popular tradition against historiographical degradation; he thus emphasized their orderliness and boundaries and the "moral economy." But he too saw the ambivalence of people's justice, which did not appeal to "reasonable conviction but rather to prejudice ... ['Rough music'] could legitimize the aggression of youths, and (if one may whisper it) youths are not always, in every historical context, protagonists of rationality or of change."[83] There was much about rough music that appealed to Thompson. And in contrast to the extremely alienated capitalistic and bureaucratic society, "rough music" still belonged to a way of life in which justice was not yet totally alienated. But: "Because law belongs to the people, and is not alienated, or delegated, it is not thereby made necessarily more 'nice' and tolerant, more cosy and folksy. It is only as nice and as tolerant as the prejudices and norms of the folk allow."[84] And some victims must have experienced the implementation of even alienating laws and the development of a bureaucratized police as liberation from the tyranny of their own people.[85]

The authorities—especially the late-absolutist administrative state—had naturally always tried to gain control over people's justice. Walter Rummel describes how the Prussian administration in the Rhineland tried to suppress village methods of rebuke like "*Katzenmusik*" (or Charivari) or riotous conviviality and excessively loud nocturnal enthusiasm.[86] While the pillory punishments were abolished in the new civil law codes in most of the German states after 1848/49, as a practice by the people they remained virulent. Thus, for example, the pillory pole at the marketplace in Flensburg remained in usage until 1864, and in numerous German towns the stone "pole-of-shame" remained part of the townscape until well into the twentieth century.[87]

Honor punishments remained an effective practice for people's justice even in the first decades of the twentieth century. During the Rhineland occupation by French and Belgian troops, resistance activists kept strict watch for any dissenters or even "traitors." Many places witnessed the formation of conspiratorial "supervisory committees for the preservation of German honor," which spied on neighbors and especially tried to determine the names of those who in any way maintained contact with members of the occupying forces.[88] Leaflets were distributed that pilloried men and women who allegedly "besmirched German honor." Illegal resistance newspapers like the *Beobachter an der Ruhr* (Watcher on the Ruhr) had rubrics like "At the Pole of Shame" or "At The Pillory." The newspaper *Rote Erde—General-Anzeiger für die werktätige Bevölkerung des Industrie-Gebiets* (Red Earth—General Gazette for the Working Population of the Industrial Region) published in its pages a "Harlot Pillory" that denounced women by their names with complete addresses.[89]

The victims of honor punishment operations were above all women who were accused of having entered into relationships with soldiers of the occupying forces. In 1924, no fewer than twenty-six men from the region around Castrop-Rauxel were put on trial because they supposedly had tied a woman to an advertising column, poured tar over her hair, and hung a sign around her neck with a mocking verse.[90] Other reports from the mining communities described cases in which women were abused, beaten, and had their hair publicly sheared. The victims hardly had a chance to defend themselves against these attacks. Women who filed complaints against the denunciatory newspapers were intimidated; others having suffered humiliation, did not want court proceedings to turn them yet again into objects of public interest.

 National Socialist acts of violence against so-called racial defilement were thus not as "medieval" as they might seem, but were instead adapted practices of honor justice. These practices had not been part of the state's criminal code since the nineteenth century, but as "Volk's justice" they remained virulent. Here, however, it is a matter of National Socialist mimicry—it is not as if one can draw a line of continuity from honor justice and Charivaris to the "racial defilement" processions of 1935. For one thing, early modern honor justice was strictly regulated and codified by the authorities. It was even stipulated which authority could pronounce what honor punishments, as well as which punishments could be applied to what specific violations. Moreover, those accused had the right to defend themselves and to plead for mercy. Additionally, the people's practice of honor punishments sought to restore the "good order" that had been violated by the "shameful" behavior of individuals. In contrast, the National Socialists did not want to restore an old order, but rather to violently assert a new racist order. Thus the forms of traditional practices of honor punishments that reemerged during the NS regime do not indicate a smooth continuity. Rather, they demonstrate much more the reservoir of practices from which National Socialists could draw in order to realize a racist order in everyday life and thereby create a new form of justice— arbitrary, situational, and supported by racial *völkisch* sentiment alone.

It was thoroughly consistent to link racism and anti-Semitism with the concept of "honor," for there was hardly another notion better suited to designating differences, boundaries, and inequality. "Honor" offered a familiar semantic field steeped in tradition with which to signify levels of and exclusions from social recognition. Whether someone was "honorable" or had heaped "shame" upon him or herself was something determined by the immediate *Gemeinschaft*, independently of whether or not these norms were also regulated by authoritative courts. The social status that someone was granted in the *Gemeinschaft* found its conceptual expression in "honor," which, with its terminological vagueness, indicated the openness of the attribution and at the same time circumscribed a specific practice.[91]

"Honor" as a social practice of inequality and the production of social order joined seamlessly with the National Socialist practice of destroying a civil society of equality and erecting a *Volksgemeinschaft* of racist inequality. On the one hand, it stood for the inclusive but thoroughly graduated meaning of "honorability," which strengthened the social hierarchy; on the other hand, it meant the severe condemnation and exclusion of those who were accused of "shame." And this openness of the concept of honor accommodated National Socialist purposes of radically changing the moral system of norms. "Honor" was in fact a suitable medium through which to impose the "*Volksgemeinschaft*." There is virtually no other concept that reveals more clearly the nexus between language and the practice of social power.

Moreover, "honor" is to a large degree determined through gender. The cases from the Middle Ages and the early modern period show that the primary concern was for the honor of the patriarchal order and the preservation of patriarchal sexual norms, the violation of which incurred honor punishments. When a man could not enforce governing authority over his wife and was even beaten by her, he was laughed at by being perched on a donkey and led through the town. But above all it pertained to women, who were made to stand at the pillory as adulteresses or prostitutes. Women were required to take care of their honor and were condemned as dishonorable if they breached the rules of "decency."

The central field of female "honorability" was sexuality. Chastity, abstinence before marriage, and an exclusive sexual commitment to the husband comprised the matrix of female honor, while promiscuity was pretty much demanded of young men. From the perspective of the patriarchal society, adultery by a woman damaged not only her own honor but also the honor of her husband or brother—a "double violation of honor" (Ute Frevert) that destroyed the social identity of two persons—whereby, in contrast, adultery by a man left his identity wholly untouched.[92] For this reason, however, the power that men acquired through this strict sexual codification was exceptionally fragile, for it rested on the absolute adherence to a normative sexual purity by the women, something that men, in the end, had no control over. Additionally, within the masculine code of honor, the ability to "conquer" other women—thus damaging their honor—was considered quite important. At any time, their women could fall in love—or, from a masculine perspective, succumb to a seducer—which also damaged masculine honor. Feminine purity was always at risk, which made men perpetually insecure and suspiciously watchful. The readiness at any moment to assert, aggressively and to the death, the honor of his woman and thus above all his own honor represents an essential pattern of masculine gender construction into the twenty-first century.

Insofar as the racists—above all the National Socialists—merged race and honor into "racial honor" (Rassenehre), they not only created a new concept but also thereby produced a social practice that perpetuated and strengthened a large portion of all the implications that came with the concept of honor. And at the same time they transformed the previous conceptual and praxeological structure in a specific and exclusive manner. Nothing characterizes this transformation more clearly than the concept of Rassenschande itself. The central focus of National Socialist action was not the (positive) perpetuation of honor as the social quality of a person; instead, the focus was on the (negative) punishment and condemnation of those people who, from a racist perspective, had "defiled" themselves and the Gemeinschaft. The National Socialists were not concerned with supporting a traditional order of decency, but rather with the implementation of a new racist-biological order of inequality—the Volksgemeinschaft.

The Nuremburg Laws

Significantly, the anti-Semitic law enacted by the Reichstag on 15 September during the NSDAP party congress at Nuremberg was called the Law for the Protection of German Blood and German Honor (Gesetz zum Schutze des deutschen Blutes und der deutschen Ehre), even though the paragraphs that followed offered no concrete formulations regarding the "defense of honor." "Honor" was so important as a central concept that it appeared in the title of the law, yet this fact did not result in any material legal stipulations.[93]

The SS leadership used the violent actions of the spring and summer of 1935 to once again radicalize anti-Semitic politics. Reporting on the excesses in the beginning of July, Heydrich wrote: "The continuous reports coming in from the entire Reich about anti-Jewish demonstrations make evident that within the territory of the Reich an ever advancing dissatisfaction with the previously inconsistent approach against Judaism is spreading. The racially oriented part of the German Volk believes that the previous measures utilized in silence against the Jews must be seen as insufficient and demands generally a more severe approach."[94] In its situation report in August, even the SD Judenreferat (Jews Section) wrote that a "determined approach to the Jewish problem" was hardly possible at the time, given the absence of clear laws. "The Volk, which on one side in accordance with its National Socialist worldview wants to see the Jews forced out of Germany, finds on the other side no activity whatsoever at the competent offices." In particular, the SD requested laws governing state citizenship, freedom of movement, and the identification of "Aryan" businesses.[95]

Meanwhile, in the ministries the preparations for a legal prohibition of "racial defilement" had already advanced. In July 1935 the Reich Ministry of Justice sent a draft of a law concerning "marriages damaging to the Volk" to Reich Interior Minister Wilhelm Frick, who took the initial step on 26 July of instructing registrars in the Reich not to perform marriages between "Aryans" and "non-Aryans."[96] On 20 August an important leadership conference took place in the Reich Economics Ministry whose participants included not only Reich Economics Minister Hjalmar Schacht, Frick, Reich Justice Minister Franz Gürtner, and other ministers and high ministerial officials, but also Reinhard Heydrich.[97] During the meeting Schacht insisted that the "prevailing lawless condition and illegal activity" needed to end. The demand to not even sell groceries to Jews was "barbarism of the worst kind." But by no means did Schacht's critique imply a deviation from anti-Semitism. The reporter for the Gestapo quoted the Reich imperial minister as follows:

I have lived with Jews for thirty years and for thirty years I have taken money from them, but not the other way around. Yet the current methods are unbearable. A system must be instilled in the predominant confusion and before this system is practically implemented, everything else must cease.[98]

At the conference Frick announced that laws that were being prepared would be "suitable for hemming in the prevalence of Jewish influence." He had no objection to a "ban on Jews" as demanded by Julius Streicher or to board signs with anti-Jewish prohibitions:

to create clarity regarding these he would turn to the Führer. If the state in this case were to demand the removal of the board signs, this would evoke an irresolvable contradiction with the party which, given the unity of the state and party, is impossible. Thus in this question, strict agreement between the party and the state would have to prevail.[99]

The Munich Gauleiter Adolf Wagner noted that the latest excesses had arisen because of divergences not only between the party and the state but also among individual departments at the level of the Reich. "But it would be wrong if the legislature waits as long as has happened now, for then it undermines the authority of the state."[100] At the end Heydrich had the floor. He complained that the police were "always the ones that suffered." The current situation could only be resolved, firstly, through legislative measures that step by step reached the objective of completely extirpating Jewish influence and, secondly, by a comprehensive political and ideological schooling and education of the *Partei-* and *Volksgenossen*. In concrete terms, Heydrich demanded the prohibition of so-called "mixed marriages," the criminal prosecution of "racial defilement," special laws for Jews, and a limitation of their freedom of movement—especially a ban on migration to large cities.[101]

The leadership conference on 20 August refutes the interpretation that the Nuremberg laws were assembled quickly, precipitously, and without preparation.[102] Rather the conference strikingly reveals that, prior to the Nuremberg party congress, a broad consensus with regard to content prevailed among the ministerial bureaucracy, the NSDAP, the Gestapo, and the SD about future legislative regulations—and, significantly, that this consensus received impetus from the pressure "from below."[103] The Reichsbürgergesetz (Reich Citizenship Law) and the Law for the Protection of German Blood and German Honor—also referred to in short as the Blutschutzgesetz—were then enacted on 15 September at the Nuremberg party congress by the Reichstag, which had been summoned to Nuremberg for the occasion. They largely fulfilled the demands raised in the Reich Economics Ministry. As a result, only a "state member of German or kindred blood" who also "demonstrates through his conduct that he is both willing and fit to faithfully serve the German Volk and Reich" could become a "Reich citizen." And only a "Reich citizen" would be granted full political rights in accordance with the law. Jewish Germans were henceforth merely "state members" who belonged to the "protective union of the German Reich," towards which they were "particularly obligated."

Introduced by a preamble that declared a deep conviction "that the purity of German blood is the perquisite for the continued existence of the German Volk," the Blutschutzgesetz not only prohibited marriages "between Jews and state members of German and kindred blood." Rather, far beyond that, it also prohibited "extra-marital intercourse between Jews and state members of German and kindred blood." Thus the racial obsession to disallow sexual contact with Jewish people became state law for the first time in Germany, which in turn enormously reinforced the already extant sexualization of "racially defiling" behavior, as the law subjected private—indeed, intimate—behavior to penalty, behavior that escaped observation by standard state and police methods of control. A prohibition of "extra-marital intercourse" could only be enforced by denunciations, and as indicated by the rapidly rising number of denunciations after the fall of 1935, it was also understood as an invitation to the *Volksgemeinschaft* to engage in snooping. Moreover, the sexualized alignment of this law was clearly shaped by a patriarchal gender perspective, in that it only punished men as the "active" part in a violation against the prohibition of "extra-marital intercourse" and in a further paragraph forbade Jews from employing female, non-Jewish domestic servants younger than forty-five years of age.

The reaction among the populace to the Nuremberg laws was varied.[104] In conservative circles the elevation of the Swastika flag to the Reich flag met with criticism. Meanwhile, according to state and police situation reports, the race laws were widely met with approval and satisfaction, for they created clear relationships and put an end to the uncontrolled excesses of the previous months. Peter Longerich has emphasized that many of the reports avoid making the impression that there was a unanimously positive reaction. Rather they were formulated in limited terms, in that they refer to "wide circles," a "larger part" or "largest part of the population." Moreover, Longerich draws attention to the fact that state authorities like the Gestapo had an eminent interest in the legislation and thus especially wanted to underscore the approval of the population.[105]

Without a doubt, after the outbreaks of collective violence police agencies were especially interested in regaining control over the politics of violence, something that will be considered more closely in the following chapter. Nonetheless, the Gestapo's situation reports can be read not only with respect to its own interests. Rather, as Bankier and Kulka have emphasized, they also take into account the general feeling that, after the violent excesses of the summer months, the laws now clearly regulated discrimination. But even though German Jews themselves might have hoped that the Nuremberg laws would create a semblance of legal security (as opposed to the assurance of illegality), it quickly became apparent that they were merely a marker in the increasingly radical Jewish policy of the NS regime.

A secret Social Democratic report from Saxony drew a thoroughly reflective picture that reveals the indifference and distance vis-à-vis the fate of the German Jews:

> The Jewish laws are not being taken seriously, for the population has other worries and is mostly of the opinion that the whole Jewish hype is only staged to distract the people from other things and give the SA something to do. But this does not mean that the badgering of the Jews has not also had the desired effect on many people. To the contrary, there are plenty of people who have been mesmerized by the persecution of the Jews and who consider the Jews to be the creators of many bad circumstances.[106]

In Spangenberg in Hesse, the National Socialists could hardly wait for the new law to become reality. In the night leading to 15 September, a torchlight procession removed "Aryan" domestic servants from the homes of Jewish families, broke down doors, destroyed furniture, and physically assaulted the Jews. The "liberators" celebrated their success with alcohol and good cheer well into the morning.[107]

Notes

1. Regarding earlier Spanish policies about pure-bloodedness vis-à-vis the Jews, see Max Sebastian Hering Torres, *Rassismus in der Vormoderne: Die "Reinheit des Blutes" im Spanien der Frühen Neuzeit* (Frankfurt am Main, 2006).

2. See the summary of the historical literature by Alexandra Przyrembel, *"Rassenschande": Reinheitsmythos und Vernichtungslegitimation im Nationalsozialismus* (Göttingen, 2003).

3. Heinrich Krieger, *Das Rassenrecht in Südwestafrika: Vergleichende Darstellung des deutschen Rechts und der deutschen Mandatszeit* (Berlin, 1940). On the Reichstag debate, see Cornelia Essner, "Zwischen Vernunft und Gefühl: Die Reichstagsdebatte von 1912 um koloniale 'Rassenmischehe' und 'Sexualität,'" *Zeitschrift für Geschichtswissenschaft* 45 (1997): 503–519; for a critique of assumptions about continuity, see Birthe Kundrus, "Von Windhoek nach Nürnberg: Koloniale 'Mischehenverbote' und die nationalsozialistischen Rassengesetzgebung," in *Phantasiereiche: Zur Kulturgeschichte des deutschen Kolonialismus*, ed. Birthe Kundrus (Frankfurt am Main, 2003), 110-131.

4. When a representative from the anti-Semitic Christsozialen Arbeiterpartei (Christian Social Workers Party) named Mumm stated that everyone in the whole Reichstag was in agreement that mixed marriages between whites and blacks were undesired, there were no objections. Cornelia Essner, "Zwischen Vernunft und Gefühl," 514.

5. See Gisela Lebzelter, "Die 'Schwarze Schmach': Vorurteile – Propaganda – Mythos," *Geschichte und Gesellschaft* 11 (1985): 37–58; Christian Koller, *"Von Wilden aller Rassen niedergemetzelt": Die Diskussion um die Verwendung von Kolonialtruppen in Europa zwischen Rassismus, Kolonial und Militärpolitik (1914–1930)* (Stuttgart, 2001); most recently, above all Sandra Maß, *Weiße Helden, schwarze Krieger: Zur Geschichte kolonialer Männlichkeit in Deutschland 1918–1964* (Cologne, 2006), 71–120.

6. Lebzelter, "Die 'Schwarze Schmach,'" 39.

7. Ebert, *Schriften, Aufzeichnungen, Reden*, vol. 2, 290.

8. A lead article "To the German Physicians" in the weekly publication entitled *Ärztliche Rundschau* from November 1920 stated: "the black disgrace: that is the mulattoization and the syphilization of our Volk, the ruin of the Volk's health, physically and spiritually! Are we to silently tolerate the fact that henceforth on the banks of the Rhine, instead of the bright songs of beautifully-featured, well-bred, spiritually upright, lively, healthy Germans, the sound will be the scratching tones of grey-speckled, low-foreheaded, broad-nosed, crude, half-animal, syphilitic Mulattos?!" *Ärztliche Rundschau*, no. 47, 20 November 1920, quoted in Lebzelter, "Die 'Schwarze Schmach,'" 50. See Katja Weller, "Die Kampagne gegen die 'Schwarze Schmach' und die Frauenbewegung zu Beginn der Weimarer Republik," in *Politische Gesellschaftsge-*

schichte im 19. und 20. Jahrhundert: Festgabe für Barbara Vogel, ed. Henning Albrecht, Gabriele Boukrif, Claudia Bruns, and Kirsten Heinsohn (Hamburg, 2006), 188–201; Maß, *Weiße Helden, schwarze Krieger*, 89–100, and in particular with respect to the truth of the allegations leveled against the "colored" occupying soldiers, 109–112.

9. Przyrembel, *"Rassenschande,"* 59–62; see Reiner Pommerin, *"Sterilisierung der Rheinlandbastarde": Das Schicksal einer deutschen farbigen Minderheit 1918–1937* (Düsseldorf, 1979).

10. Cornelia Essner, *Die "Nürnberger Gesetze" oder Die Verwaltung des Rassenwahns 1933–1945* (Paderborn, 2002), 40–49.

11. In 1923 Chamberlain also received a visit from Hitler, whom he subsequently praised in a letter as a "rare shining light" and a "divine blessing." Hitler did not only share "all of our convictions about the ruinous, yes deadly influence of Judaism on the life of the German Volk," but rather also possessed the courage for urgent measures; many had understood "but nobody dares to say it out loud, nobody dares to draw the conclusions from his thinking for his actions; nobody except for Hitler." Quoted in Harmut Zelinsky, *Richard Wagner: Ein deutsches Thema: Eine Dokumentation zur Wirkungsgeschichte Richard Wagners 1876–1976* (Berlin, 1983), 170. On Hitler's encounter with Chamberlain see Joachim Köhler, *Wagners Hitler: Der Prophet und sein Vollstrecker* (Munich, 1997) and Brigitte Hamann, *Winifred Wagner oder Hitlers Bayreuth* (Munich, 2002), 83–86.

12. Houston Stewart Chamberlain, *Die Grundlagen des 19. Jahrhunderts*. 26th printing (unabridged *Volksausgabe*) (Munich, 1940), 383.

13. Essner, *Die "Nürnberger Gesetze,"9* 32–40.

14. Przyrembel, *"Rassenschande,"* 38

15. Quoted in Essner, *Die "Nürnberger Gesetze,"* 97.

16. Ibid., 82–86.

17. Ibid., 99.

18. CVZ, 12 December 1930.

19. Przyrembel, *"Rassenschande,"* 83; regarding this incident see also Gellately, *Hingeschaut und Weggesehen*, 190. While in custody, he made the statement: "I have never been politically active and have always had a nationalist attitude."

20. Quoted in Przyrembel, *"Rassenschande,"* 83.

21. On Schlüchtern, see above 121f.; on Oberbieber, see *Westdeutscher Beobachter*, 17 December 1934.

22. In Kulka and Jäckel, *Die Juden in den geheimen NS-Stimmungsberichten 1933–1945*, there are 215 reports pertaining to the subject of "racial defilement for the period 1933–1939; half of these reports—106—are from the period 1933 to 1936, 96 of which are from the year 1935 alone.

23. Participating at the meeting on 20 December 1934 were the Reichsärzteführer Wagner, the director of the NSDAP office for racial policies Walter Groß, the "expert for racial research" in the Reich Interior Ministry Achim Gercke, the director of the NSDAP's Party Supreme Court Walter Buch, and the ministerial officials Dr. Bartels and Dr. Schultze, as well as the SS leaders Brandt and Mayer. Przyrembel, *"Rassenschande,"* 134.

24. Berlin state police report for February 1935, Kulka and Jäckel, *NS-Stimmungsberichte*, CD-ROM, doc. no. 615. Statements one month later noted: "The Volk desperately expects a legal settlement soon of this question to prevent further racial defilements." Berlin Gestapo report for March 1935, ibid., doc. no. 694.

25. Coblenz Gestapo report for February 1935, ibid., doc. no. 627.

26. Ibid.; see also the similar-sounding report by the district president in Coblenz for February and March 1935, 4 April 1935, ibid., no. 727; also, "Max Israel der Talmudjude aus Simmern," in *Der Stürmer*, no. 18, May 1935.

27. Report by Gary (Günther) Israel, quoted in Doris Wesner, *Die Jüdische Gemeinde in Simmern/Hunsrück: Familiengeschichte(n) und Schicksale aus den vergangenen Jahrhunderten* (Argenthal, 2001), 126.

28. Ibid., 127.

29. Report by the Lohra Gendarmerie, from Barbara Händler-Lachmann, Harald Händler and Ulrich Schütt, *Purim, Purim, ihr liebe Leut, wißt ihr was Purim bedeut? Jüdisches Leben im Landkreis Marburg im 20. Jahrhundert* (Marburg, 1995), 161.

30. Jakob Schlag, *Meine Erinnerungen an das "Tausendjährige Reich" und an die Juden in Lohra*, self-published (Lohra, 1991), 177–179; here from Händler-Lachmann et al., *Purim, Purim, ihr liebe Leut*, 162.

31. Ibid., 163.

32. "Rassenschande in Breslau," *Der Stürmer*, no. 5, January 1935.

33. Breslau Gestapo report for April 1935, Kulka and Jäckel, *NS-Stimmungsberichte*, CD-ROM, doc. no. 763, partially printed in *NS-Stimmungsberichte*, 129f.; Breslau district president, report for April and May 1935, *NS-Stimmungsberichte*, CD-ROM, doc. no. 883; see Przyrembel, *"Rassenschande,"* 73–75.

34. The letter is appended to the situation report of the police president dated 25 July 1935; BArch, R 58/3725, fol. 193, quoted in Przyrembel, *"Rassenschande,"* 73.

35. Quoted in Przyrembel, *"Rassenschande,"* 64.

36. See Breslau Gestapo report for June 1935, Kulka and Jäckel, *NS-Stimmungsberichte*, CD-ROM, doc. no. 935.

37. Breslau Gestapo report for April 1935, ibid., doc. no. 763.

38. Breslau Gestapo report for July 1935, ibid., doc. no. 1007.

39. Thereupon Limbach phoned the district administrator and the Gestapo in Wilhelmshaven and asked what he should do. He was told only that he should take Neemann and Wolff into protective custody if necessary. Bernhard Parisius and Astrid Parisius, "'Rassenschande' in Norden: Zur Geschichte von zwei Fotos, die das Bild Jugendlicher von der NS-Zeit prägen," *Ostfreesland: ein Kalender für jedermann* 87 (2004): 129–137; here 130.

    The reason for this action by the two SA leaders was possibly to renew pressure on the local police after the failed attempt at the end of 1934 by SA and SS to depose Bürgermeister Dr. Schöneberg and take over the police authority. On this case see Parisius and Parisius, "'Rassenschande'" in Norden"; and Hans Forster and Günther Schwickert, *Norden: Eine Kreisstadt unterm Hakenkreuz* (Norden, 1988), 160–163; Behnken, *Deutschlandberichte*, January 1935, 67f.

40. Quoted in Parisius and Parisius, "'Rassenschande' in Norden," 129.

41. "Unerhörte Provokationen durch jüdische Rassenschänder," *Ostfriesische Tageszeitung*, 23 July 1935, reprinted in Hans Forster and Günther Schwickert, *Norden: Eine Kreisstadt unterm Hakenkreuz* (Norden, 1988), 161.

    The SPD's *Deutschland-Berichte* also reported on the incident and noted that whereas "powerful groups of excitedly discussing people" had gathered on the streets, they were instead outraged. The police officers were pointedly told that they had better "worry about the Nazi pigs who mess around [*herumsauen*] daily and then rob decent Jews and girls of their honor." Behnkin, *Deutschlandberichte*, January 1935, 91. However, this report contains the evidently false information that Kurt Daluege had come personally to Norden to bring a halt to the tumult (see Parisius and Parisius, "'Rassenschande' in Norden," 135). Thus one must assume that this report is based on mere hearsay, which is also supported by the fabulated concluding sentence, namely that "the population in this case successfully asserted itself hundred-percent against the Nazis."

42. Lehmann to the Berlin C.V, 25 July 1935, CAHJP, HM2/8796, fol. 2720 (Special Archive Moscow, 721-1-3002). These seven people included Herr. Samson, who was released three hours after his arrest, Aaron Hess, Levi Altgenug, Adolf Cossen, Richard Cossen, Max Klein, and Julius Wolff. Except for Richard Cossen and Julius Wolff, all had been released again by the end of July 1935. C.V. regional association northwest Germany to Berlin headquarters, 30 July 1935, CAHJP, HM2/8796, fol. 2715 (Special Archive Moscow, 721-1-3002).

43. Robert Gellately, *Die Gestapo und die deutsche Gesellschaft: die Durchsetzung der Rassenpolitik 1933–1945* (Paderborn, 1993), 185; in second place at 24 percent were statements during interrogations. See also the study about the Düsseldorf Gestapo by Reinhard Mann, *Protest und Kontrolle im Dritten Reich: Nationalsozialistische Herrschaft im Alltag einer rheinischen Großstadt* (Frankfurt am Main, 1987); Gisela Diewald-Kenkmann, *Politische Denunziationen im NS-Regime – oder die kleine Macht der "Volksgenossen"* (Bonn, 1995); for an overview, Sheila Fitzpatrick and Robert Gellately, eds., *Accusatory Practices: Denunciation in Modern European History, 1789–1989* (Chicago, 1997); on the problem of public(s) and denunciation, see Inge Marßolek, "The 'Writings on the Wall': The Changing Public Sphere and the Jews in Germany in the Third Reich," in *On Germans and Jews under the Nazi Regime: Essays by Three Generations of Historians: a Festschrift in Honor of Otto Dov Kulka*, ed. Moshe Zimmermann (Jerusalem, 2006), 193–213.

44. Gellately, *Die Gestapo und die deutsche Gesellschaft*, 187.

45. "Albert Hirschland: Der Rasseschänder von Magdeburg," *Der Stürmer*, special edition no. 2, August 1935; for more on this see Przyrembel, *"Rassenschande,"* 192.

46. Przyrembel, *"Rassenschande,"* 192.

47. "Jud Hugo Wilhelm," *Der Stürmer*, no. 18, May 1935; Düsseldorf Gestapo report for April, Kulka and Jäckel, *NS-Stimmungsberichte*, CD-ROM, doc. no. 764.

48. Administrative district Minden, report for July 1935, Kulka and Jäckel, *NS-Stimmungsberichte*, CD-ROM, doc. no. 1081.

49. Longerich, *"Davon haben wir nichts gewusst!"* 82.

50. Ibid. According to a report by the district president of Upper Bavaria, on Sunday 5 August a large crowd of people proceeded to the Park Hotel with bands of musicians and banners that read: "Jews are unwelcome here! Bad Tölz does not want any Jews!" Since further incidents were expected, the regional district office ordered the closing of the hotel. Quoted in Broszat et al., *Bayern in der NS-Zeit*, vol. 1, 451; see also Frank Bajohr, *"Unser Hotel ist judenfrei": Bäder-Antisemitismus im 19. und 20. Jahrhundert* (Frankfurt am Main, 2003), 128f. At the beginning of June 1936, the Bad Tölz regional district office reported that the Park Hotel had now been leased to a young married couple "who [would] operate it in a purely Aryan sense." Quoted in Broszat et al., *Bayern in der NS-Zeit*, vol. 1, 461.

51. Minden Gestapo report for July 1935, Kulka and Jäckel, *NS-Stimmungsberichte*, CD-ROM, doc. no. 1021; see Erik Hoffmann, *Jüdische Nachbarn in Hessisch Oldendorf* (Hameln, 1998), 72–75.

52. C.V. regional association East Westphalia to Berlin headquarters, 26 July 1935, CAHJP, HM 2/8793, fol. 1597 (Special Archive Moscow, 721-1-2970).

53. Werner Hoffmann, Herford, to Berlin headquarters, 17 August 1935, CAHJP, HM 2/8793, fol. 1593 (Special Archive Moscow, 721-1-2970). The C.V. regional association East Westphalia reported at the end of August that the suspect was meanwhile

no longer under investigation by the state attorney because criminal actions on his part could not be substantiated. C.V. regional association East Westphalia to Berlin headquarters, 25 August 1935, CAHJP, HM 2/8793, fol. 1591 (Special Archive Moscow, 721-1-2970).

54. Quoted in Hoffmann, *Jüdische Nachbarn in Hessisch Oldendorf*, 74f.

55. See Peter Genz, "170 Jahre jüdische Gemeinde in Stralsund – ein Überblick," in *"Halte fern dem ganzen Lande jedes Verderben ..." Geschichte und Kultur der Juden in Pommern*, ed. Margret Heitmann, Julius H. Schoeps, and Bernhard Vogt (Hildesheim, 1995), 134f.

56. Stettin Gestapo report for July 1935, in Robert Thévoz, *Pommern 1934/35 im Spiegel von Gestapo-Lageberichten und Sachakten*, 2 vols. (Cologne, 1974), vol. 2, 118; see also Michael Wildt, "'Der muß hinaus! Der muß hinaus!' Antisemitismus in deutschen Nord- und Ostseebädern 1920–1935," *Mittelweg 36* 10, no. 4 (2001): 2–25, here 22.

57. Stettin Gestapo report for July 1935, in Thévoz, *Pommern 1934/35*, vol. 2, 118; see Thévoz, *Pommern 1934/35*, vol. 1, 179f.; Bogdan Frankiewicz and Wolfgang Wilhelmus, "Selbstachtung wahren und Solidarität üben: Pommerns Juden während des Nationalsozialismus," in Heitmann et al., *"Halte fern dem ganzen Lande jedes Verderben,"* 457.

58. Stettin district president report for July and August 1935, Kulka and Jäckel, *NS-Stimmungsberichte*, CD-ROM, doc. no. 1138.

59. NSDAP local chapter of Pölitz, secret appeal, 28 August 1935, ibid., doc. no. 1188.

60. Stettin Gestapo report for 30 August 1935, ibid., doc. no. 1119.

61. Wolfgang Wilhelmus, "Juden in Greifswald und Wolgast 1933–1945," in *Der faschistische Pogrom vom 9./19. November 1938 – Zur Geschichte der Juden in Pommern: Kolloquium der Sektionen Geschichtswissenschaft und Theologie der Ernst-Moritz-Arndt-Universität Greifswald am 2. November 1988* (Greifswald, 1989), 103. Paula Z. later married another man and left the town. Arnold R. emigrated in 1939 to Shanghai, while his father died shortly after the events of the summer of 1935.
It is worth pointing out that this description of the course of action, which is based on research conducted for a state exam and a report based on memory, noticeably contradicts the representation by the Greifswald district administrator, who reported that the demonstration unfolded with "exemplary discipline" and stood totally under the "auspices of a healthy German racial and *völkisch* sensibility." Greifswald district administrator, report for 08/16/1935, Kulka and Jäckel, *NS-Stimmungsberichte*, CD-ROM, doc. no. 1167.

62. Greifswald district administrator, report for 16 August 1935, Kulka and Jäckel, *NS-Stimmungsberichte*, CD-ROM, doc. no. 1167; Stettin district president, important event notice for 15–16 August 1935, ibid., CD-ROM, doc. no. 1136; Stettin district president to the Prussian minister president, 26 August 1935, in Thévoz, *Pommern 1934/35*, vol. 2, 417.

63. Stettin Gestapo report for July, in Thévoz, *Pommern 1934/35*, vol. 2, 118.

64. Joachim Haas, *Abseits der "großen" Geschichte: Opposition und Widerstand gegen den Nationalsozialismus im Raum Fulda: Versuch einer Spurensicherung* (Oberursel, 1989), 83f. One of the two workers filed charges for bodily injury and property damage. It actually came to a trial, which was stopped, however, as per the immunity act of 23 April 1936, for the KdF group had acted "merely out of excessive eagerness." The plaintiff even had to pay the court costs.

65. Stettin Gestapo report for August 1935, in Thévoz, *Pommern 1934/35*, vol. 2, 128; Stettin district president, report for July and August 1935, Kulka and Jäckel, *NS-Stimmungsberichte*, CD-ROM, doc. no. 1138.

66. District president Stettin to the Prussian minister presidents, 26 July 1935, in Thévoz, *Pommern 1934/35*, vol. 2, 316.

67. Stettin district vice-president to the Prussian minister president, 24 August 1935, in Thévoz, *Pommern 1934/35*, vol. 2, 318; Stettin Gestapo report for August 1935, in Thévoz, *Pommern 1934/35*, vol. 2, 127f.

68. Hans von Hentig, *Die Strafe*, vol. 1: *Frühformen und kulturgeschichtliche Zusammenhänge* (Berlin, 1954), 397; Grete Bader-Weiß and Karl Siegfried Bader, *Der Pranger: Ein Strafwerkzeug und Rechtswahrzeichen des Mittelalters*. (Freiburg i. Br., 1935), 38–54; entry for "Pranger" by Ruth Schmidt-Wiegand, in Adalbert Erler et al., eds., *Handwörterbuch zur deutschen Rechtsgeschichte* (HRG), vol. 3 (Berlin, 1984), col. 1877–1884; entry for "Ehrenstrafen" by W. Brückner in ibid., vol. 1 (Berlin, 1971), col. 851–853; more generally see Richard van Dülmen, *Theater des Schreckens: Gerichtspraxis und Strafrituale in der frühen Neuzeit* (Munich, 1985); Dagmar Burkhart, *Eine Geschichte der Ehre* (Darmstadt, 2006).

69. Entry for "Pranger," HRG, vol. 3, col. 1881; Gerd Schwerhoff, "Verordnete Schande? Spätmittelalterliche und frühneuzeitliche Ehrenstrafen zwischen Rechtsakt und sozialer Sanktion," in *Mit den Waffen der Justiz: Zur Kriminalitätsgeschichte des Spätmittelalters und der Frühen Neuzeit*, ed. Andreas Blauert and Gerd Schwerhoff (Frankfurt am Main, 1993), 162f.

70. Bader-Weiß and Bader, *Der Pranger*, 130; Schwerhoff, "Verordnete Schande," 174–177.

71. Bader-Weiß and Bader, *Der Pranger*, 30f., 131.

72. Ibid., 114–115. Von Hentig drew attention to the many different sexual meanings of pillar of shame (!) and, respectively, the stone of shame. Von Hentig, *Die Strafe*, vol. 1, 397–404.

73. Valentin Groebner has investigated in lucid, minute detail the by no means uncommon practice of cutting off noses in the town of Nuremburg during the late Middle Ages, a punishment that was applied first and foremost for violating sexual norms, above all for adultery. The cut-off nose was not only a symbol of castrated sexual potency but rather also indeed an emblem of the loss of face, of honor destroyed. Not men, but rather female rivals were the most frequent victims of the violent attacks. The Nuremburg poet Hans Sachs, in the Carnival play "Die Kupplerin," has the wife characteristically threaten her husband's voluptuous and dissolute lover with cutting off her nose. Valentin Groebner, *Ungestalten: Die visuelle Kultur der Gewalt im Mittelalter* (Munich, 2003), 71–93.

74. See the first chapter, "Ehre und Ehrgefühl," in Pierre Bourdieu, *Entwurf einer Theorie der Praxis auf der ethnologischen Grundlage der kabylischen Gesellschaft* (Frankfurt am Main, 1979).

75. Groebner, *Ungestalten*, 88f. It is worth remembering that into the twentieth century, loss of honor by revoking decorations, demotions, and dishonorable discharges was a common part of military criminal justice; even today, § 31 of the criminal code deals with the revocation of the civil rights (*Ehrenrechte*; literally "honorary rights") of citizens. See entry for "Ehre" in HRG, vol. 1, 846–849.

76. See entry for "Ehrenstrafen," HRG, vol. 1, col. 851–853; Bader-Weiß and Bader, *Der Pranger*, 141–146; von Hentig, *Die Strafe*, vol. 1, 411. Walter Hartinger confirms that the penal codes of absolutist Bavaria prescribed honor punishments for many types of offenses. Walter Hartinger, "Rechtspflege und Volksleben: Zur Funktion des Rechts im absolutistischen Bayern," in *Das Recht der kleinen Leute: Beiträge zur Rechtlichen Volkskunde: Festschrift für Karl-Sigismund Kramer zum 60. Geburtstag*, ed. Konrad Köstlin and Kai Detlev Sievers (Berlin, 1976), 56–59.

77. Von Hentig, *Die Strafe*, vol. 1, 420f.; Bader-Weiß and Bader, *Der Pranger*, 145f.
78. Schwerhoff, "Verordnete Schande," 173.
79. Quoted in von Hentig, *Die Strafe*, vol. 1, 422f.
80. See the exemplary description by Helga Ettenhuber, "Charivari in Bayern: Das Miesbacher Haberfeldtreiben von 1893," in *Kultur der einfachen Leute: Bayerisches Volksleben vom 16. bis zum 19. Jahrhundert*, ed. Richard van Dülmen (Munich, 1983), 180–207.
81. Natalie Zemon Davis, "The Reasons of Misrule," in N. Davis, *Society and Culture in Early Modern France: Eight Essays by Natalie Zemon Davis* (Stanford, CA, 2003), 97–123.
82. Edward P. Thompson, "Rough Music," in *Customs in Common* (New York, 1993), 467–538.
83. Ibid., 530.
84. Ibid.; see also the essay by Rainer Walz, who critically investigates the all-too-positive interpretations of village communications in the early modern period. Rainer Walz, "Agonale Kommunikation im Dorf der Frühen Neuzeit," *Westfälische Forschungen* 42 (1992): 215–251.
85. Thompson, "Rough Music," 531.
86. Walter Rummel, "Motive staatlicher und dörflicher Gewaltanwendung im 19. Jahrhundert: Eine Skizze zum Ende der frühneuzeitlichen Sozialkultur in der preußischen Rheinprovinz," in *Streitkulturen. Gewalt, Konflikt und Kommunikation in der ländlichen Gesellschaft (16.–19. Jahrhundert)*, ed. Magnus Eriksson and Barbara Krug-Richter (Cologne, 2003), 165. The fact that, in order to establish itself, the early modern territorial state had to gain control of honor—that is, of the standards of honor—is emphasized by Wolfgang Weber in "Honor, fama, gloria: Wahrnehmungen und Funktionszuschreibungen der Ehre in der Herrschaftslehre des 17. Jahrhunderts," in *Ehrkonzepte in der Frühen Neuzeit: Identitäten und Abgrenzungen*, ed. Sybille Backmann et al. (Berlin, 1998), 70–98.
87. Entry for "Pranger" in *HRG*, vol. 3, col. 1882; see the directory of existing pillories in Germany in Bader-Weiß and Bader, *Der Pranger*, 177–187; on the development of the relationship between honor and law, see also Peter Schuster, "Ehre und Recht: Überlegungen zu einer Begriffs- und Sozialgeschichte zweier Grundbegriffe der mittelalterlichen Gesellschaft," in Backmann et al., *Ehrkonzepte in der Frühen Neuzeit*, 40–66.
88. See Gerd Krüger, "Straffreie Selbstjustiz: Öffentliche Denunzierungen im Ruhrgebiet 1923–1926," *Sowi* 27, no. 2 (1998): 119–125.
89. Ibid., 120f., 122.
90. Ibid., 121. The proceedings were closed due to the London amnesty of August 1924.
91. In older research honor is understood as something substantial, conceived in a certain sense as a good that can be acquired, accumulated, and protected but also lost. This contrasts with today's understanding, which defines honor in terms of social interaction and communicative practice. See the instructive introduction by Klaus Schreiner and Gerd Schwerhoff to the volume they edited: Schreiner and Schwerhoff, eds., *Verletzte Ehre: Ehrkonflikte in Gesellschaften des Mittelalters und der Frühen Neuzeit* (Cologne, 1995); see in the same volume Martin Dinges, "Die Ehre als Thema der historischen Anthropologie: Bemerkungen zur Wissenschaftsgeschichte und zur Konzeptualisierung," 29–62.
92. See Ute Frevert, "Ehre – männlich/weiblich: Zu einem Identitätsbegriff des 19. Jahrhunderts," *Tel Aviver Jahrbuch für deutsche Geschichte* 21 (1992): 21–68; see also Martin Dinges, "Ehre und Geschlecht in der Frühen Neuzeit," in *Ehrkonzepte in der*

Frühen Neuzeit: Identitäten und Abgrenzungen, eds. Sybille Backmann et al. (Berlin, 1998), 123–147

93. "Gesetz zum Schutze des deutschen Blutes und der deutschen Ehre," *Reichsgesetzblatt (RGBl)* I, 1935, 1146f.; the "Reichsflaggengesetz" (Imperial Flag Law), *RGBl* I, 1935, 1145; and the "Reichsbürgergesetz" (Imperial Citizenship Law), *RGBl* I, 1935, 1146 were also part of the Nuremberg laws.

94. Heydrich to the Reich Chancellery, 16 July 1935; quoted in Werner Jochmann, "Die deutsche Bevölkerung und die nationalsozialistischen Judenpolitik bis zur Verkündung der Nürnberger Gesetze," in *Gesellschaftskrise und Judenfeindschaft in Deutschland 1870–1945* (Hamburg, 1988), 245f.

95. Situation report by the SD main office J I/6 (Jews), 17 August 1935, printed in Michael Wildt, *Die Judenpolitik des SD 1935–1938: Eine Dokumentation* (Munich, 1995), 69f.

96. Essner, *Die "Nürnberger Gesetze,"* 106f.

97. Numerous reports about this conference exist, although historiographies most often mention the record by the Reich Chancellery dated 22 August 1935. Documents of the Nuremberg Trial of the Major War Criminals, NG-4067. The Gestapa report I found in 1994 in the Special Archive Moscow (see Wildt, *Die Judenpolitik des SD 1935–1938*, 22f.) reveals that Heydrich also participated in the conference.

98. Gestapa II, I B 2, report on the 20 August 1935 conference held at the Reich Economics Ministry about a practical solution to the Jewish problem, Special Archive Moscow, 500-1-379, fol. 75–85. Schacht consistently aligned his position regarding the German Jews with the NS leadership. Even though he represented the viewpoint that Jewish economic activity should not be severely restricted, he at all times openly agreed with their degradation to citizens with reduced rights. The thesis in the older literature that only Schacht's resignation as Reich minister of economics in August 1937 made possible the increased severity of anti-Semitic policies is refuted by Albert Fischer, *Hjalmar Schacht und Deutschlands "Judenfrage": Der "Wirtschaftsdiktator" und die Vertreibung der Juden aus der deutschen Wirtschaft* (Cologne, 1995).

99. Gestapa II I B 2, report on the 20 August 1935 conference held at the Reich Economics Ministry, Special Archive Moscow, 500-1-379, fols. 75–85.

100. Ibid.

101. Ibid. Heydrich did not restrict himself to oral recommendations. In a brief written at the beginning of September to the conference participants he formulated his demands in detail: Heydrich to the participants of the leadership conference in the Reich Economics Ministry, 9 September 1935, printed in Wildt, *Die Judenpolitik des SD 1935–1938*, 70–73.

102. The racial expert in the Interior Ministry, Lösener, had emphasized, quasi on his own behalf, how rapidly and hectically the Nuremberg laws came into being: Bernhard Lösener, "Als Rassereferent im Reichsministerium des Innern," *Vierteljahrshefte für Zeitgeschichte* 9 (1961): 261–313. Uwe Dietrich Adam followed this interpretation and described the Nuremberg laws as a "surprising shock" in *Judenpolitik im Dritten Reich*, 125. Similarly still today, Robert Gellately writes that in September 1935, Hitler felt the time had come to promulgate new laws at the Nuremburg party congress and that the laws were hastily thrown together at the last minute—Gellately, *Hingeschaut und Weggesehen*, 174. Early opponents of this interpretation were Kulka, "Die Nürnberger Rassegesetze"; Reinhard Rürup, "Das Ende der Emanzipation: Die antijüdische Politik in Deutschland von der 'Machtergreifung' bis zum Zweiten Weltkrieg," in *Die Juden im nationalsozialistischen Deutschland*, ed. Arnold Paucker (Tübingen, 1986); and Werner Jochmann, who stressed that the Nuremberg laws had been "long

planned and intensively prepared" in Jochmann, "Die deutsche Bevölkerung und die nationalsozialistischen Judenpolitik." Cornelia Essner provides a detailed summary and a critique of sources that refutes Lösener's representation, Die "Nürnberger Gesetze," 113–134.

103. Kulka noted early on that "the laws amounted to a subsequent institutionalization of pressures and initiatives which had been previously been created and unleashed in the population by ideology and propaganda." Kulka, "Die Nürnberger Rassegesetze," 612f.

104. See Kulka, "Die Nürnberger Rassegesetze"; Kershaw, "Antisemitismus"; Bankier, The Germans and the Final Solution; and now above all Longerich, "Davon haben wir nichts gewusst!"

105. Longerich, "Davon haben wir nichts gewusst!" 98.

106. Behnken, Deutschlandberichte, September 1935, 1043.

107. Barkai and Mendes-Flohr, Aufbruch und Zerstörung, 208.

7

THE DILEMMA OF THE POLITICS OF VIOLENCE

Violence comprised the constitutive medium of National Socialist politics. And for that reason, despite all of the centralization of command authority, preserving the state's monopoly of violence was a constant problem for the NS leadership, for the local party organizations could not understand why they should renounce violence just because the "movement" had taken over the "state."

The State, according to Max Weber in his classical definition, is a human society that within a determined territory "(successfully) claims the monopoly of the legitimate use of physical force."[1] In the modern legal and constitutional state, the legitimacy of the state's use of violence is based upon the consent of the citizens who have transferred their unlimited freedom of violence (in principle) to the state. Thus from this perspective, the state can be legitimated only by the citizens, which requires that state violence assume a legal form that must generally conform to the constitution and in particular can be examined by every citizen as to its legality through independent courts.[2]

The National Socialists had no sense for the problem of limiting violence by law. To the contrary, the constitutional state and civil law were to be overcome as quickly as possible. "Legal is that which benefits the Volk" was the maxim of National Socialist legal theory,[3] and in accordance with the utilitarian reference to the "Volk" beyond the law, the application of violence was determined by National Socialists only through political calculation. Yet this did not mean that they escaped the problem of the legitimate use of violence. By severing violence from law, the National Socialists themselves created a fundamental dilemma for their order that they would never be able to resolve for the duration of their regime.

If the application of physical violence is no longer based on the consent of equal and free citizens and limited by law but instead is exclusively dependent on political claims to command authority, then there is no reason for the regime's many authorities to refrain from violence. Those who link the application of violence solely to political purposes do not really have a persuasive argument by which to insist on a monopoly of violence; there is only the claim to command authority and the discipline of obedience. Thus it was always difficult for the NS leadership to maintain control over violence after the leadership itself, in keeping with utilitarian use of violence for the benefit of the *Volksgemeinschaft*, had demanded violence "from below." To be sure, as we will see, the leadership and also the Gestapo availed themselves of the argument for claiming the state's monopoly of violence, but without understanding—let alone accepting—its decisive constitutional legitimating principle.

Hitler himself had announced the "end of the national revolution" on 6 July 1933 because a revolution was not a permanent condition and one thus had to "direct the liberated current of the revolution over into the secure bed of evolution." "There is no authority anymore from a partial area of the Reich, but rather only from the German concept of the Volk." The party had now become the state; all power resided in the Reich authority.[4] Reich Interior Minister Frick immediately added fuel to the fire with a circular that picked up the argument that the NSDAP had now become the body responsible for the state and that the authority of this state resided with the Reich regime under Hitler. Since the population was gaining confidence in the new regime precisely because of the economic revival, under no circumstances were there to be any unauthorized interventions in the economy—that is to say: no further boycott actions.[5]

At the beginning of September 1933 the Reich Economics Ministry once again made it clear that in the interests of preserving jobs for German (i.e., exclusively non-Jewish) workers and employees, activities like setting up black and white lists, refusing to include businesses in directories, banning advertising, and discouraging clientele with leaflets, signs, and sentries, for example, were banned. The Reich Economics Ministry explicitly referenced the instructions from the NSDAP party headquarters, according to which all party organizations were forbidden to engage in such actions.[6] The Prussian Interior Ministry passed the decree along and issued the following command to the police stations: "Interventions by unauthorized [persons] in retail sales operations are to be prevented by all means."[7]

In December 1934, however, Economics Minister Schacht once again had reasons to complain. In a letter to Reich Interior Minister Frick he wrote that on the occasion of the Christmas shopping season he had received reports from many places in Germany about "planned actions against non-Aryan businesses and department stores."

> Thus the buying public is prevented from entering such businesses by sentries in party organization uniforms or in civilian clothes, or after they leave the stores the names of customers are written down by the sentries; in many places signs and banners were posted, display windows were pasted over with notices and thereby rendered useless with corrosive liquids; the notices contained the demand not to buy in Jewish businesses. Further, leaflets with the same content were distributed which sometimes included directories of non-Aryan companies. Occasionally the window panes in Jewish businesses were smashed at night and in Dortmund the security guards at the large store of the Kaufmann Brothers Company were supposedly attacked by a group pasting up notices, whereby there supposedly was shooting. According to reports from the Reich Association of Jewish Frontline Soldiers, there were also actions against Jews in Niedermarsberg/ Westphalia. In a number of places, explosives, stink bombs, and tear gas bombs were thrown into Jewish businesses.[8]

According to Schacht, these actions clearly contravened many different decrees; moreover, he himself, in a letter written in mid November to the state regime, had advocated an undisturbed Christmas shopping season. Schacht continued:

> After the representations in the materials submitted to me and after the recent descriptions by eye-witnesses to my case workers, I cannot help but have the impression that the police did not intervene in each case with the required severity.... An unpunished act of illegality serves to bring forth a situation of legal insecurity that shakes the faith in the authority of the state not only for non-Aryan state members but for the Volk as a whole and gives uncontrollable elements the opportunity to engage in anti-state activities.[9]

This last argument could not have failed to make an impression on Frick, for he forwarded Schacht's letter to the Prussian secret state police office and to all state administrations with the request "to make sure that the expressed concerns are remedied. At the same time, I am drawing attention to the fact that lately the cases of so-called Volk's justice have become exceptionally frequent. The resulting unrest and legal insecurity must in any case be stopped."[10]

From the perspective of the NSDAP, on the other hand, the problem was rather that there were still far too many people maintaining contact with Jewish Germans. In August 1934 the party leadership complained "that party members are lacking in the requisite aloofness vis-à-vis Judaism" and ordered that all party members were forbidden from any "interactions with Jews in public and in local establishments."[11] In February 1935, in a directive issued against bureaucratism in the party, political leaders were requested to "resist the danger of the emergence of a party bureaucracy without any frontline spirit whatsoever." "Only if the same living frontline spirit prevails everywhere in the party can we maintain the confidence that we National Socialists all together need to perform the fruitful work for our German Volk as the Führer intends [im Sinne des Führers]."[12] That was by no means a call for violent action, but the decree could surely invigorate those who understood their party role in the sense of a "living frontline spirit." In April Heß further strengthened the directive that forbade party members from having any off-duty contact with Jews and especially from shopping in Jewish stores.[13] Hitler, too, made sure that anti-Semitic pressure at the local level remained high. After Hitler himself apparently heard repeated complaints about signs with statements like "Jews are not wanted," "Jews enter this place at their own risk," etc., he decided in April 1935 that such signs were completely unobjectionable.[14]

Thus the party groups were not entirely wrong when they believed that in a certain sense they were acting with highest of mandates. According to the district president in Wiesbaden:

> The opinion cannot be eradicated from the conceptions circulating in subordinated party offices that the Führer is in a certain sense two-faced. Certain directives, particularly in the area of the Jewish question, had to be decided with respect to foreign countries. The Führer's true will, however, is known to every genuine National Socialist from his world view. With that one acts as the Führer intends [im Sinne des Führers]. This idea explains why Parteigenossen and members of the SA were significantly involved in the most diverse violent activities and special actions against the Jews which, after the incidents at the Kurfürstendamm in Berlin, became even more intense.[15]

The Münster Gestapo similarly reported that in wide circles of the NSDAP, particularly the SA, the opinion prevailed "that now the time had come to solve the Jewish question completely. People want—as one says—to roll up and tackle the Jewish problem from below and believe that the regime will have to follow."[16]

But it was precisely this lack of uniformity in the policies against the German Jews that troubled the NS regime, especially during the violent excesses of 1935. The situation reports indicate that there was no such thing as a consistent anti-Semitic political position. To the contrary, the reports of both the Gestapo and the district presidents complained about the contradictions between the party organization and the central politics of Berlin, particularly that of the Reich Economics Ministry, which did not want to see the economic activity of Jewish business people impaired and opposed any calls for boycotts. Thus in many instances the police would intervene against the boycott actions of local NSDAP groups in order to enforce the political directives from the center.

In Schlüchtern, the NSDAP district leader Puth, who was both the Bürgermeister and the chief of the local police, had a life-sized effigy of a Jew set up in the center of town on the main street and plastered with anti-Semitic signs. He brusquely refused the directive from the district administrator to remove the figure and the signs. The confrontation escalated to such an extent that Puth relieved the district administrator of his party offices and banned him from wearing the uniform. Meanwhile Puth himself, at the initiative of the Kassel state police, was threatened with the loss of his police authority.[17]

One can repeatedly observe, elaborated the Kassel Gestapo in its report, "that political leaders polemicize against administrators and officials, whereby they refer to laws and administrative ordinances as if they only exist on paper. Even directives from the state police agency, particularly as to the Jewish question, were initially ignored because, according to the perspective of the party agencies, they were not compatible with the goals of the National Socialist state."[18] Two months later the Kassel Gestapo concluded:

> The relationship between the party and the state agencies is by and large frictionless. Disagreements, however, repeatedly arise regarding the Jewish question. The party agencies rightly feel themselves obligated to intervene against the relations with Jews or against the support of Jews by German *Volksgenossen*. But this sometimes happens in a manner which contravenes the provisions that have been decreed by the Reich regime. This often results in embarrassing situations for the authorities, particularly for police officials, also for the reason that, against their will, they gain the reputation of being friends with the Jews when they act in accordance with the state's directives. A few of the Bürgermeisters in the Kassel administrative district refused to comply with the directive of the district administrator on the removal of board signs with anti-Jewish inscriptions because they,

being at the same time [party] officers, had received contrary orders from the competent [party] district leader.... Very often the party must go in a different direction than the administrations in the fight against anti-state efforts. The result is that the orders of the party do not correspond with the directives from the state agencies. The police official, who is at the same time also a [party] officer, can therefore be badly conflicted in the question about fulfilling his duties.[19]

Similarly, the district administrator in Fritzlar-Homberg complained that police officers who actively protected Jews acquired the reputation, against their wills, of being "*Judenfreunde*" (friends of the Jews).[20]

Thus from their perspective, the police found themselves in a precarious position between the ministerial directives from the center and actions at the local level. Police officers who had to enforce the directives from the center also came into conflict with local party groups, whose leaders often exercised the state function of the Bürgermeister, which further obscured the already blurred line between party politics and state executive functions. Additionally, these police officers fell under public suspicion of being "*Judenfreunde*" and of wanting to protect Jews, which, with few exceptions, was probably not their intention. If the police agreed with the regime's anti-Semitic politics and at the same time always found themselves having to enforce the legal rights of Jews and implement state directives, then from their perspective this dilemma could only be resolved if Jews were declared second-class citizens and stripped of any legal rights that they might assert as citizens of the German state.

The Hanover Gestapo focused on this self-created dilemma in one of its situation reports:

Because of the events during the last week, the anti-Semitic mood among the broad masses has significantly increased. Apart from a few unreconstructed exceptions, the sharp rejection of the encroachments of Judaism is generally welcomed. But the great majority of the population does not understand the pointless individual actions and acts of terror which were observed in these last few days right here in Hanover. Transgressions occurred repeatedly, in which members of NS organizations participated, about which the broad masses in the street openly expressed their displeasure.... It is quite especially regrettable and detrimental to state authority if the population is a witness and must observe that police officials who previously had behaved with extraordinary reserve are dubbed "*Judenhöriger*" [slaves of the Jews] and "*Judenfreund*" [friend of the Jews] during dutiful interventions against rowdies and provocateurs.[21]

The police, particularly the Gestapo, had a strong interest in making sure they did not lose control of the violence. The Gestapo repeatedly condemned "individual actions." After the central directive issued by the party leadership in April proved to have little effect, the Gestapo pressured Gau and district leaders of the NSDAP to rein the party organizations in. In May, Cologne-Aachen Gauleiter Grohé sharply criticized "individual actions" and warned that the police would relentlessly pursue perpetrators. This at least had an effect for a while.[22] The Gestapo in Pomerania came to an arrangement with the Gau leadership by which the NSDAP district leadership would be responsible for removing boycott signs—"insofar as their contents [represented] a threat."[23] The district administrator in Bad Kreuznach reported on a serious conflict with a district leader who opposed a directive to remove signs like "the Jews are our misfortune" from municipal buildings and properties. Instead, he actually did the opposite, ordering that such signs be erected at all of the community's points of entry. The district administrator wanted to write a special report "because I consider the current condition to be unsustainable for the party and the administration, while the Jew, from whom this condition does not remain hidden, is laughing up his sleeve and exploiting the situation."[24] Similarly, the police president in Stettin defended himself against the possible suspicion that he wanted to protect the Jews: "As the Gauleitung knows, I have complete understanding for the struggle against Judaism and Jewish arrogance, but as a police administrator I am responsible for assuring that the regulations issued by the ministries are complied with and that public security and order are not disturbed and that criminal actions like gross misconduct and property damage do not occur."[25]

At the end of July 1935 in Berlin, after actions threatened to get out of control, Police President Helldorf again issued an official notification that individual actions were prohibited.[26] Only a few days later, Martin Bormann also turned against "self-help actions," and on 8 August Hitler himself stirred and forbade any "wild actions." On the next day the party leadership issued another communiqué to each Gauleiter in which these actions—which had, in fact, been initiated by the party—were condemned by Hitler's authority.[27] Even Julius Streicher fell in line, opposing "individual actions" in a major speech given on 15 August at the Berlin Sportpalast. The Berlin Gestapo reported with satisfaction:

The speech by Gauleiter Streicher on 15/08/35 in the Sportpalast has produced further clarity in the Jewish question. The opinion among *Parteigenossen* was often that the administrative measures to combat individual actions were officially approved of by the party in the interests of the reputation abroad, but that it actually tolerated and promoted the running battle [*Kleinkrieg*] against the Jews. In the meantime, the wave of individual actions has ebbed.[28]

On 20 August, Reich Interior Minister Frick issued a directive to all police agencies, including the local NSDAP chapters, with corresponding instructions to the Gauleitung, in which he wrote:

> The Führer and Reich chancellor has ordered that the individual actions against Jews by members of the NSDAP, its organization, and its affiliated associations must absolutely stop. After this, anyone who still participates in or incites individual actions against Jews must henceforth be considered a provocateur, rebel, and enemy of the state. I therefore request that from now such actions be ruthlessly opposed and that absolute peace, security, and order be maintained by any means. Illegalities are to be prevented using the most severe police methods, if necessary. In particular, criminal acts of property damage, physical injury, coercion, trespass, breach of the public peace, and riotous assembly should not be tolerated under any circumstances, no matter who is targeted by these criminal acts.[29]

This directive makes it sound like Frick wanted to defend what Ernst Fraenkel would call the Normative State from the Prerogative State, as if the concern was with guaranteeing legal norms and prosecuting criminal actions. But just a few weeks later, the regime's leadership engaged in a brief internal correspondence about what was to be considered an individual action. This correspondence makes it clear that the concern was not with norms but with measures. In mid October, the Reich Economics Ministry turned to both the NSDAP chancellery and also the Reich Interior Ministry. Given the repeated prohibition of all "individual actions," the question arose as to what that actually meant, and the Reich Economics Ministry itself suggested a definition, namely "that individual actions are to be understood as any measures which are not based on an expressed directive by the Reich regime or the Reich directorship of the NSDAP." Both Martin Bormann and the state secretary for the Reich Interior Ministry promptly confirmed that they agreed with the definition, thereby mutually affirming that the regime leadership was not interested in the question as to whether such actions were against the law but only whether or not they were ordered from above.[30]

This dichotomy in the attitude of the police, on the one hand supporting the regime's anti-Semitic policies and on the other hand understanding itself as a state organ in charge of safeguarding public order—that is, upholding state laws and directives—is also reflected in the population's reaction to the boycott actions. The reports repeatedly mention criticisms because of property damage. Thus in April 1935 the Cologne Gestapo wrote: "The general population has little understanding for the boycott actions against Jewish businesses that took place in the last weeks. In particular, they point out that the damage that results from smashing display windows and smearing shutters and houses does not impact the Jewish business owners but rather the insurance companies."[31] And the Trier Gestapo pointed out that the disaffection was further increased by the fact that "Christian employees of these Jewish businesses had to remove such smeared paint."[32]

In his investigation of public opinion in National Socialist Germany, David Bankier has argued more forcefully than anyone that the reports reveal a very widespread apathy and indifference to Jewish neighbors and that complaints were voiced not about the persecution of people but rather only about the damage caused to things.[33] But Peter Longerich has objected, holding that reports by the police and other state agencies always pursued specific interests and by no means provided an objective representation of what occurred.[34] The emphasis on property damage as a criminal offense naturally reinforces the appeal to the state as an authority that enforces order, whereas the mention of empathy, sympathy, or even open contradiction calls into the questions the efficacy of National Socialist anti-Semitic policies and would have necessitated not the police but rather more "enlightenment." Nonetheless, the aforementioned criticisms about the actions show the extent to which National Socialist policies regarding violence were also a question of "negotiation" between the different agents of violence. In 1935 the actions of the local SA, NSDAP, and HJ activists went way beyond limits that would have still been respected in 1933 and 1934. The fact that the questions about property damage now played such a central role as an argument reveals a limit in the expansion of violence. But it is impossible to know whether damage to property was the actual reason for the objection or a way to establish limits using the language of the state and criminal law. In the arguments put forward by the police, violating these limits would necessarily call the state organs into action. But this did not allow the institutions of the National Socialist state to escape the dilemma of their own politics of violence.

As much as the regime leadership tried to instrumentalize violence "from below," it was also unable to escape the logic of violence, which cannot simply be engaged and disengaged. Longerich concludes that "despite discernible frictions and tactical oppositions," the party leadership, party bases, and state apparatus "by and large [worked] together in harmony on the 'Jewish question' in 1935 as well."[35] But this only conceals the contradictions and oppositions, for the violent actions at the local level did not threaten the state organ's exclusive claim to the application of violence merely in terms of political theory. Rather, for the NS movement, "violence from below" was always a central medium of politics, not simply an instrument that could be deployed against political opponents and bureaucratic and legal obstacles. National Socialist politics were genuinely violent. The Gestapo agencies therefore had to learn that they could obviously not completely control these actions, that these actions continued despite central decrees, and that local party functionaries, by invoking the "will of the Führer," opposed state directives.

The "Individual Actions" Continue

The efforts to produce "racial legislation" in the summer of 1935 can thus also be interpreted as an attempt to end local violent actions and to regain control over the use of the violence. Indeed, state police agencies reported that the number of local violent actions declined after the proclamation of the Nuremberg laws.[36] Even so, the reports regarding "Einzelaktionen" (individual actions) did not decrease,[37] and letters from the local chapters of the C.V. indicate that the actions were effective and the Jews were becoming increasingly isolated in daily life. According to the East Prussian regional association, there was external peace, but business was very bad because the population was intimidated. Hairdressers, bakers, and butchers had put up signs saying that Jews were unwelcome.[38] The northwest German regional association reported that Jewish doctors were suffering badly because non-Jewish private patients stayed away, Jewish lawyers hardly had any non-Jewish clients, and only a few days earlier the last Jewish employee at the Tietz department store was fired.[39]

The C.V also reported from Anhalt and Magdeburg that many businesses throughout the entire Gau had put up signs stating "Jews are not wanted." Large banners were strung up in Magdeburg with slogans like "Anyone who buys from Jews is a traitor to the Volk" or "Brand the servants of the Jews." Notices posted in the Junkers factory in Dessau, the sugar factory in Stendal, and other companies threatened workers with immediate dismissal if they shopped in Jewish businesses.[40] Reports from Rhineland-Westphalia stated that the bureaucrats, employees, and workers at municipal operations for a large number of towns were being threatened with losing their jobs for shopping in Jewish businesses. The effects were "devastating."[41] In 1935 only a single Jewish family still lived in Rothenfelde near Herford, operating a butcher shop that mostly supplied the area's guesthouses, hotels, and health spa. At the beginning of August a protest assembly and a subsequent procession of demonstrators demanded that these establishments stop receiving supplies from the Jewish butcher. Additionally, the names of all of the establishments that had been shopping there were made public in a pillory display case. This action "fully ruined the business of the very well-respected butcher. Nobody in the population can risk entering the shop without being put in the pillory display case."[42]

In Stargard and Pyritz, Jews were no longer being served by hairdressers. In Gützkow, all of the businesses were prohibited from selling to Jews, and with the exception of a single colonial goods store, all of the businesses complied with the prohibition. The regional association in Pomerania determined that, even after the so-called individual actions were over, reviving the Jewish businesses was out of the question. "The threats which had not really caught on earlier—that anyone who maintains any kind of a relationship with Jews exposes himself to the most serious economic and personal danger—have become so effective that, as our friends correspondingly report, anyone who today still in any way visits the Jews must be described as a hero."[43] Summarizing in a report to the Reich Economics Ministry, the Berlin headquarters of the CV wrote:

> The measures against Jewish retail stores which were pursued with particular emphasis in the months of July and August have so sharply constricted the economic situation of Jewish retail operations, particularly in the provinces of East Prussia, Pomerania, Grenzmark, Hanover, Hesse-Nassau, in East Frisia and also in the states of Anhalt, Lippe, Hesse and in the Palatinate, that they must be considered as being in extreme economic danger. A not inconsiderable part of the companies is already destroyed and forced into liquidation. Even though, since the end of August, a series of the most severe measures has been lifted, the fear of being called to account for shopping in Jewish businesses continues to have such an effect that the business situation, especially in the small and mid-sized towns, has not improved.[44]

Jemgum

Jemgum was a town of about 1,200 residents in East Frisia, which had a small Jewish community of less than a dozen people.[45] It had become known that Frieda Pinto, the sister of a the Jewish butcher Levy Pinto, and her fiancé Adolf Cohen from Wittmund, who was also a butcher by trade, wanted to move in together in Jemgum. Shortly after Cohen's arrival, a procession of demonstrators formed in the community, carrying a banner that read: "We protest the influx of Talmud Jews." The crowd of people gathered in front of the Pinto family home and chanted words like "Judah out! Judah die!" and "We demand that the Jew Cohen leaves Jemgum."

The protest went beyond mere chanting—windows were also smashed. Thereupon the Bürgermeister and village police officer came to the scene and promised the crowd they would make sure that Adolf Cohen left. The police report records the subsequent events as follows:

> Bürgermeister Meyer and I betook ourselves in front of the house door, calmed the crowd, and promised them to make sure that the Jew would leave Jemgum. Thereupon we betook ourselves in the house and impressed upon the Jew to leave Jemgum soon, for he had to see that the residents of Jemgum had raised a most severe protest against his move [to Jemgum]. Cohen immediately declared his agreement, that he would leave Jemgum within a half an hour. Meyer and I went outside, informed the crowd of this, and asked it to disperse quietly and peacefully, which then occurred. Cohen asked for protection so that he could leave [Jemgum] unimpeded. Bürgermeister Meyer and I then accompanied Cohen to the ferry and had him taken across. A larger crowd of people followed us to the ferry. At the ferry office I requested the crowd to accompany [us] no further. Bürgermeister Meyer and Cohen then went to the ferry dock. Since the ferry skipper Kroon had received the command from Blockleiter Sinning not to take the Jew across, he came to me and asked for permission. I granted this to him. On the way back we discovered that the crowd had completely dissipated. Then I informed the district administrator about the incident by telephone. Overnight the broken windowpanes were replaced by a third party.[46]

A few weeks later, Adolf Cohen once again became the target of anti-Semitic attacks in Wittmund. According to the Gestapo report, on 12 November forty to fifty people, probably mostly SA and NSDAP members from Wittmund, gathered in front of the house of an innkeeper and farmer named Eilt Tammen in Abens, a village near Wittmund. They were demonstrating against the fact the Cohen had been slaughtering animals for Tammen. And as in Jemgum, they likewise started to smash the windows of the guesthouse. The crowd, which in the meantime had naturally increased with the addition of spectators from the village, demanded that Cohen be handed over. But fortunately he had already left Tammen's house and departed from the village, so there was no further violence.[47]

Gladenbach

Especially vicious attacks occurred in Gladenbach, a small community near Marburg in Hesse of around 1,800 residents with a Jewish community of slightly more than 100 people.[48] As early as March 1933, a crowd had gathered in front of the house of the Adler family shouting phrases like "Jews out! Beat the Jews to death!" An SA member named Karl Zunz forced his way into the house and found a neighbor, a dentist named Hupfeld, who had come to protect the Adler family. Zunz tore Hupfeld out of the house and turned him over to the crowd, which insulted him as a "Jewish lackey" and abused him as badly as it did members of the Adler family.[49] A few days later a crowd went to the house of Sally Stern, who supposedly had said that Hitler could "kiss his ass," dragged him from his residence, and forced him to proceed through the community. According to later findings of the Marburg district court, Stern was so scared that he had screaming fits. He had to stop every fifty meters to ring a bell and loudly proclaim that he took back his alleged statement. Additionally, he also had to insult himself as a "sow-Jew."[50]

On a late night in August 1935, groups once again came together in front of a number of houses, smashing windows by throwing stones and attempting to break through doors in order to gain entry to houses by force. Furniture was destroyed, inhabitants were beaten, and at the Grünstein residence the water line was broken, which caused the entire house to flood. The synagogue was attacked as well. The violent action persisted until early morning and unleashed panic among the twenty-six families in Gladenbach for a number of days. According to the C.V. report, many people fled Gladenbach for a number of days, and others spent the night of the pogrom in the forest, inadequately clothed.[51]

After the Jewish citizens filed complaints in the days that followed, the state attorney investigated the events and even visited the demolished houses. But three days later, as Sally Stern left the courthouse after being questioned, a crowd of people was again waiting for him and threatened him so fiercely that he fled back into the courthouse and requested police protection. Julius Levi, who wanted to drive August Schiff home from the court, was likewise attacked by the crowd. He ran to an apothecary in order to call the court and request assistance, but the pharmacist refused to help and instead sent Levi back into the street. Only the courageous intervention by a noncommissioned officer in the Reichswehr, who protected Levi and Schiff from the crowd, as well as the two police officers who escorted Sally Stern, enabled them to get home.[52]

In the night leading to 3 September, between two and three o'clock, masked men again forced their way into the homes of three Jewish families in Gladenbach, destroyed the furnishings, and beat the completely defenseless and mostly elderly people with clubs and sticks, injuring some of them severely. As the perpetrators left the home of Julius Meier, they threatened to come again in a week and "cut the Jews' throats."[53] On 10 September, Max Schiff wrote to the C.V. that the Jewish families had fled Gladenbach and no longer dared to return.[54]

Only six of the thirty-five Jewish families who lived in Gladenbach in 1933 returned during the next months, and many of these left the community again in the following period. After the violent excesses and the flight of many Gladenbach Jews, there was virtually a liquidation sale of businesses and properties, so that many non-Jewish Gladenbach residents became homeowners for a low price. At the beginning of November 1938, only thirteen Jewish people still lived in Gladenbach and businesses with Jewish proprietors no longer existed. The synagogue, which had been spared destruction because neighbors were anxious that a fire might spread to their houses, was later confiscated by the town. In the end, only an elderly married couple, Adolf and Sara Stern, still lived in Gladenbach, and they then moved to Frankfurt in June 1940. The Jewish history of a town—where a Jewish family was first registered in 1610 and where forty to fifty Jewish families lived at the end of the nineteenth century, where citizens of Jewish faith at times sat on the municipal council, and where as late as 12 March 1933 Max Schiff was reelected as an independent candidate—was over. Some managed to escape abroad; most sought refuge in large cities, particularly Frankfurt am Main; and a third of the Gladenbach Jews were murdered in the Shoah.[55]

Wolfhagen

Wolfhagen was a small Hessian town near Kassel with just under 3,000 residents. Its Jewish community was centuries old, but compared to its considerable size in the nineteenth century it had shrunk to just 65 people in 1934.[56] In November 1935 it was the scene of a noteworthy incident. A farmer named August Kepper had purchased bedroom furnishings from an iron goods dealer named Albert Katzenstein. Even as the furniture was being loaded, a crowd of people gathered, insulting Kepper as a "Jewish lackey" and the like. Faced with an increasingly threatening situation, Kepper decided to leave some of the furniture with Katzenstein for the time being and drive home with what he had already loaded. But the crowd followed him to his property, smashed his windows, and was just about to throw the furniture into a nearby stream when the police finally intervened, taking Kepper into custody and ordering his son to take the furniture back again—accompanied by two gendarmes! Nonetheless, furniture was thrown from the wagon along the way.

The next day, while customers once again frequented Katzenstein's store, another crowd of people gathered—the C.V. report mentions forty to fifty people—who became so threatening that Katzenstein closed his store. Even though the C.V. immediately turned to the Reich Economics Ministry and the latter apparently promised to intervene, the action had its desired effect. Responding to a letter from Albert Katzenstein, which explained that the ministry was going to provide assistance and that he could collect his furniture unimpeded, Kepper responded:

> Dear Herr Katzenstein! I am making reference to your esteemed letter from yesterday and was glad to hear that you have applied yourself so energetically; but I have no confidence in the promise that you have received, because I have realized that all of the authorities are against me. Even the police president in Kassel has submitted to the actions of the [NSDAP] district leadership by issuing an arrest warrant against me without examining the matter from a legal perspective. Even the lawyers do not want put themselves in opposition to the district leadership, and so I see myself without rights and exposed to the public. I have given up on the furniture purchase to avoid everything else. I am now sending back the things in my possession (keys, screws, etc.). I am exceptionally sorry, but surely you will understand. With kind regards.[57]

"Illusion of the Grace Period"

When Hitler sent troops into the demilitarized Rhineland at the beginning of March 1936, he accomplished a foreign policy coup. This was something that the regime's top leaders had hoped for more than they had expected, for despite all fears, the French army did not oppose the advancing German troops and the protests by the allies and the League of Nations against the breach of the Treaty of Versailles remained without effect.[58] Victor Klemperer noted on 8 March in his diary: "Three months ago I would have been convinced that we would have been at war on the same evening. Today, vox populi (my butchers): 'they are risking nothing.' General conviction, and ours also, that everything will remain quiet. A new 'act of liberation' by Hitler, the nation celebrates—what is internal freedom, what do we care about the Jews?"[59]

The suggestion of success, the belief that everything seemed to work for Hitler, resonated far beyond the supporters of the National Socialists and widely throughout the German population. The Reichstag "elections" on 29 March turned into a triumphal procession of the "Führer."[60] The *Deutschland-Berichte* of the exiled SPD records in detail the propagandistic spectacles and the mobilization of the population that took place in even the smallest communities. For example, in the fourteen days before the election in Endorf in Upper Bavaria, a community with around 1,700 residents, there were eight election-related rallies, and leaflets were distributed nine times. At a Saturday rally, one day before the election, 2,000 people from other communities in the area were summoned together. The election day itself began early in the morning with a large musical awakening and the firing of twenty shots from a small cannon. All private automobiles were utilized in the service of the election. By eleven o'clock, around 80 percent of the people in Endorf had already cast their vote. At noon the SA began searching for anyone who had not yet voted. There was no opportunity to stay away from the election. The SA detained a businessman who wanted to depart by train in the morning because he could not present a voting receipt, and he was returned to the poll location. Voting booths were hardly used, and many voters did not even bother marking the ballot because, according to the election workers, it was not necessary. And so it happened, determined the report, that with a voter turnout of 100 percent, 100 percent of the votes were cast for the "Führer." By contrast, in Breitenberg near Passau, a small community with around 800 residents, there were actually thirteen "no" votes. Thereupon, on the Monday after the election, a straw puppet with a rope around its neck was strung up in the village linden tree. Hanging from the puppet was a large sign stating that the "13 traitors of the Volk" would suffer the same fate.[61]

Thus Uwe Adam's conclusion that the year 1936 was a "period of external peace and quasi legal security" for the German Jews is now considered outdated and has been revised by more recent research.[62] The widespread conception that still persists today, namely that the terror against the Jews was halted during the Olympiad in Berlin, was disputed even at the time by the *Deutschland-Berichte*. According to these reports, there were admittedly no large-scale anti-Semitic actions during the Olympic Games, "but the everyday running battle did not diminish or stop for a moment."[63] Victor Klemperer noted on 17 August: "In the *Stürmer* (which is displayed on every corner) I recently saw a picture: two girls at a seaside resort, bathing costume. Above: 'Forbidden to Jews,' below: 'How nice that we are now amongst ourselves again.'"[64]

Even though Gestapo agencies were consistently reporting at the beginning of 1936 that the number of so-called "individual actions" was clearly declining, the excesses had by no means wholly ebbed. The reports repeatedly mention smashed display windows, vandalized cemeteries, and damaged synagogues, and there were indeed more violent attacks as well. In February in Steinau in Hesse, two lawyers who had come to the district court from elsewhere to represent their client, a livestock trader named Levy, were intercepted by around twenty people shouting words like "Get out of here, we don't need any Jews in Steinau!" and "Get the Jews out!" Pushed and shoved, the lawyers were brought back to the train station.[65] In another community in the middle of February, an unemployed man was led through the streets by the HJ with a sign that read "I am a servant to the Jews" because he had purchased cloth from a Jewish merchant.[66] In March, Jews who wanted to walk in the evenings from the Neukirchen train station to Rhina had stones thrown at them, in one case so intensely that the person under attack had to run back to Neukirchen and ask the gendarmes for protection.[67] At the beginning of April, a notice from the HJ Scharführer that appeared in the *Hünfelder Kreisblatt* stated:

> Warning to whom it may concern. The leader of the Schar 4/13/167 advises: Rothenkirchen. In our village the HJ placed signs at the village entrances with the inscription "Forbidden to Jews!" These signs were effective for a time. Then the "sons of Israel" tried to enter the village using detours. Now the "chosen people" are brazenly going past the signs. We hereby would like to warn all whom this concerns. The youth of Rothenkirchen is not willing to put up with such conduct. Also warned are those who still believe that they must deal with Jews. We are the New Age![68]

The boycott actions also remained aggressive. During the Sunday Christmas market on 20 December 1936 in Cham in Bavaria, the customers who shopped in stores owned by Jews were photographed, starting in the morning. According to the police report, in the early afternoon a large crowd of people gathered in front of the Eisfeld shoe store, shouting slogans like "Judah die!" and "Do not buy from Jews!" and trying to prevent customers from shopping. The pressure eventually became so strong that Eisfeld closed his store. Thereupon the crowd moved through the streets of Cham to the other Jewish businesses, forcing them to close.[69]

The Cham district office reported that the activists included functionaries of the HJ, DAF, and SA, and many young people were supposedly in the crowd as well.[70] This impression was also made by the reports by the Jewish victims in Cham. In a protest letter to the Bavarian Economics Ministry, the Association of Bavarian Israelite Communities wrote that "around thirty young people, who were later also joined by adults and a number of other followers" organized a procession around Cham. They chanted the following slogans: "Judah, die!" "Jews—Gustloff's murderers!"[71] "The Jews are our misfortune," and "Do not buy from the Jews!"

The demonstrators had torn the shutters from most of the stores and even nailed the doors shut from the outside on two stores. In its letter, the association drew attention to an appeal in the *Bayerische Ostmark* (which appeared in Cham) two days before the action, in which *"Volksgenossen"* were encouraged to act "according to the commandments of the National Socialist *Volksgemeinschaft*" when Christmas shopping. In particular, the article stated: "Do not wait for laws! Every German within his Volk has a political mission to fulfill. If we recognize the political mission, then nobody needs to wait for laws and implementation instructions about the activity of the Jews in the German economy."[72]

The regime leadership also struck a more severe note. At the end of August 1936 in an internal memorandum on the four-year plan, Hitler demanded that the German army be ready for deployment and that the German economy be ready for war in four years, threatening to create a law that "makes all of Judaism responsible for any damages that are caused to the German economy and thereby the German Volk by individual exemplars of this criminal society [*Verbrechertums*]."[73] At the end of September 1936, a conference in the Reich Interior Ministry among high-ranking regime officials regarding future Jewish policy established as a common goal the "emigration of the Jews under any circumstances." Therefore the range of economic opportunities for Jews had to be restricted; in particular, Jews had to be excluded from itinerant trades.[74] This impacted precisely those people who, because of the economic boycott measures, could now earn money only as traveling merchants. In January 1937, of a total of around 8,000 Jewish physicians, only 3,300 were still practicing; of 4,000 lawyers, only around 2,200. Even though the re-armament program had for some time already resulted in full employment, around 30,000 to 40,000 Jewish workers were unemployed and without prospects for work.[75]

Spurred on by the Spanish Civil War, the party congress in September 1936 targeted Bolshevism and the "international Jewish revolutionary headquarters in Moscow," as Hitler noted in his opening speech, in a special way.[76] Goebbels proclaimed that "the idea of Bolshevism ... could only have been born in the brain of Jews" and that the "Bolshevik practice in its terrifying cruelty is imaginable only as perpetrated by the hands of Jews."[77] The local party groups apparently understood the Führer's appeal very well. The Bürgermeister of Bodenmais in Lower Bavaria issued a proclamation in January 1937 that stated:

> I hereby expressly forbid the accommodation of Jews in Bodenmais. The Nuremberg laws and the Führer's explication at the 1936 party congress should have taught even the last of the *Volksgenossen* how important the

treatment of the Jewish question is. Jews and Bolshevism are two inextricable concepts and therefore I do not want to see any Jews in my community.[78]

In front of 800 district leaders of the NSDAP, Hitler explained the tactics of his politics against the German Jews:

> Of course, I do not immediately want to violently challenge an opponent to a fight. I do not say "Fight!" because I want to fight. Rather I say, "I want to destroy you! And now, Intelligence, help me maneuver you into the corner so that you cannot strike and then you will receive the stab in the heart." That is it![79]

The speech has survived as an audio recording. Hitler increasingly works himself up, finally shouting the last three words as loudly as possible like an explosion. The applause that followed was raging.[80] At the end of November Joseph Goebbels noted in his diary that he had discussed the "Jewish question" with Hitler at length: "the Jews must get out Germany, yes, out of all of Europe. This will still take some time, but it will and must happen. The Führer is strongly determined in this."[81]

At the NSDAP party congress in September 1936, Hitler fomented fiercely against "Jewish World-Bolshevism" and invoked his racist perspective of the world, stating that the Jews were "neither spiritually nor morally a superior [race], but rather in both cases a through and through inferior race."[82] Two months later he revealed to his closest military leaders that he was determined to go to war, whereby the first objective had to be the "lightning quick" subjugation of Czechoslovakia and Austria.[83] This is the background against which the stricter course of action against the German Jews needs to be seen. In a Germany that was itself ready for war, the Jews, for one, were considered to be "natural" opponents who allegedly wanted to cause damage to German efforts.[84] Additionally, Jewish wealth was coveted in order to finance rearmament. "Aryanization" and war preparation were directly related. Of the ca. 50,000 Jewish businesses that still existed in the German Reich at the beginning of 1933, only around 9,000 still existed in July 1938, and 3,600 of these were in Berlin.[85] Those who left Germany had to pay so many taxes and fees that they retained only a tiny portion of their assets with which to start anew.[86]

The boycott movement against Jewish businesses reached a scale that was almost impossible to bear. Quite a few proprietors, particularly in small and mid-sized communities, had to give up. At the end of March 1937, the C.V. received the following letter from Christburg in East Prussia:

As of a few days ago, the situation in Christburg is unsustainable. Last week our stairs and entrances were besmirched. In the night of Friday, from the 26th to the 27th, display windows, doors, and houses were again badly besmirched. There are now always SS people in uniform standing with cameras in front of our two Jewish businesses and impeding entry to the businesses. On the street we are harassed and are not allowed to show ourselves. Yesterday I encountered a serious incident: a SA man and a drunk civilian entered my store in the evening and demanded that I come into the street. We are without protection here and even employees of the magistrate participate in the boycott. My plea is not intended to support [legal] charges. Naturally, I am refraining from that. My letter is only supposed to have the purpose that you or pass this along [sic] to a competent authority to help us get out of here, that is to lease out or sell my two properties as soon as possible ....[87]

Of the fourteen Jewish families that were still living in Christburg at the end of 1934, only a few remained. In July 1938 the last Jewish family left the town.[88]

Notes

1. Weber, *Wirtschaft und Gesellschaft*, 822. Violence, insisted Weber, is naturally not the normal or only means of the state, but it was specific to the state.

2. See the concise overview of the problem by Grimm, "Das staatliche Gewaltmonopol."

3. The sentence comes from Hans Frank, who was Adolf Hitler's lawyer for many years. After 1933 he was the chairman for the Association of National Socialist Jurists and president of the Academy for German Law. As of 1939 he was the governor-general of Poland and responsible for millions of murders. "I brought this idea to expression for the first time in 1926 during a lecture to jurists in the Union room in Munich and repeated it in the Reichstag, where I gave it the following formulation: Everything that benefits the Volk is right; everything that does it harm is wrong." Hans Frank, ed., *Nationalsozialistisches Handbuch für Recht und Gesetzgebung* (Munich, 1935), xiv; see Dieter Willoweit, "Deutsche Rechtsgeschichte und 'nationalsozialistischen Weltanschauung': das Beispiel Hans Frank," in *Rechtsgeschichte im Nationalsozialismus: Beiträge zur Geschichte einer Disziplin*, ed. Michael Stolleis and Dieter Simon (Tübingen, 1989); for a biography see Dieter Schenk, *Hans Frank: Hitlers Kronjurist und Generalgouverneur* (Frankfurt am Main, 2006).

4. Hitler's speech to the Reich governors in Berlin, 6 July 1993, quoted here in Hitler, *Hitler: Reden und Proklamationen*, part I, vol. 1, 286f.

5. RMdI, Frick, circular dated 10 July 1933, Institut für Zeitgeschichte, *Akten der Partei-Kanzlei der NSDAP*, part I, microfiche no. 101 21256–259. Two weeks later Heß prohibited any unauthorized violence and ordered that measures be taken against party organizations that did not obey. StdF, Verfügung, 24 July 1933, quoted in Bessel, *Political Violence and the Rise of Nazism*, 124.

6. Reich Economics Ministry, circular dated 1 September 1933, "Ministerialblatt für die preußische Verwaltung," cols. 1115–1118.
7. Prussian Interior Ministry, circular, II E 2492/33, "Ministerialblatt für die preußische Verwaltung," col. 1115.
8. Schacht to Frick, 12 December 1934, printed in Paul Sauer, ed., *Dokumente über die Verfolgung der jüdischen Bürger in Baden-Württemberg durch das nationalsozialistischen Regime 1933–1945*, 2 vols. (Stuttgart, 1966), vol. 1, doc. no. 145, 169–171.
9. Ibid.
10. Frick to the Gestapa and all state regimes, 26 December 1934, printed in ibid., 171.
11. Decree Heß, 16 August 1934, published in *Verordnungsblatt der Obersten SA-Führung*, no. 34, 24 September 1934; Institut für Zeitgeschichte, *Akten der Partei-Kanzlei der NSDAP*, microfiche no. 101, 07626f.
12. Decree Heß, 19 February 1935, Institut für Zeitgeschichte, *Akten der Partei-Kanzlei der NSDAP*, part II, microfiche no. 13825.
13. Directive Heß, 11 April 1935, mentioned in the decree by the Karlsruhe Gestapo, 13 May 1935, in Sauer, *Dokumente über die Verfolgung der jüdischen Bürger*, vol. 1, doc. no. 43, 57; see also Walk, *Das Sonderrecht für die Juden im NS-Staat*, 551. In its mid February 1935 situation report, the Berlin Gestapa wrote that it had requested the Deputy Führer "to again prohibit relations with Jews in a decree to the organizations." Gestapa II 1 B 2, "Lagebericht Juden," 19 February 1935, Special Archive Moscow, 501-1-18, 63–69; also Kulka and Jäckel, *NS-Stimmungsberichte*, CD-ROM, doc. no. 551, partially printed in *NS-Stimmungsberichte*, 116.
14. The note by Hitler's adjutant Wiedemann to Bormann dated 30 April 1935 states: "Re: signs 'Jews are prohibited from entering.' I have told the Führer about the reservations that are being felt because of the Olympiad regarding these signs. This has not changed anything about the Führer's decision that there is nothing objectionable about these signs." Institut für Zeitgeschichte, *Akten der Partei-Kanzlei der NSDAP*, microfiche no. 124 05038. A collection of official and party correspondence regarding the erection of such anti-Semitic signs can be found in Sauer, *Dokumente über die Verfolgung der jüdischen Bürger*, vol. 1, 52–56.
15. District president Wiesbaden, August 1935, Kulka and Jäckel, *NS-Stimmungsberichte*, CD-ROM, doc. no. 1141. The NSDAP Gauleitung in Cologne-Aachen also determined that the "more detailed and stricter treatment of the Jewish question" contributed to the "increase of the party's activity." "Notwithstanding the fundamental nature of this question and the awakened *völkisch* instinct which generally makes its treatment desirable, with the subject of the Jewish question, department store, Jewish business etc. we have revived the temperament of the resigned middle-class." NSDAP Gauleitung Cologne-Aachen, March 1935, Kulka and Jäckel, *NS-Stimmungsberichte*, CD-ROM, doc. no. 748.
16. Münster Gestapo report, May 1935, Kulka and Jäckel, *NS-Stimmungsberichte*, CD-ROM, doc. no. 865.
17. Schlüchtern district administrator report for January and February 1935, 19 February 1935, printed in Klein, *Regierungsbezirk Kassel*, 341; Kassel Gestapo report for January 1935, 5 February 1935, printed in Klein, *Lageberichte der Geheimen Staatspolizei*, 217.
18. Ibid., 218.
19. Kassel district president, January/February 1935, 27 February 1935, printed in Klein, *Regierungsbezirk Kassel*, 356. The Coblenz Gestapo makes similar complaints in its report for February 1935, Kulka and Jäckel, *NS-Stimmungsberichte*, CD-ROM, doc. no. 627.

20. District administrator for Fritzlar-Homberg, report for January/February 1935, 19 February 1935, printed in Klein, *Regierungsbezirk Kassel*, 316.

21. Hanover Gestapo, special report, 18 August 1935, Kulka and Jäckel, *NS-Stimmungs-berichte*, CD-ROM, doc. no. 1093.

22. Cologne Gestapo report, May 1935, ibid., doc. no. 837; NSDAP Gauleitung Co-logne-Aachen, May 1935, ibid., doc. no. 920.

23. Köslin Gestapo report, June 1935, ibid., doc. no. 944.

24. District administrator Bad Kreuznach, report for June 1935, ibid., doc. no. 976.

25. Police president Stettin, May 1935, ibid., doc. no. 873.

26. Evidently the disruptions were initiated by low-level party organizations, for the Berlin Gau leadership prohibited all NSDAP, SA, SS, and HJ members from participating in such actions under threat of expulsion from the party. The police had instructions to intervene immediately and to inform the Gau leadership of the names of the gang leaders. These instructions were not primarily concerned with protecting Jewish citizens, but rather with maintaining public order and the state's monopoly of violence. On 30 June the police vice-president held a conference in the Berlin town hall with the Oberbürgermeister, Gestapo representatives, the NSDAP Gau leadership, and the SA. Together they decided upon a comprehensive catalogue of anti-Semitic communal measures in order, as the protocol stated, to "carry out the struggle against the Jews in Berlin without public demonstrations and individual actions." Gestapa, II 1 B 2, to Heydrich, 31 July 1935; Special Archive Moscow, 500-1-379, fols. 51–53; regarding this catalogue of measures, see Wolf Gruner, "'Lesen brauchen sie nicht zu können …' Die 'Denkschrift über die Behandlung der Juden in der Reichshauptstadt auf allen Gebieten des öffentlichen Lebens' vom Mai 1938," *Jahrbuch für Antisemitismusforschung* 4 (1995): 305–341.

27. Circular by the Deputy Führer to all Gauleiter, quoted in Adam, *Judenpolitik im Dritten Reich*, 121. Hitler's directive of 8 August is mentioned in a circular by the Baden Gauleiter and Reich Governor Wagner dated 15 August 1935. Sauer, *Dokumente über die Verfolgung der jüdischen Bürger*, vol. 1, 67.

28. Berlin Gestapo, Kulka and Jäckel, *NS-Stimmungsberichte*, CD-ROM, doc. no. 1089.

29. Directive RMdI, signed Frick, 20 August 1935, transcription with the decree issued by the Baden Interior Ministry to the regional district offices, 28 August 1935. Printed in Sauer, *Dokumente über die Verfolgung der jüdischen Bürger*, vol. 1, no. 52, 67.

30. Reich Economics Ministry to the Deputy Führer, 10 October 1935; Stuckart to Reich Economics Ministry, 25 October 1935; Bormann to Reich Economics Ministry, 31 October 1935, CAHJP HM2/8814, fols. 585–588 (Special Archive Moscow, 721-1-3254).

31. Cologne Gestapo report, April 1935, Kulka and Jäckel, *NS-Stimmungsberichte*, CD-ROM, doc. no. 770.

32. Trier Gestapo report for April 1935, ibid., doc. no. 789.

33. Bankier, *The Germans and the Final Solution*, 74.

34. Longerich, *"Davon haben wir nichts gewusst!"* 98.

35. Longerich, *Politik der Vernichtung*, 74.

36. See the reports for September from the Arnsberg Gestapo, Kulka and Jäckel, *NS-Stimmungsberichte*, CD-ROM, doc. no. 1203; Breslau Gestapo, ibid., doc. no. 1210; Lüneberg Gestapo, ibid., doc. no. 1221; Magdeburg Gestapo, ibid., doc. no. 1222; Munich police directorate, ibid., doc. no. 1226; Oldenbourg Gestapo, ibid., doc. no. 1227; Palatinate district president, ibid., doc. no. 1255.

37. Aachen Gestapo report for September 1935, ibid., doc. no. 1202: "Generally it must unfortunately be said that excesses against Jews in the month of September have

increased." See also the September reports from the Bavarian Gestapo, ibid., doc. no. 1208; Berlin Gestapo, ibid., doc. no. 1209; and Trier Gestapo, ibid., doc. no. 1237.

38. C.V. Grenzmark district association to Berlin headquarters, 17 August 1935, Special Archive Moscow, 721-1-243, fol. 125.

39. C.V. regional association northwest Germany, 6 September 1935, CAHJP, HM2/8814, fol. 1447f. (Special Archive Moscow, 721-1-3258).

40. C.V. central German regional association to Berlin headquarters, 6 September 1935, CAHJP, HM 2/8814, fol. 1439f. (Special Archive Moscow, 721-1-3258).

41. C.V. Rhineland-Westphalia regional association to Berlin headquarters, 6 September 1935, CAHJP, HM 2/8814, fols. 1429–1433 (Special Archive Moscow, 721-1-3258); see also other reports from 10 October 1935, CAHJP, HM 2/8803, fols. 1583–1586 and 24 October 1935, ibid., fols. 1564–1569, which describe the unchanged and continuing boycott, providing many local examples.

42. Werner Hoffmann, Herford, to the Berlin C.V 17 August 1935, Special Archive Moscow, 721-1-213, fol. 264.

43. C.V. Pomerania regional association to Berlin headquarters, 6 September 1935, CAHJP, HM 2/8814, fol. 1434 (Special Archive Moscow, 721-1-3258).

44. C.V. Berlin, signed by Brodnitz and Reichmann, to Reich Economics Ministry, 12 September 1935, CAHJP, HM2/8814, fol. 1401f. (Special Archive Moscow, 721-1-3258); further regional C.V. report in Longerich, *Politik der Vernichtung*, 117. Marion Kaplan poignantly describers how the experience of hostility resulted in the difficult and painful decision to emigrate. Kaplan, *Between Dignity and Despair*, 62–73.

45. Obenaus, *Handbuch der jüdischen Gemeinden in Niedersachsen und Bremen*, vol. 2, 906.

46. Gendarmerie Jemgum, report dated 13 September 1935, Kulka and Jäckel, *NS-Stimmungsberichte*, CD-ROM, doc. no. 1285; see also the report by the Aurich district president dated 13 September 1935, ibid., doc. no. 1241; also the daily report by the Aurich Gestapo dated 13 September 1935, ibid., doc. no. 1205. At the end of 1939, only six members of the Pinto family were still living in Jemgum. They were then brought to Leer and a little later to Berlin. At this point, the traces of three family members disappear, while the other three were deported to Riga and Auschwitz and murdered. Obenaus, *Handbuch der jüdischen Gemeinden in Niedersachsen und Bremen*, vol. 2, 907.

47. Aurich Gestapo, daily report for 12 November 1935, Kulka and Jäckel, *NS-Stimmungsberichte*, CD-ROM, doc. no. 1415. "Thirty-one of the demonstrators could be identified," concluded the Gestapo report, "and proceedings have been initiated against them because of breach of the peace." The reports that follow never make any mention of a sentencing.

48. Jürgen Runzheimer, *Abgemeldet zur Auswanderung: Die Geschichte der Juden im ehemaligen Landkreis Biedenkopf* (Biedenkopf, 1992), 36.

49. This was the finding of the Marburg district court in 1953 in its judgment against the SA member Zunz. Landgericht Marburg/Lahn, 7 KLs 4/53 and 7/53, 16 September 1953, Yad Vashem Archives, Jerusalem, TR-10/346. The judgment and other court documents are also printed in Klaus Moritz and Ernst Noam, *NS-Verbrechen vor Gericht 1945–1955: Dokumente aus hessischen Justizakten* (Wiesbaden, 1978), 77–90.

50. Ruling by the Marburg district court, 16 September 1953, Landgericht Marburg/Lahn, 7 KLs 4/53 and 7/53, 16 September 1953, Yad Vashem Archives, Jerusalem, TR-10/346. At the time, a number of perpetrators had to appear before court and address charges of trespass, bodily injury, and property damage, and numerous participants received prisons sentences of several weeks. But the district repealed the

sentences in 1935 and closed the proceedings. Runzheimer, *Abgemeldet zur Auswanderung*, 41.

51. Ruling by the Marburg district court, 16 September 1953, Landgericht Marburg/ Lahn, 7 KLs 4/53 and 7/53, 16 September 1953, Yad Vashem Archives, Jerusalem, TR-10/346. See especially the report by the C.V. regional association Hesse-Nassau and Hesse to Berlin headquarters, 16 August 1935, Special Archive Moscow, 721-1- 2556, fols. 117–120. The report by the Wiesbaden district president dated 30 August 1935 also makes brief mention of the excesses, printed in Klein, *Regierungsbezirk Kassel*, 901f. See also Runzheimer, *Abgemeldet zur Auswanderung*, 48–50.

52. Report by Hermann Hammerschlag to the C.V. regional association Hesse, 18 August 1935, Special Archive Moscow, 721-1-2556, fol. 116.

53. C.V. regional association Hesse to the Wiesbaden district president, 3 September 1935, Special Archive Moscow, 721-1-2556, fol. 108f.

54. Appendix to a brief by the C.V. regional association Hesse to Berlin headquarters, 16 September 1935, Special Archive Moscow, 721-1-2556, fols. 99–101. Some of Gladenbach's Jewish families sought compensation for the destruction, and by order of the Wiesbaden district court in 1936 they received between RM 30 and 600 as "compensation for tumult damages" (*Tumultschädenersatz*), as the bureaucratic language put it.

55. Arnsberg, *Die jüdischen Gemeinden in Hessen*, vol. 1, 266; see the list of persons in Runzheimer, *Abgemeldet zur Auswanderung*, 117–129. Schiff had to give up his mandate as early as 29 March 1933 because of Göring's ordinance "to eliminate deficiencies in municipal administration," dated 22 March 1933. Runzheimer, *Abgemeldet zur Auswanderung*, 36.

56. See Paul Görlich, *Wolfhagen: Geschichte einer nordhessischen Stadt* (Wolfhagen, 1980), 344–354. In 1874 the Jewish community in Wolfhagen still included about 300 persons, which amounted to 10 percent of the population.

57. Appendix to the brief by Albert Katzenstein to the C.V. Berlin, 24 November 1935, CAHJP, HM2/8793, fol. 1318 (Special Archive Moscow, 721-1-2969).

58. "Am I ever glad! My God! Am I ever glad that this went off so smoothly!" Hitler supposedly said to Hans Frank at the end of March as both men were traveling back to Berlin in a special train after a triumphant rally in Cologne. Kershaw, *Hitler*, vol. 1, 741.

59. Klemperer, *Ich will Zeugnis ablegen bis zum letzten*, vol. 1, 250.

60. See Kershaw, *Der Hitler-Mythos*, 100–103.

61. Behnkin, *Deutschlandberichte*, April 1936, 431.

62. Adam, *Judenpolitik im Dritten Reich*, 153.

63. Behnkin, *Deutschlandberichte*, August 1936, 973. With regard to the Olympiad, Heß issued an order to desist from using particularly offensive formulations in anti-Jewish signs in a January 1936 circular to NSDAP organizations. And Bormann, in a letter one month later to the Reich Nutrition Ministry, made it clear that in individual cases one could show some restraint for "foreign policy considerations" (the matter concerned a boycott against livestock traders from the Netherlands who stemmed from Jewish families). But in principle, he added, "the objective of the NSDAP, to eventually shut out Judaism from all the German Volkstum's spheres of life, is firmly fixed." Quoted in Longerich, *Politik der Vernichtung*, 116.

64. Klemperer, *Ich will Zeugnis ablegen bis zum letzten*, vol. 1, 372.

65. Kassel Gestapo report for February 1936, in Klein, *Regierungsbezirk Kassel*, 387.

66. Ibid.

67. In April and May, young people in Rhina threw stones at those attending a Jewish religious service and bombarded the synagogue so intensely that the service had to be cancelled. C.V. regional association Hesse to the Hünfeld district administrator, 30 June 1936, Special Archive Moscow, 721-1-2514, fol. 17f.

68. C.V. regional association Hesse to the Hünfeld district administrator, 20 May 1936, Special Archive Moscow, 721-1-2514, fols. 21–23. In February 1936, the C.V. reported on attacks by adolescents and schoolchildren against Jewish fellow students, adults, and particularly the elderly in other communities in Hesse like Gmünden, Grebenstein, Frankenberg, Schlüchtern, Hoof, Bad Wildungen, and Salmünster. C.V. Berlin to regional association Hesse, 2 March 1936, Special Archive Moscow, 721-1-2514, fol. 52f; see also Kaufman, "The Daily Life of the Village and Country Jews in Hessen," 173–179.

69. Cham district office report for 20–21 December 1936 ("Tagesbericht: Vorkommnisse gegen jüdische Geschäfte in Cham"), Kulka and Jäckel, *NS-Stimmungsberichte*, CD-ROM, doc. no. 2037; Munich state police report for December 1936, ibid., doc. no. 2027; extracts printed in Broszat et al., *Bayern in der NS-Zeit*, vol. 1, 464.

70. Cham district office report for 20–21 December 1936 ("Tagesbericht: Vorkommnisse gegen jüdische Geschäfte in Cham"), Kulka and Jäckel, *NS-Stimmungsberichte*, CD-ROM, doc. no. 2037

71. The NSDAP Landesgruppenleiter in Switzerland, Wilhelm Gustloff, was shot to death by a young Jew named David Frankfurter in February 1936. The National Socialist press made a big propagandistic show of the trial against Frankfurter in Switzerland in December 1936. Longerich, *"Davon haben wir nichts gewusst!"* 101–103.

72. Association of Bavarian Israelite Communities to the State Ministry for Economics, Munich, 23 December 1936, CAHJP, HM2/8768, fols. 1431–1433 (Special Archive Moscow, 721-1-2546).

73. The memorandum is documented by Wilhelm Treue, "Hitlers Denkschrift zum Vierjahresplan 1936," *Vierteljahrshefte für Zeitgeschichte* 3 (1955): 184–210; see also Kershaw, *Hitler*, vol. 2, 53–56.

74. Note by State Secretary in the Reich Interior Ministry Stuckart about the conference on 29 September 1936, printed in Hans Mommsen and Susanne Willems, eds., *Herrschaftsalltag im Dritten Reich: Studien und Texte* (Düsseldorf, 1988), 445–452; see also Barkai, *Vom Boykott zur "Entjudung,"* 127; Wolf Gruner, *Öffentliche Wohlfahrt und Judenverfolgung: Wechselwirkungen lokaler und zentraler Politik im NS-Staat (1933–1942)* (Munich, 2002), 87f.; Longerich, *Politik der Vernichtung*, 119f.

75. Barkai, *Vom Boykott zur "Entjudung,"* 78f.

76. Hitler, *Hitler: Reden und Proklamationen*, part I, vol. 2, 638.

77 Quoted in Friedländer, *Years of Persecution*, 183.

78. Quoted in the monthly report of the district president for Lower Bavaria and Upper Palatinate, 5 February 1937, Kulka and Jäckel, *NS-Stimmungsberichte*, CD-ROM, doc. no. 2068.

79. Hitler, speech to the district leaders at Ordensburg Vogelsang, 29 April 1937, printed in Adolf Hitler, *"Es spricht der Führer": 7 exemplarische Hitler-Reden*, edited with commentary by Hildegard von Kotze and Helmut Krausnick, with collaboration from F. A. Krummacher (Gütersloh, 1966), 148.

80. This is the analysis in Friedländer, *Years of Persecution*, 188.

81. Goebbels, *Tagebücher*, part I, vol. 4, 429.

82. Hitler, *Hitler: Reden und Proklamationen*, part I, vol. 2, 728–730. Goebbels had an even more hysterical tone in his party congress speech on 11 September: "Without fear, we want to point our finger at the Jew as the inspirer, the author, and the

beneficiary of this terrible catastrophe [Goebbels was referring to the Spanish Civil War—M.W.]: look, that is the enemy of the world, the destroyer of cultures, the parasite among the nations, the son of chaos, the incarnation of evil, the ferment of decomposition, the visible demon of the decay of humanity." Quoted in Friedländer, *Years of Persecution*, 184.

83. Minutes of the Conference in the Reich Chancellery, 5 November 1937 (Hoßbach Protocol), in *Trial of the Major War Criminals before the International Military Tribunal, Nuremberg, 14 November 1945 – 1 October 1946* (Nuremberg, 1947), vol. 25, 402–413; see Walter Bußmann, "Zur Entstehung und Überlieferung der 'Hoßbach'-Niederschrift." *Vierteljahrshefte für Zeitgeschichte* 16 (1968): 373–384; Bradley F. Smith, "Die Überlieferung der Hoßbach-Niederschrift im Lichte neuer Quellen," *Vierteljahrshefte für Zeitgeschichte* 38: (1990): 329–336. The so-called Blomberg-Fritsch affair then offered the welcome opportunity to reorganize and reshuffle the Wehrmacht in order to bind it more tightly to the NS leadership. Hitler himself took over the supreme command of the Wehrmacht. For details, see Kershaw, *Hitler*, vol. 2, 87–104.

84. See Adam, *Judenpolitik im Dritten Reich*, 166–203; Ludolf Herbst, *Das nationalsozialistischen Deutschland 1933–1945: Die Entfesselung der Gewalt: Rassismus und Krieg* (Frankfurt am Main, 1996), 200–217. Victor Klemperer learned about the dismissal of Economics Minister Schacht, who opposed a forced rearmament policy (but who in any event remained the Reich Bank president) in a small announcement in the newspaper at the end of November 1937, yet Klemperer nonetheless noted presciently that later historiography might very well see this small point as the beginning of the end. "Only: how many years separate this beginning from the final end?" Klemperer, *Ich will Zeugnis ablegen bis zum letzten*, vol. 1, 386 (entry for 28 November 1837).

85. Barkai, *Vom Boykott zur "Entjudung*," 78–80.

86. The revenue obtained from the so-called Reich flight tax alone for the financial year 1935/36 amounted to around RM 45 million; in 1936/37, it was almost 70 million; in 1937/38, it was over 81 million; and in 1938/39 it was 342 million. In the fourth quarter of 1938—a high point in emigration after the November pogrom—the revenue from the "Reich flight tax" surpassed that from property taxes. Longerich, *Politik der Vernichtung*, 125.

87. Extract from this letter cited in C.V. regional association East Prussia to Berlin headquarters, 31 March 1937, CAHJP, HM2/8783, fol. 1767f. (Special Archive Moscow, 721-1-2804).

88. See the entry "Christburg/Dzierzgoń," in *The Encyclopedia of Jewish Life Before and During the Holocaust*, ed. Shmuel Spector and Geoffrey Wigodor, 3 vols. (New York, 2001), vol. 1, 257.

8

POGROM

A major reason why the pogrom in November 1938 has such a significant place in the politics of memory in postwar Germany[1] is that it destroyed the self-conception of a society, even under National Socialist conditions. "Descent into Barbarism" was the subtitle for Wolfgang Benz's 1988 essay on the November pogrom,[2] wholly concurring with the narratives of those societies that describe themselves as civilized, externalizing as "barbaric" this violence that appears to them "wild," "excessive," irrational, and inexplicable. Admittedly, anti-Jewish pogroms had taken place earlier in Germany, for example in Pomerania in the summer of 1881 or in the region around Konitz in West Prussia in the spring of 1900. But they were regionally contained and the state authorities quickly intervened, not so much because they wanted to help the Jews but rather to restore "peace and order."[3] Moreover, the event in November 1938 so clearly distinguished itself from these excesses that, even with the understanding that the violent action was ordered from above and carried out exclusively by the SA, one still has to explain the unlimited brutality and destructive rage.

First, we should establish that the pogrom in November was by no means an isolated occurrence. The pogroms in 1938 began in March in Austria with the country's Anschluss to the German Reich. As early as the evening prior to the arrival of German troops on 12 March, Austrians in Vienna and elsewhere fully vented their anti-Semitic resentment. Jewish businesses were plundered, Jews were arbitrarily arrested, driven out of apartments, and abused, and personal enrichment was the order of the day.[4] Remembering that 11 March in Vienna, Carl Zuckmayer wrote in his autobiography:

> On this day all hell broke loose. The Underworld opened its gates and released its lowest, most despicable and unclean spirits. The city transformed itself into a nightmare-painting by Hieronymus Bosch: Lemurs and demi-demons seemed to crawl out of the filth and rise from holes in the ground. The air was filled with a relentlessly piercing, desolate, hysterical screeching, coming from male and female throats, a shrilling that persisted for days and nights. And all people lost their faces, and looked like distorted grimaces: some of them in fear, the others in falsehood, and others in wild hate-filled triumph.[5]

Hans Reichmann in Berlin learned about the reports from Austria in the Berlin office of the C.V.:

> On the next day, I listen to every report about the entry of the troops, hear children screeching and the Austrian BDM in Linz shouting "*Heil*" until finally in the evening hours the Führer steps out on the balcony of the Linz town hall. At the same time I see, in spirit, swarms of fleeing people and think about German Jews, for whom Vienna had just opened up as a new asylum. But I did not yet know at the time what horrible misdeeds this influx of troops would evoke. The Reich representatives and we impatiently await news from Vienna. Two or three weeks pass before the first unofficial dispatches from the religious community in Vienna appear in Berlin. What we hear is horrifying. It exceeds all experiences of March and April 1933. Again somewhat later, a representative of the Viennese Jewish attorneys approaches me. He still does not take the development seriously, believes that the mob rule [*Strassenherrschaft*] will ebb away, that the conditions will stabilize on the basis of the German Jewish laws. The German bureaucracy is apparently of the same opinion: the Justice Ministry transfers the principles for the continuance of Jews in the legal profession that apply for Germany to Austria. But suddenly there are reports and mass arrests the likes of which we have until then never experienced in Germany.[6]

In Vienna, Adolf Eichmann, who arrived as an SD representative shortly after the troops, organized the anti-Jewish policies, extorting several hundred thousand Reichsmarks from the Jewish religious community. He thereby demonstrated that, in contrast to the cumbersome methods of the ministerial bureaucracies, the SD had sufficient criminal energy to have the Jews themselves finance their own expulsion. The newly founded Viennese Central Office for Jewish Emigration became the model for

Berlin and Prague.[7] Tens of thousands fled from the terror. By the spring of 1939, 190,000 Austrian Jews had left their country, thousands of them violently expelled across the border by the SA and SS, particularly into Switzerland.[8]

In the spring of 1938, succeeding the events in Austria, anti-Semitic excesses recurred in Germany as well. In March the district president of Lower Franconia reported that violent acts against Jews had taken place in a number of localities.[9] In the night leading to 2 April, unknown perpetrators set off an explosive in the gate entrance to Richard Mayer's house in Böchingen near Landau in the Palatinate. The pressure from the explosion lifted the courtyard gate from its hinges and destroyed the windows in Mayer's house as well as those of his neighbors; according to the district president's report, wooden debris landed twenty meters away.[10] In Goldbach by Aschaffenburg in Bavaria, the Jewish livestock trader Heinrich Schönfeld and other Jewish merchants had their stairs torn away and their doorways walled off with stones. The gendarmerie in nearby Hösbach reported that Schönfeld testified that at around two o'clock a larger number of people, yelling and hollering, smashed all of the closed windows and shutters, calling out repeatedly: "Judah must die, Judah must get out!" Schönfeld himself collapsed due to the excitement and was unconscious for some time.[11]

In Alzenau in Bavaria, a crowd of about 100 people, according to the gendarmerie report, moved from a May Day dance at the tavern to the manufactured goods store of Hugo Hamburger and cried: "Out with the stinking Jew, the defiler of the national holiday." On the next evening this action was repeated, targeting the merchant Simon Oppenheimer. Only after the police came and took Oppenheimer into custody did the crowd calm down and disperse.[12] In Hessian Hanau, on a Friday night in mid May, all of the entrances to the synagogue were walled off, making religious services on the Sabbath impossible. The synagogue remained closed for days because there were no bricklayers available in Hanau who were willing to reopen it.[13]

People in Gelnhausen in Hesse had the same idea. According to the Gestapo's daily report, on the night leading to 4 June 1938 "the access to the synagogue and to a Jewish store were blocked by stacking up stones."[14] Manfred Meyer would later fill in the details that lurked behind the dry language of the report. Born in Gelnhausen in 1904, and having emigrated to the United States in 1939, Meyer sent a statement to Gelnhausen in 1986 in which he recalled the event:

> We then experienced the worst three days in the year 1938 as we were celebrating our so-called Feast of Weeks, seven weeks after our Easter feast.

In 1938 it fell on a Sunday and Monday. On Friday evening the entire congregation was, as usual, still in the synagogue for religious service. Saturday morning around 7:30, synagogue-helper Stein said to my father, we cannot get into the synagogue because both entrances have been walled off. My brother, who was a courageous young man, got Siegfried Weiss. They went to the synagogue, reaching the synagogue courtyard from the community center (which today is no longer standing) through a kitchen window; [they] opened the doors from within and managed to tear down the wall toward the outside, for the mortar was still very fresh. The work had hardly been done when hundreds of screaming people gathered in the courtyard and bombarded the courtyard by throwing stones, destroying all the windows in the synagogue and the windows of the room in the community center that was still being used by the congregation. Herr Weiss and my brother stayed in the synagogue in order to protect themselves from the crowd's hail of stones. How, after hours, they got away safely that time remains a mystery to me even today.

By a roundabout path they both then managed to sneak home. We had no connection of any kind with Jewish friends, for no one dared to let himself be seen in the street. In the night from Saturday to Sunday, the mob smashed the windows of all the Jewish residences, even those in the synagogue and community center which had not yet been hit. At the same time, at the manufactured goods store of S.H. Scheuer, they walled off the large main entrance and at the private home at 17 Schmidtgasse they barricaded the entrance door with an angle iron so that nobody could get out. The mob did not know that the entire Scheuer family had driven to Frankfurt for the holidays.[15]

On Tuesday, Heinrich and Richard Scheuer were summoned to the Bürgermeister's office, where they were informed that the Jewish community itself would have to cover the resulting damages to the synagogue and private homes. Furthermore, the office wished for Gelnhausen to be "Jew free" by 1 September and "generously" indicated that Jewish families would be left in peace until that time.[16] This was the final reason for the Gelnhausen Jews to leave a community that had become their enemy. The synagogue was sold to a non-Jewish grocer and thus not destroyed in November. Ten days before the pogrom, on 1 November 1938, the *Kinzig-Wacht*, under the proud headline, "Gelnhausen is Finally Jew Free," reported that the last Jewish family, Siegfried Weiß and his wife Selma née Scheuer, had left Gelnhausen.[17]

In May and June, excesses flared up again in Berlin as well. Jewish businesses were vandalized and synagogues were damaged, in the course of which, according to an SD report, Jewish stores were plundered and destroyed and violence broke out.[18] A year later Hans Reichmann recalled:

I knew where they were to leave the mark of the *"kochende Volksseele"* [boiling soul of the Volk] from the path of the "smear brigades" in 1935. At that time, the *"kochende Volksseele"* had been appeased by the "Nuremberg laws." It took five days for the brigades to move from defaced Neu-Kölln to Alexanderplatz and from there further toward the West. New streets were "conquered" daily this time as well. In so doing there were grotesque spectacles: the business of a Reich-German Jew, for example, is defaced, but the neighboring shop which belongs to a Polish Jew is carefully avoided. A completely defaced business dares to open again. Suddenly the police are on the spot and force it to close because an open Jewish business has a "provocative" effect. In the night from Saturday the 11th to Sunday the 12th of June, they do some thorough work. Each Jewish business, and a few non-Jewish ones as well whose owners are mistakenly thought to be Jews, bears the inscription "Jew," "Itzig," or "Sarah" in awkward giant letters. Some display windows, where the Hitler Youth paint brigades especially exerted themselves, depict gallows or grotesque Jewish faces, drawn with the skill of schoolchildren. I travel on the deck of a bus along the Kurfürstendamm in order to observe the mood of the Volk, walk past the defaced display windows and mix with the pedestrians. Now and then a mocking word, sometimes a quiet repudiation, but in general there is silence.[19]

Hitler turned against further excesses, evidently because of foreign policy concerns. Upon a resolution by the Gauleitung and the Berlin police president, which was preceded by a "personal intervention by the Führer from Berchtesgarden," anti-Jewish actions were initially prohibited as of 21 June.[20] Yet Hans Reichmann recalled that there were raids on Jewish cafés and restaurants throughout the entire summer.

It happened like this: suddenly the notorious police captain Schneider appeared with his contingent of police cars and the constables and criminal investigators cordoned off the restaurants. He had the harmless guests show him their identity cards, knocked cigarettes out of the mouths of the elderly, put protesters in handcuffs, and took off to Alexanderplatz with a haul of thirty, fifty, sixty people. There they kept the catch for days, even weeks, for the Jewish question is indeed now being resolved legally. No Jewish guest-house, no restaurant however remote was safe from these lightning raids. The Jews had already retreated to ghetto establishments, but even here there was no peace. The result was intense intimidation. The cafés were empty.[21]

Once again, the security police exploited the "unleashed anger of the Volk" to intensify its own politics against the Jews. At a leadership meeting on 1 June 1938, Reinhard Heydrich informed his officers that "by order of the Führer, certain things [were] implemented in the western part of the Reich. For this purpose it is necessary to send all available work forces over there." Heydrich recommended arresting KZ prisoners, "work-shy and anti-social elements," and Jews with criminal records.[22] On the same day, the Reich Criminal Investigation Office issued a decree signed by Heydrich, according to which, for the week between 13 and 18 June, each criminal investigation agency was to "take at least two-hundred male persons (asocials) capable of work into preventative custody." It also determined that "furthermore, likewise for the week from 13 to 18 June, all male Jews in the district of the criminal investigation agency who have been given prison sentences of more than one month are to be taken into preventative custody by police."[23] The June action, where far more than 10,000 people—including 1,500 Jews—were arrested and taken to concentration camps, signified a drastic intensification of state police measures. Initial reports about the inhumane conditions in the concentration camps soon reached the C.V. in Berlin. Harry Stein's findings regarding the Jews in Buchenwald applied likewise to the other concentration camps: "no other group of prisoners in the summer of 1938 was more harassed."[24]

The year 1938 has been described as the "year of fate" (Avraham Barkai), the moment when the persecution of the Jews took a decisive turn. In March the Jewish communities lost their status as corporations under civil law. In April Göring issued an ordinance requiring the registration of Jewish assets, which systematically recorded the property that was to be seized. With the third amendment of the Reich Citizenship Law in June, which defined which companies were to be considered "Jewish," together with a decree by the Reich Interior Ministry one month later on taking inventories of all "Jewish" companies, the NS leadership wanted to make certain that not even a single business could escape its measures. The Law to Amend the Regulations on Trades and Professions (Gesetz zur Änderung der Gewerbeordnung) of 6 June 1938 was to effect the expulsion of Jews from those professions where they were still allowed to work.[25] Reichmann reported on the chicaneries to which Jewish dealers were exposed. The itinerant trade licenses that they were issued in one office were taken away again by the Gestapo two doors down the hall. The Gestapo threatened to imprison the Jewish lawyer who wanted to represent the complaints of the dealers, unless he made certain that the complaints were withdrawn.[26]

The SD's situation report for the first quarter of 1938 determined with satisfaction "that the regime's measures taken in recent times against the Jews in the area of economics were, from the perspective of the Reich, very successful." It continued: "On the other hand, this has limited to a severe degree the opportunities for the Jews to emigrate from Germany."[27]

The SD was well aware of the contradiction between impoverishing the Jews on the one hand and thus on the other hand decisively limiting their opportunities to emigrate, especially since the newly added Austrian Jews made the problem even worse. Shutting the Jews out of the economy resulted in falling revenues for Jewish communities and aid organizations. And these until now had in large part provided the financial means for Jews who were willing to emigrate but had few assets.

Five years after the party's seizure of power, the National Socialist anti-Semitic policies had come to a dead end, even though in balance they appeared successful. The ministerial bureaucracy had successfully expedited the legal exclusion of Jews from public life. The special laws for the Jews had been continuously woven to increasingly refine their ramifications. Their expulsion from the economy with respect to the liberal professions had been largely successful, and the "Aryanization" of Jewish companies had significantly advanced. But the impoverished Jews hardly had the opportunity anymore to leave the country voluntarily, for they did not possess the capital required by the countries that might welcome their immigration. Only young people and wealthy Jews could still hope to start again in another country, although the conference arranged by US President Roosevelt in 1938 in France at Evian-les-Bain on Lake Geneva to support the persecuted Jews revealed that no country was prepared to increase its immigration quotas.[28]

Accordingly, those who remained behind consisted of the poor, the elderly, and those who were unable to imagine that the Germans could treat them any worse than they already had and thus stubbornly clung to "their" Germany.[29] At the beginning of September, the SD had to admit:

> The emigration opportunities, however, are so strongly in decline due to international measures that one can hardly speak of a regulated emigration anymore—except for the Ostmark to a certain extent. Even if the necessary support from foreign Jewish organizations is made available and the Reich releases foreign currencies, in the future this question will not be easy to solve.[30]

The Pogrom-Prone Mood in the Early Fall of 1938

The atmosphere in Germany after the events in June remained charged with violence. The crisis in the Sudetenland staged by the NS regime led to an increasingly shrill press campaign in support of the "oppressed" Sudetenland Germans in Czechoslovakia who were supposed to be brought "home into the Reich." At the same time, fears were growing that another war would have to be fought for the Sudetenland. Official reports spoke of a "genuine war psychosis" and even "panic."[31] In many instances, money was withdrawn from banks and savings accounts as a precautionary measure, and in the border regions suitcase retailers were thriving.[32] An HJ report from Bavaria about the mood of the youth "in the critical days" highlighted the generational differences. According to the report, older people especially—those who had experienced the war of 1914–1918—were expressing doubts. Asked by frightened women about whether there would be a war, a local leader of the NS Women's Auxiliary told them not to worry and to "just trust in the Führer."[33]

Hans Reichmann, who at this time was staying with his wife in Baden-Baden, likewise reported on the tension-filled atmosphere that prevailed during those days:

> We also do not miss any reports from German radio, which shrieks its hate-propaganda into the world every half hour. In between we listened to Luxemburg and for the first time the voice of Chamberlain sounded from English radio. We pounced on the newspapers in order to approximately guess from Kircher's lead articles in the *Frankfurter Zeitung* what Hitler desired in the end. But the articles say something different twice each day, and the picture of the situation does not become clear.... I listened to the populace: nowhere was there enthusiasm, but the bourgeois strata believed the German propaganda: "the Strasbourger broadcaster lies" and "How calm our people are!"—"The Czechs have mobilized, tonight our mobilization will follow. Very well."—"Now we must see who wins, fascism or bolshevism. We shall see." But then: "Frau Städele, who always said *Heil Hitler* so loudly, she doesn't say it anymore either."—"They came to get my husband in the night. Tomorrow he is supposed to go to Czechia. What is supposed to become of all this?" Those were scraps of conversation that we gathered.... Certain agitation materials made me recognize in horror that they cheaply, cynically, and remorselessly wanted to burden the Jews with the blame for the war.... Streicher prepared a special edition of the *Stürmer* —"The Jews and the War"—which was supposed to pillory the Jews as warmongers and war criminals [*Kriegsschuldige*] in a fashion even cruder and more dangerous than Rosenberg.[34]

Here was the way to release the loaded tension: blame the Jews. While the faith in Hitler during those tense weeks prior to the Munich Agreement was apparently endangered but unbroken, the emotions were directed elsewhere—against the Jews. In Rauenthal in the Rhine district, a Jewish man and a Jewish woman allegedly told their neighbor that, in light of the foreign-political situation, they would be in power again within two years. The following night they were torn from their homes and, clad only in nightshirts, chased through the town with a whip.[35] According to the SD, in Nassau an der Lahn on 27 September at around nine o'clock there was a "Volk's demonstration [*Volksauflauf*] against the resident Jews" who had gathered in a house. The house was literally besieged. Window shutters and windows were smashed until the police arrested the alleged gang leader, Walter Rosenthal.[36] In Unsleben near Bad Neustadt on the Saale, a resident manufacturer named Theo Mittel allegedly said something similar to Sudetenland Germans who had fled there from Czechoslovakia because of the tensions: what goes around comes around. Thereupon a group of Sudetenland Germans gathered in front of Mittel's house, forced open the courtyard gate, and beat Mittel so severely that, according to the report, his cries could be heard from far away.[37]

Similarly, violence broke out in Mellrichstadt on 30 September after a Jew allegedly stated that, because of the trifling matter of the Sudetenland Germans, the whole world would mobilize. The interior of the Mellrichstadt synagogue, benches, ritual objects, candelabras, and other furnishings were completely destroyed. As stated in the report by the district president, the first attack was carried out by only a few perpetrators, and then a crowd that had gathered in the meantime joined in the destruction. Afterward the display window of the Mantel fabric store was smashed and the display was plundered, while the windows were smashed in the Jewish residences in Mellrichstadt. The district president also reported excesses in the communities in Main-Franconia.[38]

In its monthly report for September, the SD noted that "during the last reporting period, the mood among the Jews in the territory of the Reich was determined almost exclusively by the foreign-political situation, which gave occasion for the most wide-ranging kinds of rumors about the possible treatment of the Jews in the case of war. In a few cases, there were reports of impudent behavior by Jews—those who hoped for a German defeat in the case of war. But the Jews in general were afraid of being brought to concentration camps or rendered harmless in other ways." The attitude of the population against the Jews had "intensified under the pressure of foreign-political developments."[39]

Peter Longerich has pointed out that a pogrom-prone mood prevailed especially amongst party activists. At the end of October, the SD stated "that actions against the Jewish population resulted in part because party members believed the moment had come for the final liquidation of the Jewish question."[40] In some districts the NSDAP initiated its own "Aryanization," rounding up Jews and violently forcing them to sell their property, houses, businesses, and real estate at pitifully low prices, so they could then drive them out of the community.[41] The SD reported from western Germany that on 20 and 22 September in Beveringen, Neuen-kirchen, and Fürstenau, synagogues were broken into and their furnishings destroyed, and Jewish cemeteries were desecrated.[42] Also on 20 September, NSDAP members in Bechhofen in Middle Franconia forced the last three Jewish residents to leave the community. The SD reported: "They were taken from their homes, beaten and spat upon, kicked and driven through the community, some of them barefoot. Even the children, upon encouragement, participated in this demonstration."[43] As in Bechhofen, all of the Jewish families were also driven out of Wilhermsdorf in the district of Neustadt an der Aisch, according the district president. "These communities, like the entire district of Feuchtwangen, are henceforth completely Jew free."[44]

The Munich Agreement, concluded on 29 September, saw Chamberlain complying with German demands and agreeing to the annexation of the Sudetenland. Nonetheless, the anti-Jewish excesses continued in the south and southwest, where they had taken on what the SD described in its monthly report for October as "in part [a] pogrom-like character." In numerous towns and small communities, the synagogues were destroyed or set ablaze, and the windows of Jewish residences were smashed. "In the Gau of Franconia and in Württemberg, the Jews in individual communities were in part forced by the population to leave their homes immediately, bringing with them only what was most necessary."[45]

In a number of small communities in Hunsrück, Jewish families were assaulted in their homes; furniture was destroyed and people were driven off. They often fled to relatives or acquaintances in the closest larger towns and, according to the C.V. report, did not dare return to their home communities.[46] The district president in the Palatinate reported that in many places synagogues and private homes were attacked. During the night in Rülzheim in the district of Germersheim, windows were smashed in almost all of the houses where Jews lived, and slogans like "Hang the Jews," "War provocateurs," and "Jews dead" were smeared on them in red paint. "The population," noted the district president, "wants the Jews out of the villages and takes vengeance in this way for the impudent behavior of the Jews during the tense period in September. This justification for the actions of the population resonates throughout all of the reports."[47]

On 14 October in Leutershausen, a small Franconian community with around 1,400 inhabitants, the windows of a Jewish residence and synagogue were smashed and cow manure was thrown in front of their entrances. Two days later, numerous citizens of Leutershausen forced their way into Jewish homes, smashed their furnishings, and abused the inhabitants. Around forty or fifty people broke into the synagogue and destroyed the entire inventory. Thereupon most of the twenty or so Leutershausen Jews fled from the town in panic. Of those Jews who remained, seven more had left by the middle of December, and by February 1939 all the Jews had left Leutershausen.[48]

The neighboring local NSDAP chapter in Windsbach reacted with its own leaflet regarding the acts of violence in Leutershausen:

> In the last critical weeks, the Jew had the firm intention of hounding a part of the peoples of the world into a frightful war. The German nation was to be defeated and obliterated. Millions of people were to be slaughtered and murdered. Towns and villages of the German Gaue were to be destroyed. More than hundreds of thousands of German families would have faced unspeakable suffering. That was the will of the Jews.... Our unshakeable will is: in a short time, Windsbach must be Jew free.[49]

Even today, the severity and brutality of the November pogrom have not been sufficiently explained. The principle of command and obedience is undoubtedly a necessary part of the reason, but it is not sufficient, for SA troops could easily be ordered, even at night, to set synagogues and residences ablaze, but the destructive rage revealed during the pogrom could not be commanded. The destructive emotions also cannot simply be explained by anti-Semitic hatred alone, even though without such hatred this kind of excessive violence would hardly have been possible. Drawing conclusions based on the description of the preceding events, the emotionalism and the obsession that dominated the November pogrom can only be explained with reference to the violent tensions built up during 1938, especially the tensions that brought Europe to the brink of war. In a fatal inversion during the search for those responsible for the threat of war, by focusing not on the actual war provocateurs but on the Jews, who were wholly blameless in the affair, the tension could be released without having to implicate the NS regime and especially Hitler, who were actually to blame. The fact that this inversion of reality was plausible to so many people reveals that they were more willing to accept anti-Semitic justifications and to see or even make the innocent suffer than to question their own worldview. The fact that the November pogrom, as an aggressive release of a highly charged fear of war, could become so brutal and destructive reveals the intensity of the emotions—the deep fear—that prevailed in Germany in the fall of 1938 and could turn into such destructive rage. The reports indicate that the smaller pogroms in the provinces, which all took place weeks before the assassination by Herschel Grynszpan, no longer sought merely to discriminate against and isolate Jewish neighbors but were clearly set on expelling the Jews and extinguishing Jewish culture in Germany.

November Pogrom

The immediate cause of Herschel Grynszpan's assassination of the embassy staff member Ernst vom Rath in Paris was a renewed massive police action against the Jews. On 26 October, as a reaction to the Polish government's anti-Semitic intentions to revoke the state citizenship of Polish citizens living abroad and to mark their passports accordingly so that they could not return to Poland—a measure that in the first instance targeted Jewish Poles—Himmler issued a residency ban for Polish Jews and ordered that they had to leave the German Reich within three days. In a targeted large-scale action, the Gestapo apprehended 17,000 Polish Jews and violently deported them at the Polish border. Since Poland denied these people entry, they wandered aimlessly in no-man's land without any help, foodstuffs, or sanitation. Only after Poland and Germany came to an agreement days later about extending the time limits for deportations did Himmler cancel the action.[50]

It was this coldly calculated and brutal measure by the NS state that drove the young Herschel Grynszpan, whose parents had been among those deported, to undertake an assassination in Paris, where on 7 November 1938 he shot the German embassy staff member Ernst vom Rath.[51] By the evening of the assassination, the propaganda ministry was instructing all newspapers to report "in the biggest way possible about the assassination"; the news must "completely dominate the front page." Care was to be taken not to direct the articles against France but rather "against the international Jewish criminal rabble."[52]

On the afternoon of 9 November, when news arrived about Rath's death, leading representatives of the Reich's Deputation of the German Jews and the C.V. tried to avert the impending danger and together sent a telegram expressing condolences to Hitler, in which they emphasized that German Jews, like all well-mannered people, detested political murder and the assassination in Paris.[53] But those in the NS leadership who had been waiting for just such a situation in order to finally strike out against the Jews were by no means willing to be restrained.

The first anti-Jewish excesses occurred in Kassel as early as the evening of 7 November. A group of around thirty men forced their way into the synagogue, laid waste to the interior, and burned prayer scrolls and other religious objects in the forecourt while a few hundred people watched. A large crowd—the Gestapo report mentioned 1,000 people—then moved to the Café Heinemann, which was owned by a Jewish proprietor, and destroyed its interior as well. Next in line was the building on Große Rosenstraße that housed the Jewish elementary school, the community administration, and association office and meeting rooms. The excesses persisted until one o'clock in the morning, with people destroying and partially looting another twenty businesses. The attacks and lootings continued the next day as well.[54] Anti-Jewish excesses also occurred on the following day in other localities within the Kassel region, like Felsberg, Guxhagen, and Hersfeld.[55] The Bürgermeister in Bebra reported that after news of the assassination was broadcast on the radio on 7 November and the NSDAP district leader called for vengeance at a party meeting that night, individual groups moved through the town around midnight, smashing the windows of Jewish stores and also engaging in looting. The interior of the synagogue and the Jewish school were completely destroyed. On the same night, the district leader Braun drove to the county seat of Rotenburg and, with support of the local SA leader, also organized a pogrom there.[56]

Admittedly, on the next day, 8 November, the district president in Kassel issued an order to all police agencies that the "demonstrations against the Jews flaring up here and there" were to be "stopped immediately."[57] But in accordance with press instructions from the center, the daily newspapers were filled with fierce and prominently displayed anti-Semitic articles—the *Kurhessische Landeszeitung* reported on the first page about the previous day's "demonstrations by the population"—so that the activists knew what to do.

Correspondingly, that day there were anti-Jewish excesses in a number of Hessian communities. The local gendarmerie in Kirchhain reported that in the night of 8 November "large gangs" attacked houses owned by Jews and completely destroyed the interior of the local synagogue. The crowds of people had "dwelt horribly [*fürchterlich gehaust*]" in some of the buildings.[58] Kirchhain Jews were so brutally beaten that in the spring of 1939 the NSDAP Gau court in Kassel initiated proceedings against thirteen party members because "on the occasion of the Jewish action in Kirchhain on 11/08/1938 [they] abused Jews in an especially raw fashion." But they were all acquitted because the accused "acted in the approved framework of this action against the Jews."[59]

In Abterode in the district of Eschwege, the NSDAP Ortsgruppenleiter incited a political meeting, whereupon the synagogue was demolished, the Westheim Jewish department store was plundered, and a number of Jewish residences were devastated. The livestock trader Max Ronsheim was dragged through the streets to the synagogue, ridiculed, beaten, and spat upon. The perpetrators even wanted to throw him from the synagogue gallery, but this was evidently prevented by the urgent protests of a few of those present.[60] During the night leading to 9 November in Bad Hersfeld, a crowd of about 1,000 people destroyed Jewish homes and burned down the synagogue.[61] On the evening of 9 November in Felsberg in the district of Melsungen, a crowd destroyed the synagogue, demolished houses, and dragged Jewish residents from their homes and abused them so badly that one of those residents, Robert Weinstein, died on the same evening as a result of the violence.[62]

Wolfhagen

The morning of 9 November in Wolfhagen witnessed the arrival of SS troops from the neighboring town of Arolsen, the location of the office of the SS Obergruppenführer Hereditary Prince Josias von Waldeck and an SS garrison. They forced their way into the Jewish school and a Jewish apartment building and set off explosives. The director of the local health insurance company at the time supposedly guided the destructive troops.[63] Many Wolfhagen citizens participated in the pogrom, which lasted the entire day. Jewish homes were plundered and demolished, and in the evening the synagogue was set ablaze as well. It was still morning when, in light of the pogrom's brutality, the NSDAP district leader in Wolfhagen telephoned the Gauleitung in Kassel, only to be told to "stay out" of it. Not until the late afternoon did the notice come from the Gauleitung that "demonstrations" against the Jewish population were prohibited.[64]

At eleven o'clock in the evening on 9 November—that is, an hour before Goebbels mobilized the Gauleiters in Munich for the pogrom—the Kassel district president sent a radio message to all police agencies that all excesses against the Jews, including property damage, were to be prevented. As a result, in a few small communities like, for example, Burghaun in the district of Hünfeld, gendarmes tried to protect Jewish residences and synagogues during the night. Seven hours later, at around 6:30 a.m. on the morning of 10 November, they received a radio message from Chief Daluege of the regular police that the "demonstrations and actions [are] understandable" and were to be accompanied by only the regular police, "in weak force and plain clothes," in order to prevent looting.[65]

In Wolfhagen the pogrom continued on 10 November as well. In the afternoon, the director of the local SD took note of a call from Bürgermeister Vaihinger, who said to him:

> I just learned from Herr District Administrator Dr. Elze that a fire is to be started this evening at the marketplace where the Jewish inventory that has been thrown into the streets is to be burned. I must hereby officially forbid this. Incidentally, he had to express his deepest aversion to the fact that the SS stood at the fore of this action. It was no longer the Volk's anger but rather the purest vandalism. He is certainly no *Judenfreund*, but this course of action absolutely did not have his approval.[66]

Emden

The order to commit arson was received by the Emden NSDAP district leader from the Gauleitung in Oldenburg on 9 November at around 10:30 p.m. by telephone.[67] The district leader then consulted with the other party functionaries, the Bürgermeister, the director of the criminal investigators, and also the leaders of the district fire department. And around 4:00 a.m., the Emden synagogue was blazing brightly. Around midnight, the SA had been drummed up by SA Standartenführer Kroll, who gave the order that all Jews were to be arrested and brought to the schoolyard of the Neutor school, if necessary by force of weapons. The Jews were to be compelled to sleep overnight out in the open, and Jewish businesses were to be destroyed. In groups of four, the SA troops moved through the Emden neighborhoods, forced their way into homes with extreme violence, beat and abused the residents without regard for whether they were women, children, or elderly, and dragged them to the Neutor school.

Walter Philipson, who was twenty-three years old at the time, recalled forty years later:

> In the evening after 8 o'clock, the large torchlight procession marched along the Brückstraße to the Herrentor school. I looked out the window and said to my father: "Well, tonight things are going to happen." I always had a nose for this. "They will smash the windows in again, like in 1933," my father said.... At 3:30 they came back from the Herrentor school. I suddenly heard: "Jews out. Death to the Jews!" At first mainly on Oldersumer Straße, for that was where my bedroom faced. Then I went to the front to see what was happening on Brückstraße. And there I happened to hear how they were raging at [the place of] Gans the clockmaker. They had dragged the woman into the street and screamed: "Sarah, turn over your money!" or something like that. And in that moment I hear how they are taking beams from the burned-out Gasthaus Church and are bashing in the door panels of our house.

Walter Philipson ran into his parents' bedroom in order to warn them. As if he had failed to grasp what was happening, his 70-year-old father had gone down the stairs in a nightshirt.

> He thought he was supposed to open the door for them. But they had already smashed in the door panels. He went on the stairs—we had a straight stairway with twenty steps, with linoleum. He stood at the top and they immediately shot him in the chest, a shot through the lung. It came out the back again through the nightshirt, a shot that went directly through.

Mother and son were dragged off to the Neutor school, and the father was left where he had fallen while the SA laid waste to the residence.

> My father was fully conscious, [and he] watched how they threw the furniture out the window, how they took clubs and smashed everything. Then the two [SA men] who had remained upstairs, took him and chased him—barefoot and with a shot through the lung—through the streets of the town to the Neutor school. The neighbors saw it. He could not make it any more. "Do you want to run, you Jew!" With hooks to the chin, they beat him upright. He later said that he did not know how he got there. And there they immediately threw him to the ground; and he had lost so much blood! As he and other injured people then arrived at the Neutor school—it was 5 o'clock in the morning at the time and icy cold—he lay down on the ground and continued to cry: "I am dying, I am dying!" They had thrown him a sack; it was quickly soaked through with blood. Then my mother had tremendous courage. She said to the SA man: "may I get a blanket for my husband? You can accompany me, I will not run away." Then he pulled his dagger and said: "your husband shall perish in the same way that Herr vom Rath perished." That was the answer, and father was left lying [on the ground].[68]

Around three hundred Emden Jews were interned in the schoolyard. They were beaten, tortured, and humiliated by the SA. They were forced to engage in mock mounted combat and cockfights, crawl on all fours, and bark like dogs. In the morning the women, children, and elderly were released. The police finally brought Walter Philipson's father to the hospital for treatment. In the early morning of 11 November, the remaining men were led through the streets to the train station. Walter Philipson remembers:

> Many workers were underway on bicycles. Many got off their bicycles. At that time I still had good nerves and watched the expressions on the faces, because I always thought: what are the Emdeners saying about this? I saw how they stood there, very stiff—that I noticed.... In Oldenburg we had to go through the town to the police jail and we waited there until more transports came from the surrounding area. The town was a cordon of school children and other people; they spat upon us and threw stones at us.[69]

The men were taken to KZ Sachsenhausen, where Salomon Löwenstein and Hermann Sax died because of the terrible prison conditions. Daniel Beer, who like Louis Philipson had been shot during the night of the pogrom, died at the end of November as a result of the wound. Walter Philipson's mother no longer had the confidence to live in her own home, for even after 10 November thieves and looters repeatedly came at night and stole, among other things, a coin and stamp collection. After his release in the spring of 1939, Walter Philipson immediately emigrated to Palestine. His parents remained in Emden and were deported in the final transport in 1941 to Litzmann/Lodz, where the trail vanishes.[70]

Norden

In the neighboring town of Norden, after setting the synagogue ablaze in the early morning hours of 10 November, the SA gathered the Norden Jews, including women and the elderly, some dressed only in pajamas or bathrobes, and drove them to the slaughterhouse.[71] There they were tortured by the SA men, who had them do calisthenics and climb over barriers in the stalls, and threw them into the filthy straw and beat them with electrically charged poles that were used to herd livestock. The Jewish people were individually interrogated as to where they had hidden money, jewelry, and other valuables. And while the one group of SA men continued to torture, another group went to the residences, stealing money and other goods, destroying the furniture, and demolishing the interiors. The money was paid into a special account; the amount therein was later reported as RM 21,364.52. In total, cash and valuables amounting to RM 150,000 were "confiscated," according to estimates in the final report of the Wilhelmshaven Gestapo, which was investigating because of theft. It had been discovered that "a larger portion of the valuables and cash taken from the Jews was not delivered to the offices of the party and its organization."[72]

Frau Samson, one of the Jewish victims, called the police as early as the morning of 10 November and led a criminal investigator through the devastated house. The entire contents of a study had been stolen, and the last horse, together with a wagon and fifteen to twenty nosebags, were taken from the stable. Ultimately the criminal investigators found the contents of the study, horse, wagon, and nosebags in the possession of the SS Sturmbann leader. The SS got revenge a few days later by once again forcing their way into the Samson family home, destroying what was still intact and so badly abusing Frau Samson that she collapsed with a stroke. After the women and elderly were released from the slaughterhouse on the morning of 10 November, the remaining seventeen men were turned over to the police. First they were forced to work on cleaning up the ruins of the synagogue, and the next day, together with Jewish men from Marienhafen and Dornum, they were brought to Oldenburg, after which they were taken to the Sachsenhausen concentration camp.[73]

Treuchtlingen

The pogrom in Treuchtlingen in Middle Franconia, a town of around 4,200 people in the 1930s including more than 100 Jewish citizens, began in the early morning hours of 10 November 1938.[74] Around midnight, the Weißenburg SA Standartenführer Georg Sauber was ordered by telephone to come to Nuremberg to receive the assignment to destroy the synagogues and apprehend the male Jews. After that he drove personally to Treuchtlingen to pass along appropriate instructions to the local SA Standartenführer Peter Engelhardt. The Treuchtlingen SA people were awakened and gathered between three and four at the Feuerwehrplatz, not far from the synagogue. While the men were still being divided into squads and receiving the order from Engelhardt to drive the Treuchtlingen Jews from their homes and destroy the interiors, other SA men were already setting fire to the synagogue. A witness remembered how the men stood at the house of the cantor Moses Kurzweil, which was structurally connected to the synagogue, and shouted: "Jew, open up, get out, we are setting fire to your house, or we will burn you up!" And then they kicked in the door and forced their way into the synagogue, which was soon emitting flames. Arriving at the scene, the fire department protected only the surrounding "Aryan" houses, allowing the Treuchtlingen synagogue to burn to its foundations.

Awakened by the noise and the fire alarm, an increasing number of Treuchtlingen citizens met in front of the burning synagogue and went with the SA squads to the Jewish residences. The SA men made up the core of the squads of thugs, but the other men, women, and youth from Treuchtlingen also participated in the destruction, urging the thugs on to greater actions, verbally abusing Jewish neighbors, and looting the stores. Those Treuchtlingen residents who did not become perpetrators turned away and closed their windows. Only very few are known to have tried to help.

Moritz Mayer, who was a grocer in Treuchtlingen at the time, reported in his memoirs, which he recorded immediately upon his emigration to Palestine in 1939:

> On 10 November between 4–5 o'clock I heard footsteps in the garden. When I looked out the window, 8–10 men (SA) were standing there, heavily armed with axes, hatchets, daggers and revolvers. By the time I awoke my wife and my eleven-year-old son, a man was already in the bedroom, ordered us to go to the basement and immediately began to smash everything into pieces: wash basin, mirrors, windows, furniture, doors, etc. After we (including my sister-in-law and daughter) had been in the basement a short while, I was called upstairs. When my daughter wanted to accompany

me, she was pushed back. I was yelled at: "You rascal, you must know that you have been made fair game for us ever since tonight at midnight, give us your documents." Before I could unlock the desk, I received such a blow to my face that my glasses fell off and broke, my right eye strongly swelled up, and my pupil was injured. The doctor later explained that the blow could have blinded me. Then I was dumped in a corner and furniture was randomly thrown at me. The fact that I only received three flesh wounds and did not receive a serious injury can only be described as extraordinary luck. Meanwhile the entire house was demolished in the manner mentioned above. In the kitchen, all of the dishes were smashed; in the basement, a full can of conserves was thrown at my wife's head; the women themselves had to smash wine bottles and canning jars. After the SA came the plebs and then the school youth; each party continued to destroy and to steal.[75]

The crowd proceeded against the other Treuchtlingen Jews in a similar fashion. According to the findings of the Nuremberg district court, in the Gutmann family home an SA man threatened the son with a pickaxe. The other men demolished the interiors of the ground floor rooms, knocked over shelves, and smashed the dishes. The non-Jewish wife and sons appealed to the women A. and H. (who were later charged), also pointing out that they were Christians. The women just laughed maliciously.

Albert Neuburger's hardware store, not far from the burning synagogue, was stormed by the crowd and plundered. According to a witness who later testified in court, everything was destroyed and the display windows were totally emptied. Inside everything was completely strewn about and, together with other Treuchtlingen residents, the witness was climbing around on the merchandise. Bottles of wine were taken out of Neuburger's basement in laundry baskets, and people had thrown all kinds of things down from the stairs of the Weinmann house, especially clothes, hats, and boxes. According to the evidentiary findings of the later proceedings, even HJ boys had trampled on the pieces of furniture and battered an overturned linen cupboard.

People stole material, suits, and the like from the shelves of Bacharach's textile store. A sum of RM 3,000 was stolen from the Jewish Hänlein family. A crowd of Treuchtlingen residents gathered in front of the house of the Jewish eye-doctor, Dr. Meyerson, and urged on the SA thugs inside. A woman supposedly called out: "That is far too little. Bring them out, the Jew-sows!" The Meyerson residence was demolished as well. Accused of having established a secret connection with a radio broadcaster in Strasbourg, the doctor was taken to the town hall and abused. A few days later he took his own life, and his wife died soon thereafter in 1939.

Albert Mayer was wounded with a dagger in the basement of his house. SA men shoved a bottle with a broken neck into the mouth of his under-age daughter, demanding that she drink. An older man was so badly beaten that he and his wife reported to the gendarmerie station in Treuchtlingen on the morning of 11 November and requested to be taken into protective custody because they were afraid of further mistreatment.[76]

Many Treuchtlingen Jews, especially women and children, fled hastily to the train station to escape the inferno—some barely dressed, taking with them only what they could carry. Along the way they were chased and beaten. Moritz Mayer and his wife were allowed to pack some linens and clothing "and had [to go] between a cordon formed by the mob and amidst its malicious laughter to the train station. Other members of the community were already there, after others had already left with an earlier train."[77] The train station supervisor was one of the few upstanding people in Treuchtlingen. During this night he apparently stopped every train that was passing through so that the people could flee from Treuchtlingen.[78]

On the morning of 10 November, the crowd was still not satisfied and tried to prevent the husband of the housekeeper G., who worked for the Meyersons, from driving to work, shouting: "pull him off the motorcycle, the *Judenknecht*." The pogrom finally subsided at around ten o'clock. The Treuchtlingen Bürgermeister reported on 15 November to the fire insurance office in Eichstätt that the synagogue and the residence of the cantor Moses Kurzweil had burned down completely, and that all of the Jewish properties—a total of twenty-one houses or apartments—were destroyed.[79] According to a report dated 11 November from the regional office in Weißenburg to the Gestapo in Nuremberg, of the ninety-three Treuchtlingen Jews, only two men and a woman over sixty years of age remained in the town. Four Jews had been taken into custody, and the rest had left the town.[80] In the middle of 1939, Bürgermeister Günter reported proudly to the district administrator in Weißenburg "that since 10 November 1938, Treuchtlingen is free of Jews."[81]

Pogroms in Europe

Significantly, pogrom is a Russian word that refers to collective violence against civilians and is associated with theft, rape, and murder. After the extensive anti-Semitic excesses against Jews following the assassination of Alexander II in 1881, the word became common and was taken over by other languages, for violent anti-Semitic excesses were by no means limited to Russia. Nor were pogroms during the first half of the twentieth century a German peculiarity, for they also took place in other European countries.[82]

In French-occupied Algeria, members of the large Jewish community could look upon a history reaching back into antiquity. After they received state citizenship in 1870, there were a number of anti-Semitic pogroms. Similarly after the First World War there repeatedly were pogroms in the North African colonies against the native Jews.[83] The so-called Dreyfus Affair was set in motion by the wrongful accusation and conviction in 1894 of Alfred Dreyfus, a Jewish officer in the general staff, for alleged treason. This exposed the virulent anti-Semitism in France. After the public victory of the Dreyfusards, the anti-Semitic movement lost momentum for a number of decades, but it revived in 1936 with the election victory of the Popular Front under the socialist Léon Blum, who stemmed from a Jewish family, even though there were also always voices among French fascists who distanced themselves from anti-Semitism.[84]

The Jeunesses Patriotes in particular became prominent as activists, demanding among other things a complete boycott of Jewish businesses in France during the mid 1930s.[85] Louis-Ferdinand Céline's notorious pamphlet, *Bagatelles pour un massacre*, called openly for anti-Semitic violence, and a new generation of young militant anti-Semites took over from the "old right" of the Action Française and its figurehead Charles Maurras.[86] In Belgium, too, racist anti-Semitic groups formed repeatedly within the political right, like the Volksverwering (Defense of the People), from which the German occupation would later recruit collaborators for the persecution and extermination of the Belgian Jews.[87]

In the Netherlands, the Nationaal-Socialistische Beweging (NSB) under Anton Adriaan Mussert won the approval of around 300,000 voters in the parliamentary elections, which corresponded to 8 percent and surprisingly made the NSB the fifth-strongest party.[88] Even though Mussert did not adopt the anti-Semitism of the German National Socialists and actually tolerated Jewish members, more radical anti-Semites nonetheless pushed for a clear racist position in the "Jewish question." The 1937 party program of the NSB contained clear anti-Semitic statements and thenceforth Jews were prohibited from membership in the organization.[89]

Even though Italian fascism initially lacked strict biological statements and at the beginning Mussolini's party even had around 590 Jewish members (about 0.2 percent), its conception of a homogenous and pure Italian people was completely based on race.[90] The emphasis on "natural differences" led also in Italy to fascistic violent actions against national minorities and Jews. A propaganda campaign against the Jews was established after the fascists seized power in October 1922. Similar to developments within the French sphere of influence, anti-Jewish pogroms occurred especially in the North African colonies, which contained Jewish communities that were hundreds of years old. In August 1923 the Italian fascists led a "punitive expedition" in the Jewish quarter of Tripoli, after conflicts had previously broken out during which an Italian soldier was killed.[91] After an assassination attempt on Mussolini in October 1926, anti-Semitic hatred was unleashed in violent excesses, during which fascist troops devastated the main synagogue in Padua. Two years later an anti-Semitic article in the party newspaper *Il Populo di Romo*, supposedly written by Mussolini himself, set off a new anti-Jewish wave.[92]

The Abyssinian War in 1935/36 especially accelerated Italian racism—not merely in the party program, where the inhabitants of the African colonies were defined as "inferior people," but also in practice. The Italians ruthlessly waged war against the black civilian population. The Italian air force destroyed villages, fields, and herds of livestock, and in many cases even deployed poison gas. Soldiers looted, raped, and murdered to such an extent that even Badoglio, the supreme commander, was prompted to take steps against the unrestrained violence in order to save the "honor and prestige of Italy." "Punitive expeditions," gruesome executions, and murderous arson were among the practices of the occupying regime.[93] Before National Socialist Germany increased pressure on allied Italy to enact anti-Semitic laws in 1938, racist politics had already taken shape in Italy. These politics were not evoked from the outside but rather developed within the fascist regime itself, particularly through the violent practices in Africa.

In Poland, anti-Semitism had raged for a long time, well nourished by the Catholic Church. By virtue of the Polish-Soviet War of 1920–1921, it obtained an additional political and anti-Bolshevist charge.[94] After Polish troops were able to push back the Red Army, which had almost reached Warsaw, the Jewish minority in the reconquered villages and towns was accused of collaboration and spying for the Soviets. The Polish *soldateska* shot to death innocent Jewish people and destroyed and plundered houses, businesses, and apartments. When the American negotiating delegation under President Wilson, which had traveled to the Paris peace conference, learned of the atrocities, it successfully requested that a group of American observers led by Henry Morgenthau be sent to Poland to investigate the incidents. While visiting the town of Pinsk at the beginning of June 1919, two of the delegates even became eyewitnesses to such a pogrom, where thirty-one Jews were murdered and hundreds of Jewish-owned businesses were plundered and devastated.[95]

The National Democratic movement, also called Endek and led by Roman Dmowski, was one of the most important political forces in Poland. It was also a "standard-bearer of anti-Semitism" (Dietrich Beyrau) and demanded the expulsion of the Jewish minority. With an aggressive and violent boycott campaign, Endek members—young people in particular—terrorized Jewish merchants in order to make their lives unbearable and compel them to give up their businesses and emigrate. *"Nie kupujcie u Z·ydów"* (Do not buy from Jews) was the chief slogan of Endek, presented as a demand put to the Polish nation.[96]

After the death of Pilsudski in 1935, who had ended the brief democratic phase in Poland after 1918 with a military coup in 1926 and established an authoritarian military regime, the anti-Semitic excesses reached their zenith—with growing support by the population for an ethnic nationalization of Polish society. At the universities, Jewish students were persecuted and beaten, and a few were even murdered. In 150 towns and villages, Endek supporters organized violent anti-Jewish actions. In Przytyk, for example, a brawl between Jewish and Polish youth was enough to escalate the violence into bloody excesses during which a Polish farmer died. The man's funeral, in turn, sparked a pogrom against the Jewish population in Przytyk: "Kill them! Do not forget what they have done to our brother! Kill them!" screamed the crowd. Groups of twenty to thirty men stormed houses with Jewish inhabitants, beat the people, devastated the residences, and threw the furniture from the windows. A Jewish married couple was murdered and their children severely injured, though they were saved by a Polish neighbor. Only after police arrived from Radom did the pogrom subside.[97] Between 1935 and 1937 an estimated 2,000 Jewish people were injured and twenty to thirty were killed, while thousands fled from the violence within their communities—not to mention the property damage that was caused. The number of dead was not concentrated in a few large towns but rather spread across many communities in the Polish provinces, which reported one or two murdered Jews in each case.[98] The anti-Semitic activists were by no means alone. The actions were accompanied, supported, and encouraged by large crowds.[99]

The primate of the Catholic Church, Cardinal August Hlond, admittedly condemned the violence in a pastoral letter. But the relevant sentences were short and vague, while the letter itself contained clear anti-Semitic allegations, namely that the Jews were the leading edge of godlessness, bolshevism, and infiltration, and that there would be a Jewish problem as long as there were Jews in the country.[100] Even the ruling military regime bet heavily on anti-Semitism in order to retain the support of the population, making a serious effort in 1937 to negotiate with the French regime to realize an old anti-Semitic project, namely the resettlement of the Jews in Madagascar.[101] In March 1938 the Polish regime issued a denaturalization decree according to which all Polish state citizens who resided abroad for more than five years would lose their state citizenship.

The decree was directed in the first instance against Polish Jews. There were 56,000 Polish Jews living in Germany alone. In turn, this decree prompted the National Socialist regime, which by no means wanted to tolerate thousands of stateless Jews in Germany, to deport around 17,000 people over the Polish border into no man's land—including the parents of Herschel Grynszpan.

These few examples show that pogrom-prone anti-Semitism was hardly specific to Germany but rather a European phenomenon. Even in Great Britain during the 1930s, there were numerous violent anti-Jewish attacks on houses and businesses, and even directly against people.[102] Yet although these forms of violence were surprisingly similar—consider, for example, the aggressive boycott actions in Germany and in Poland—there were also apparent differences that distinguished the November pogrom from the excesses in other European countries. As opposed to the rest of Europe, in Germany a movement that was not merely fascist but also radically anti-Semitic had first seized power and then permanently changed the state. As authoritarian and undemocratic as the Pilsudski regime was in Poland, as much as it discriminated against the Jews, that regime can still not be characterized as fascistic or radically anti-Semitic. Even in Italian fascism, which unquestionably became more radically racist as a result of violent practices in the North African colonies in the 1930s, anti-Jewish excesses remained locally contained.

In Germany, however, violence against the Jews was part of the political praxis of the National Socialist movement from its very beginning. And because after 1933 the regime leadership was anxious to maintain control over the violent actions by the party organization, it repeatedly engaged in violence or allowed violence to run its course in order to radicalize anti-Semitic politics. In November 1938 the time had apparently come when Hitler, pressured by Goebbels, no longer shied away from setting in motion a nationwide and centrally commanded violent action. Whereas in April 1938 the regime leadership had still placed great value upon making sure that the centrally ordained and locally implemented boycott action was disciplined and took place without excessive violence, this time the central command issued to the party organization directly sought the unmediated implementation of destruction and arson.

To be sure, after the extent of the devastation became apparent, the NS leadership immediately wanted to give the pogrom the appearance of a disciplined action. As early as the morning of 10 November, the propaganda ministry issued instructions to the press that reports on the pogrom were not to be presented as big stories and that no photographs were to be published.[103] But this did not make the local events witnessed by most Germans disappear. There was no sign of discipline at the local level.

Instead, the destructive rage and vandalism had literally been laid bare for all to see.[104]

Without doubt, most of the German population did not approve of the pogrom—every historical investigation agrees upon this point.[105] Yet it was not so much sympathy for the Jewish victims as the destruction of property that was the focal point of criticism. If one considers the background and situation reports, there was definitely support for "retribution" for the assassination of Rath, although the form of this retributive action met in part with severe disapproval. In contrast, the "atonement fee" of RM 1 billion that Göring imposed upon the German Jews by decree two days after the pogrom, which also compelled them to pay for the damages they suffered, was seen as "just punishment."[106] David Bankier has referred to this attitude toward the fate of the Jews as "moral insensibility."[107] Significantly, this charge of indifference also applies to the Christian churches, which watched the widespread destruction of the places of worship and sanctuaries of the god they shared and did nothing.

Peter Longerich has warned against too quickly adopting the assessments in the background and situation reports and presented a series of evidence indicating that the disapproval of the pogrom went deeper than is apparent in the official reports.[108] On 10 November, the Berlin journalist and Nazi opponent Ruth Andreas-Friedrich noted in her diary:

> At 9:30 I drive to the editorial office. The Kurfürstendamm is a single sea of shards. At the corner of Fasanenstraße the people are immobilized. A silent mass that stares sheepishly in the direction of the synagogue, the dome of which is veiled in smoke.... If one could only find out who is for it and who is against it! I start to investigate the mood of the Volk. Everywhere I go, in the best case I find a Volk's malaise, and in the worst an abysmal despair. "One does not even dare to look a person in the eye," explains even our boss at work, who is rumored to be infected with Nazism. "Anti-Semitism—fine! But not like this." Only tall Meyer, our "political fellow," rubs his hands in satisfaction. "Finally we have shown them, the cursed pack," he says triumphantly.[109]

Despite the apparent distance within the population to the acts of the pogrom, it cannot be overlooked, firstly, that within a few hours during the night, the party leadership had successfully managed to mobilize thousands of members for an unprecedented destructive action. According to the evaluation of fifty-one postwar legal proceedings by Dieter Obst, the people involved were not social outsiders or predominantly adolescents but rather were mostly representative of the majority—men between the ages of thirty and fifty from all levels of society.[110] Even if one wants to suggest that the pogrom perpetrators were limited to these activists alone, the kinds of acts that these "completely normal men" were prepared to do and capable of doing are still significant.

Secondly, empirical descriptions reveal that, apart from the SA and SS troops, many people participated in the pogrom in a variety of ways.[111] Many residents, especially in smaller communities, were awakened by fire department sirens and ran to the burning synagogues and other locations to find out what was going on. Many of these witnesses did not immediately turn their backs on the events or attempt to help their beleaguered Jewish neighbors. Instead, they remained and thus became accomplices in the pogrom.[112] Others spurred the thugs on and helped to further excite the violent mood and increase the mortal terror of the Jewish victims. Many people took part in the destruction and vandalism, and many participated in the looting. This often occurred after the squads of thugs had left a home and the Jewish residents had been dragged off, driven away, or left behind in utter fear.[113]

Thirdly, the arrests of the Jewish men upon the instructions of Heydrich and the Gestapo Chief Müller[114] took place the next day in complete public view and involved brutal mistreatment. Thus in Saarbrücken, the 130 arrested Jewish men had to form a procession. One man had a drum hung around his neck, a second was given a gong, and, singing and beating, they had to move through the streets. Upon arrival at the synagogue, the men were forced to kneel and sing religious songs and dance. On the way back to the train station, clad in pajamas, nightshirts, or trousers, they were doused on this November morning with a stream of water from the town's sprinkler truck until they were completely soaked. In Meppen the Jewish men were driven through the town and forced to lie down in front of the SA Standartenhaus and kiss the ground while the SA men kicked and walked all over them. The victims had to carry signs and banners with statements like "We are the murderers of Rath," "We are wretched Jews and have betrayed the Fatherland," or "Exodus of the Jews." And they had to sing folk songs like "Muß I denn zum Städele hinaus," "Nun ade mein lieb Heimatland," and "Das Wandern ist des Müllers Lust." They were often accompanied by a horde of people, including children and youth, who jeered, beat, and kicked the procession—for the victims, the march to the train station was like running a gauntlet. In some places, entire school classes were summoned to witness the spectacle and spit upon or beat the victims.[115]

Fourthly, the rulers had evidently issued orders to spare human lives and refrain from causing bodily harm, but anyone who issues such orders of destruction knows or at least consciously accepts that the dynamics of such destructive violence will not desist from abuse and murder. Even now, no precise figures are available to quantify the entire extent of the pillaging, rapes, physical injuries, and murders that occurred during these days. In a letter to Göring two days after the pogrom, Heydrich himself placed the number of dead at thirty-six; the highest party court of the NSDAP later mentioned ninety-one deaths in an internal report but emphasized that the police investigations were still not complete.[116] The actual number of those murdered must in fact have amounted to hundreds. The NS leadership had issued a de facto authorization to kill. Jews could be robbed, abused, beaten, and killed in full public view; meanwhile the state's security forces would not intervene and the perpetrators did not have to fear subsequent punishment. In so doing, a threshold was crossed. Notwithstanding all of the regime's efforts to never repeat such a pogrom, there was no going back. With the November pogrom, the authorization for violence on the one hand and the Jewish victims' experience of absolute helplessness on the other hand had become unavoidable.

To the victims, the collapse of any form of law during this night and the rule of absolute violence must have appeared as a descent into barbarism. One can therefore understand that the decisive experience people remembered was not the deportations toward death in the late fall of 1941 but the unleashed violence of the mob in November 1938. Even after the war, the experience of a renewed eruption of street violence, whether by Ernst Fraenkel during the student unrests in Berlin in the 1960s or by the board member of the Jewish community in Leipzig, Getzel Taube, during the June 1953 uprising in the GDR, would reawaken the memory of absolute lawlessness and unlimited arbitrary violence that could only be crushed by state power.[117]

Effects

The NS leadership's displeasure about the destruction found expression immediately after the pogrom. The central conference in the Reich Ministry of Aviation on 12 November was supposed "to summarize the Jewish question," as Göring put it at the outset. The formulation of his criticism was both brutal and unmistakable: "I would have liked it better if you had beaten two-hundred Jews to death and had not destroyed such assets."[118]

Significantly, questions about insurance played a big role at the conference, for the devastating and plundering mob paid no heed to the fact that merchants were usually insured against glass damage, theft, and fire. A "very large catastrophe" had been created for the insurance industry, complained its representative Hilgard, who had been especially invited to the conference in the Reich Aviation Ministry. A single business, the Margraf jewelry store on Unter-den-Linden in Berlin, had reported damages of RM 1.7 million because the store had been completely plundered. Fire damages pertained primarily to the synagogues, and the parties insured were almost exclusively Jewish congregations. But with respect to glass damages, the injured parties were mainly non-Jewish building owners because the Jewish merchants were mostly only renters. The glass sheeting necessary for replacements could not be provided solely by German industry; rather, Belgian glass had to be imported at an estimated cost of RM 3 million, which in turn would reduce the German Reich's foreign exchange balance.[119]

For his part, Göring did not want the state to lose any revenue, nor did he want insured Jews to receive any money. He delegated the settlement of the damages mostly to the lucrative German insurance industry, confiscated the payments to German Jews, and imposed upon them the above mentioned contribution of RM 1 billion as an "atonement fee." Consequently, the regime enacted the coercive "Aryanization" of any remaining Jewish companies through official trustees. The Reich Education Ministry ordered the dismissal of all remaining Jewish students. Himmler revoked the driving licenses of Jews and a police regulation enabled district presidents to limit the spatial and temporal freedom of movement of Jews—a first measure toward ghettoization.[120] Concrete planning for the implementation of forced labor had already begun in the summer of 1938. Now the corresponding ordinances were being issued to enlist "all unemployed and capable Jews" (as stipulated in the foundational decree by the Reich Institute for Labor on 20 December) in work brigades for forced labor.[121]

After the pogrom, the organization and conceptual leadership of the persecution of the Jews was taken over by the SS and the police. At the conference on 12 November, Heydrich had proudly reported that the newly founded Central Office for Jewish Emigration in Vienna had successfully managed to "remove" 50,000 Jews, whereupon he received approval from Göring to create a similar office for the German Reich.[122] Heydrich recommended an "emigration action" that would have to stretch out over "at least eight to ten years" because no more than 8,000 to 10,000 people could be "removed" a year. The Jews were to be isolated—though not in ghettos, because they could not be supervised by police—and were to wear a symbol. "As much as the Jews have been removed from economic life," noted Heydrich, "in the end the basic problem is always that the Jew must be removed from Germany."[123]

The policy of forced expulsion was expressly encouraged by Hitler. As Göring informed the Gauleiters, district presidents, and Reich governors in December 1938, the primary principle according to Hitler was as follows: "The point of all our considerations and measures is the intention of expelling the Jews abroad as quickly and effectively as possible, to use all emphasis to force emigration and thereby remove anything which hinders emigration."[124]

At the 12 November conference, Göring had already demonstrated the future trajectory of National Socialist politics:

> If the German Reich in any foreseeable time is involved in a foreign-political conflict, then it is self-evident that in Germany we will also in the first instance think about carrying out a large reckoning with the Jews. Beyond that, the Führer now finally wants to make a foreign-political proposal, initially to the powers that have raised the Jewish question, so as to actually resolve the Madagascar question. He discussed this with me on 9 November. There is no longer any other way. He also wants to say to the other states: "Why are you always talking about the Jews?—Take them!"[125]

On 30 January 1939 Hitler gave a speech to the Reichstag in which he invited European powers to come up with a "solution to the Jewish question" and concluded with the threat that if it came to war, the result would not be the "Bolshevization of Earth" but rather the "destruction of the Jewish race in Europe."[126] In March 1939 Germany occupied the rest of the Czech Republic, in violation of the Munich Agreement, and half a year later it attacked Poland. In the shadow of the war, the "solution of the Jewish question" henceforth took the form of systematic mass murder.

Notes

1. Harald Schmid, *Erinnern an den "Tag der Schuld": Das Novemberpogrom von 1938 in der deutschen Geschichtspolitik* (Hamburg, 2001).
2. Wolfgang Benz, "Rückfall in die Barbarei: Bericht über den Pogrom," in *Von der "Reichskristallnacht" zum Völkermord*, ed. Walter H. Pehle (Frankfurt am Main, 1988), 13–51; see also Michael Wildt, "Sind die Nazis Barbaren? Betrachtungen zu einer geklärten Frage," *Mittelweg 36* 15, no. 2 (2006): 8–26.
3. Christhard Hoffmann, "Politische Kultur und Gewalt gegen Minderheiten: Die antisemitischen Ausschreitungen in Pommern und Westpreußen 1881," *Jahrbuch für Antisemitismusforschung* 3 (1994): 93–120; Smith, *The Butcher's Tale*.
4. Hans Safrian and Hans Witek, *Und keiner war dabei: Dokumente des alltäglichen Antisemitismus in Wien 1938* (Vienna, 1988), 71.
5. Carl Zuckmayer, *Als wär's ein Stück von mir* (Stuttgart, 1966), 71.
6. Reichmann, *Deutscher Bürger und verfolgter Jude*, 60.
7. Hans Safrian, *Die Eichmann-Männer* (Vienna, 1993); Gabriele Anderl, "Die 'Zentralstellen für jüdische Auswanderung' in Wien, Berlin und Prag – ein Vergleich," *Tel Aviver Jahrbuch für deutsche Geschichte* 23 (1994): 275–299; see David Cesarani, *Eichmann: His Life and Crimes* (London, 2004).

8. Jacob Toury, "Ein Auftakt zur 'Endlösung': Judenaustreibungen über nichtslawische Reichsgrenzen 1933–1939," in *Das Unrechtsregime: Internationale Forschung über den Nationalsozialismus*, ed. Ursula Büttner with collaboration by Werner Johe and Angelika Voß (Hamburg, 1986), vol. 2, 164–196.

9. Thus in Adelsberg, Burgsinn Gemünden, and Mittelsinn in the district of Gemünden, the windows of Jewish businesses, private homes, and synagogues were smashed; in Kleinlangheim near Nißingen, a Jew was allegedly injured by a thrown stone. District president of Lower Franconia and Aschaffenburg, report for March 1938, Kulka and Jäckel, *NS-Stimmungsberichte*, CD-ROM, doc. no. 2399.

10. District president Pfalz, report for April, Kulka and Jäckel, *NS-Stimmungsberichte*, CD-ROM, doc. no. 2415.

11. Gendarmerie Hösbach, report dated 19 April 1938, printed in Kulka and Jäckel, *NS-Stimmungsberichte*, 270–272.

12. Gendarmerie Alzenau, report for May 1938, Kulka and Jäckel, *NS-Stimmungsberichte*, CD-ROM, doc. no. 2447; see Herbert Schultheis, *Juden in Mainfranken 1933–1945 unter besonderer Berücksichtigung der Deportationen Würzburger Juden* (Bad Neustadt a. d. Saale, 1980), 109f., 149f.

13. SD-Außenstelle Hanau II 112, reported dated 15 May 1938, Kulka and Jäckel, *NS-Stimmungsberichte*, CD-ROM, doc. no. 2435. Weeks later, when a company could be found that would reopen the entrances, the town imposed a boycott on the company and canceled its other municipal contracts.

14. Frankfurt am Main. Gestapo report dated 18 June 1938, Kulka and Jäckel, *NS-Stimmungsberichte*, CD-ROM, doc. no. 2462; a facsimile of the document is pictured in Gelnhäuser Historischen Gesellschaft e.V., *Zur Geschichte der Juden in Gelnhausen*, 18.

15. Meyer, "Jüdisches Leben in Gelnhausen," 66.

16. Gelnhäuser Historischen Gesellschaft e.V., *Zur Geschichte der Juden in Gelnhausen*, 15f.

17. Facsimile of the article in ibid., 16. See also Scheuer, "Das Ende der israelitischen Kultusgemeinde."

18. SD-Hauptamt II 112, report dated 1 July 1938, BArch, R 58/996 (Kulka and Jäckel, *NS-Stimmungsberichte*, CD-ROM, doc. no. 2458); see also SD-OA Ost to SD-Hauptamt, 24 June 1938; Special Archive Moscow, 500-1-645; see in detail Longerich, *Politik der Vernichtung*, 172–185; also Gruner, "'Lesen brauchen sie nicht zu können.'"

19. Reichmann, *Deutscher Bürger und verfolgter Jude*, 73. In a 10 July speech to police officers in his capacity as the Berlin Gauleiter, Goebbels encouraged them to "engage in constant encroachments against the Jews." Stabskanzlei SD-Hauptamt an Abteilung II 112, 22 June 1938; Special Archive Moscow, 500-1-645. In his diary, he noted on 11 June: "Spoke in front of 300 police officers in Berlin about the Jewish question. I really heated things up. Against any sentimentality. The catchword is not law but chicanery. The Jews must get out of Berlin." Goebbels, *Tagebücher*, part I, vol. 5, 340. Jewish businesses and synagogues were also attacked and Jewish proprietors physically assaulted in Magdeburg and Frankfurt am Main. Teletype SD Leipzig to SD-Hauptamt, 22 June 1938; SD-OA Fulda-Werra to SD Hauptamt, 23 June 1938; Special Archive Moscow, 500-1-645, fol. 10f.

20. Stabskanzlei SD-Hauptamt to Abteilung II 112, 22 June 1938, Special Archive Moscow, 500-1-645; likewise the corresponding references in Goebbels's entries for 21 to 24 June 1938. Goebbels, *Tagebücher*, part I, vol. 5, 353–358.

21. Reichmann, *Deutscher Bürger und verfolgter Jude*, 81f.

22. File note Dr. Spengler, 1 June 1938; Special Archive Moscow, 500-1-645.
23. Decrees by the Reich Criminal Investigation Office, signed by Heydrich, to the criminal investigation agencies, 1 June 1938, printed in Wolfgang Ayaß, ed., *"Gemeinschaftsfremde": Quellen zur Verfolgung von "Asozialen" 1933–1945*, no. 5, *Materialien aus dem Bundesarchiv* (Coblenz, 1998), 134f.; Wolfgang Ayaß, *"Asoziale" im Nationalsozialismus* (Stuttgart, 1995), 147–165.
24. Harry Stein, *Juden in Buchenwald 1937–1942*, ed. the Gedenkstätte Buchenwald (Weimar, 1992), 24.
25. See Barkai, *Vom Boykott zur "Entjudung,"* 128–137.
26. Reichmann, *Deutscher Bürger und verfolgter Jude*, 68.
27. SD Hauptamt II 112, quarterly report January to March 1938, printed in Wildt, *Die Judenpolitik des SD 1935–1938*, 180–195.
28. See Susanne Heim, "'Deutschland muß ihnen ein Land ohne Zukunft sein': Die Zwangsemigration der Juden 1933–1938," in *Arbeitsmigration und Flucht*, vol. 11, *Beiträge zur nationalsozialistischen Gesundheits- und Sozialpolitik* (Berlin, 1993): 59–65.
29. In 1933 over 35 percent of the Jewish population was under thirty and 10 percent was over sixty-five years old; in 1939, these percentages had changed to almost 19 and over 21 percent. In 1938 around 48 percent of all Jews were employed; in 1939 it was just over 15 percent. Almost three-quarters of all Jews over fourteen were listed as "unemployed independents" in the census lists—that is, they lived from their savings and had to make do the best they could. Barkai, *Vom Boykott zur "Entjudung,"* 168f.
30. SD-Hauptamt II 112, situation report for August 1936, Special Archive Moscow, 500-3-316, partially printed in Kulka and Jäckel, *NS-Stimmungsberichte*, 292f.
31. Kershaw, *Der Hitler-Mythos*, 165; Hellmuth Auerbach, "Volksstimmung und veröffentlichte Meinung in Deutschland zwischen März und November 1938," in *Machtbewußtsein in Deutschland am Vorabend des Zweiten Weltkrieges*, ed. Franz Knipping and Klaus-Jürgen Müller (Paderborn, 1984), 274–293; Engelbert Schwarzenbeck, *Nationalsozialistische Pressepolitik und die Sudetenkrise 1938* (Munich, 1979).
32. Dieter Obst, *"Reichskristallnacht": Ursachen und Verlauf des antisemitischen Pogroms von November 1938* (Frankfurt am Main, 1991), 57.
33. Kershaw, *Der Hitler-Mythos*, 167f. The regime's attempt to heighten the willingness to go to war with a parade of troops in Berlin on 27 September failed. Only a few hundred Berlin residents watched in silence as the division marched past. Kershaw, *Hitler*, vol. 2, 174f.; a vivid eyewitness account is provided by Ruth Andreas-Friedrich, *Der Schattenmann: Tagebuchaufzeichnungen 1938–1945* (Frankfurt am Main, 1983), 9–12.
34. Reichmann, *Deutscher Bürger und verfolgter Jude*, 97, 100–102.
35. SD-Unterabschnitt Wiesbaden, report for 27 September 1938, Kulka and Jäckel, *NS-Stimmungsberichte*, 295.
36. Ibid.
37. District office Bad Neustadt/Saale, report for September 1938, Kulka and Jäckel, *NS-Stimmungsberichte*, CD-ROM, doc. no. 2518. The case is also briefly mentioned in Obst, *"Reichskristallnacht,"* 59.
38. Telegram of the SA-OA Süd to the SD-Hauptamt Berlin, 4 October 1938, Special Archive Moscow, 500-1-630, fol. 7; Main-Franconia district president, report for September 1938, Kulka and Jäckel, *NS-Stimmungsberichte*, 296; see Herbert Schultheis, *Juden in Mainfranken 1933–1945*.
39. SD-Hauptamt II 112, report for September 1938, Special Archive Moscow, 500-3-316, printed in Kulka and Jäckel, *NS-Stimmungsberichte*, 294f. Otto Dov Kulka, who

was one of the first historians to scientifically evaluate the background and situation reports, indicated in 1982 that these excesses had not yet been mentioned in the historiography even though they clearly anticipated the November pogroms. Otto Dov Kulka, "'Public Opinion' in Nazi Germany and the 'Jewish Question,'" *The Jerusalem Quarterly* 25 (1982): 121–144, here 138.

40. SD-Hauptamt II 112 to II 1, 31 October 1938, Special Archive Moscow, 500-1-187, quoted in Longerich, *Politik der Vernichtung*, 193f.

41. Obst, *"Reichskristallnacht,"* 27–29.

42. Report from the SD-Oberabschnitts West, 24 September 1938; Special Archive Moscow, 500-1-630, fol. 3.

43. Report of the SD-OA Süd, 11 October 1938, Special Archive Moscow, 500-1-630, fol. 6. In any event, the "nature and execution of this measure" evoked "tremendous outrage" from a large part of the Catholic population. For their own protection, the three men were taken into custody and released three days later after they had promised to leave Bechhofen.

44. District president of Upper and Middle Franconia, report for September 1938, Kulka and Jäckel, *NS-Stimmungsberichte*, 296f.

45. SD-Hauptamt II 112, report for October 1938, Special Archive Moscow, 500-3-316, printed in Kulka and Jäckel, *NS-Stimmungsberichte*, 297–299.

46. C.V. regional association Rhineland-Left Bank to Berlin headquarters, 3 October 1938, Special Archive Moscow, 721-1-2914, fol. 2.

47. Palatinate district president, report for October 1938, Kulka and Jäckel, *NS-Stimmungsberichte*, 301–303; similar violent actions against synagogues and private homes were reported in Lower Bavaria, Swabia, Baden-Württemberg, Rhineland, and Westphalia.

48. SD-OA Süd to SD-Hauptamt Berlin, 20 October 1938, Special Archive Moscow, 500-1-630, fols. 15–17; see Baruch Z. Ophir and Falk Wiesemann, eds., *Die jüdischen Gemeinden in Bayern 1918–1945: Geschichte und Zerstörung* (Munich 1979), 195.

49. Quoted in the report by the SD-OA Süd about "Ausschreitungen gegen Juden im Oberabschnittbereich," 25 October 1938; Special Archive Moscow, 500-1-630, fol. 31.

50. See Trude Maurer, "Abschiebung und Attentat: Die Ausweisung der polnischen Juden und der Vorwand für die 'Kristallnacht,'" in *Der Judenpogrom 1938: Von der "Reichskristallnacht" zum Völkermord*, ed. Walter H. Pehle (Frankfurt am Main, 1988), 52–73; Sybil Milton, "Menschen zwischen Grenzen: Die Polenausweisung 1938," *Menora: Jahrbuch für deutsch-jüdische Geschichte* 1 (1990): 184–206; also the memoirs of Marcel Reich-Ranicki, who as a young man was among those deported, Marcel Reich-Ranicki, *Mein Leben* (Stuttgart, 1999), 157–160.

51. On the November pogrom see especially the comprehensive account by Obst, *"Reichskristallnacht"*; Wolfgang Benz, "Der Novemberpogrom 1938," in *Die Juden in Deutschland 1933–1945: Leben unter nationalsozialistischer Herrschaft*, ed. Wolfgang Benz (Munich, 1988), 499–544; Longerich, *Politik der Vernichtung*, 190–207.

52. DNB-Rundruf (20:37 o'clock), 7 November 1938, in Hans Bohrmann and Gabriele Toepser-Zeigert, eds., *NS-Presseanweisungen der Vorkriegszeit: Edition und Dokumentation* (Munich, 1999), vol. 6/III, 1050, no. 3176.

53. Reichmann, *Deutscher Bürger und verfolgter Jude*, 111.

54. Report by the Kassel Gestapo about the excesses on 7–8 November 1938, printed in Wolf-Arno Kropat, *Kristallnacht in Hessen: Der Judenpogrom vom November 1938*

(Wiesbaden, 1988), 31f.; Jörg Kammler et. al., *Volksgemeinschaft und Volksfeinde: Kassel 1935–1945: Eine Dokumentation* (Fuldabrück, 1984), 248.

55. Thus Dieter Obst probably assumes correctly that this was the result of an independently initiated action by the regional Gauleitung. Obst, *"Reichskristallnacht,"* 67f. In the revised and expanded edition of his documentation, Wolf-Arno Kropat even assumes that the Gestapo in Kassel itself helped organize the excesses. Wolf-Arno Kropat, *"Reichskristallnacht": Der Judenpogrom vom 7. bis 10. November 1938 – Urheber, Täter, Hintergründe* (Wiesbaden, 1997).

56. Report by the Bürgermeister of the town of Bebra to the district administrator of the district of Rotenburg an der Fulda, 23 November 1938, printed in Kropat, *Kristallnacht in Hessen*, 32f.

57. Order from the Kassel district president to all police agencies, 8 November 1938, printed in Kropat, *"Reichkristallnacht,"* 207.

58. Report from Gendarmerie Chief Mai to the commander of the gendarmerie in Kassel, 9 November 1938, printed in Kropat, *Kristallnacht in Hessen*, 38f. The report continues: "All of the benches standing in the gallery were thrown down into the center of the synagogue. All of the lighting sources as well as a large candelabra were demolished. Of the other Jewish buildings, violent acts were perpetrated at two of them, the interiors were completely demolished. Closets were rummaged through and everything that was made of glass was smashed. In one place there was looting. Thus a type-writer was broken out of its case. Pieces of clothing were carried off in packages and hidden. Subsequent searches in the adjacent gardens recovered many of the stolen objects.… With the still on-going investigation, new thefts are repeatedly coming to light. From one Jewish house, items of high value were stolen."

59. Judgment by the Kurhessian Gau court of the Kassel NSDAP, dated 17 March 1939, printed in Moritz and Noam, *NS-Verbrechen vor Gericht*, 199–201.

60. Kropat, *"Reichskristallnacht,"* 64.

61. The district leader in Witzenhausen reported to the Kassel Gau propaganda office that during the night from 8 to 9 November "thousands of *Volksgenossen*" had gathered to demonstrate against the assassination. In the process, the synagogue, Jewish residences, and in particular "the private home of a familiar impudent Jew from Witzenhausen named Hecht" were attacked and "seriously damaged." Kropat, *Kristallnacht in Hessen*, 37. In an express letter dated 9 November 1938 to the chief of the regular police (Ordnungspolizei), the chief of the security police reported on the excesses in various Hessian locations—according to Kropat, by 9 November the pogroms had spread to eleven of the fifteen regional districts in Hesse. BArch, R 58/979, printed in Kropat, *"Reichskristallnacht,"* 207f.

62. BArch, R 58/979, printed in Kropat, *"Reichskristallnacht,"* 207f.

63. Berthold Kommallein, Notizen zur Geschichte der Stadt Wolfhagen, typed manuscript, n.d., 21. I greatly thank the director of the Wolfhagen town archives, Dr. Sven-Hinrich Siemers, for providing a copy of this text. The original is located in the Wolfhagen municipal archives.

64. Kropat, *"Reichskristallnacht,"* 70f.

65. See the report by the gendarmerie in Burghaun, 12 November 1938; also the radio message by the chief of the regular police to all police agencies, 10 November 1938, 6:30 a.m., both printed in ibid., 212f. and 216f.

66. Quoted in ibid., 240f.

67. See *Das Ende der Juden in Ostfriesland: Ausstellung der Ostfriesischen Landschaft aus Anlaß des 50. Jahrestages der Kristallnacht* (Aurich, 1988), 47–52. According to Obst,

the order from Munich for the pogrom arrived at the different Gau capital towns between 22 and 22:30 hrs. Obst, *"Reichskristallnacht,"* 111.

68. Interview with Walter Philipson on 22 May 1982 in Claudi and Claudi, *Die wir verloren haben,* interview 16: 9–11.

69. Ibid., 16:16.

70. Because of the boycott campaigns and persecutions since 1933, the number of Jewish families in Emden had already strongly declined. In the fall of 1938, only 430 Jewish citizens still lived in the town, 25 percent fewer than when the National Socialists first took power. In 1941 only 164 remained in Emden, mostly older people, who in October of that year were deported to their deaths. See the entry for "Emden" in Obenaus, *Handbuch der jüdischen Gemeinden in Niedersachsen und Bremen,* 533–569.

71. See Lina Gödeken, *Rund um die Synagoge in Norden: Die Geschichte der Synagogengemeinde seit 1866* (Aurich, 2000), 300–315; *Das Ende der Juden in Ostfriesland,* 60–63; see the description of the course of events in the judgment issued by the Aurich jury court, 18 December 1948, 2 Ks 8/48, Yad Vashem Archives, TR-10/453. Of the seven perpetrators who were charged after the war with first-degree arson, breach of peace, first-degree deprivation of liberty, grievous bodily harm, and crimes against humanity, three were sentenced to between eighteen months and four years of prison and the other four were acquitted.

72. Aurich State Archives of Lower Saxony, Rep. 109 E/341, Mappe II, Bl. 364ff., referenced in Gödeken, *Rund um die Synagoge in Norden,* 306.

73. Ibid., 307f. In May 1939, only 91 of the 204 Jewish residents registered in 1933 still lived in Norden. At the beginning of 1940, the remaining 34 Jews still living in Norden also had to leave. A little more than half of the Jewish people who lived in Norden in 1933 were able to flee abroad. At least 94 were murdered in the ghettos and concentration camps of Eastern Europe, including many who had fled to neighboring Holland only to once again fall into the hands of National Socialists after the invasion in 1940. See the entry for "Norden" in Obenaus, *Handbuch der jüdischen Gemeinden in Niedersachsen und Bremen,* 1122–1139.

74. The description that follows about the course of the pogrom in Treuchtlingen is based on findings, evidence, and witness testimony of proceedings in the district court of Nuremburg-Fürth against Nora A. and others for breach of peace, looting, physical injury, and more. Judgment and legal opinion dated 9 May 1946 (KLs 16/14), archive of the town administration of Treuchtlingen 063/19. Of the 52 men and women charged, 39 were convicted of breach of peace and in part of theft, coercion, deprivation of liberty, and severe bodily harm. They were sentenced to as much as two years in prison—including five women who received prison sentences ranging from three months to two years. See also Michael Wildt, "Violence against Jews in Germany 1933–1939", in *Probing the Depths of German Antisemitism: German Society and the Persecution of the Jews, 1933–1941,* ed. David Bankier (New York, 2000), 181–209.

75. Moritz Mayer, reported memoir, typed, 1939, Yad Vashem Archives, Jerusalem, Record Group 033/80.

76. Gendarmerie station Treuchtlingen to the Weißenburg district office, 11 November 1938, Yad Vashem Archives, Jerusalem, M1DN/203, fol. 295. The elderly people were both admitted to the Weißenburg prison and released a week later.

77. Moritz Mayer, reported memoir, typed, 1939, Yad Vashem Archives, Jerusalem, Record Group 033/80.

78. Bernhard Tachauer, who later emigrated to Canada, hastily fled from an anti-Semitic mob in his home community of Marktbreit in the district of Kitzingen and did not have any money. On his way to Munich, he had to wait at the Treuchtlingen railway

station. He described the situation as follows: "I am thankful to the train station supervisor who was working in the night from the 9th to the 10th of November, 1938. He did not betray me to the police, but rather let me get onto the train without a ticket and even arranged with the conductor to bring me to Munich." *Treuchtlinger Kurier*, 19–20 November 1988.

79. Treuchtlingen Bürgermeister to the fire insurance office in Eichstätt, 15 November 1938, archive of the town administration of Treuchtlingen 063/19.
80. Regional district office Weisenburg to the Nuremberg state police, 11 November 1938, Yad Vashem Archives, Jerusalem, M1DN/203, fol. 293.
81. Treuchtlingen Bürgermeister to the Weisenburg district administrator, 29 June 1939, Yad Vashem Archives, Jerusalem, M1DN/203, fol. 352.
82. See Herbert A. Strauss, ed. *Hostages of Modernization: Studies on Modern Antisemitism 1870–1933/39*, vol. 3/1: *Germany – Great Britain – France* (Berlin, 1993), 455–666; Hermann Graml, Angelika Königseder, and Juliane Wetzel, eds. *Vorurteil und Rassenhaß: Antisemitismus in den faschistischen Bewegungen Europas* (Berlin, 2001); William I. Brustein, *Roots of Hate: Anti-Semitism in Europe before the Holocaust* (Cambridge, 2003); on the concept of "pogrom," see Werner Bergmann, "Pogrome," in *Internationales Handbuch der Gewaltforschung*, ed. Wilhelm Heitmeyer and John Hagan (Wiesbaden, 2002), 441–460.
83. Juliane Wetzel, "Frankreich und Belgien," in *Dimension des Völkermords: Die Zahl der jüdischen Opfer des Nationalsozialismus*, ed. Wolfgang Benz (Munich, 1996), 107f.
84. See Philippe Burrin, "Faschismus und Antisemitismus in Frankreich," in Graml et al., *Vorurteil und Rassenhaß*, 119–129.
85. Andreas Wirsching, *Vom Weltkrieg zum Bürgerkrieg? Politischer Extremismus in Deutschland und Frankreich 1918–1933/39: Berlin und Paris im Vergleich* (Munich,1999), 498.
86. Ulrich Bielefeld, *Nation und Gesellschaft: Selbstthematisierungen in Deutschland und Frankreich* (Hamburg, 2003), 327f.
87. Lieven Saerens, "Belgische Gruppierungen der 'Neuen Ordnung' und die Juden (1918–1944)," in Graml et al., *Vorurteil und Rassenhaß*, 131–150.
88. Konrad Kwiet, "Mussert, 'Mussert-Juden' und die 'Lösung der Judenfrage' in den Niederlanden," in Graml et al., *Vorurteil und Rassenhaß*, 157f. Two years later, however, the NSB suffered a clear defeat and ended up with only 4.2 percent of the votes
89. Ibid., 160.
90. Juliane Wetzel, "Der Mythos des 'braven Italieners': Das faschistische Italien und der Antisemitismus," in Graml et al., *Vorurteil und Rassenhaß*, 57.
91. Ibid., 56; see also Reichardt, *Faschistische Kampfbünde*, 628–631.
92. Wetzel, "Der Mythos des 'braven Italieners,'" 58.
93. Aram Mattioli, *Experimentierfeld der Gewalt: Der Abessinienkrieg und seine internationale Bedeutung 1935–1941* (Zurich, 2005), 112–117, 140–156.
94. See in general Frank Golczewski, *Polnisch-jüdische Beziehungen 1881–1922: Eine Studie zur Geschichte des Antisemitismus in Osteuropa* (Wiesbaden, 1981); Yisrael Gutman, Ezra Mendelsohn, Jehuda Reinharz, and Chone Shmeruk, eds. *The Jews of Poland between Two World Wars* (London, 1989); Herbert A. Strauss, ed. *Hostages of Modernization: Studies on Modern Antisemitism 1870–1933/39*, vol. 3/2: *Austria– Hungary – Poland – Russia* (Berlin, 1993), 963–1173.
95. David Cymet, "Polish State Antisemitism as a Major Factor Leading to the Holocaust," *Journal of Genocide Research* 1, no. 2 (1999): 169–212, here 176f.; see also the case study on the pogrom in Lwów in November 1918, William W. Hagen, "The Moral Economy of Ethnic Violence: The Progrom in Lwów, November 1918," *Geschichte und Gesellschaft* 31 (2005): 203–226.

96. Joanna Michlic-Coren, "Anti-Jewish Violence in Poland, 1918–1939 and 1945–1947," *Polin: Studies in Polish Jewry* 13 (2000): 40; William W. Hagen, "Before the 'Final Solution': Toward a Comparative Analysis of Political Anti-Semitism in Interwar Germany and Poland," *Journal of Modern History* 68, no. 2 (1996): 368–371.

97. Michlic-Coren, "Anti-Jewish Violence in Poland," 55.

98. Ibid., 37; see also Emanuel Melzer, "Antisemitism in the Last Years of the Second Polish Republic," in Gutman et al., *The Jews of Poland between Two World Wars*, 126–137.

99. Michlic-Coren, "Anti-Jewish Violence in Poland," 42.

100. Cymet, "Polish State Antisemitism," 170; see Ronald Modras, *The Catholic Church and Antisemitism in Poland, 1933–1939* (Chur, 1994).

101. See Magnus Brechtken, *"Madagaskar für die Juden": Antisemitische Idee und politische Praxis 1885–1945* (Munich, 1997), 81–164; Hans Jansen, *Der Madagaskar-Plan: Die beabsichtigte Deportation der europäischen Juden nach Madagaskar* (Munich, 1997), 109–174.

102. Gisela Lebzelter, "Political Anti-Semitism in England 1918–1939," in Strauss, *Germany – Great Britain – France*, 396–412.

103. DNB broadcast, 10 November 1938, in Bohrmann and Toepser-Zeigert, *NS-Presseanweisungen der Vorkriegszeit*, vol. 6/III, 1060f., no. 3209; see Longerich, *"Davon haben wir nichts gewusst!"* 125–129.

104. See the vivid photographs of the destruction by the pogrom in the German provinces in Hesse and Springer in *Vor aller Augen*, 89–116.

105. Kershaw, "Antisemitismus"; Bankier, *The Germans and the Final Solution*, 85–88; Obst, *"Reichskristallnacht,"* 319–348; Longerich, *"Davon haben wir nichts gewusst!"* 129–135.

106. The "Verordnung zur Wiederherstellung des Straßenbildes bei jüdischen Gewerbetrieben," (*RGBl* I, 1581), dated 12 November 1938, compelled Jewish store owners to alleviate the damages caused by National Socialists gangs at their own expense. The "Verordnung über eine Sühneleistung der Juden deutscher Staatsangehörigkeit" (*RGBl*, 1579), also dated 12 November 1938, imposed upon the German Jews a levy of RM 100 million. The levy was later expanded to include stateless Jews and increased to RM 1,000 million. Adam, *Judenpolitik im Dritten Reich*, 209–216.

107. Bankier, *The Germans and the Final Solution*, 81.

108. Longerich, *"Davon haben wir nichts gewusst!"* 134.

109. Andreas-Friedrich, *Der Schattenmann*, 28–30.

110. Obst, *"Reichskristallnacht,"* 137.

111. In this respect, the sources used by Dieter Obst, namely the postwar legal proceedings, have only a limited potential, for they dealt only with the actions of those who were legally charged, who were almost exclusively members of the SA and SS. They did not deal with the involvement of the rest of the crowd. The case of Treuchtlingen is thus an unusual example, for in this case fifty-two men and women from Treuchtlingen faced charges in court. In order to depict the event it is therefore necessary to also rely on the testimony of Jewish survivors, as is usually the case in most local studies.

112. Dieter Obst collected cases of help and support in his investigation, although the fact that these consist of postwar testimonies needs to be taken into consideration. Obst, *"Reichskristallnacht,"* 319–333.

113. A tabulation by the Reich Economic Group "Insurance" in December 1938 calculated the damages at RM 49.5 million, including RM 39 million in fire damages, RM

6.5 million in glass damages, and RM 3.5 million in break-in damages. Longerich, *Politik der Vernichtung*, 203.

114. On 9 November, just before midnight, Gestapo Chief Müller sent a secret telex to all state police agencies stating, among other things: "1. Shortly throughout Germany there will actions against the Jews, particularly against their synagogues. They are not to be disturbed. Yet working with the regular police, it is to be ensured that looting and other excesses are prevented.... 3. Preparations are to be made for the arrest of around 20–30,000 Jews in the Reich. In particular, wealthy Jews are to be selected." Secret telex from Gestapa II, signed Müller, to all state police offices and agencies, 9 November 1938, 23:55, printed in *IMG*, vol. 25, 376–378 (374-PSJ). In parallel, Heydrich dispatched a similar-sounding telex to all state police agencies—express telex from Heydrich to all state police and SD agencies, 10 November 1938, 1:20, printed in *IMG*, vol. 31, 515–518 (3051-PSJ).

115. See the many cases described in Obst, *"Reichskristallnacht,"* 279–307; on the participation of children and youth, see especially 263–270.

116. Heydrich to Göring, 11 November 1938, printed in *IMG*, vol. 32, 1–2 (3058-PS); report of the Obersten Parteigerichts to Göring, 13 February 1939, printed in ibid., 20–29 (3063-PS).

117. See the interview with Ernst Fraenkel in the *Berliner Morgenpost* dated 17 September 1967—and also Rudolf Wolfgang Müller, "'... wenn es morgens um 6 Uhr klingelte, war es der Milchmann' – Ernst Fraenkel und die West-Berliner Studentenbewegung 1967," in *Vom Sozialismus zum Pluralismus: Beiträge zu Werk und Leben Ernst Fraenkels*, ed. Hubertus Buchstein and Gerhard Göhler (Baden-Baden, 2000), 97–113. Also the biographical interview with Getzel Taube in Lutz Niethammer, Alexander von Plato, and Dorothee Wierling, *Die volkseigene Erfahrung: Eine Archäologie des Lebens in der Industrieprovinz der DDR: 30 biographische Eröffnungen* (Berlin, 1991). I thank Dorothee Wierling for directing me to this interview.

118. Stenographic and partially hand-written record of the conference in the Reich Aviation Ministry, 12 November 1938, printed in *IMG*, vol. 28, 499–540, quote on 518. This brutal anti-Semitic tone prevailed during the entire conference.

119. Ibid., 511–517.

120. See Friedländer, *Years of Persecution*, 280–293.

121. See above all Wolf Gruner, *Der Geschlossene Arbeitseinsatz deutscher Juden: Zur Zwangsarbeit als Element der Verfolgung 1938–1943* (Berlin, 1997).

122. On 24 January, as commissioner of the four-year plan, Göring announced the creation of the Central Office for Jewish Emigration, appointing Heydrich as its director. Anderl, "Die 'Zentralstellen für jüdische Auswanderung,'" 275–288.

123. Transcription of the conference at the Reich Aviation Ministry, 12 November 1938, printed in *IMG*, vol. 28, 532. Directly after the conference, the SD-Hauptamt began working on such a characteristic symbol. In any event, on 6 December Göring reported that Hitler rejected a symbol for the Jews; see Heim, "'Deutschland muß ihnen ein Land ohne Zukunft sein,'" 71. The wearing of a "Jewish star" was then decreed by the Reichstag in September 1941.

124. Göring, speech on 6 December 1938, in Susanne Heim and Götz Aly, "Staatliche Ordnung und 'organische Lösung': Die Rede Hermann Görings 'Über die Judenfrage' vom 6. Dezember 1938," *Jahrbuch für Antisemitismusforschung* 2 (1992): 384.

125. Transcription of the conference in the Reich Aviation Ministry, 12 November 1938, printed in *IMG*, vol. 28, 539.

126. See Kershaw, *Hitler*, vol. 2, 214; Hans Mommsen, "Hitler's Reichstag Speech of 30 January 1939," *History & Memory* 9 (1997): 147–161.

Conclusion

THE PRODUCTION OF THE VOLKSGEMEINSCHAFT

Inclusion and Exclusion

The concept of the *Volksgemeinschaft* owed its strength and popularity to the First World War, when it was necessary to unite the Germans behind the imperial war flag. The statement by Wilhelm II that he henceforth no longer recognized parties but only Germans expressed simply but pointedly the political necessity to mobilize the entire population for the war. It also addressed the need for inclusion and integration with the grand totality, which not only Social Democrats but also German Jews desired. The fact that social class divisions quickly reemerged within the society at war and that old anti-Semitic resentments once again spread may have damaged the *Volksgemeinschaft* as an accurate conceptual reflection of reality. Yet it lost none of its magic as a promise for the future, particularly since it was based in the myth of an experienced past.

The Revolution of 1919 and the constitution of the Weimar Republic brought the "Volk" as an association of citizens into the political area, and more than one hundred years after the French Revolution the divine right of kings was also declared illegitimate in Germany; in its place the

Volk was declared sovereign. But the *Volksgemeinschaft* remained on the political agenda. Admittedly, the ambivalence was situated within the constitution itself, for it did not merely constitute the Volk as an association of citizens that determined its Reichstag representatives in free, secret, and equal elections. Rather, it also anchored a preconstitutional Volk in its preamble, a Volk that previously existed and, as it says in the text, granted itself this constitution. In addition, there were constitutionally installed anti-representative stabilizers, like the equally ranked position of the Reich president, who was elected in a plebiscite "by the entire German Volk."

Carl Schmitt clearly recognized these ambivalences and at the same time tried to force upon them an anti-representative and anti-liberal interpretation by declaring that the identity and homogeneity of the political Volk was a prerequisite to any democratic constitutional order. The state of citizens that Hugo Preuß had in mind failed to appeal to a majority of German constitutional theorists, who were fixated on an authoritative state. The Socialist Democrats were the leading force during the Revolution and overcame the rule of the councils to successfully install a parliamentary state, but despite the Gotha Program and the concept of a "*Volksstaat*" they did not have a well-articulated constitutional theory that went beyond the demand for a parliamentary system. The attempts by Hugo Preuß, Friedrich Meinecke, and Friedrich Ebert to create a bond between the Germans and the new constitution by means of the concept of the *Volksgemeinschaft* was bound to fail, for the parliamentary system inevitably requires the existence of political parties and party conflict, and a Republic of state citizens cannot be resolved into a single unified Volk and *Gemeinschaft*.

Yet *Gemeinschaft* was the "idol of this age," as it was put by Helmuth Plessner, a shrewd observer at the time.[1] Nearly all of the parties propagated the *Volksgemeinschaft* as a political program—with both gradual and fundamental differences. The Catholic Center Party, which was fundamentally critical of the secular concept of *Volkssouveränität* (people's sovereignty), placed too much value on the hierarchical social order of estates based on natural law as an image of divine creation for it to be able to accept the egalitarian aspect of the *Volksgemeinschaft*—the elimination of classes and the equality of all productive people. For the Social Democrats, the working class had long since become, in the course of its history, the large majority of the Volk, which in the end stood opposite a small, receding, and illegitimately powerful minority of industrialists and large landowners. However, within this socially determined perspective, leveling class society through the construction of an ethnic *Volksgemeinschaft* that also included capitalists and Junkers lay outside the political program. Nonetheless, the tendency toward including all producers within a genuine *Volksgemeinschaft* was unmistakable, even if the concept retreated to the background in Social Democratic journalism after the death of Friedrich Ebert (apart from Hermann Heller, who, as an expert in constitutional law, tried to create a basis for the *Volksgemeinschaft* in democratic terms).

But insofar as even the parties that were loyal to the constitution propagated the *Volksgemeinschaft*, they provided terminological nourishment for a destructive opponent, for the populist-integrative appeal to unity and *Gemeinschaft* in opposition to "brotherly strife" and "party conflict" undermined republican political culture, which requires discussion and compromise. This appeal repudiated the public sphere of civil society, which is defined by argument and debate.

In contrast, the political right understood the *Volksgemeinschaft* predominantly in its anti-republican and exclusionary dimensions. The right-wing parties, especially the NSDAP, were by no means concerned with the inclusion of all Germans, but rather only with the community of the *Volksgenossen*, an ethnic *Volksgemeinschaft* that excluded all German Jews from the outset. Even though the right-wing political rhetoric naturally placed the *Volksgemeinschaft* at center stage, the *Volksgemeinschaft* was produced above all by sharply and violently drawing boundaries—that is, by exclusion. In the reciprocal relationship between inclusion and exclusion, which defines the construction of any group, the conceptual and practical reference point with respect to ethnicity was undoubtedly the exclusion of anyone who, according to an ethnic perspective based on blood mythology and racial biology, did not belong to the *Volksgemeinschaft*.

Anti-Semitism played the decisive role in this process. For embedded within the preconstitutional construction of the Volk—outside the state—as a "natural community of blood [*Blutsgemeinschaft*]" that must seek its own political order (which just so happened not to be the civil order of the national state) was an inextricable racist, anti-Semitic boundary. Anti-Semitism constituted the National Socialist *Volksgemeinschaft*, and it also fueled its radicalism and destructive potential. With only an inclusionary concept, the German *Volksgemeinschaft* would have been satisfied with full employment and a revision of the Versailles Treaty according to the borders of 1938. Instead, anti-Semitic, racist passions propelled it further to expand borders, define exclusionary differences, continually produce the *Volksgemeinschaft* anew, and realize an ethnic-racist order in Europe.

These boundaries were not merely drawn in theory but above all in practice—that is, with violence. In contrast to the "quilldrivers" and "knights of ink," Hitler stylized himself as a rhetorician of anti-Semitism who wanted not to convince but rather, using the power of speech, to incite action. National Socialist anti-Semitism proved itself by its actions. Only through action could a serious effort be made to exclude the Jews from the German *Volksgemeinschaft* and thereby begin the production of that *Volksgemeinschaft*. Violence for the National Socialists was not merely a means for politics; it *was* politics. Violence not only made it possible to represent but also, above all, to *experience* the political, understood as the difference between friend and foe (according to Carl Schmitt, as an "utmost degree of intensity of a union or a separation, of an association or dissociation").[2]

Violence—*violentia*—stands in opposition to law. To be sure, the constitutional state must undoubtedly possess the power to deploy violence as means of physical coercion against the breach of law. Yet the basis of a legal order can never be violence but only the recognition by everyone of the rationality, if not also the reasonableness, of the law, as well as the legitimacy and legality of the institutions that deploy violence and guarantee the legal order. And vice versa: all those who consciously disregard the state's monopoly of violence and organize their own violent militias call into question the legitimacy of the state and likewise the validity of the law. Reichswehr putschists, National Socialists, and Communist revolutionaries wanted to destroy the Weimar constitutional order. Their violent actions were supposed to challenge the civil constitutional state, provide evidence of its helplessness and thus publicly delegitimize it. The SA and other violent militias created lawless spaces, zones within which a state of emergency obtained, where decisionism, arbitrariness, and violence prevailed.

The Weimar Republic, which had insufficient civic support for its legal institutions, could not master this political violence. Every violent action attacked the constitutional state's claim to the monopoly of violence, and only the determined deployment of police and sustained criminal prosecution of the violence could have repelled these attacks and gained the citizens' confidence in the state's ability to provide security. In its final phase, the Weimar Republic was no longer up to the task of coping with the ubiquitous political violence. The threat was less one of civil war, as many feared, but of the constitutional state's collapse under the pressure of such violence and the growing number of people who hoped for a new political order that would bring security, unity, and an end to the divisions within the society.

In any event, the violence of the National Socialist terror groups was not merely directed against political enemies—the "Reds"—who with their own violent militia represented an equal opponent. The SA also beat up unarmed civilian Jewish citizens who hardly had a chance to defend themselves. The asymmetry of this violence, which distinguished the National Socialists from the Communists in an essential way, was racist at its core, for the intention here was not to demonstrate superiority over a political enemy. It was not merely about defeating someone; rather, the violent perpetrators wanted to inflict harm and to destroy. It was about annihilation—a violence that no longer reckoned with resistance but simply wanted to inflict violence on its own. It was not merely instrumental violence but, as Jan Philipp Reemtsma has put it, "autotelian violence."[3]

Nonetheless, despite all of its weaknesses, the Weimar Republic offered the structures of a constitutional state. The police took action against violent militias, governments declared states of emergency in order to put down revolutionary coups with the help of the military, and, importantly, there were independent courts where victims of discrimination and violence could file complaints against the perpetrators. Political parties like the SPD, social organizations like the C.V., and even courageous individuals like the Oberbürgermeister of Oldenburg in 1923 were able to mobilize the public against violence. This is why 30 January 1933—which at first glance only looks as if a new Reich chancellor was appointed by the Reich president—in fact marks a decisive break: from this point forward, the enemies of law took over the regime.

The electoral campaign for the Reichstag elections on 5 March 1933 was already overshadowed by massive propaganda and the ruthless use of state violence by the governing National Socialists. In particular, the Reichstag fire in the night leading to 27 February provided the NS leadership with a welcome opportunity to sanction state terror. By means of the Decree for the Protection of the Volk and the State on 28 February, essential fundamental rights like freedom of the individual, inviolability of the home, privacy of postal correspondence and telephone communication, freedom of opinion and assembly, freedom of association, and protection of property were suspended. Ernst Fraenkel aptly referred to this decree as the "constitutional charter of the Third Reich."[4] The Reichstag Fire Decree consciously avoided declaring a military state of emergency and transferring executive power to a military commander, as had previously been usual. Instead, it strengthened the power of the police in the NS regime and demonstrated how little the National Socialist leadership thought in terms of the traditional categories of a state of emergency or state of siege.

The decree was supposed to give the regime full freedom of action—or, more generally formulated, the political was to be withdrawn from the sphere of law. In his analysis of the NS regime published in 1941 as *The Dual State* during his exile in the United States, Ernst Frankel noted:

> The political sphere is a vacuum as far as law is concerned. Of course it contains a certain element of factual order and predictability but only in so far as there is a certain regularity and predictability in the behavior of officials. There is, however, no legal regulation of the official bodies. The political sphere in the Third Reich is governed neither by objective nor by subjective law, neither by legal guarantees nor jurisdictional qualifications. There are no legal rules governing the political sphere. It is regulated by arbitrary measures (*Massnahmen*), in which the dominant officials exercise the discretionary prerogatives. Hence the expression "Prerogative State" (*Massnahmenstaat*).[5]

Specific to the National Socialist regime was that its regulating principle was not based on state and law but on Volk and race. At the center of National Socialist thought was not the state but rather the Volk. This was made perfectly clear by Hitler himself in *Mein Kampf*:

> But in general it should never be forgotten that the highest purpose of a human being is not the preservation of a state or even a regime, but rather the protection of his kind. We, as Aryans, are only able to conceive of the state as the living organism of a *Volkstum*, which not only assures the preservation of this *Volkstum* but also, by further cultivation of its spiritual and conceptual capabilities, leads it to the highest freedom.[6]

Therefore the NS regime did not waive the juridical foundation of its order as a *Volksherrschaft* (popular government). The *Volksgemeinschaft* did not do away with the idea of the sovereign Volk. But it defined and regulated the Volk in racial-biological terms, cleansed of "Jews," "foreign races," the "inferior," and those "foreign to the community." All authority was to proceed from this racially defined *ethnos*—not from the *demos*, the Volk of the constitutional state, nor from the assembly of free citizens regardless of their gender, religion, skin color, or heritage. Thus it is difficult to base the *Volksgemeinschaft* as understood by the National Socialists on Jean-Jacques Rousseau, whose political philosophy was intended to create a social collective that did not impinge on human freedoms. Yet on the other hand, Rousseau's social contract did not rule out the possibility that sovereignty of socialized individuals could be based on the exclusion and oppression of others. Rousseau openly conceded that the civil liberties of the Greek *polis* rested on the bondage of its slaves.

In his writings, Carl Schmitt maliciously recognized the incoherence of Rousseau's concept and used the model to understand the sovereign Volk not as an association of free and equal citizens but to postulate equality as something substantial: "each real democracy is based not only on the equal treatment of that which is equal, but also, as an inevitable consequence, on the unequal treatment of that which is unequal. Thus democracy necessarily requires, first, homogeneity, and second—if need be—the elimination or annihilation of the heterogeneous."[7] After 1933, Schmitt began using the word "*Artgleich*" (of the same kind or species) instead of "*Gleichartige*" (similar) in some of his formulations.[8] Schmitt's adaptation of Rousseau's argument allowed the *Volksgemeinschaft* to become sovereign — that is, make a claim for popular government—without losing its particular racial-biologically defined character.

Furthermore, Rousseau's concept that only the assembled Volk that declares its will can be sovereign, and that this sovereignty is both indivisible and inalienable, thus prohibiting any representation of the Volk's will, provided the opportunity to criticize the Weimar constitutional state and simultaneously reclaim for oneself the representation of genuine democracy. By opposing identity and representation, Schmitt developed the argument that the unity of the Volk could not be represented by means of a parliament but could only be formed through identity. "Where the Volk as the subject of a constitution-granting power appears, the form of the state defines itself by the idea of an identity; the nation is there; it need not and cannot be represented."[9] Accordingly, if the parliament claims to represent the unity of the Volk, it stands in opposition to genuine democracy.

Indeed, Rousseau's theory of the absolute sovereignty of the people opens a horizon of expectations that is very difficult to reconcile with the everyday experience of representative democracies. The statement that all authority proceeds from the people evokes a power that is not exhausted by the practice of regular elections. Within the representative structures of the constitutional state, the constitutive power of the people—the "*pouvoir constituent*" (Emmanuel Joseph)—retains a certain unfulfilled magnitude that is fenced off by legal theory yet has the potential to awaken the political passions that under certain conditions compel the people to man the barricades.

Thus *Volksgemeinschaft* does not necessarily imply a regression toward premodernity. It serves also as a programmatic formula by which to abolish modernity—to surmount the modern using modern means. Popular government without representation—this formula would express the political *telos* of the National Socialist's *Volksgemeinschaft* rhetoric. It was from here that National Socialism drew the obsession and the intensity of political emotion with which it fought against the constitutional state in order to replace it with a new, identity-based political order.

Thus it becomes clear that the *Volksgemeinschaft* makes reference to something that has been ostracized from civil society, namely, an undifferentiated longing for power and identity. By no means does it exhaust itself in a merely inclusive order of equality and common interest, but as such it must always be produced in opposition to the social reality of self-interest and heterogeneity. In this sense the *Volksgemeinschaft* amounts to the promise of a meta-modern order of racial inequality in which the Volk, producing and protecting its homogeneity, experiences itself as sovereign.

Division

The production of the *Volksgemeinschaft* could not, therefore, proceed only through gratification, self-dramatization, conformity or terror, regulation, and law. This transformation was a political process that encompassed the entire society, not only in the large cities but also, and particularly, in the provinces—the villages and smaller communities where the Nazis had admittedly taken over leadership positions but still had not acquired political power. The persecution of the Jews as "*Volksfeinde*" and "racial opponents of the German Volk" was the quintessential political instrument to destroy the Volk of the state and produce the *Volksgemeinschaft*.

In terms of local political practice this meant creating social distance, stigmatizing any solidarity and empathy with the persecuted in order to isolate the Jews, strip them of rights, and even declare them fair game. One can hardly underestimate what it meant for local Jewish families when Jewish members were excluded from local associations—sport clubs, choirs, gun clubs—or local fire departments, all of which in the course of 1933 adopted an "Aryan paragraph" in their association bylaws. Additionally, there was the boycott movement, which was by no means limited to 1 April 1933. In the large cities, under the watchful eyes of foreign observers and concentrated control by the police, the boycott was initially halted after 1 April. But in the small towns and villages of the provinces, the boycott created a political arena in which local party and SA groups could transform the social, cultural, and political order of the community. The boycott made it possible to experiment with a variety of forms of action, from public placards and banners, standing sentry in front of stores, and merely requesting that customers not enter the stores, to verbal abuse and the application of violence.

Certainly, there was still resistance. Not everyone wanted the National Socialist persecution of the Jews to prevent them from engaging in rational economic behavior and buying goods where they were least expensive. Mature and trusting business relationships were especially important in the livestock market; as a result, National Socialists had great difficulty motivating farmers to break off their relationships with Jewish livestock traders. In many places, drastic state measures were required. And without doubt, there were many for whom the Jewish merchant was an upright and trustworthy neighbor, someone they had known for years and whom they were reluctant to abandon simply because of pressure. The secret and bashful purchases after business hours mentioned repeatedly in memoirs and in the C.V. files are indications of such an attitude toward people's Jewish neighbors.

Finally, many people repudiated the violent actions during which display windows were smashed, homes smeared with paint, or Jewish proprietors beaten and abused. Wanton destruction of property is rarely considered acceptable, particularly since a modern bourgeois society also includes companies that insure glass; thus groups that destroyed windows at night caused material harm not only to Jewish proprietors but also to the German insurance industry. Yet the nonmaterial damages of such violence—the threat under which Jewish Germans suffered in their communities, where they had lived and felt secure for a long time—can hardly be underestimated.

But non-Jewish customers were also targeted by local activist groups. NSDAP members were prohibited from having contact with Jews in any case. After 1933 all state employees were pressured, under threat of losing their jobs, to yield to anti-Semitic policies and refrain from visiting Jewish doctors, seeking counsel from Jewish lawyers, and shopping in Jewish stores. But National Socialist boycott demands reached far beyond that to all "Germans." What was, prior to 1933, formulated as an appeal to national duty, *völkisch* virtue, and solidarity with one's "German" brother took on a more severe tone after the seizure of power. Henceforth, those who stood by their relationships to Jews were considered "traitors" of the *Volksgemeinschaft* and publicly stigmatized in the *Stürmer-Kästen*, often identified by their full names and addresses. This social pressure was especially effective in smaller communities where the residents knew each other. Being brought to the "pillory" was something only those with the most uncompromising spirits could bear.

There was no legal basis for these actions, and accordingly the Jewish victims hoped to obtain law and order by filing complaints with the state institutions. The fact that these authorities denied them, and even prior to the Nuremberg laws violated the practice of treating citizens as equals before the law, indicates the fragility of the bourgeois legal order as well as the National Socialists' determination to destroy it. From his exile in London in 1939, the former syndic of the Centralverein deutscher Staatsbürger jüdischen Glaubens, Hans Reichmann, wrote: "We were accustomed to considering the constitutional state as the self-evident prerequisite for community life; for us it was completely unproblematic because for five generations we had lived with the ideas of a constitutional state. For us, the constitutional state was a fact, not a goal. Of course we did not know what a non-constitutional state [Unrecht-Staat] is."[10]

Honor and Shame

By focusing on codified state law, the academic debate about state and legal theory often fails to notice that other legal orders obtain within society that are not regulated by the constitution. Occasionally legal textbooks refer to these with the concept of customary law. But the category of honor goes beyond the regulation of everyday conflicts, for it signifies a specific social behavior, culturally and historically variable, compliance with which was not merely customary but customarily required. During premodernity, breaches of honor were subject to authoritative criminal codes and punished by the neighborhood, village, and religious community. In the process of creating the modern state, which also meant the unification and state regulation of law, this people's justice was increasingly suppressed, but it never disappeared.

The many practices by which breaches of honor were punished persisted into the twentieth century. To "pillory" was not understood literally, although in many German towns like Breslau the pillory pole was preserved as a monument, even though it no longer served a judicial function. But in a more figurative and still very violent sense, these practices persisted. Honor was always defined through violence, and the examples from the Rhineland while under French occupation in the 1920s reveal that the public humiliation and abuse of women were the order of the day.

This calls attention to a second characteristic of honor—that is, gender. Honor was always linked with sexuality—with safeguarding the sexual patriarchal order. To be sure, men who were deceived by their wives, for example, or who married young women at an advanced age became objects of traditional honor punishments. But in the first instance, honor justice was targeted at women, who were required to protect their purity and were severely punished if that purity was violated. This did not change in the twentieth century: violence and gender remained the two decisive characteristics of honor.

In addition, honor became racially charged. That which in premodernity represented an order to regulate social behavior became, under racial-biological auspices, a practice of irrevocable ostracism. The public stigmatization was supposed ban the person from the "community of blood" (*Blutsgemeinschaft*), since according to racial theories of contagion—popularized to a large extent by Arthur Dinter's novel *The Sin against the Blood*—a non-Jewish woman remained "poisoned" for the rest of her life due to merely a single contact with a Jewish man.

As opposed to the boycott actions, which did not meet with the unanimous assent of the population, the local National Socialist chapters apparently discovered that their "racial defilement" actions opened up a political field where Jews could be not merely segregated but expelled from the *Volksgemeinschaft* and where the punishment of "breaches of honor" by non-Jewish Germans—especially the "disgrace" of women—could be practically implemented with approval.

The cases of "racial defilement" spread like wild fire throughout the Reich in 1935, that is (to emphasize this point again), months before the enactment of the Nuremberg laws. The practice of public humiliation and abuse became current throughout the German Reich. For Jewish men, the "racial defilement" processions were only the first phase of punishment, after which they were generally taken into "protective custody" and brought to a concentration camp. Non-Jewish women did not need to expect additional state measures after being publicly "dishonored," but they were often so socially ostracized that they lost their jobs and felt compelled to leave their communities.

If one considers the images of those processions, which—in contrast to the nightly attacks on Jewish businesses and residences—took place in broad daylight, the crowds that accompanied them are striking: women, children, and adolescents are running along, laughing, taunting, insulting, and spitting at the victims. The voyeuristic action, the approval, and the participation in the violent punishment of a breach of "racial honor" cannot be overlooked. With the "racial defilement" actions of 1935, the National Socialists had found a field where, with the approval of non-Jewish *Volksgenossen*, they could effectively draw the boundaries of the *Volksgemeinschaft*. The flood of denunciations of Jewish and non-Jewish neighbors because of alleged "racial defilement" after the enactment of the Nuremberg laws also provides evidence that this addressed a political passion that, in contrast to other anti-Semitic policies that targeted, for example, economic behavior, could be successfully mobilized by the National Socialists.

Popular Justice (*Volksrecht*)

At first glance one might think that these "racial defilement" processions represented a form of unlimited violence that, liberated from the enclosure of civil law, could unfold without restrictions. Upon closer consideration, however, these forms of defilement processions reveal the outline of a different legal order, an alternative to civil law. Beginning with the public denunciations, naming those who had "disgraced" honor, making them stand at the pillory, listing their "disgraceful acts" on signs hung around their necks, parading them through the community, publicly dishonoring female victims by cutting off their hair, and actively approving of the "punishment" in crowds that berated, abused, and spat upon the accused—these are all obvious forms of a traditional people's honor justice, which the modern state had excluded through the codification of civil law but could never make disappear. National Socialist activists in local communities were able to latch onto these traditional judiciary practices and successfully gain approval and consensual participation—with one fundamental difference.

National Socialism was not concerned with reinstituting the traditional "good" order that was threatened by the claims of the modern centralized state. Rather, it sought to destroy the civil legal order. Judging by its external form and its practices, it might appear as if medieval and early modern practices had been revitalized. But in reality, it was National Socialist mimicry, for the punitive practice of honor served to replace civil equality and the rule of law with racial inequality and the rule of the *Volksgemeinschaft*. The apparent medieval practices of "racial defilement" processions revealed the order of "*Volksrecht*," in which the members of the legal order were not supposed to be equal. Rights were not to be constitutionally determined and published in written laws that were understood by all, and upon which all could call upon equally before the courts. The National Socialist "*Volksrecht*" was established by the "Volk" of the village; the "Volk" pronounced judgment and likewise carried out the sentence: "*Volksrecht*" as a radical and violent critique of the civil legal code.

Honor as a system of order beyond codified law offered an appropriate political field to assert a new racial order of society and law, not merely as a supplement but in conscious opposition to civil law. Hitler's social Darwinist stylization of struggle as a "legal principle," his pejorative remarks about jurists and strict rejection of any normative limitation of the possibilities of action are familiar: "There is only one law in the world," wrote Hitler in 1928, "and this law lies in one's own strength."[11] And even though the standard legal objection is justified, namely that where "might is right" law does not really exist, in my view it would be insufficient to reduce the legal will of the National Socialists to arbitrariness and the pure quest for power.

The National Socialists targeted the civil code as an expression of a "French-Enlightenment and liberal-materialist ethos, particularly the implementation of foreign, Roman-Jewish legal thought."[12] In its place, National Socialist legal theory formulated a completely different source of law: the appeal to an unwritten, supralegal law of the Volk. The core of National Socialist law was not the individual human being, nor was it subjective rights, which provide the linchpin of the civil legal order; rather, it was the law of the community—of the *Volksgemeinschaft*. "Law," according to Karl Larenz, "is, according to us, the life-form of the *Volksgemeinschaft*, its real form of being. It is not brought to the *Gemeinschaft* from outside, but rather is always provided as its immanent organization and order."[13]

In his influential 1934 essay "On the Three Types of Juristic Thought," Carl Schmitt distinguished between normativism as a way of thinking about laws and rules, decisionism as legal thought based on the decisions of judges, and finally the doctrine of concrete order, which refers to the concrete communities within the Volk. "For the doctrine of concrete order," wrote Schmitt, "'order' is also juristically not in the first instance a regulation or a sum of regulations, but rather, the other way around—the regulation is only a part of and a means for order."[14] Admittedly, the thesis that applied law was less to be found in written law books than in the customary legal practice of the respective members of a community was not new. But Schmitt's doctrine of concrete order combined with the concept of a *Volksgemeinschaft* represented a turning point in the development of National Socialist legal theory. As Ernst Fraenkel put it:

> The idea that the community constitutes the sole source of law has a corollary, the doctrine that there can be no law outside the community.... Those who stand outside the community are actual or potential enemies. Relations within the community are marked by prevalence of peace, order and justice. Relations with those outside the community are marked by power, war and destruction.[15]

To be sure, Schmitt was not concerned with allowing concrete *Gemeinschaften*, insofar as they only comprised an ordered whole, to be comparable sources of law for concrete orders. This would, in fact, lead to a kind of liberalism of autonomous groups—for Schmitt, undoubtedly a horrifying vision. Only in connection with the National Socialist conception of the *Gemeinschaft* did the concept first obtain its decisionistic element, for the only groups recognized as agents of concrete order were those that were accepted as a "*Gemeinschaft*" in the National Socialist sense of the term. "The doctrine of community," according to Fraenkel, "is the pivot of the whole National-Socialist system."[16]

The doctrine of concrete order legitimated the arrangement of different *Gemeinschaften* into racial hierarchies as well as the local practice of anti-Semitic violence. While the German *Volksgemeinschaft* could live in relative legal security, other groups, above all the Jews and beyond them all so-called *Fremdvölkische* and *Gemeinschaftsfremde*, were pushed beyond the protection of the law and persecuted without restriction. "*Volksrecht*," as practiced by the local NSDAP groups in their actions against Jewish citizens, found a form to mimic in the traditional honor justice practices that had always existed alongside the state's authoritative law. In terms of its actual content, however, it was not directed toward the restoration of a traditional order but rather toward creating the new order of a racist, anti-Semitic *Volksgemeinschaft*.

Self-Empowerment

The violent actions contained even more political potential. Above and beyond the destruction of the civil legal order, violence provided the experience of unmediated physical power. "This is the root of power," writes the sociologist Heinrich Popitz. "People can exercise power over others because they can injure others."[17] Nowhere are power and helplessness experienced more directly than in the practice or suffering of physical violence. People are in many ways capable of both inflicting and being exposed to injury. The exposure of the human body, its physical vulnerability, and the threat of death are not abstract but concrete experiences. People do not merely feel pain, fear, and passion; they also know about these feelings and can imagine them in anticipation.

> Just how overpowering the dominance of people over people can be is revealed in the direct act of injury more fully than by any other form of power. The direct act of injury recalls the permanent vulnerability of people to the actions of others, their openness to injury, the fragility and exposure of their bodies and their person.[18]

For the victim, nothing remains the same after the violent act. The inner constitution is permanently damaged; the confidence in one's own strength and integrity is irrevocably shaken. According to Wolfgang Sofsky, violence "impacts [the person] in its inner self and overthrows [the person] as a whole, in its totality. If one only considers the effects of violence as a physical, external action then one has not yet understood it in the least."[19] The humiliation, degradation, and evidence of inferiority persist, especially if it is not a situation where two equally ranked contestants are taking measure of their strengths. The experience of weakness stands diametrically opposed to, yet in necessary linkage with, the certainty of strength. Only the surrender of the defeated offers the feeling of victory for the stronger party.

Under equal conditions the loser can request a rematch and, in a reenactment of the contest or in a contest with someone else, has the opportunity to transform his defeat into a victory. But the asymmetrical conditions of the NS regime excluded precisely this kind of opportunity. The overwhelming violence of the perpetrator corresponded with the complete and humiliating helplessness of the person, one that extinguished the person's dignity. The chance of the ostracized victim to defend himself was taken away. The right of self-defense was construed as impermissible resistance, while the attackers were able to feel secure in their own structural superiority even before they took action.

The violence was public and was supposed to put the victim's helplessness and the perpetrator's power on display. The visible humiliation of the victim was a constituent part of the action. These actions took place not merely as images in the *Stürmer-Kasten* but physically, in the market place or in front of the town hall, in a central location within the community—a place where everybody passed by and could see the publicly humiliated person, left exposed to abuse. The purpose of these violent acts was to compel even non-participating passers-by to take a position. Only connivance granted the legal violation its desired success, something that Sebastian Haffner clearly recognized in the scene in the library of the Berlin district court in March 1933.

It is significant that those who were supposed to uphold the law and prevent criminal acts only intervened late or not at all. Instead of stepping in to protect victims from further abuse, the police allowed the violent operations to proceed before shutting them down. And even then, the police did not take steps against the perpetrators but rather took the Jewish victims into custody. In contrast, the often youthful perpetrators could feel secure that they had the more or less blatant approval of their adult superiors, even those who in their official capacity were supposed to guarantee public order.

The more or less undisguised complicity at the local level, which in practice suspended the applicable legal order for the Jews, denied them protection, and abandoned them to violence, was, as politics "from below," just as necessary as the decrees, laws, and measures "from above" in order to produce the *Volksgemeinschaft*. In the moment where the law vis-à-vis a group could be broken without consequences, the boundary of the *Volksgemeinschaft* was already drawn, including on the one side all of the *Volksgenossen* while on the other side excluding all Jews and other *Fremdvölkische* and *Gemeinschaftsfremde*.

The numerous cases described here indicate that it would be a mistake to look only at the activists. Just as the perpetrators were people who did not merely receive orders and carry out directives but rather helped define the situation and the violent act, likewise the spectators, passers-by, and bystanders played an elemental role as people who granted tolerance and approval or acted as accomplices. The victims had to endure their helplessness, while the *Volksgenossen* could experience their empowerment in every day life, and even those who did not directly participate but rather only stood by and watched could take part complicitly in the exercise of power.

At the same time, violence provided community. Everyone could participate and be included without having to take individual responsibility or leadership. Even the most cowardly was allowed to beat, shove, and inflict violence without fear of the victim mounting a defense. With the participation of the community, the violence against the victim was multiplied, on the one hand, and on the other hand the perpetrator's fear of being injured or incurring other damage to his or her own person decreased. In the collective act of violence against Jews, the exclusion of the "other" was executed in a brutal way. And likewise, for the individual perpetrator violence meant a powerful experience of "self-affirmation" (Alf Lüdtke). Taking shape within action was that *Volksgemeinschaft* of which the NS propaganda merely spoke: a community that had an enemy whose persecution and exclusion became the touchstone of its existence, a community that did not define itself through laws that could always have established boundaries, a community that created itself through action and could be experienced as self-intensification.

The different motives might have been completely variable: greed, jealousy, and malevolence might have animated the actors just as much as an explicit enmity toward Jews. And even among the anti-Jewish motivations there might have been various motives and purposes. In this respect, the communal act is evidence of neither shared motivations nor a uniform *Weltanschauung*. Yet the various motivations merged together in the communal act. The violent actions transcended the possible differences in motivation between the participants in the collective actions. Regardless of the intentions that propelled the act, the violence was always directed toward Jews. And in each case, official racial-biological anti-Semitism provided a trite and publicly sanctioned legitimation even for those who merely acted out of greed, revenge, or other driving factors that were not necessarily anti-Jewish. Indeed, and worse yet, anti-Semitic practice made it possible to uninhibitedly act out all feelings and resentments that would otherwise be socially penalized.

The NS regime collectivized violence and allowed the *Volksgenossen* to participate in it. By the beginning of the war in 1939 or the attack against the Soviet Union in 1941, those HJ adolescents who participated in the actions against German Jews in 1935/36 might very well have been the young Wehrmacht soldiers whose violence against Polish, Russian, Ukrainian, and Latvian Jews we are still trying to explain. Even so, there is no inevitable path from the violent actions against Jews in the German provinces to the genocide against European Jews. To the contrary, the reports from local and regional organizations of the C.V. reveal the ambivalence of the violent situations, whose logic could be wholly shut down or interrupted by civic courage and intrepid intervention. Each violent action broke through boundaries. And insofar as that the breach of law went unpunished, these actions changed the order, making possible new and different options for action that had not been available before. Radicalization is not an inevitable, teleological process of causalities, but rather of opportunities that are taken or not taken.

In such a way actions change the conditions for future actions. Opportunities emerge that previously did not exist. The violent actions against the Jews did not create the *Volksgemeinschaft*, but this practice of violence anticipated the reality of the *Volksgemeinschaft*, even if it was spatially and temporally limited. Violence made a social condition concrete—indeed, made it something that could be physically experienced in that it suspended the old order and established a new political order of racist inequality. "For many," writes Alf Lüdtke, "who saw themselves excluded from the 'commanding heights' of society and state, the act of violence proved to be a 'liberating' form of politics. Actors and claqueurs took part in political rule in *their* way."[20] In violent actions, the Nationalist Socialist Volk realized itself as politically sovereign and produced for itself the order of a racist *Volksgemeinschaft* in which each member could participate and experience power: *Volksgemeinschaft* as self-empowerment.

Notes

1. Helmuth Plessner, *Grenzen der Gemeinschaft: Eine Kritik des sozialen Radikalismus (1924)* (Frankfurt am Main, 2002), 28.
2. Schmitt, *Concept of the Political*, 26.
3. Jan Philipp Reemtsma, "Die Natur der Gewalt als Problem der Soziologie," *Mittelweg 36* 15, no. 5 (2006): 14.

4. Fraenkel, *The Dual State*, 3.

5. Ibid.

6. Hitler, *Mein Kampf*, 104, 434.

7. Carl Schmitt, *Die geistesgeschichtliche Lage des heutigen Parlamentarismus* [1923] (Berlin, 1996), 13 (quotation translated by Bernard Heise).

8. Schmitt, *Der Begriff des Politischen*, 27, 20. I owe the reference to the significant reversal of the syllables from "gleichartig" to "artgleich" to Lutz Niethammer, *Kollektive Identität: Heimliche Quellen einer unheimlichen Konjunktur* (Reinbek, 2000), 101–105.

9. Schmitt, *Verfassungslehre*, 205 (quote translated by Bernard Heise).

10. Reichmann, *Deutscher Bürger und verfolgter Jude*, 67.

11. *Völkischer Beobachter*, 23 September 1928, quoted in Rüthers, *Die unbegrenzte Auslegung*, 105.

12. Quoted in Diethelm Klippel, "Subjektives Recht und germanisch-deutscher Rechtsgedanke in der Zeit des Nationalsozialismus," in *Die Deutsche Rechtsgeschichte in der NS-Zeit: Ihre Vorgeschichte und ihre Nachwirkungen*, ed. Joachim Rückert and Dietmar Willoweit (Tübingen, 1995), 42.

13. Quoted in Rüthers, *Die unbegrenzte Auslegung*, 124.

14. Schmitt, *Über die drei Arten des rechtswissenschaftlichen Denkens*, 13 (quotation translated by Bernard Heise).

15. Fraenkel, *The Dual State*, 140–141; see the foundational study by Stolleis, "Gemeinschaft und Volksgemeinschaft Zur juristischen Terminologie im Nationalsozialismus."

16 Fraenkel, *The Dual State*, 142.

17. Heinrich Popitz, *Phänomene der Macht*, exp. 2nd ed. (Tübingen, 1992), 25.

18. Ibid., 43.

19. Wolfgang Sofsky, *Traktat über die Gewalt* (Frankfurt am Main, 1996), 70.

20. Alf Lüdtke, "Thesen zur Wiederholbarkeit: 'Normalität' und Massenhaftigkeit von Tötungsgewalt im 20. Jahrhundert," in *Kulturen der Gewalt: Ritualisierung und Symbolisierung von Gewalt in der Geschichte*, ed. Rolf Peter Sieferle and Helga Breuninger (Frankfurt am Main, 1998), 280.

BIBLIOGRAPHY

Abbes, Otto. *Hersfelds jüdische Geschichte 1330 bis 1970*. Bad Hersfeld, 2002.

Adam, Uwe Dietrich. *Judenpolitik im Dritten Reich*. Düsseldorf, 1972.

Agamben, Giorgio. *Homo sacer: Die souveräne Macht und das nackte Leben*. Frankfurt am Main, 2002.

Ahlheim, Hannah. *"Deutsche, kauft nicht bei Juden!" Antisemitismus und politischer Boykott in Deutschland 1924 bis 1935*. Göttingen, 2011.

Albrecht, Richard. *Der militante Sozialdemokrat: Carlo Mierendorff 1897–1943*. Berlin, 1987.

Anderl, Gabriele. "Die 'Zentralstellen für jüdische Auswanderung' in Wien, Berlin und Prag – ein Vergleich." *Tel Aviver Jahrbuch für deutsche Geschichte* 23 (1994): 275–299.

Andreas-Friedrich, Ruth. *Der Schattenmann: Tagebuchaufzeichnungen 1938–1945*. Frankfurt am Main, 1983.

Angress, Werner T. and Bradley F. Smith. "Diaries of Heinrich Himmler's Early Years." *Journal of Modern History* 31 (1959): 206–224.

Anschütz, Gerhard. *Die Verfassung des Deutschen Reiches vom 11. August 1919: Ein Kommentar für Wissenschaft und Praxis*. 3rd ed. 12th printing. Berlin, 1930.

Arendt, Hannah. *On Violence*. New York, 1970.

———. "Organisierte Schuld." In Hannah Arendt, *Die verborgene Tradition: Acht Essays*, 32–45. Frankfurt am Main, 1976.

———. "Was heißt persönliche Verantwortung unter einer Diktatur?" In Hannah Arendt, *Nach Auschwitz: Essays & Kommentare 1*, 81–97. Berlin, 1989.

Arnsberg, Paul. *Die jüdischen Gemeinden in Hessen: Anfang, Untergang, Neubeginn*. 2 vols. Frankfurt am Main, 1971.

Aschheim, Steven E. *Brothers and Strangers: The East European Jews in German and German Jewish Consciousness, 1800/1923*. Madison, WI, 1999.

Asmus, Burkhard. *Republik ohne Chance? Akzeptanz und Legitimation der Weimarer Republik in der deutschen Tagespresse zwischen 1918 und 1923.* Berlin, 1994.

Auerbach, Hellmuth. "Volksstimmung und veröffentlichte Meinung in Deutschland zwischen März und November 1938." In *Machtbewußtsein in Deutschland am Vorabend des Zweiten Weltkrieges,* ed. Franz Knipping and Klaus-Jürgen Müller, 274–293. Paderborn, 1984.

Ayaß, Wolfgang. *"Asoziale" im Nationalsozialismus.* Stuttgart, 1995.

———, ed. *"Gemeinschaftsfremde": Quellen zur Verfolgung von "Asozialen" 1933–1945.* Coblenz, 1998.

Bader-Weiß, Grete and Karl Siegfried Bader. *Der Pranger: Ein Strafwerkzeug und Rechtswahrzeichen des Mittelalters.* Freiburg i. Br., 1935.

Bajohr, Frank. *"Arisierung" in Hamburg: Die Verdrängung der jüdischen Unternehmer 1933–1945.* Hamburg, 1997.

———. *Parvenüs und Profiteure: Korruption in der NS-Zeit.* Frankfurt am Main, 2001.

———. "The 'Folk Community' and the Persecution of the Jews: German Society under National Socialist Dictatorship, 1933–1945." *Holocaust and Genocide Studies* 20 (2006): 83–206.

———. *"Unser Hotel ist judenfrei": Bäder-Antisemitismus im 19. und 20. Jahrhundert.* Frankfurt am Main, 2003.

Bajohr, Frank and Michael Wildt, eds. *Volksgemeinschaft: Neue Forschungen zur Gesellschaft des Nationalsozialismus.* Frankfurt am Main, 2009.

Balistier, Thomas. *Gewalt und Ordnung: Kalkül und Faszination der SA.* Münster, 1989.

Ball-Kaduri, Kurt Jakob. *Vor der Katastrophe: Juden in Deutschland 1934—1939.* Tel Aviv, 1967.

Bankier, David. *The Germans and the Final Solution: Public Opinion under Nazism.* Oxford, 1992.

Barkai, Avraham. "The C.V. Archives in Moscow: A Reassessment." *Leo Baeck Institute Yearbook* 45 (2000): 173–182.

———. "The German Volksgemeinschaft from the Persecution of the Jews to the 'Final Solution.'" In *Confronting the Nazi Past: New Debates on Modern German History,* ed. Michael Burleigh, 84–97. London, 1996.

———. *Vom Boykott zur "Entjudung": Der wirtschaftliche Existenzkampf der Juden im Dritten Reich, 1933–1943.* Frankfurt am Main, 1988.

———. *"Wehr Dich!" Der Centralverein deutscher-Staatsbürger jüdischen Glaubens 1893–1938.* Munich, 2002.

Barkai, Avraham and Paul Mendes-Flohr. *Aufbruch und Zerstörung 1918–1945.* Vol. 4, *Deutsch-Jüdische Geschichte der Neuzeit.* Munich, 1997.

Baumann, Ulrich. *Zerstörte Nachbarschaften: Christen und Juden in badischen Landgemeinden 1862–1940.* Hamburg, 2000.

Beck, Dorothea. *Julius Leber: Sozialdemokrat zwischen Reform und Widerstand.* Berlin, 1983.

Beer, Udo. *Die Juden, das Recht und die Republik: Verbandswesen und Rechtsschutz 1919–1933.* Frankfurt am Main, 1986.

Behmer, Markus. *Von der Schwierigkeit, gegen Illusionen zu kämpfen: Der Publizist Leopold Schwarzschild – Leben und Werk vom Kaiserreich bis zur Flucht aus Europa.* Münster, 1997.

Behnken, Klaus, ed. *Deutschlandberichte der Sozialdemokratischen Partei Deutschland (Sopade) 1934 bis 1940.* Reprint. Frankfurt am Main, 1980.

Benz, Wolfgang. "Der Novemberpogrom 1938." In *Die Juden in Deutschland 1933–1945: Leben unter nationalsozialistischer Herrschaft*, ed. Wolfgang Benz, 499–544. Munich, 1988.

———. "Prolog. Der 30. Januar 1933." In *Die Juden in Deutschland 1933–1945: Leben unter nationalsozialistischer Herrschaft*, ed. Wolfgang Benz, 15–33. Munich, 1988.

———. "Rückfall in die Barbarei: Bericht über den Pogrom." In *Von der 'Reichskristallnacht' zum Völkermord*, ed. Walter H. Pehle, 13–51. Frankfurt am Main, 1988.

Benz, Wolfgang and Barbara Distel, eds. *Terror ohne System: Die ersten Konzentrationslager im Nationalsozialismus 1933–1935*. Vol. 1, *Geschichte der Konzentrationslager, 1933–1945*. Berlin, 2001.

Bergmann, Werner. "Pogrome." In *Internationales Handbuch der Gewaltforschung*, ed. Wilhelm Heitmeyer and John Hagan, 441–460. Wiesbaden, 2002.

Bergmann, Werner and Juliane Wetzel. "'Der Miterlebende weiß nichts': Alltagsantisemitismus als zeitgenössische Erfahrung und spätere Erinnerung (1919–1933)." In *Jüdisches Leben in der Weimarer Republik/Jews in the Weimar Republic*, ed. Wolfgang Benz, Arnold Paucker, and Peter Pulzer, 173–196. Tübingen, 1998.

Berichte und Protokolle des Achten Ausschusses über den Entwurf einer Verfassung des Deutschen Volkes. No. 21 of *Berichte der verfassunggebenden Deutschen Nationalversammlung 1919*. Berlin, 1920.

Bessel, Richard. *Political Violence and the Rise of Nazism: The Storm Troopers in Eastern Germany 1925–1934*. London, 1984.

Bielefeld, Ulrich. *Nation und Gesellschaft: Selbstthematisierungen in Deutschland und Frankreich*. Hamburg, 2003.

Böckenförde, Ernst-Wolfgang. "Der Zusammenbruch der Monarchie und die Entstehung der Weimarer Republik." In Ernst-Wolfgang Böckenförde, *Recht, Staat, Freiheit: Studien zur Rechtsphilosophie, Staatstheorie und Verfassungsgeschichte*, 306–343. Frankfurt am Main, 1991.

Bohrmann, Hans and Gabriele Toepser-Zeigert, eds. *NS-Presseanweisungen der Vorkriegszeit: Edition und Dokumentation*. Munich, 1999.

Borut, Jacob. "'Bin Ich doch ein Israelit, ehre Ich auch den Bischof mit': Village and Small-Town Jews within the Social Spheres in Western Germany Communities during the Weimar Republic." In *Jüdisches Leben in der Weimarer Republik/Jews in the Weimar Republic*, ed. Wolfgang Benz, Arnold Paucker, and Peter Pulzer, 117–133. Tübingen, 1998.

———. "Gewalttätiger Antisemitismus im Rheinland und in Westfalen in der Zeit der Weimarer Republik." *Geschichte im Westen* 22 (2007): 9–40.

Bourdieu, Pierre. *Entwurf einer Theorie der Praxis auf der ethnologischen Grundlage der kabylischen Gesellschaft*. Frankfurt am Main, 1979.

Bracher, Karl Dietrich, Wolfgang Sauer, and Gerhard Schulz. *Die nationalsozialistischen Machtergreifung: Studien zur Errichtung des totalitären Herrschaftssystems in Deutschland 1933/34*. 2nd ed. Cologne, 1962.

Brakelmann, Günter. "Hoffnungen und Illusionen evangelischer Prediger zu Beginn des 'Dritten Reiches': gottesdienstliche Feiern aus politischen Anlässen." In *Die Reihen fast geschlossen: Beiträge zur Geschichte des Alltags unterm Nationalsozialismus*, ed. Detlev Peukert and Jürgen Reulecke, 129–148. Wuppertal, 1981.

Brechtken, Magnus. *"Madagaskar für die Juden": Antisemitische Idee und politische Praxis 1885–1945*. Munich, 1997.

Brenner, Michael. *Jüdische Kultur in der Weimarer Republik*. Munich, 2000.

Breuer, Stefan. *Nationalismus und Faschismus: Frankreich, Italien und Deutschland im Vergleich*. Darmstadt, 2005.

———. *Ordnungen der Ungleichheit – die deutsche Rechte im Widerstreit ihrer Ideen 1871–1945*. Darmstadt, 2001.

Brocke, Michael, Margret Heitmann, and Harald Lordick, eds. *Zur Geschichte und Kultur der Juden in Ost- und Westpreußen*. Hildesheim, 2000.

Broszat, Martin. *Der Staat Hitlers: Grundlegung und Entwicklung seiner inneren Verfassung*. Munich, 1969.

Broszat, Martin, Elke Fröhlich, and Falk Wiesemann, eds. *Bayern in der NS-Zeit: Soziale Lage und politisches Verhalten der Bevölkerung im Spiegel vertraulicher Berichte*, vol. 1. Munich, 1977.

Browning, Christopher. *Ordinary Men: Reserve Police Battalion 101 and the Final Solution in Poland*. New York, 1992.

Bruendel, Steffen. *Volksgemeinschaft oder Volksstaat: Die "Ideen von 1914" und die Neuordnung Deutschlands im Ersten Weltkrieg*. Berlin, 2003.

Bruns, Claudia. "Ricarda Huch und die Konservative Revolution." *WerkstattGeschichte* 25 (2000): 5–33.

Brustein, William I. *Roots of Hate: Anti-Semitism in Europe before the Holocaust*. Cambridge, 2003.

Buchloh, Ingrid. *Die nationalsozialistischen Machtergreifung in Duisburg: Eine Fallstudie*. Duisburg, 1980.

Buddrus, Michael. *Totale Erziehung für den totalen Staat: Hitlerjugend und nationalsozialistischen Jugendpolitik*, 2 vols. Munich, 2003.

Burkhart, Dagmar. *Eine Geschichte der Ehre*. Darmstadt, 2006.

Burrin, Philippe. "Faschismus und Antisemitismus in Frankreich." In *Vorurteil und Rassenhaß: Antisemitismus in den faschistischen Bewegungen Europas*, ed. Hermann Graml, Angelika Königseder, and Juliane Wetzel, 119–129. Berlin, 2001.

Bußmann, Walter. "Zur Entstehung und Überlieferung der 'Hoßbach'-Niederschrift." *Vierteljahrshefte für Zeitgeschichte* 16 (1968): 373–384.

Buttaroni, Susanna and Stanislaw Musial, eds. *Ritualmordlegenden in der europäischen Geschichte*. Vienna, 2002.

Büttner, Ursula, ed. *Die Deutschen und die Judenverfolgung im Dritten Reich*. Frankfurt am Main, 2003.

Cesarani, David. *Eichmann: His Life and Crimes*. London, 2004.

Chamberlain, Houston Stewart. *Die Grundlagen des 19. Jahrhunderts*. 26th printing (unabridged *Volksausgabe*). Munich, 1940.

Chickering, Robert. *Imperial Germany and the Great War, 1914–1918*. Cambridge, 1998.

Claudi, Marianne and Reinhard Claudi. *Goldene und andere Zeiten: Emden – Stadt in Ostfriesland*. Emden, 1982.

———, eds. *Die wir verloren haben: Lebensgeschichten Emder Juden*. Aurich, 1988.

Cohn, Willy. *Verwehte Spuren: Erinnerungen an das Breslauer Judentum vor seinem Untergang*, ed. Norbert Cohns. Cologne, 1995.

Comité des Delegations Juives, ed. *Das Schwarzbuch: Tatsachen und Dokumente: Die Lage der Juden in Deutschland 1933*. Paris, 1934.

Cymet, David. "Polish State Antisemitism as a Major Factor Leading to the Holocaust." *Journal of Genocide Research* 1, no. 2 (1999): 169–212.

Das Ende der Juden in Ostfriesland: Ausstellung der Ostfriesischen Landschaft aus Anlaß des 50. Jahrestages der Kristallnacht. Aurich, 1988.

Davis, Belinda. *Home Fires Burning: Food, Politics, and Everyday Life in World War I Berlin*. London, 2000.

Davis, Natalie Zemon. "The Reasons of Misrule." In N. Davis, *Society and Culture in Early Modern France: Eight Essays by Natalie Zemon Davis*. Stanford, CA, 2003.

Diewald-Kenkmann, Gisela. *Politische Denunziationen im NS-Regime – oder die kleine Macht der "Volksgenossen."* Bonn, 1995.

Dinges, Martin. "Die Ehre als Thema der historischen Anthropologie: Bemerkungen zur Wissenschaftsgeschichte und zur Konzeptualisierung." In *Verletzte Ehre: Ehrkonflikte in Gesellschaften des Mittelalters und der Frühen Neuzeit*, ed. Klaus Schreiner and Gerd Schwerhoff, 29–62. Cologne, 1995.

Dippel, John V. H. *Die große Illusion: Warum deutsche Juden ihre Heimat nicht verlassen wollten*. Berlin, 1997.

Dörner, Bernward. *"Heimtücke": Das Gesetz als Waffe: Kontrolle, Abschreckung und Verfolgung in Deutschland 1933–1945*. Paderborn, 1998.

Dülmen, Richard van. *Theater des Schreckens: Gerichtspraxis und Strafrituale in der frühen Neuzeit*. Munich, 1985.

Ebert, Friedrich. *Schriften, Aufzeichnungen, Reden*. 2 vols. Dresden, 1926.

Eiber, Ludwig. *Arbeiter unter der NS-Herrschaft: Textil- und Porzellanarbeiter im nordöstlichen Oberfranken 1933–1939*. Munich, 1979.

Erler, Adalbert et al., eds. *Handwörterbuch zur deutschen Rechtsgeschichte*. Berlin, 1971–1998.

Eschenhagen, Wieland. *Die "Machtergreifung": Tagebuch einer Wende nach Presseberichten vom 1. Januar bis 6. März 1933*. Darmstadt and Neuwied, 1982.

Essner, Cornelia. *Die "Nürnberger Gesetze" oder Die Verwaltung des Rassenwahns 1933–1945*. Paderborn, 2002.

———. "Zwischen Vernunft und Gefühl: Die Reichstagsdebatte von 1912 um koloniale 'Rassenmischehe' und 'Sexualität.'" *Zeitschrift für Geschichtswissenschaft* 45 (1997): 503–519.

Ettenhuber, Helga. "Charivari in Bayern: Das Miesbacher Haberfeldtreiben von 1893." In *Kultur der einfachen Leute: Bayerisches Volksleben vom 16. bis zum 19. Jahrhundert*, ed. Richard van Dülmen, 180–207. Munich, 1983.

Fest, Joachim. "Franz von Papen und die Konservative Kollaboration." In Joachim Fest, *Das Gesicht des Dritten Reiches: Profile einer totalitären Herrschaft*, 209–224. Munich, 1993.

Fischer, Albert. *Hjalmar Schacht und Deutschlands "Judenfrage": Der "Wirtschaftsdiktator" und die Vertreibung der Juden aus der deutschen Wirtschaft*. Cologne, 1995.

Fischer, Conan. *Stormtroopers: A Social, Economic, and Ideological Analysis, 1929–1935*. London, 1983.

Fitzpatrick, Sheila and Robert Gellately, eds. *Accusatory Practices: Denunciation in Modern European History, 1789–1989*. Chicago and London, 1997.

Fitzpatrick, Sheila and Alf Lüdtke. "Energizing the Everyday. On the Breaking and Making of Social Bonds in Nazism and Stalinism." In *Beyond Totalitarianism. Stalinism and Nazism Compared*, ed. Michael Geyer and Sheila Fitzpatrick, 231-265. Cambridge and New York, 2009.

Flade, Roland. *Juden in Würzburg 1918–1933*. Würzburg, 1985.

Flasch, Kurt. *Die geistige Mobilmachung: Die deutschen Intellektuellen und der Erste Weltkrieg: Ein Versuch*. Berlin, 2000.

Föllmer, Moritz. "The Problem of National Solidarity in Interwar Germany." *German History* 23, no. 2 (2005): 202–231.

Forster, Hans and Günther Schwickert. *Norden: Eine Kreisstadt unterm Hakenkreuz*. Norden, 1988.

Fraenkel, Ernst. "Die representative und plebiszitäre Komponente im demokratischen Verfassungsstaat." In *Deutschland und die westlichen Demokratien*, ed. Alexander v. Brünneck, 153–203. Frankfurt am Main, 1991.

———. *The Dual State: A Contribution to the Theory of Dictatorship*. New York, 1941.

François-Poncet, André. *Als Botschafter in Berlin 1931–1938*. Mainz, 1949.

Frank, Hans, ed. *Nationalsozialistisches Handbuch für Recht und Gesetzgebung*. Munich, 1935.

Frankiewicz, Bogdan. "Das Schicksal der Juden in Pommern nach 1933." In *Der faschistische Pogrom vom 9./19. November 1938 – Zur Geschichte der Juden in Pommern. Kolloqium der Sektionen Geschichtswissenschaft und Theologie der Ernst-Moritz-Arndt-Universität Greifswald am 2. November 1938*, no editor, 41–52. Greifswald, 1989.

Frankiewicz, Bogdan and Wolfgang Wilhelmus. "Selbstachtung wahren und Solidarität üben: Pommerns Juden während des Nationalsozialismus." In *"Halte fern dem ganzen Lande jedes Verderben": Geschichte und Kultur der Juden in Pommern*, ed. Margret Heitmann, Julius H. Schoeps, and Bernhard Vogt, 453–471. Hildesheim, 1995.

Frei, Norbert. "'Volksgemeinschaft': Erfahrungsgeschichte und Lebenswirklichkeit der Hitler-Zeit." In Norbert Frei, *1945 und wir: Das Dritte Reich im Bewußtsein der Deutschen*, 107–108. Munich, 2005.

Freud, Sigmund. "Zeitgemäßes über Krieg und Tod." In *Studienausgabe*, vol. 9, 33–60. Frankfurt am Main, 1982.

Frevert, Ute. "Ehre – männlich/weiblich: Zu einem Identitätsbegriff des 19. Jahrhunderts." *Tel Aviver Jahrbuch für deutsche Geschichte* 21 (1992): 21–68.

Freytagh-Loringhoven, Axel Freiherr von. *Die Weimarer Verfassung in Lehre und Wirklichkeit*. Munich, 1924.

Friedländer, Saul. *Nazi Germany and the Jews*. Vol. 1, *The Years of Persecution, 1933–1939*. London, 1997.

———. *Nazi Germany and the Jews*. Vol. 2, *The Years of Extermination, 1939–1945*. New York, 2007.

Fries, Helmut. *Die große Kartharsis: Der Erste Weltkrieg in der Sicht deutscher Dichter und Gelehrter*. 2 vols. Constance, 1995.

Fritzsche, Peter. *Wie aus Deutschen Nazis wurden*. Munich, 1999.

Gasten, Elmar. *Aachen in der Zeit der nationalsozialistischen Herrschaft 1933–1944*. Frankfurt am Main, 1993.

Geiger, Theodor. "Die Panik im Mittelstand." *Die Arbeit* 7 (1930): 637–654.

Geisthövel, Alexa. "Augusta-Erlebnisse: Repräsentationen der preußischen Königin 1870." In *Neue Politikgeschichte: Perspektiven einerhistorischen Politikforschung*, ed. Ute Frevert and Heinz-Gerhard Haupt, 82–114. Frankfurt am Main, 2005.

Gellately, Robert. *Die Gestapo und die deutsche Gesellschaft: die Durchsetzung der Rassenpolitik 1933–1945*. Paderborn, 1993.

———. *Hingeschaut und Weggesehen: Hitler und sein Volk*. Stuttgart, 2002.

Gelnhäuser Historischen Gesellschaft e.V., ed. *Zur Geschichte der Juden in Gelnhausen während der nationalsozialistischen Vergangenheit: Ein Stadtrundgang*. Gelnhausen, 1996.

Genschel, Helmut. *Die Verdrängung der Juden aus der Wirtschaft im Dritten Reich*. Göttingen, 1966.

Genz, Peter. "170 Jahre jüdische Gemeinde in Stralsund – ein Überblick." In *"Halte fern dem ganzen Lande jedes Verderben ..." Geschichte und Kultur der Juden in Pommern*, ed. Margret Heitmann, Julius H. Schoeps, and Bernhard Vogt, 119–144. Hildesheim, 1995.

Gerstenberger, Heide and Dorothea Schmidt, eds. *Normalität oder Normalisierung? Geschichtswerkstätten und Faschismusanalyse*. Münster, 1987.

Geyer, Martin H. *Verkehrte Welt: Revolution, Inflation und Moderne, München 1914–1924*. Göttingen, 1998.

Gillessen, Günther. *Hugo Preuß, Studien zur Ideen- und Verfassungsgeschichte der Weimarer Republik*. Berlin, 2000.

Gödeken, Lina. *Rund um die Synagoge in Norden: Die Geschichte der Synagogengemeinde seit 1866*. Aurich, 2000.

Goebbels, Joseph. *Die Tagebücher von Joseph Goebbels, im Auftrag des Instituts für Zeitgeschichte und mit Unterstützung des Staatlichen Archivdienstes Rußlands, Teil I: Aufzeichnungen 1923–1941*. Edited by Elke Fröhlich. Munich, 2000-2008

Goebbels, Joseph, *Joseph Goebbels Tagebücher 1924–1945*. Edited by Ralf Georg Reuth. Munich, 1992.

Golczewski, Frank. *Polnisch-jüdische Beziehungen 1881–1922: Eine Studie zur Geschichte des Antisemitismus in Osteuropa*. Wiesbaden, 1981.

Goldhagen, Daniel Jonah. *Hitler's Willing Executioners: Ordinary Germans and the Holocaust*. New York, 1996.

Gordon, Sarah. *Hitler, Germans, and the "Jewish Question."* Princeton, 1984.

Görlich, Paul. *Wolfhagen: Geschichte einer nordhessischen Stadt*. Wolfhagen, 1980.

Götz, Norbert. *Ungleiche Geschwister: Die Konstruktion von nationalsozialistischer Volksgemeinschaft und schwedischem Volksheim*. Baden-Baden, 2001.

Graml, Hermann. *Reichskristallnacht: Antisemitismus und Judenverfolgung im Dritten Reich*. Munich, 1988.

———. "Zur Debatte über den Reichstagsbrand." In *Der Reichstagsbrand und der Prozess vor dem Reichsgericht*, ed. Dieter Dieseroth, 27–34. Berlin, 2006.

Graml, Hermann, Angelika Königseder, and Juliane Wetzel, eds. *Vorurteil und Rassenhaß: Antisemitismus in den faschistischen Bewegungen Europas*. Berlin, 2001.

Grill, Johnpeter Horst. "The Nazi Party's Rural Propaganda Before 1928." *Central European History* 15 (1982): 149–185.

Grimm, Dieter. "Das staatliche Gewaltmonopol." In *Herausforderungen des staatlichen Gewaltmonopols: Recht und politisch motivierte Gewalt am Ende des 20. Jahrhunderts*, ed. Freia Anders and Ingrid Gilcher-Holtey, 18–38. Frankfurt am Main, 2006.

Groebner, Valentin. *Ungestalten: Die visuelle Kultur der Gewalt im Mittelalter*. Munich, 2003.

Gruner, Wolf. *Der Geschlossene Arbeitseinsatz deutscher Juden: Zur Zwangsarbeit als Element der Verfolgung 1938–1943*. Berlin, 1997.

———. "'Lesen brauchen sie nicht zu können …' Die 'Denkschrift über die Behandlung der Juden in der Reichshauptstadt auf allen Gebieten des öffentlichen Lebens' vom Mai 1938." *Jahrbuch für Antisemitismusforschung* 4 (1995): 305–341.

———. *Öffentliche Wohlfahrt und Judenverfolgung: Wechselwirkungen lokaler und zentraler Politik im NS-Staat (1933–1942)*. Munich, 2002.

Gusy, Christoph. *Die Weimarer Reichsverfassung*. Tübingen, 1997.

———. "Verfassungsumbruch und Staatsrechtswissenschaft: Die Verfassung des Politischen zwischen Konstitutionalismus und demokratischer Republik." In *Neue Politikgeschichte: Perspektiven einer historischen Politikforschung*, ed. Ute Frevert and Heinz-Gerhard Haupt, 166–201. Frankfurt am Main, 2005.

Gutleben, Burkhard. "Volksgemeinschaft oder zweite Republik? Die Reaktionen des deutschen Linksliberalismus auf die Krise der 30er Jahre." *Tel Aviver Jahrbuch für deutsche Geschichte* 17 (1988): 259–284.

Gutman, Yisrael, Ezra Mendelsohn, Jehuda Reinharz, and Chone Shmeruk, eds. *The Jews of Poland between Two World Wars*. London, 1989.

Guttmann, Barbara. *Weibliche Heimarmee: Frauen in Deutschland 1914–1918*. Weinheim, 1989.

Haas, Joachim. *Abseits der "großen" Geschichte: Opposition und Widerstand gegen den Nationalsozialismus im Raum Fulda: Versuch einer Spurensicherung*. Oberursel, 1989.

Haffner, Sebastian. *Geschichte eines Deutschen: Die Erinnerungen 1914–1933*. Stuttgart, 2000.

———. *Von Bismarck zu Hitler: Ein Rückblick*. Munich, 1987.

Hagen, William W. "Before the 'Final Solution': Toward a Comparative Analysis of Political Anti-Semitism in Interwar Germany and Poland." *Journal of Modern History* 68, no. 2 (1996): 351–382.

———. "The Moral Economy of Ethnic Violence: The Progrom in Lwów, November 1918." *Geschichte und Gesellschaft* 31 (2005): 203–226.

Hamann, Brigitte. *Winifred Wagner oder Hitlers Bayreuth*. Munich, 2002.

Händler-Lachmann, Barbara, Harald Händler and Ulrich Schütt. *Purim, Purim, ihr liebe Leut, wißt ihr was Purim bedeut? Jüdisches Leben im Landkreis Marburg im 20. Jahrhundert*. Marburg, 1995.

Hartenstein, Wolfgang. *Die Anfänge der Deutschen Volkspartei 1918–1920*. Düsseldorf, 1962.

Hartinger, Walter. "Rechtspflege und Volksleben: Zur Funktion des Rechts im absolutistischen Bayern." In *Das Recht der kleinen Leute: Beiträge zur Rechtlichen Volkskunde: Festschrift für Karl-Sigismund Kramer zum 60. Geburtstag*, ed. Konrad Köstlin und Kai Detlev Sievers, 50–68. Berlin, 1976.

"Hauptdaten zur Geschichte der israelitischen Kultusgemeinde." In *Festschrift Ehemalige Synagoge Gelnhausen*, compiled by the Geschichtsverein Gelnhausen, 108. Gelnhausen, 1986.

Hauschildt, Dieter. "Vom Judenboykott zum Judenmord. Der 1. April 1933 in Kiel." In *"Wir bauen das Reich": Aufstieg und erste Herrschaftsjahre des Nationalsozialismus in Schleswig-Holstein*, ed. Erich Hoffmann and Peter Wulf, 335–360. Neumünster, 1981.

Hecht, Cornelia. *Deutsche Juden und Antisemitismus in der Weimarer Republik*. Bonn, 2003.

Heid, Ludger. "'Er ist ein Rätsel geblieben': Oskar Cohn – Politiker, Parlamentarier, Poale-Zionist." In *Jüdisches Leben in der Weimarer Republik/Jews in the Weimar Republic*, ed. Wolfgang Benz, Arnold Paucker, and Peter Pulzer, 25–48. Tübingen, 1998.

Heim, Susanne. "'Deutschland muß ihnen ein Land ohne Zukunft sein': Die Zwangsemigration der Juden 1933–1938." In *Arbeitsmigration und Flucht*. Vol. 11, *Beiträge zur nationalsozialistischen Gesundheits- und Sozialpolitik*, 48–81. Berlin, 1993.

Heim, Susanne and Götz Aly. "Staatliche Ordnung und 'organische Lösung': Die Rede Hermann Görings 'Über die Judenfrage' vom 6. Dezember 1938." *Jahrbuch für Antisemitismusforschung* 2 (1992): 378–404.

Heller, Hermann. "Sozialismus und Nation (1925)." In Hermann Heller, *Gesammelte Schriften*, vol. 1, 437–526. Leiden, 1971.

Hentig, Hans von. *Die Strafe: Vol. I: Frühformen und kulturgeschichtliche Zusammenhänge*. Berlin, 1954.

Herbst, Ludolf. *Das nationalsozialistischen Deutschland 1933–1945: Die Entfesselung der Gewalt: Rassismus und Krieg*. Frankfurt am Main, 1996.

Herzl, Theodor. *Der Judenstaat: Versuch einer modernen Lösung der Judenfrage: Text und Materialien 1896 bis heute*. Edited with an afterword by Ernst Piper. Berlin, 2004.

Heß, Jürgen C. *"Das ganze Deutschland soll es sein": Demokratischer Nationalismus in der Weimarer Republik am Beispiel der Deutschen Demokratischen Partei.* Stuttgart, 1978.

Hesse, Klaus and Philipp Springer. *Vor aller Augen: Fotodokumente des nationalsozialistischen Terrors in der Provinz.* Essen, 2002.

Hettling, Manfred, Andreas Reinke, and Norbert Conrads, eds. *In Breslau zu Hause? Juden in einer mitteleuropäischen Metropole der Neuzeit.* Hamburg, 2003.

Hilberg, Raul. *Die Vernichtung der europäischen Juden.* Extended paperback ed. Frankfurt am Main, 1990.

Hilberg, Raul. *Perpetrators, Victims, Bystanders: The Jewish Catastrophe 1933–1945.* New York, 1992.

Hilberg, Raul. *Unerbetene Erinnerung.* Frankfurt am Main, 2008.

Hill, Leonidas E. and Walter Gyssling. "The Centralverein and the Büro Wilhelmstrasse, 1929–1933." *Leo Baeck Institute Yearbook* 38 (1993): 193–208.

Hitler, Adolf. *"Es spricht der Führer": 7 exemplarische Hitler-Reden.* Edited with commentary by Hildegard von Kotze and Helmut Krausnick, with collaboration from F. A. Krummacher. Gütersloh, 1966.

———. *Hitler: Reden und Proklamationen 1932–1945, Part I: Triumph, Vol. 1: 1932–1934, Vol. 2: 1935–1938.* Edited by Max Domarus. Leonberg, 1988.

———. *Mein Kampf.* 349th–351st printing. Munich, 1938.

———. *Sämtliche Aufzeichnungen 1905–1924.* Edited by Eberhard Jäckel and Axel Kuhn. Stuttgart, 1980.

Hoffmann, Christhard. "Politische Kultur und Gewalt gegen Minderheiten: Die antisemitischen Ausschreitungen in Pommern und Westpreußen 1881." *Jahrbuch für Antisemitismusforschung* 3 (1994): 93–120.

———. "Verfolgung und Alltagsleben der Landjuden im nationalsozialistischen Deutschland." In *Jüdisches Leben auf dem Lande: Studien zur deutsch-jüdischen Geschichte,* ed. Monika Richard and Reinhard Rürup, 373–398. Tübingen, 1997.

Hoffmann, Erik. *Jüdische Nachbarn in Hessisch Oldendorf.* Hameln, 1998.

Holz, Klaus. *Nationaler Antisemitismus: Wissenssoziologie einer Weltanschauung.* Hamburg, 2001.

Horne, John and Alan Kramer, *German atrocities, 1914: a history of denial.* New Haven, 2001.

Huber, Ernst Rudolf, ed. *Dokumente zur deutschen Verfassungsgeschichte: Vol. 4: Deutsche Verfassungsdokumente 1919–1933.* 3rd ed. Stuttgart, 1991.

Hüppauf, Bernd, ed. *Ansichten vom Krieg: Vergleichende Studien zum Ersten Weltkrieg in Literatur und Gesellschaft.* Königstein, 1984.

IMG (Internationaler Militärgerichtshof). *Der Prozeß gegen die Hauptkriegsverbrecher in Nürnberg 14.11.1945–1.10.1946.* 42 vols. Nuremberg, 1948.

Institut für Zeitgeschichte, ed. *Akten der Partei-Kanzlei der NSDAP: Rekonstruktion eines verlorengegangenen Bestandes,* Part I. Munich, 1983.

Jäckel, Eberhard and Jürgen Rohwer, eds. *Der Mord an den Juden im Zweiten Weltkrieg.* Stuttgart, 1985.

Jamin, Mathilde. *Zwischen den Klassen: Zur Sozialstruktur des SA Führerschaft.* Wuppertal, 1984.

Jansen, Hans. *Der Madagaskar-Plan: Die beabsichtigte Deportation der europäischen Juden nach Madagaskar.* Munich, 1997.

Jarausch, Konrad and Larry E. Jones, eds. *In Search of a Liberal Germany: Studies in the History of German Liberalism from 1789 to the Present.* New York, 1990.

Jaschke, Hans-Gerd and Martin Loiperdinger. "Gewalt und NSDAP vor 1933: Ästhetische Okkupation und physischer Terror." In *Faszination der Gewalt: Politische Strategie und Alltagserfahrung*, ed. Rainer Steinweg, 123–155. Frankfurt am Main, 1983.

Jegelka, Norbert. "'Volksgemeinschaft': Begriffskonturen in 'Führer' ideologie, Recht und Erziehung (1933–1945)." In *Das Volk: Abbild, Konstruktion, Phantasma*, ed. Annette Graczyk, 115–128. Berlin, 1997.

Jens, Inge. *Dichter zwischen rechts und links: die Geschichte der Sektion Dichtkunst an der Preußischen Akademie der Künste*. 2nd ed.. Leipzig, 1994.

Jochmann, Werner. "Die Ausbreitung des Antisemitismus in Deutschland 1914–1923." In Werner Jochmann, *Gesellschaftskrise und Judenfeindschaft in Deutschland 1870–1945*, 99–170. Hamburg, 1988.

———. "Die deutsche Bevölkerung und die nationalsozialistischen Judenpolitik bis zur Verkündung der Nürnberger Gesetze." In Werner Jochmann, *Gesellschaftskrise und Judenfeindschaft in Deutschland 1870–1945*, 236–354. Hamburg, 1988.

———. *Gesellschaftskrise und Judenfeindschaft in Deutschland 1870–1945*. Hamburg, 1988.

———. *Nationalsozialismus und Revolution: Ursprung und Geschichte der NSDAP in Hamburg 1922–1933: Dokumente*. Frankfurt am Main, 1963.

Junker, Detlef. *Die Deutsche Zentrumspartei und Hitler 1932/33: Ein Beitrag zur Problematik des politischen Katholizismus in Deutschland*. Stuttgart, 1969.

Kaiser, Elfriede. "Handel und Gewerbe bei den Gelnhäuser Juden." In *Festschrift Ehemalige Synagoge Gelnhausen*, edited by Magistrat der Barbarossastadt Gelnhausen and compiled by the Geschichtsverein Gelnhausen, 67–74. Gelnhausen, 1986.

Kammler, Jörg et. al. *Volksgemeinschaft und Volksfeinde: Kassel 1935–1945: Eine Dokumentation*. Fuldabrück, 1984.

Kaplan, Marion. *Between Dignity and Despair: Jewish Life in Nazi Germany*. New York, 1998.

Kater, Michael H. *Studentenschaft und Rechtsradikalismus in Deutschland 1918–1933: Eine sozialgeschichtliche Studie zur Bildungskrise in der Weimarer Republik*. Hamburg, 1975.

Kaufman, Menahem. "The Daily Life of the Village and Country Jews in Hessen from Hitler's Ascent to Power to November 1938." *Yad Vashem Studies* 22 (1992): 147–198.

Kershaw, Ian. "Antisemitismus und die NS-Bewegung vor 1933." In *Vorurteil und Rassenhaß: Antisemitismus in den faschistischenBewegungen Europas*, ed. Hermann Graml, Angelika Königseder, and Juliane Wetzel, 29–47. Berlin, 2001.

———. *Der Hitler-Mythos: Führerkult und Volksmeinung*. Stuttgart, 1999.

———. *Hitler*. 2 vols. Stuttgart, 1998–2000.

———. "The Persecution of the Jews and German Popular Opinion in the Third Reich." *Leo Baeck Institute Yearbook* 26 (1981): 261–289.

Klein, Thomas, ed. *Der Regierungsbezirk Kassel 1933–1936: Die Berichte des Regierungspräsidenten und der Landräte*. Darmstadt, 1985.

———, ed. *Die Lageberichte der Geheimen Staatspolizei über die Provinz Hessen-Nassau 1933–1936*. Cologne, 1986.

Klemperer, Victor. *Curriculum Vitae: Erinnerungen 1881–1918*. Berlin, 1996.

———. *Ich will Zeugnis ablegen bis zum letzten: Tagebücher 1933–1945*. Vol 1. Edited by Walter Nowojski with collaboration by Hadwig Klemperer. Berlin, 1995.

Klier, John D. and Shlomo Lambroza, eds. *Pogroms: Anti-Jewish Violence in Modern Russian History*. Cambridge, 1992.

Klippel, Diethelm. "Subjektives Recht und germanisch-deutscher Rechtsgedanke in der Zeit des Nationalsozialismus." In *Die Deutsche Rechtsgeschichte in der NS-Zeit: Ihre Vorgeschichte und ihre Nachwirkungen*, ed. Joachim Rückert and Dietmar Willoweit, 31–54. Tübingen, 1995.

Knipping, Ulrich. *Die Geschichte der Juden in Dortmund während der Zeit des Dritten Reiches.* Dortmund, 1977.

Knütter, Hans-Helmuth. "Die Linksparteien." In *Entscheidungsjahr 1932: Zur Judenfrage in der Endphase der Weimare Republik,* ed. Werner E. Mosse and Arnold Paucker, 323–345. Tübingen, 1966.

Kocka, Jürgen. *Klassengesellschaft im Krieg: Deutsche Sozialgeschichte 1914–1918.* Göttingen, 1973.

Köhler, Joachim. *Wagners Hitler: Der Prophet und sein Vollstrecker.* Munich, 1997.

Kolb, Eberhard. *Die Weimarer Republik.* Vol. 16, *Oldenbourg Grundriß der Geschichte.* 6th ed. Munich, 2002.

Koller, Christian. *"Von Wilden aller Rassen niedergemetzelt": Die Diskussion um die Verwendung von Kolonialtruppen in Europa zwischen Rassismus, Kolonialund Militärpolitik (1914–1930).* Stuttgart, 2001.

Kossert, Andreas. "Die jüdische Gemeinde Ortelsburg: Ein Beitrag zur Geschichte der Juden in Masuren." In *Zur Geschichte und Kultur der Juden in Ost- und Westpreußen,* ed. Michael Brocke, Margret Heitmann, and Harald Lordick, 87–124. Hildesheim, 2000.

Krieger, Heinrich. *Das Rassenrecht in Südwestafrika: Vergleichende Darstellung des deutschen Rechts und der deutschen Mandatszeit.* Berlin, 1940.

Kropat, Wolf-Arno. *Kristallnacht in Hessen: Der Judenpogrom vom November 1938.* Wiesbaden, 1988.

———. *"Reichskristallnacht": Der Judenpogrom vom 7. bis 10. November 1938 – Urheber, Täter, Hintergründe.* Wiesbaden, 1997.

Krucker, Lucia. "Zur Geschichte der Jüdischen Gemeinde in Schlüchtern." *Unsere Heimat* 4 (1988): 31–68.

Krüger, Gerd. "Straffreie Selbstjustiz: Öffentliche Denunzierungen im Ruhrgebiet 1923–1926." *Sowi* 27, no. 2 (1998): 119–125.

Kruse, Wolfgang. "Kriegsbegeisterung? Zur Massenstimmung bei Kriegsbeginn." In *Eine Welt von Feinden: Der Große Krieg 1914–1918,* ed. Wolfgang Kruse, 159–166. Frankfurt am Main, 1997.

Kühnel, Horst. *Juden in Breslau 1850–1945: Beiträge zu einer Ausstellung.* Munich, 1993.

Kulka, Otto Dov. "Die Nürnberger Rassegesetze und die deutsche Bevölkerung im Lichte geheimer NSLage- und Stimmungsberichte." *Vierteljahrshefte für Zeitgeschichte* 32 (1984): 582–624.

———. "Jewish Society in Germany as Reflected in Secret Nazi Reports on 'Public Opinion' 1933–1945." In *On Germans and Jews under the Nazi Regime: Essays by Three Generations of Historians: A Festschrift in Honor of Otto Dov Kulka,* ed. Moshe Zimmermann, 261–279. Jerusalem, 2006.

———. "'Public Opinion' in Nazi Germany and the 'Jewish Question.'" *The Jerusalem Quarterly* 25 (1982): 121–144.

———, ed. *Deutsches Judentum unter dem Nationalsozialismus. Band 1: Dokumente zur Geschichte der Reichsvertretung der deutschen Juden 1933–1939.* Tübingen, 1997.

Kulka, Otto Dov and Eberhard Jäckel, eds. *"Die Juden in den geheimen NS-Stimmungsberichten 1933–1945."* Düsseldorf, 2004; also CD-ROM. English edition: *The Jews in the Secret Nazi Reports on Popular Opinion in Germany, 1933—1945.* New Haven, 2010.

Kundrus, Birthe. *Kriegerfrauen: Familienpolitik und Geschlechterverhältnisse im Ersten und Zweiten Weltkrieg.* Hamburg, 1995.

Kurlander, Eric. *Living with Hitler: Liberal Democrats in the Third Reich.* New Haven, 2009.

Kwiet, Konrad. "Mussert, 'Mussert-Juden' und die 'Lösung der Judenfrage' in den Niederlanden." In *Vorurteil und Rassenhaß: Antisemitismus in den faschistischen Bewegungen Europas,* ed. Hermann Graml, Angelika Königseder, and Juliane Wetzel. Berlin, 2001.

Landau, Edwin. "Mein Leben vor und nach Hitler." In *Jüdisches Leben in Deutschland: Selbstzeugnisse zur Sozialgeschichte.* Vol. 3: 1918–1945, ed. Monika Richarz, 99–108. Stuttgart, 1982.

Large, David Clay, "'Out with the Ostjuden': The Scheunenviertel Riots in Berlin, November 1923." In *Exclusionary Violence: Antisemitic Riots in Modern History,* ed. Christhard Hoffmann, Werner Bergmann, and Helmut Walser Smith, 123–140. Ann Arbor, 2002.

Lebzelter, Gisela. "Die 'Schwarze Schmach': Vorurteile – Propaganda – Mythos." *Geschichte und Gesellschaft* 11 (1985): 37–58.

———. "Political Anti-Semitism in England 1918–1939." In *Hostages of Modernization: Studies on Modern Antisemitism 1870–1933/39,* Vol. 3/1: *Germany – Great Britain – France,* ed. Herbert A. Strauss, 385–424. Berlin, 1993.

Lefèvre, Andrea. "Lebensmittelunruhen in Berlin 1920–1923." In *Der Kampf um das tägliche Brot: Nahrungsmangel, Versorgungspolitik und Protest 1770–1990,* ed. Manfred Gailus and Heinrich Volkmann, 346–360. Opladen, 1994.

Lehnert, Detlef. *Verfassungsdemokratie als Bürgergenossenschaft: Politisches Denken, Öffentliches Recht und Geschichtsdeutungen bei Hugo Preuß: Beiträge zur demokratischen Institutionenlehre in Deutschland.* Baden-Baden, 1998.

———. "Verfassungsdispositionen für die politische Kultur der Weimarer Republik: Die Beiträge von Hugo Preuß im historisch-konzeptiven Vergleich." In *Pluralismus als Verfassungs- und Gesellschaftsmodell: Zur Politischen Kultur in der Weimarer Republik,* ed. Detlef Lehnert and Klaus Megerl, 11–47. Opladen, 1993.

———. "Von der politischkulturellen Fragmentierung zur demokratischen Sammlung: Der 'Volksblock' des 'Reichsbannerlagers' und die katholischen Republikaner." In *Pluralismus als Verfassungs- und Gesellschaftsmodell: Zur politischen Kultur in der Weimarer Republik,* ed. Detlef Lehnert and Klaus Megerle, 77–129. Opladen, 1993.

Lepper, Herbert, ed. *Volk, Kirche, Vaterland: Wahlaufrufe, Aufrufe, Satzungen und Statuten des Zentrums 1870–1933.* Düsseldorf, 1998.

Lepsius, Oliver. *Die gegensatzaufhebende Begriffsbildung: Methodenentwicklungen in der WeimarerRepublik und ihr Verhältnis zur Ideologisierung der Rechtswissenschaft unter dem Nationalsozialismus.* Munich, 1994.

Liepach, Martin. "Das Krisenbewusstsein des jüdischen Bürgertums in den Goldenen Zwanzigern." In *Juden, Bürger, Deutsche: Zur Geschichte von Vielfalt und Differenz 1800–1933,* ed. Andreas Gotzmann, Rainer Liedtke, and Till van Rahden, 395–417. Tübingen, 2001.

———. "Zwischen Abwehrkampf und Wählermobilisierung: Juden und die Landtagswahl in Baden 1929." In *Jüdisches Leben in der Weimarer Republik/Jews in the Weimar Republic,* ed. Wolfgang Benz, Arnold Paucker, and Peter Pulzer, 9–23. Tübingen, 1998.

Liermann, Hans. *Das deutsche Volk als Rechtsbegriff im Reichs- Staatsrecht der Gegenwart.* Berlin, 1927.

Lindenberger, Thomas and Alf Lüdtke, eds. *Physische Gewalt: Studien zur Geschichte der Neuzeit.* Frankfurt am Main, 1995.

Lindenberger, Thomas. *Straßenpolitik: Zur Sozialgeschichte der öffentlichen Ordnung in Berlin 1900 bis 1914.* Bonn, 1995.

Linsmayer, Ludwig, ed. *Der 13. Januar: Die Saar im Brennpunkt der Geschichte.* Saarbrücken, 2005.

Lohalm, Uwe. *Völkischer Radikalismus: Die Geschichte des Deutschvölkischen Schutz- und Trutz-Bundes 1919–1923.* Hamburg, 1970.

Longerich, Peter. *"Davon haben wir nichts gewusst!": Die Deutschen und die Judenverfolgung 1933–1945.* Munich, 2006.

————. *Politik der Vernichtung: Eine Gesamtdarstellung der nationalsozialistischen Judenverfolgung*. Munich, 1998. English edition: *Holocaust: The Nazi Persecution and the Murder of the Jews*. Oxford, 2010.

————. *Die braunen Bataillone: Geschichte der SA*. Munich, 1989.

Lösener, Bernhard. "Als Rassereferent im Reichsministerium des Innern." *Vierteljahrshefte für Zeitgeschichte* 9 (1961): 261–313.

Löwith, Karl. *Mein Leben in Deutschland vor und nach 1933: Ein Bericht*. Stuttgart, 1986.

Lüdtke Alf. "'Ehre der Arbeit': Industriearbeiter und Macht der Symbole: Zur Reichweite symbolischer Orientierungen im Nationalsozialismus." In *Arbeiter im 20. Jahrhundert*, ed. Klaus Tenfelde, 343–392. Stuttgart, 1991.

————. "'Formierung der Massen' oder: Mitmachen und Hinnehmen? 'Alltagsgeschichte' und Faschismusanalyse." In *Normalität oder Normalisierung? Geschichtswerkstätten und Faschismusanalyse*, ed. Heide Gerstenberger and Dorothea Schmid, 15–34. Münster, 1987.

————. "Funktionseliten: Täter, Mit-Täter, Opfer? Zu den Bedingungen des deutschen Faschismus." In *Herrschaft als soziale Praxis*, ed. Alf Lüdtke, 559–590. Göttingen, 1991.

————. "The Appeal of Exterminating 'Others': German Workers and the Limits of Resistance." In *The Third Reich: The Essential Readings*, ed. Christian Leitz, 155–177. Oxford, 1999.

————. "Thesen zur Wiederholbarkeit: 'Normalität' und Massenhaftigkeit von Tötungsgewalt im 20. Jahrhundert." In *Kulturen der Gewalt: Ritualisierung und Symbolisierung von Gewalt in der Geschichte*, ed. Rolf Peter Sieferle and Helga Breuninger, 280–289. Frankfurt am Main, 1998.

Lüpke, Reinhard. *Zwischen Marx und Wandervogel: Die Jungsozialisten in der Weimarer Republik 1919–1931*. Marburg, 1984.

Mai, Gunther. "'Verteidigungskrieg' und 'Volksgemeinschaft': Staatliche Selbstbehauptung, nationale Solidarität und soziale Befreiung in Deutschland in der Zeit des Ersten Weltkrieges (1900–1925)." In *Der Erste Weltkrieg: Wirkung, Wahrnehmung, Analyse*, ed. Wolfgang Michalka, 583–602. Munich, 1994.

Mann, Klaus. *Kind dieser Zeit*. Berlin, 1932.

Mann, Reinhard. *Protest und Kontrolle im Dritten Reich: Nationalsozialistische Herrschaft im Alltag einer rheinischen Großstadt*. Frankfurt am Main, 1987.

Marßolek, Inge. "The 'Writings on the Wall': The Changing Public Sphere and the Jews in Germany in the Third Reich." In *On Germans and Jews under the Nazi Regime: Essays by Three Generations of Historians: A Festschrift in Honor of Otto Dov Kulka*, ed. Moshe Zimmermann, 193–213. Jerusalem, 2006.

Mason, Timothy W. *Arbeiterklasse und Volksgemeinschaft: Dokumente und Materialien zur deutschen Arbeiterpolitik 1936–1939*. Opladen, 1975.

Maß, Sandra. *Weiße Helden, schwarze Krieger: Zur Geschichte kolonialer Männlichkeit in Deutschland 1918–1964*. Cologne, 2006.

Matthäus, Jürgen. "Kampf ohne Verbündete: Der Centralvereindeutscher Staatsbürger jüdischen Glaubens 1933–1938." *Jahrbuch für Antisemitismusforschung* 8 (1999): 248–277.

Mattioli, Aram. *Experimentierfeld der Gewalt: Der Abessinienkrieg und seine internationale Bedeutung 1935–1941*. Zurich, 2005.

Mauersberg, Jasper. *Ideen und Konzeption Hugo Preuß' für die Verfassung der deutschen Republik 1919 und ihre Durchsetzung im Verfassungswerk von Weimar*. Frankfurt am Main, 1991.

Maurer, Trude. "Abschiebung und Attentat: Die Ausweisung der polnischen Juden und der Vorwand für die 'Kristallnacht.'" In *Der Judenpogrom 1938: Von der "Reichskristallnacht" zum Völkermord*, ed. Walter H. Pehle, 52–73. Frankfurt am Main, 1988.

———. *Ostjuden in Deutschland 1918–1933*. Hamburg, 1986.

Meinecke, Friedrich. "Bemerkungen zum Entwurf der Reichsverfassung." In *Werke, Vol. II: Politische Schriften und Reden*, 299–312. Edited with an introduction by Georg Kotowski. Darmstadt, 1968.

Melzer, Emanuel. "Antisemitism in the Last Years of the Second Polish Republic." In *The Jews of Poland between Two World Wars*, ed. Yisrael Gutman, Ezra Mendelsohn, Jehuda Reinharz, and Chone Shmeruk, 126–137. London, 1989.

Mendes-Flohr, Paul. "The Kriegserlebnis and Jewish Consciousness." In *Leben in der Weimarer Republik/Jews in the Weimar Republic*, ed. Wolfgang Benz, Arnold Paucker, and Peter Pulzer, 225–237. Tübingen, 1998.

Mergel, Thomas. "Führer, Volksgemeinschaft und Maschine: Politische Erwartungsstrukturen in der Weimarer Republik und dem Nationalsozialismus 1918–1936." In *Politische Kulturgeschichte der Zwischenkriegszeit 1918–1939*, ed. Wolfgang Hardtwig, 91–127. Göttingen, 2005.

———. *Parlamentarische Kultur in der Weimarer Republik: Politische Kommunikation, symbolische Politik und Öffentlichkeit im Reichstag*. Düsseldorf, 2002.

Meyer, Manfred. "Jüdisches Leben in Gelnhausen." In *Gelnhäuser Heimat-Jahrbuch: Jahreskalender für Familie und Heim in Stadt und Land zwischen Vogelsberg und Spessart*, no editor, 62–68. N.p., 1988.

Meyer, Marcus. "Ein schwieriger Patient: Ein Bremer Rechtsanwalt und der 'Judenboykott' im April 1933. *Arbeiterbewegung und Sozialgeschichte: Zeitschrift für die Regionalgeschichte Bremens im 19. und 20. Jahrhundert* 11 (2003): 16–29.

Michlic-Coren, Joanna. "Anti-Jewish Violence in Poland, 1918–1939 and 1945–1947." *Polin: Studies in Polish Jewry* 13 (2000): 34–61.

Miller, Susanne. *Die Bürde der Macht: Die deutsche Sozialdemokratie 1918–1920*. Düsseldorf, 1978.

Milton, Sybil. "Menschen zwischen Grenzen: Die Polenausweisung 1938." In *Menora: Jahrbuch für deutsch-jüdische Geschichte*. Vol. 1. Munich, 1990.

Möbius, Ben. "Das Vaterland der 'vaterlandslosen Gesellen': Sozialdemokratischer Patriotismus am Vorabend des Ersten Weltkrieges." In *Politische Gesellschaftsgeschichte im 19. und 20. Jahrhundert*, ed. Henning Albrecht, Gabriele Boukrif, Claudia Bruns, and Kirsten Heinsohn, 13–29. Hamburg, 2006.

Modras, Ronald. *The Catholic Church and Antisemitism in Poland, 1933–1939*. Chur, 1994.

Möller, Hans. "Geschichte und Geschichten aus Schlüchtern." In *Ausschnitte aus 1250 Jahre Stadtgeschichte*. ed. the town of Schlüchtern, 121. N.p., n.d.

Möller, Horst. *Weimar: Die unvollendete Demokratie*. Munich, 1985.

Mommsen, Hans. *Die verspielte Freiheit: Der Weg der Republik von Weimar in den Untergang 1918 bis 1933*. Vol. 8, *Propyläen Geschichte Deutschlands*. Berlin, 1989.

———. "Hitler's Reichstag Speech of 30 January 1939." *History & Memory* 9 (1997): 147–161.

———. "Volksgemeinschaft." In *Lexikon zur Geschichte und Politik im 20. Jahrhundert, Vol. 2: L–Z*, ed. Carola Stern et al., 830. Cologne, 1971.

Mommsen, Hans and Dieter Obst. "Die Reaktion der deutschen Bevölkerung auf die Verfolgung der Juden." In *Herrschaftsalltag im Dritten Reich*, ed. Hans Mommsen and Susanne Willems, 387–394. Düsseldorf, 1988.

Mommsen, Hans and Susanne Willems. *Herrschaftsalltag im Dritten Reich: Studien und Texte*. Düsseldorf, 1988.

Mommsen, Wolfgang. *Max Weber und die deutsche Politik 1890–1920*. Expanded 2nd edition. Tübingen, 1974.

Mommsen, Wolfgang, ed. *Kultur und Krieg: Die Rolle der Intellektuellen, Künstler und Schriftsteller im Ersten Weltkrieg*. Munich, 1996.

Morgenthaler, Sibylle. "Countering the Pre-1933 Nazi Boycott against Jews." *Leo Baeck Institute Year Book* 36 (1991): 127–149.

Moritz, Klaus and Ernst Noam. *NS-Verbrechen vor Gericht 1945–1955: Dokumente aus hessischen Justizakten*. Wiesbaden, 1978.

Morsey, Rudolf, ed. *Das "Ermächtigungsgesetz" vom 24. März 1933: Quellen zur Geschichte und Interpretation des "Gesetzes zur Behebung der Not von Volk und Reich."* Düsseldorf, 1992.

Morsey, Rudolf. *Die Deutsche Zentrumspartei 1917–1923*. Düsseldorf, 1966.

Mühlen, Patrik von zur. *"Schlagt Hitler an der Saar!" Abstimmungskampf, Emigration und Widerstand im Saargebiet 1933–1935*. 2nd. ed. Bonn, 1981.

Müller, Joachim. *Die "Ideen von 1914" bei Johann Plenge und in der zeitgenössischen Diskussion: Ein Beitrag zur Ideengeschichte des Ersten Weltkrieges*. Neuwied, 2001.

Müller, Reinhard. "Hitlers Rede vor der Reichswehrführung 1933: Eine neue Moskauer Überlieferung." *Mittelweg 36* 11, no. 1 (2001): 73–90.

Müller, Rudolf Wolfgang. "'… wenn es morgens um 6 Uhr klingelte, war es der Milchmann': Ernst Fraenkel und die West-Berliner Studentenbewegung 1967." In *Vom Sozialismus zum Pluralismus: Beiträge zu Werk und Leben Ernst Fraenkels*, ed. Hubertus Buchstein and Gerhard Göhler, 97–113. Baden-Baden, 2000.

Niethammer, Lutz. *Kollektive Identität: Heimliche Quellen einer unheimlichen Konjunktur*. Reinbek, 2000.

Niethammer, Lutz, Alexander von Plato, and Dorothee Wierling. *Die volkseigene Erfahrung: Eine Archäologie des Lebens in der Industrieprovinz der DDR: 30 biographische Eröffnungen*. Berlin, 1991.

Niewyk, Donald L. "Solving the 'Jewish Problem': Continuity and Change in German Antisemitism, 1871–1945." *Leo Baeck Institute Yearbook* 35 (1990): 335–370.

Nolte, Paul. *Die Ordnung der deutschen Gesellschaft: Selbstentwurf und Selbstbeschreibung im 20. Jahrhundert*. Munich, 2000.

Nolzen, Armin. "The Nazi party and Its Violence against Jews, 1933–1939: Violence as a Historiographical Concept." *Yad Vashem Studies* 31 (2003): 245–285.

Obenaus, Herbert (with collaboration from David Bankier), ed. *Historisches Handbuch der jüdischen Gemeinden in Niedersachsen und Bremen*. 2 vols. Göttingen, 2005.

Obst, Dieter. *'Reichskristallnacht': Ursachen und Verlauf des antisemitischen Pogroms von November 1938*. Frankfurt am Main, 1991.

Ophir, Baruch Z. and Falk Wiesemann, eds. *Die jüdischen Gemeinden in Bayern 1918–1945: Geschichte und Zerstörung*, Munich and Vienna, 1979.

Osterrath, Franz. "Der Hofgeismarkreis der Jungsozialisten." *Archiv für Sozialgeschichte* 4 (1964): 525–569.

Papen, Franz von. *Der Wahrheit eine Gasse*. Munich, 1952.

Parisius, Bernhard and Astrid Parisius. "'Rassenschande' in Norden: Zur Geschichte von zwei Fotos, die das Bild Jugendlicher von der NS-Zeit prägen." *Ostfreesland: ein Kalender für jedermann* 87 (2004): 129–137.

Pätzold, Kurt. *Faschismus, Rassenwahn, Judenverfolgung: Eine Studie zur politischen Strategie und Taktik des faschistischen deutschen Imperialismus (1933–1935)*. East Berlin, 1975.

Paucker, Arnold. *Der jüdische Abwehrkampf gegen Antisemitismus und Nationalsozialismus in den letzten Jahren der Weimarer Republik*. 2nd ed. Hamburg, 1969.

Paul, Gerhard. *Aufstand der Bilder: Die NS-Propaganda vor 1933*. Bonn, 1990.

————. *"Deutsche Mutter – heim zu Dir!" Warum es mißlang, Hitler an der Saar zu schlagen: Der Saarkampf 1933–1935.* Cologne, 1984.

————. "Von Psychopathen, Technokraten des Terrors und 'ganz gewöhnlichen' Deutschen: Die Täter der Shoah im Spiegel der Forschung." In *Die Täter der Shoah: Fanatische Nationalsozialisten oder ganz normale Deutsche?* ed. Gerhard Paul, 13–90. Göttingen, 2002.

Peukert, Detlev. *Volksgenossen und Gemeinschaftsfremde: Anpassung, Ausmerze und Aufbegehren unter dem Nationalsozialismus.* Cologne, 1982.

Peukert, Detlev and Jürgen Reulecke, eds. *Die Reihen fast geschlossen: Beiträge zur Geschichte des Alltags unterm Nationalsozialismus.* Wuppertal, 1981.

Phelps, Reginald R. "Hitlers 'grundlegende' Rede über den Antisemitismus." *Vierteljahrshefte für Zeitgeschichte* 16 (1968): 390–420.

Plessner, Helmuth. *Grenzen der Gemeinschaft: Eine Kritik des sozialen Radikalismus (1924).* Frankfurt am Main, 2002.

Plum, Günter. "Wirtschaft und Erwerbsleben." In *Die Juden in Deutschland 1933–1945: Leben unter nationalsozialistischer Herrschaft,* ed. Wolfgang Benz, 268–313. Munich, 1988.

Pommerin, Reiner. *"Sterilisierung der Rheinlandbastarde": Das Schicksal einer deutschen farbigen Minderheit 1918–1937.* Düsseldorf, 1979.

Popitz, Heinrich. *Phänomene der Macht.* Exp. 2nd ed. Tübingen, 1992.

Pötzsch, Hansjörg. *Antisemitismus in der Region: Antisemitische Erscheinungsformen in Sachsen, Hessen, Hessen-Nassau und Braunschweig 1870–1914.* Wiesbaden, 2000.

Preuß, Hugo. "Das Verfassungswerk von Weimar." In Hugo Preuß, *Staat, Recht und Freiheit: Aus 40 Jahren deutscher Politik und Geschichte,* 421–428. Hildesheim, 1964.

————. "Denkschrift zum Entwurf des allgemeinen Teils der Reichsverfassung vom 3. 1. 1919." In *Staat, Recht und Freiheit: Aus 40 Jahren deutscher Politik und Geschichte,* 368–394. Hildesheim, 1964.

————. "Volksgemeinschaft?" In *Um die Reichsverfassung,* 17–22. Berlin, 1924.

————. "Volksstaat oder verkehrter Obrigkeitsstaat." In *Staat, Recht und Freiheit: Aus 40 Jahren deutscher Politik und Geschichte,* 365–368. Hildesheim, 1964.

Protokoll über die Verhandlungen des außerordentlichen Parteitages der Unabhängigen Sozialdemokratischen Partei Deutschlands vom 2. bis 6. März 1919 in Berlin. Berlin, 1919.

Protokoll über die Verhandlungen des Parteitags der Sozialdemokratischen Partei Deutschlands, abgehalten in Görlitz vom 18. bis 24. September 1921. Berlin, 1921.

Przyrembel, Alexandra. *"Rassenschande": Reinheitsmythos und Vernichtungslegitimation im Nationalsozialismus.* Göttingen, 2003.

Puschendorf, Peter. "Sandersleben." In *Wegweiser durch das jüdische Sachsen-Anhalt,* ed. Jutta Dick and Marina Sassenberg, 174–180. Potsdam, 1998.

Puschner, Uwe. *Die völkische Bewegung im wilhelminischen Kaiserreich: Sprache – Rasse – Religion.* Darmstadt, 2001.

Rahden, Till van. *Juden und andere Breslauer: Die Beziehungen zwischen Juden, Protestanten und Katholiken in einer deutschen Großstadt von 1860 bis 1925.* Göttingen, 2000.

Raithel, Thomas and Irene Strenge. "Die Reichstagsbrandverordnung: Grundlegung der Diktatur mit den Instrumenten des Weimarer Ausnahmezustandes." *Vierteljahrshefte für Zeitgeschichte* 48 (2000): 413–460.

Reemtsma, Jan Philipp. "Die Gewalt spricht nicht: Zum Verhältnis von Macht und Gewalt." In Jan Philipp Reemtsma, *Die Gewalt spricht nicht: Drei Reden,* 7–46. Stuttgart, 2002.

————. "Die Natur der Gewalt als Problem der Soziologie." *Mittelweg 36* 15, no. 5 (2006): 2–25.

———. "'Wie hätte ich mich verhalten?' Gedanken über eine populäre Frage." In *Wie hätte ich mich verhalten?" und andere nicht nur deutsche Fragen: Reden und Aufsätze*, 9–29. Munich, 2001.

Rehme, Günther, Konstantin Haase, and Klaus Hesse. *"...mit Rumpf und Stumpf ausrotten": Zur Geschichte der Juden in Marburg und Umgebung nach 1933*. Marburg, 1982.

Reichardt, Sven. *Faschistische Kampfbünde: Gewalt und Gemeinschaft im italienischen Squadrismus und in der deutschen SA*. Cologne, 2002.

———. "Gewalt, Körper, Politik: Paradoxien in der deutschen Kulturgeschichte der Zwischenkriegszeit." In *Politische Kulturgeschichte der Zwischenkriegszeit 1918–1939*, ed. Wolfgang Hardtwig. Vol. 21, *Geschichte und Gesellschaft Sonderhefte*, 205–239. Göttingen, 2005.

Reichmann, Hans. *Deutscher Bürger und verfolgter Jude: Novemberpogrom und KZ Sachsenhausen 1937 bis 1939*. Edited with an introduction by Michael Wildt. Munich, 1998.

Reich-Ranicki, Marcel. *Mein Leben*. Stuttgart, 1999.

Reichsgeschäftsstelle der DDP Berlin, ed. *Staat und Wirtschaft: Rede von Gustav Schneider, Bundesvorsitzender des Gewerkschaftsbundes der Angestellten, auf dem Reichsparteitag der Deutschen Demokratischen Partei in Weimar am 6. April 1924*. Berlin, n.d.

Reifferscheid, Gerhard. "Die NSDAP in Ostpreußen: Besonderheiten ihrer Ausbreitung und Tätigkeit." *Zeitschrift für die Geschichte und Altertumskunde Ermlands* 39 (1978): 61–85.

Repgen, Konrad and Hans Booms, eds. *Akten der Reichskanzlei: Regierung Hitler 1933–1938, Part I: 1933/34, Vol.1: 30. Januar bis 31. August 1933*. Comp. by Karl-Heinz Minuth. Boppard am Rhein, 1983.

Roden, Günter von, et al. *Geschichte der Duisburger Juden*. Duisburg, 1986.

Rummel, Walter. "Motive staatlicher und dörflicher Gewaltanwendung im 19. Jahrhundert: Eine Skizze zum Ende der frühneuzeitlichen Sozialkultur in der preußischen Rheinprovinz." In *Streitkulturen: Gewalt, Konflikt und Kommunikation in der ländlichen Gesellschaft (16.–19. Jahrhundert)*, ed. Magnus Eriksson and Barbara Krug-Richter, 157–178. Cologne, 2003.

Runzheimer, Jürgen. *Abgemeldet zur Auswanderung: Die Geschichte der Juden im ehemaligen Landkreis Biedenkopf*. Biedenkopf, 1992.

Ruppert, Karsten. *Im Dienst am Staat von Weimar: Das Zentrum als regierende Partei in der Weimarer Demokratie 1923–1930*. Düsseldorf, 1992.

Rürup, Reinhard. "Das Ende der Emanzipation: Die antijüdische Politik in Deutschland von der 'Machtergreifung' bis zum Zweiten Weltkrieg." In *Die Juden im nationalsozialistischen Deutschland*, ed. Arnold Paucker, 97–114. Tübingen, 1986.

Rüthers, Bernd. *Die unbegrenzte Auslegung: Zum Wandel der Privatrechtsordnung im Nationalsozialismus*. Exp. 6th ed.. Tübingen, 2005.

Saerens, Lieven. "Belgische Gruppierungen der 'Neuen Ordnung' und die Juden (1918–1944)." In *Vorurteil und Rassenhaß: Antisemitismus in den faschistischen Bewegungen Europas*, ed. Hermann Graml, Angelika Königseder, and Juliane Wetzel, 131–150. Berlin, 2001.

Safrian, Hans. *Die Eichmann-Männer*. Vienna, 1993.

Safrian, Hans and Hans Witek. *Und keiner war dabei: Dokumente des alltäglichen Antisemitismus in Wien 1938*. Vienna, 1988.

Sauer, Paul, ed. *Dokumente über die Verfolgung der jüdischen Bürger in Baden-Württemberg durch das nationalsozialistischen Regime 1933–1945*. 2 vols. Stuttgart, 1966.

Schenk, Dieter. *Hans Frank: Hitlers Kronjurist und Generalgouverneur*. Frankfurt am Main, 2006.

Scheuer, Richard. "Das Ende der israelitischen Kultusgemeinde in der ehemals freien Reichsstadt Gelnhausen." In *Festschrift Ehemalige Synagoge Gelnhausen*, ed. Magistrat der Barbarossastadt Gelnhausen, comp. Geschichtsverein Gelnhausen, 75–82. Gelnhausen, 1986.

Scheuerman, William E. *Carl Schmitt: The End of Law*. Lanham, MD, 1999.

Schildt, Axel. "Ein konservativer Prophet moderner nationaler Integration: Biographische Skizze des streitbaren Soziologen Johann Plenge (1874–1963)." *Vierteljahrshefte für Zeitgeschichte* 35 (1987): 523–570.

Schlag, Jakob. *Meine Erinnerungen an das "Tausendjährige Reich" und an die Juden in Lohra*. Self-published. Lohra, 1991.

Schleunes, Karl A. The *Twisted Road to Auschwitz: Nazi Policy toward German Jews 1933–1939*. Urbana, 1970.

Schmid, Harald. *Erinnern an den "Tag der Schuld": Das Novemberpogrom von 1938 in der deutschen Geschichtspolitik*. Hamburg, 2001.

Schmitt, Carl. *Die Diktatur: Von den Anfängen des modernen Souveränitätsgedankens bis zum proletarischen Klassenkampf* (1921). Berlin, 1994.

———. *Die geistesgeschichtliche Lage des heutigen Parlamentarismus* (1923). Berlin, 1996.

———. *Der Begriff des Politischen: Text von 1932 mit einem Vorwort und drei Corollarien*. Berlin, 1996.

———. *The Concept of the Political*. Translation, Introduction, and Notes by George Schwab. Chicago, 2007.

———. *Über die drei Arten des rechtswissenschaftlichen Denkens*. Hamburg, 1934.

———. *Verfassungslehre* (1928). Berlin, 1993.

Schneider, Michael. *Unterm Hakenkreuz: Arbeiter und Arbeiterbewegung 1933 bis 1939*. Bonn, 1999.

Schneider, Uwe and Andreas Schumann, eds. *"Krieg der Geister": Erster Weltkrieg und literarische Moderne*. Würzburg, 2000.

Schoenbaum, David. *Die braune Revolution*. Cologne, 1968. *Hitler's Social Revolution: Class and Status in Nazi Germany, 1933—1939*. Garden City, 1966.

Scholder, Klaus. *Die Kirchen und das Dritte Reich*. Vol. 1. Berlin, 1977.

Scholem, Gerschom and Betty Scholem. *Scholem, Betty – Gershom Scholem, Mutter und Sohn im Briefwechsel 1917–1946*. Edited by Itta Shedletzky. Munich, 1989.

Schönekäs, Klaus. "'Christenkreuz über Hakenkreuz und Sowjetstern': Die NSDAP im Raum Fulda." In *Hessen unterm Hakenkreuz: Studien zur Durchsetzung der NSDAP in Hessen*, ed. Eike Henning et al. 127–179. Frankfurt am Main, 1983.

Schreiber, Karl. "800 Jahre Stadtrechte Gelnhausen." In *Gelnhausen, die Barbarossastadt: 800 Jahre Stadtrechte*, edited for the Stadtverwaltung Gelnhausen, 47–54. Bad Homburg, 1970.

Schreiner, Klaus and Gerd Schwerhoff, eds. *Verletzte Ehre: Ehrkonflikte in Gesellschaften des Mittelalters und der Frühen Neuzeit*. Cologne, 1995.

Schüler-Springorum, Stefanie. *Die jüdische Minderheit in Königsberg/ Preußen 1871–1945*. Göttingen, 1996.

Schultheis, Herbert. *Juden in Mainfranken 1933–1945 unter besonderer Berücksichtigung der Deportationen Würzburger Juden*. Bad Neustadt a. d. Saale, 1980.

Schumann, Dirk. *Politische Gewalt in der Weimarer Republik 1918–1933: Kampf um die Straße und Furcht vor dem Bürgerkrieg*. Essen, 2001.

Schuster, Peter. "Ehre und Recht: Überlegungen zu einer Begriffsund Sozialgeschichte zweier Grundbegriffe der mittelalterlichen Gesellschaft." In *Ehrkonzepte in der Frühen Neuzeit: Identitäten und Abgrenzungen*, ed. Sybille Backmann et al., 40–66. Berlin, 1998.

Schwarzenbeck, Engelbert. *Nationalsozialistische Pressepolitik und die Sudetenkrise 1938.* Munich, 1979.

Schwerhoff, Gerd, "Verordnete Schande? Spätmittelalterliche und frühneuzeitliche Ehrenstrafen zwischen Rechtsakt und sozialer Sanktion." In *Mit den Waffen der Justiz: Zur Kriminalitätsgeschichte des Spätmittelalters und der Frühen Neuzeit,* ed. Andreas Blauert and Gerd Schwerhoff, 158–188. Frankfurt am Main, 1993.

Seeligmann, Chaim and Givat Brenner. "Die Reichstagswahlen des 14. September 1930 im Spiegel der jüdischen Presse in Deutschland." *Tel Aviver Jahrbuch für deutsche Geschichte* 17 (1988): 169–192.

Sieg, Ulrich. *Jüdische Intellektuelle im Ersten Weltkrieg: Kriegserfahrungen, weltanschauliche Debatten und kulturelle Neuentwürfe.* Berlin, 2001.

Siegel, Tilla. "Lohnpolitik im nationalsozialistischen Deutschland." In *Angst, Belohnung, Zucht und Ordnung: Herrschaftsmechanismen im Nationalsozialismus,* ed. Carola Sachse et al., 104–129. Opladen, 1982.

Smith, Bradley F. "Die Überlieferung der Hoßbach-Niederschrift im Lichte neuer Quellen." In *Vierteljahrshefte für Zeitgeschichte* 38 (1990): 329–336.

Smith, Helmut Walser. *The Butcher's Tale: Murder and Anti-Semitism in a German Town.* New York, 2002.

Sofsky, Wolfgang. *Traktat über die Gewalt.* Frankfurt am Main, 1996.

Sontheimer, Kurt. *Antidemokratisches Denken in der Weimarer Republik.* Munich, 1962.

Spector, Shmuel and Geoffrey Wigodor, eds. *The Encyclopedia of Jewish Life Before and During the Holocaust.* 3 vols. Jerusalem and New York, 2001.

Stein, Harry. *Juden in Buchenwald 1937–1942.* Edited by Gedenkstätte Buchenwald. Weimar, 1992.

Steinert, Marlis. *Hitlers Krieg und die Deutschen.* Düsseldorf, 1970.

Steinwascher, Gerd. *Judenverfolgung in Schaumburg 1933–1945.* Bückeburg, 1988.

Stier-Somlo, Fritz. *Deutsches Reichs- und Landesstaatsrecht,* vol 1. Leipzig, 1924.

Stolleis, Michael. "Gemeinschaft und Volksgemeinschaft Zur juristischen Terminologie im Nationalsozialismus." *Vierteljahrshefte für Zeitgeschichte* 20 (1972): 16–38.

———. *Gemeinwohlformeln im nationalsozialistischen Recht.* Berlin, 1974.

———. *Geschichte des öffentlichen Rechts in Deutschland: Dritter Band: Staats- und Verwaltungsrechtswissenschaft in Republik und Diktatur 1914–1945.* Munich, 1999.

Stöver, Bernd. *Volksgemeinschaft im Dritten Reich: Die Konsensbereitschaft der Deutschen aus der Sicht sozialistischer Exilberichte.* Düsseldorf, 1993.

Strauss, Herbert A., ed. *Hostages of Modernization: Studies on Modern Antisemitism 1870–1933/39, Vol. 3/1: Germany –Great Britain – France, 3/2: Austria– Hungary – Poland – Russia.* Berlin, 1993.

Swett, Pamela E. *Neighbors and Enemies: The Culture of Radicalism in Berlin 1929–1933.* Cambridge, 2004.

Tambiah, Stanley J. *Leveling Crowds: Ethnonationalist Conflicts and Collective Violence in South Asia.* Berkeley, 1996.

Tausk, Walter. *Breslauer Tagebuch 1933–1940.* Berlin, 1988.

Teuber, Werner. *Jüdische Viehhändler in Ostfriesland und im nördlichen Emsland 1871–1942: Eine vergleichende Studie zu einer jüdischen Berufsgruppe in zwei wirtschaftlich und konfessionell unterschiedlichen Regionen.* Cloppenburg, 1995.

Thamer, Hans-Ulrich. *Verführung und Gewalt: Deutschland 1933–1945.* Revised ed. Berlin, 1994.

Thévoz, Robert. *Die Geheime Staatspolizei in den preußischen Ostprovinzen 1934–1936: Pommern 1934/35 im Spiegel von Gestapo-Lageberichten und Sachakten.* 2 vols., Cologne, 1974.

Thiele, Ulrich. *Advokative Volkssouveränität: Carl Schmitts Konstruktion einer "demokratisch-en" Diktaturtheorie im Kontext der Interpretation politischer Theorien der Aufklärung.* Berlin, 2003.

Thompson, Edward P. "Rough Music." In Edward P. Thompson, *Customs in Common,* 467–538. New York, 1993.

Tilitzki, Christian. *Alltag in Ostpreußen 1940–1945: Die geheimen Lageberichte der Königsberger Justiz 1940–1945.* Leer, 1991.

Torres, Max Sebastian Hering. *Rassismus in der Vormoderne: Die "Reinheit des Blutes" im Spanien der Frühen Neuzeit.* Frankfurt am Main, 2006.

Toury, Jacob. "Ein Auftakt zur 'Endlösung': Judenaustreibungen über nichtslawische Reichsgrenzen 1933–1939." In *Das Unrechtsregime: Internationale Forschung über den Nationalsozialismus,* ed. Ursula Büttner with collaboration by Werner Johe and Angelika Voß, vol. 2, 164–196. Hamburg, 1986.

———. "Gab es ein Krisenbewußtsein unter den Juden während der 'guten Jahre' der Weimarer Republik 1924–1929." *Tel Aviver Jahrbuch für deutsche Geschichte* 17 (1988): 145–168.

Treue, Wilhelm. *Deutsche Parteiprogramme 1861–1954.* Göttingen, 1954.

———. "Hitlers Denkschrift zum Vierjahresplan 1936." *Vierteljahrshefte für Zeitgeschichte* 3 (1955): 184–210.

Triepel, Heinrich, ed. *Quellensammlung zum Deutschen Reichsstaatsrecht.* Exp. 4th ed. Tübingen, 1926.

Trippe, Christian F. *Konservative Verfassungspolitik 1918–1923: Die DNVP als Opposition in Reich und Ländern.* Düsseldorf, 1995.

Uhlig, Heinrich. *Die Warenhäuser im Dritten Reich.* Cologne, 1956.

Ullrich, Volker. *Kriegsalltag: Hamburg im Ersten Weltkrieg.* Cologne, 1982.

Ulrich, Bernd G. *Nationalsozialismus und Antisemitismus in Anhalt: Skizzen zu den Jahren 1932 bis 1942.* Dessau, 2005.

Vaget, Hans Rudolf. *Im Schatten Wagners: Thomas Mann über Richard Wagner.* Frankfurt am Main, 1999.

———. "Wagner-Kult und nationalsozialistische Herrschaft: Hitler, Wagner, Thomas Mann und die 'nationale Erhebung.'" In *Richard Wagner im Dritten Reich,* ed. Saul Friedländer and Jörn Rüsen, 264–282. Munich, 2000.

Verhandlungen der Verfassunggebenden Deutschen Nationalversammlung 1919/20. Berlin, 1920.

Verhey, Jeffrey. *Der "Geist von 1914" und die Erfindung der Volksgemeinschaft.* Hamburg, 2000.

Vestring, Sigrid. *Die Mehrheitssozialdemokratie und die Entstehung der Reichsverfassung von Weimar 1918/19.* Münster, 1987.

Vogelsang, Thilo. "Neue Dokumente zur Geschichte der Reichswehr 1930–1933." *Vierteljahrshefte für Zeitgeschichte* 2 (1954): 397–436.

Volkov, Shulamit. "Das geschriebene und das gesprochene Wort: Über Kontinuität und Diskontinuität im deutschen Antisemitismus." In Shulamit Volkov, *Antisemitismus als kultureller Code: Zehn Essays,* 54–75. Exp. 2nd ed. Munich, 2000.

Walk, Joseph. *Das Sonderrecht für die Juden im NS-Staat: Eine Sammlung der gesetzlichen Maßnahmen und Richtlinien: Inhalt und Bedeutung.* 2nd ed. Heidelberg, 1996.

Walter, Dirk. *Antisemitische Kriminalität und Gewalt: Judenfeindschaft in der Weimarer Republik.* Bonn, 1999.

Walter, Franz. *Nationale Romantik und revolutionärer Mythos: Politik und Lebensweisen im frühen Weimarer Jungsozialismus.* Berlin, 1986.

Walz, Rainer. "Agonale Kommunikation im Dorf der Frühen Neuzeit." *Westfälische Forschungen* 42 (1992): 215–251.

Wassermann, Henry and Eckhart G. Franz. "'Kauft nicht beim Juden': Der politische Antisemitismus des späten 19. Jahrhunderts." In *Juden als Darmstädter Bürger*, ed. Eckhart G. Franz, 123–136. Darmstadt, 1984.

Weber, Max. "Der Reichspräsident." In *Max Weber Gesamtausgabe*, sect. I, vol. 16, 220–224. Tübingen, 1988.

———. *Wirtschaft und Gesellschaft: Grundriß der verstehen den Soziologie*. 5th ed. Tübingen, 1980.

———. "Zur Neuordnung Deutschlands." In *Max Weber Gesamtausgabe*, sect. I, vol. 1, 91–146. Tübingen 1988.

Weber, Wolfgang. "Honor, fama, gloria: Wahrnehmungen und Funktionszuschreibungen der Ehre in der Herrschaftslehre des 17. Jahrhunderts." In *Ehrkonzepte in der Frühen Neuzeit: Identitäten und Abgrenzungen*, ed. Sybille Backmann et al., 70–98. Berlin, 1998.

Wehler, Hans-Ulrich. *Deutsche Gesellschaftsgeschichte*. Vol. 3, *Von der "Deutschen Doppelrevolution" bis zum Beginn des Ersten Weltkrieges 1849–1914*. Munich, 1995.

———. *Deutsche Gesellschaftsgeschichte*. Vol. 4, *Vom Beginn des Ersten Weltkrieges bis zur Gründung der beiden deutschen Staaten 1914–1949*. Munich, 2003.

Weisbrod, Bernd. "Der Schein der Normalität: Zur Historisierung der 'Volksgemeinschaft.'" In *Geschichte als Möglichkeit: Über die Chance von Demokratie: Festschrift für Helga Grebing*, ed. Karsten Rudolph et al., 224–242. Essen, 1995.

Weller, Katja. "Die Kampagne gegen die 'Schwarze Schmach' und die Frauenbewegung zu Beginn der Weimarer Republik." In *Politische Gesellschaftsgeschichte im 19. und 20. Jahrhundert: Festgabe für Barbara Vogel*, ed. Henning Albrecht, Gabriele Boukrif, Claudia Bruns, and Kirsten Heinsohn, 188–201. Hamburg, 2006.

Welzer, Harald. *Täter: Wie aus ganz normalen Menschen Massenmörder werden*. Frankfurt am Main, 2005.

Wertheimer, Jack. *Unwelcome Strangers: East European Jews in Imperial Germany*. New York, 1991.

Wesner, Doris. *Die Jüdische Gemeinde in Simmern/Hunsrück: Familiengeschichte(n) und Schicksale aus den vergangenen Jahrhunderten*. Argenthal, 2001.

Wetzel, Juliane. "Der Mythos des 'braven Italieners': Das faschistische Italien und der Antisemitismus." In *Vorurteil und Rassenhaß: Antisemitismus in den faschistischen Bewegungen Europas*, ed. Hermann Graml, Angelika Königseder, and Juliane Wetzel, 49–74. Berlin, 2001.

———. "Frankreich und Belgien." In *Dimension des Völkermords: Die Zahl der jüdischen Opfer des Nationalsozialismus*, ed. Wolfgang Benz, 105–135. Munich, 1996.

Wieland, Lothar. *Belgien 1914: Die Frage des belgischen "Franktireurkrieges" und die deutsche öffentliche Meinung von 1914 bis 1936*. Frankfurt am Main, 1984.

Wiesemann, Falk. "Juden auf dem Lande: die wirtschaftliche Ausgrenzung der jüdischen Viehhändler in Bayern." In *Die Reihen fast geschlossen: Beiträge zur Geschichte des Alltags unterm Nationalsozialismus*, ed. Detlef Peukert and Jürgen Reulecke, 381–396. Wuppertal, 1981.

Wildt, Michael. *An Uncompromising Generation: The Nazi Leadership of the Reich Security Main Office*. Madison, WI, 2010.

———. "'Der muß hinaus! Der muß hinaus!' Antisemitismus in deutschen Nord- und Ostseebädern 1920–1935." *Mittelweg 36* 10, no. 4 (2001): 2–25.

———. *Die Judenpolitik des SD 1935–1938: Eine Dokumentation*. Munich, 1995.

———. "Ernst Fraenkel und Carl Schmitt: Eine ungleiche Beziehung." In *Geschichte als Experiment: Studien zu Politik, Kultur und Alltag im 19. und 20. Jahrhundert: Festschrift für Adelheid von Saldern*, ed. Daniela Münkel and Jutta Schwarzkopf, 35–48. Frankfurt am Main, 2004.

———. "Sind die Nazis Barbaren? Betrachtungen zu einer geklärten Frage." *Mittelweg 36* 15, no. 2 (2006): 8–26.

———. "Violence against Jews in Germany 1933–1939." In *Probing the Depths of German Antisemitism: German Society and the Persecution of the Jews, 1933–1941*, ed. David Bankier, 181–209. New York, Oxford, and Jerusalem, 2000.

———. "Volksgemeinschaft und Führererwartung in der Weimarer Republik." In *Politische Kultur und Medienwirklichkeiten in den 1920er Jahren*, ed. Ute Daniel et al., 181-204, Munich, 2010.

Wilhelmus, Wolfgang. "Juden in Greifswald und Wolgast 1933–1945." In *Der faschistische Pogrom vom 9./19. November 1938 – Zur Geschichte der Juden in Pommern: Kolloquium der Sektionen Geschichtswissenschaft und Theologie der Ernst-Moritz-Arndt-Universität Greifswald am 2. November 1988*, 98–112. Greifswald, 1989.

Willoweit, Dieter. "Deutsche Rechtsgeschichte und 'nationalsozialistischen Weltanschauung': das Beispiel Hans Frank." In *Rechtsgeschichte im Nationalsozialismus: Beiträge zur Geschichte einer Disziplin*, ed. Michael Stolleis and Dieter Simon, 25–42. Tübingen, 1989.

Winkler, Heinrich August. *Der Schein der Normalität: Arbeiter und Arbeiterbewegung in der Weimarer Republik 1924 bis 1930*. 2nd ed. Berlin, 1988.

———. *Der Weg in die Katastrophe: Arbeiter und Arbeiterbewegung in der Weimarer Republik 1930 bis 1933*. Berlin, 1987.

———. "Klassenbewegung oder Volkspartei? Zur Programmdiskussion in der Weimarer Sozialdemokratie 1920–1925." *Geschichte und Gesellschaft* 8 (1982): 9–54.

———. *Von der Revolution zur Stabilisierung: Arbeiter und Arbeiterbewegung in der Weimarer Republik 1918 bis 1924*. Berlin, 1984.

———. *Weimar 1918–1933: Die Geschichte der ersten deutschen Demokratie*. Munich, 1993.

Wirsching, Andreas. *Vom Weltkrieg zum Bürgerkrieg? Politischer Extremismus in Deutschland und Frankreich 1918–1933/39: Berlin und Paris im Vergleich*. Munich, 1999.

Wittrock, Christine. *Das Unrecht geht einher mit sicherem Schritt Notizen über den Nationalsozialismus in Langenselbold und Schlüchtern*. Hanau, 1999.

Wolff, Theodor. *Tagebücher 1914–1919*. Edited by Bernd Sösemann. Boppard, 1984.

Yahil, Leni. *Die Shoah: Überlebenskampf und Vernichtung der europäischen Juden*. Munich, 1998.

Zelinsky, Hartmut. *Richard Wagner: Ein deutsches Thema: Eine Dokumentation zur Wirkungsgeschichte Richard Wagners 1876–1976*. Berlin, 1983.

Zentrale für Heimatdienst, ed. *Der Geist der neuen Volksgemeinschaft: Eine Denkschrift für das deutsche Volk*. Berlin, 1919.

Ziątkowski, Leszek. *Die Geschichte der Juden in Breslau*. Wrocław, 2000.

Zimmermann, Peter. *Theodor Haubach (1896–1945): Eine politische Biographie*. Hamburg, 2004.

Zuckmayer, Carl. *Als wär's ein Stück von mir*. Stuttgart, 1966.

INDEX OF PLACES & NAMES

Lightning Source UK Ltd.
Milton Keynes UK
UKOW03f0351030714

234483UK00006B/89/P